THE CRUSADES

For Kenneth
in old friendship
Hans

THE
CRUSADES

SECOND EDITION

BY
HANS EBERHARD MAYER

TRANSLATED BY
JOHN GILLINGHAM

OXFORD UNIVERSITY PRESS
1988

Oxford University Press, Walton Street, Oxford OX2 6DP
Oxford New York Toronto
Delhi Bombay Calcutta Madras Karachi
Petaling Jaya Singapore Hong Kong Tokyo
Nairobi Dar es Salaam Cape Town
Melbourne Auckland
and associated companies in
Beirut Berlin Ibadan Nicosia

Oxford is a trade mark of Oxford University Press

Published in the United States
by Oxford University Press, New York

© 1965 W. Kohlhammer GmbH, Stuttgart
This translation © Oxford University Press 1972, 1988

British Library Cataloguing in Publication Data
Mayer, Hans Eberhard
The crusades. —— 2nd ed.
1. Crusades
I. Title   II. Geschichte der Kreuzzüge.
English
909.07   D157
ISBN 0-19-873098-5
ISBN 0-19-873097-7 Pbk

Library of Congress Cataloging in Publication Data
Mayer, H. E. (Hans Eberhard), 1932–
The Crusades.
Rev. translation of the original German ed. published
in 1965 under title: Geschichte der Kreuzzüge.
Bibliography: p.
1. Crusades. I. Title.
D157.M3813 1988   940.1'8   87-24795
ISBN 0-19-873098-5
ISBN 0-19-873097-7 Pbk

Typeset by Cotswold Typesetting Limited, Gloucester
Printed in Great Britain
at the University Press, Oxford
by David Stanford
Printer to the University

PREFACE TO THE FIRST EDITION

FOR every author there is a special pleasure in seeing his work translated into another language; the fact of translation gives him some confidence that he has written something of value. Naturally I hope that this is true of this book. But there were, in addition, some very practical and down-to-earth considerations which led to the English translation of my *Geschichte der Kreuzzüge* (first published as a paperback, Stuttgart 1965). The English-speaking reader is fortunate in having excellent—indeed the best—general books on the crusades at his disposal. He can choose between Sir Steven Runciman's three-volume *History of the Crusades*, a *tour de force* of English historical writing, and the important collective work, *History of the Crusades*, edited by Kenneth M. Setton (Institute for Advanced Study, Princeton) in which both American and European scholarship may be seen at their best. Both works are indispensable for anyone who wishes to study the crusades at all seriously. But what has hitherto been lacking is an account of the crusades which is brief as well as being based on modern scholarship. To find good, short histories in English we have to go back to W. B. Stevenson's book, *The Crusaders in the East* (1907), and to the masterly article by Ernest Barker in the 1911 edition of the *Encyclopaedia Britannica*. In their day these sketches were excellent examples of English historical scholarship, but inevitably the questions now asked by historians are often very different ones. So there is a gap which this book attempts to fill. I hope that it will be useful to university students as well as to those members of the general public who are interested in the crusades. To this end I have made some additions and alterations to the text in order to take account of the most recent research; but the essential character of the German edition remains, I hope, unchanged. In particular, the bibliographical notes have been brought up to date and I would like to take this opportunity to draw special attention to the very important two-volume work by Joshua Prawer, *Histoire du royaume latin de Jérusalem*. The first volume was published in 1969. Since I have not been able to take account of works published after December 1970 I have not had the advantage of seeing the second volume which, although officially a 1970 publication, was not available until May 1971. And, of course, it still remains true that anyone who wishes to study the crusades in greater detail must turn to Runciman and Setton as well as to the specialist literature to which I refer in the notes.

Faced by the perennial problem of the transliteration of oriental place and personal names, the translator and I decided, in the interests of readability and a simpler type, to renounce all diacritical signs. In most cases we have deliberately adopted Runciman's system of transliteration in order to make things easier for anyone who wishes to go on to read Runciman's work.

I dedicate this book to the Nestor of German medieval historians, Friedrich Baethgen, in honour of his eightieth birthday. He was professor of history, first at Königsberg and then at Berlin, at that time outstanding among German universities. For the crucial decade after the Second World War he was President of one of the most distinguished of all research institutes for medieval history. This was the Monumenta Germaniae Historica which had owed its origin to the patriotic spirit which characterized the approach to history in the period of the Wars of Liberation against Napoleon. Later in the nineteenth century the Monumenta Germaniae set a new standard of scholarship in the quality of the editions of historical texts in medieval Latin which were produced under its auspices. For nine years Friedrich Baethgen was also President of the Bayerische Akademie der Wissenschaften. But it is, of course, his writings rather than his offices which made him well-known in the English-speaking academic world.

Friedrich Baethgen it was who gave me the chance to join the Monumenta Germaniae. It was the decisive moment of my career. For twelve years I served the Monumenta Germaniae and so it was that a close bond was created which no change in the external circumstances of my life has been able to alter. It was not just the length of time which created this bond. It was also the meticulous work which was expected of me by the members of the Institute, and especially by my immediate superior, Theodor Schieffer; it was being given the opportunity to learn much; above all, it was the consciousness of belonging to a living tradition, a tradition established by some of the greatest names in German historical learning—the scholars who had made the Monumenta Germaniae famous. Thus in dedicating this book in gratitude to Friedrich Baethgen who opened for me the doors of the Monumenta Germaniae, I would also like to express my thanks to the Monumenta Germaniae Historica for those twelve years when I enjoyed complete freedom to research.

I cannot conclude without first thanking others. During the preparation of this translation both my German publisher, W. Kohlhammer, and the Clarendon Press have always been most helpful. My good friend and eminent colleague, Karl Leyser, of Magdalen College, Oxford, constantly encouraged me to have the book translated. I was extremely fortunate to find in John Gillingham, of The London School of Economics, a translator who is also a medievalist. I would like to pay my particular thanks to him for the boundless patience with which he has answered my questions and accommodated my wishes. On questions of content I have had the benefit of his friendly criticism and wide historical knowledge. It has been a most enjoyable co-operative effort; I could not have wished for a better translator.

When I see this book in print I shall look back with nostalgia to the months when, among other things, I put the finishing touches to the English edition; to the untroubled months when I was a guest in the gracious atmosphere of a scholar's paradise—the villa of Dumbarton Oaks in Georgetown, Washington D.C.

Washington D.C.
January 1971

PREFACE TO THE SECOND EDITION

AFTER the original German edition (1965) had been reprinted five times, Messrs Kohlhammer of Stuttgart decided to let me completely revise it, although it was still selling well. I am both happy and grateful that Oxford University Press decided that there should also be a completely revised English edition.

The alterations are very substantial, ranging from nuances reflecting new shades of opinion to whole sections which have been added or completely rewritten. During the past twenty years research has tended to concentrate on the history of the crusader states and the revisions necessarily reflect this development. Consequently, in quantity as well as in quality, the main changes are to be found in chapters 4, 6, 8, and 14. Inevitably this has made the book somewhat longer, so, in order to keep this growth within tolerable limits, I have omitted chapter 15 with its brief perspective on the crusades from the fourteenth to the sixteenth centuries. In the notes I have omitted most references to primary sources in order to make more room for the scholarly literature. This will in any case lead the reader to the sources. I have taken account of most of the literature published up to 1985, a year in which the harvest worldwide was particularly good in this field.

We are now witnessing in Britain, which today supplies more historians of the crusades than any other country, a growing interest in the crusading movement as such, both before and after 1291, both ideologically and as a series of events. But this new emphasis in the direction of research is only beginning to emerge and I have left this to be dealt with in books by English colleagues which are now in the making. I have, however, added a few details of particular interest to English readers. Once again I must thank John Gillingham, the translator of this book, for looking after the English translation of the revision.

I take pleasure in thanking my staff in Kiel, above all Mrs Annelie Gutow, but also Dr Thomas Vogtherr and Ms Susanne Dammann, for their unfailing help in producing this book. More than I can say I owe to the scholars with whom, during the last thirty years, I have been privileged to share the joys of research in this field: Claude Cahen, Marie-Luise Favreau-Lilie, Bernard Hamilton, Rudolf Hiestand, Robert B. C. Huygens, Jonathan Riley-Smith, and R. C. Smail. *Meliora eis, falsa mihi.*

Kiel,
January 1986

CONTENTS

LIST OF MAPS

I

THE MEDITERRANEAN REGION IN 1095

THE geography of the world as men pictured it in the late eleventh century differed hardly at all from the conceptions formulated in classical times. It is important to note this before taking a closer look at the history of the crusades for, when the crusades were over, this, together with much else, had changed. Although the teaching of Ptolemy of Alexandria was generally accepted in the early Middle Ages, his theory of the spherical shape of the earth had been almost completely forgotten owing to the great influence of the encyclopaedist, Isidore of Seville. But by the end of the crusading period a growing acquaintance with Ptolemy's own writings had given a new lease of life to this theory. Above all, a very great deal had been learnt about the inhabited world which lay east of Europe. This was new knowledge, based on the descriptions of travellers, and not merely the revival of traditional learning. By contrast, in the earlier period between the heyday of the Roman Empire and the start of the crusades, the frontiers of the known world had remained relatively stable, although some advances had been made as a result of the spread of Christianity into Germany, Scandinavia, and some parts of the Byzantine Empire.

From a European point of view the centre of gravity of the world of 1095 still lay in the Mediterranean lands. It was here that the pope lived; here were the capitals of the eastern and western empires, Constantinople and Rome. The imperial crown of the West was worn, it is true, by the kings of Germany, but a king of Germany (or rather, to use his contemporary title, a king of the Romans) could obtain that crown only from the hand of the pope and at Rome. Moreover, with the exception of Spain, the Mediterranean Sea was the great dividing line between the two world-religions, Christianity and Islam. Broadly speaking, the north coast was Christian, the south coast Muslim. In places where the Muslims had advanced north of this line they had either already been forced to retreat, as in France (c. 973) and Sicily (1091), or they were now in the process of being pushed back.

It might have been expected that Europe would be united as it gathered its strength for a vigorous counter-attack on the Muslims whose invasions had caused so much misery during the eighth, ninth, and tenth centuries. But although the continent had recovered from the direct consequences of these invasions and those of the Vikings and Magyars, and was once again in the ascendant, there was still no question of there being anything remotely approaching a coherent European political structure such as had once been supplied by the Carolingian Empire. Indeed on the eve of the crusades Europe was caught up in fierce internecine struggles. In the Investiture Contest the papacy, reformed and strengthened during the course of the eleventh century, attempted to shake off the protecting hand of the secular power. The visible symbol of this power was the royal practice of installing bishops and abbots in their offices by investing them with ring and staff. By virtue of the so-called 'proprietary church law' (*Eigenkirchenrecht*), the king then claimed rights of lordship over them. In the nature of things the pope's most important opponent in this contest was the emperor. Henry IV (1056–1105) broke completely with the pope and recognized an anti-pope, Guibert of Ravenna, as Clement III (1080–1100). The climax of the Investiture Contest—Henry IV's penance at Canossa (1077) and then the collapse of the position of his papal opponent, Gregory VII (1073–85)—was, it is true, already past; none the less the emperor was still excommunicated and agreement a long way off. It did not come until the Concordat of Worms in 1122. At any rate when a pope planned a crusade he left the emperor out of his reckoning.

But neither could he count upon the kings of France and England. Philip I of France (1060–1108) had been excommunicated in 1094 for sending his wife Bertha packing. William Rufus of England (1087–1100), a son of William the Conqueror, was still preoccupied with the consolidation of Norman power in England. His policies, anyway, were usually extremely anti-clerical. North Italy was caught up in the imperial–papal struggle; south Italy had only recently been subjugated by the Normans who had driven out the Byzantines and Saracens. In the Iberian peninsula the kings of Asturia-Leon, Navarre, Aragon, and Portugal were all engaged in expelling the Muslims, though not until 1492 was complete success finally achieved.

Since 1054 not even the Christian Church had been at one. On the surface, the schism, still unhealed today, was the result firstly of an interpolation of the creed by the West which the Eastern Church was unable to accept, and secondly of the liturgical problem of whether leavened or unleavened bread should be used at communion. But just as important as the growing differences in theology and ritual were matters of politics—church politics like the question of the primacy of Rome and secular politics like the rivalry between the two 'Roman' empires of East and West. The cultural differences between the Greek-speaking East and the Latin West were too great for the unity of Christendom to survive for long.

Not that all relations between East and West had been broken off since 1054.[1] On the contrary, the wish for a union of the Churches permeated papal policy throughout the Middle Ages, and time and again it had an influence on the history of the crusades. In Rome it was recognized that the schism in no way freed the West from a responsibility towards their Christian brothers in the East. Even before the crusades in 1074 Gregory VII had wanted to organize an expedition to help the Eastern Empire against the invading Seldjuks—though presumably he hoped thereby to reap advantages of his own. Then in 1078 he completely reversed his policy when a marriage alliance which he had just helped to arrange between Robert Guiscard, the Norman ruler of south Italy, and a Byzantine princess, fell through as the result of a palace revolution in Constantinople. Pope Gregory excommunicated the new emperor and then the next one—Alexius Comnenus (1081–1118), who also obtained the imperial throne by means of a palace revolution. In him, after long years of internal dissension, Byzantium had again found an energetic ruler. In these circumstances there was no immediate chance of a union of the Churches.

In 1071 the Normans had captured Bari, the last Byzantine stronghold in Italy. Ten years later, just when Alexius Comnenus ascended the throne, they moved on to attack the empire itself at Epirus. With Venetian help Alexius was able to drive the Normans back; then Robert Guiscard had to return home to deal with unrest in south Italy, where he died in 1085. The Venetians came out of it best, for they obtained far-reaching commercial privileges in return for their help. These privileges undermined the traditional trading system of Byzantium, established the long-lasting political influence of Venice in the Adriatic and provided a spring-board for further expansion towards Constantinople, the Eastern Mediterranean, and the Levant.

For Byzantium, however, the Muslims presented a greater threat than the Normans. Very soon after Muhammad's death it had become clear that the new religion was possessed of an enormous political energy. Borne up by the idea of the jihad, the holy war, the Arabs forced their way east and west in a breathtaking expansion of power. (Whereas the Christian holy war was, in theory if not always in practice, a defensive undertaking, the jihad was right from the beginning a war of aggression.) In the second half of the seventh century they conquered the whole of North Africa. In 711 the Ommayad Tariq crossed the Straits of Gibraltar and destroyed the Visigothic kingdom of Spain. Not until 732, when the Carolingian Charles Martel won the Battle of Poitiers, was the Arab torrent dammed. But the Arab conquest was not confined to this part of Europe. In the East they posed a serious threat to Byzantium. In the West they overran Sicily in the ninth century and established themselves in south Italy, where, in 982, they decisively defeated the Roman Emperor Otto II. From bases on the coast of Provence they devastated south France and Switzerland. They controlled the Alpine passes, and it was on the Great St. Bernard that they captured Majolus, the universally venerated Abbot of Cluny in 972. This notorious ambush marked a turning point. Gradually energetic counter-attacks were organized and the Arabs were driven out of France and, by the Normans, out of Italy and Sicily. In Spain, however, they were more firmly established and here the *Reconquista* lasted until the end of the Middle Ages.

Islam too was torn by schism, between Sunnite and Shi'ite. The development of this split must be traced in rather more detail since it had considerable influence on Muslim history in the period of the crusades.[2] It went back to the situation at the death of Muhammad. One group recognized Abu Bakr, one of Muhammad's close associates, as caliph, i.e. as the prophet's representative. The other group believed that Ali—as Muhammad's cousin and son-in-law—had a better claim by virtue of his kinship. And in fact Ali did become the fourth caliph. Ali's supporters called themselves Shi'ites (Shi'atu Ali means Ali's party) and would recognize only his descendants as caliphs. The opposing party called themselves Sunnites because they believed that they had held fast to the correct tradition. (Sunna means the orally transmitted sayings of Muhammad.) The Abbasid caliphs of Baghdad were Sunnites since they had to be very orthodox in order to make up for being upstarts who had wiped out the legitimate Ommayad caliphs of Damascus.

On the other side because Ali had had several wives it was inevitable that the Shi'ites too would split up. They all agreed that the line of Imams (the successors of Ali) would have to come to an end at some time, because the last Imam would work on in concealment in order to reappear as the Mahdi, an eschatological saviour who would bring justice to the world and convert all men to the Shi'a. But they could not agree on which of the Imams was the last one. Depending on the number of Imams they recognized the different Shi'ite sects were known as the 'Fivers', the 'Seveners', and the 'Twelvers'. The last made up the moderate wing of the Shi'ites, while the 'Seveners' who regarded the seventh Imam, Ismail, as the Mahdi—and were therefore called the Ismailites—formed an extremist group. Thanks to their leaning towards social revolution and to their close links with the Muslim guilds they were able to increase their numbers and, in 909, to found the Fatimid caliphate of North Africa (after 973 at Cairo) as a rival to the Abbasids of Baghdad.

The Fatimid caliph was not looked upon as the Mahdi. Even so he soon became as dependent on the army and bureaucracy as was his rival in Baghdad. When, in 1094, al-Afdal the vizier of Egypt chose a pliable younger son, al-Mustali, as the new caliph, thus passing over Nizar, the eldest son of the previous ruler, the Fatimids lost the support of the Ismailites. Within the Ismailite movement the centre of gravity shifted to its extreme wing, the Nizarites, the Persian branch of which became famous as the Assassins. The name derived from a corrupt Latin form of hashish, the drug with which they were said to intoxicate themselves. Tightly organized under a kind of 'Grandmaster' they elevated murder to the level of a religious duty as well as a political weapon. Early in the twelfth century some of them settled in North Syria. Savagely persecuted by the Sunnites they became a source of insecurity and terror for Sunnite and Christian alike. The troubadours of the thirteenth century gave eloquent expression to the fear felt by the Christians. Above all the Assassins fought to prevent the creation of a united Sunnite front which would have been directed against them just as much as against the Christian states formed as a result of the First Crusade. In this way they gave indirect help to the crusading states.

The world of Islam which had once been a domain of the Arabs was given a new political structure by the arrival of Turks from Central Asia.[3] Originally shamanist in their beliefs the Turks became Sunnite Muslims during the tenth century. In a sense they saved Islam because they brought to it the warrior spirit of the nomad just at the time when the political drive of the Arabs was fading. Particularly important were the Seldjuks, Turkish tribesmen who within little more than fifty years built up an immense empire which stretched from Khorassan and Persia to the Caucasus, from Mesopotamia to Syria and Palestine and as far as the Hijaz, the birthplace of Islam. The orthodox caliphs were freed from the Shi'ite overlordship of the Persian Buyids only to become tools in the hands of the Seldjuk sultans. Sultan Alp-Arslan (1063–73) pushed still further west and in 1071 defeated the Byzantine army at Manzikert in eastern Anatolia. From that date on Turks migrated almost imperceptibly into Anatolia and slowly but surely undermined the Byzantine provincial administration. The reign of Sultan Malik Shah (1077–92) witnessed the final expulsion of the Byzantines out of what was the real power house of their empire. This left the Greek Church of Anatolia in a difficult position and at the same time it added to the problems facing pilgrims on the land route to the Holy Land, though not so much as scholars once thought. But for Byzantium the loss of Anatolia remained a catastrophe.

It cannot be proved that the Turks actually did oppress the Christians in the East, as western sources, among them the speech attributed to Urban II at Clermont, maintained. In the conquered districts the native Christians were treated just as they always had been by the Muslims—as a subject minority population who paid taxes but who enjoyed the protection of Islamic law and a certain measure of freedom of worship. What happened to them at the time of the conquest was the inevitable result of war and was felt by all sections of the population. In particular the non-Melkite Churches of the East, Jacobites and Nestorians who did not speak Greek and who had been oppressed by the Greek Orthodox Church on account of their leanings towards monophysitism and other heresies, had no reason at all to regret the change. Their writers sang the praises of Malik Shah, who after the disturbances of the conquest symbolized the restoration of order, just as loudly as did the Muslim chroniclers. Apart from the persecution under Caliph Hakim (1009), there is no evidence of

anti-Christian pogroms in the eleventh century. The persecution unleashed in Jerusalem by the Turcoman Atsiz in 1078 was definitely anti-
Fatimid in character and the Christians were probably spared. It is
significant that no appeal for help was ever sent to the West by the eastern
Christians. When Urban II and the propagandists for the crusade
emphasized the persecution of the Eastern Christians it was either because
they did not know the real situation or because they wanted to arouse a
vague feeling of resentment in Europe.

In Europe too the Byzantine emperor had a Turkish problem to face.
The Petchenegs, a tribe of Turkish origin now settled in the Danube
valley, allied with the Seldjuks of Asia Minor, and in 1091–2 they attacked
Byzantium on two fronts. But in April 1091 Alexius, with characteristic
forcefulness, defeated the Petchenegs so decisively that they practically
disappeared from history. In Asia Minor, however, the Seldjuks were too
firmly established for Alexius to be able to strike as effectively against
them. He had to be content with coming to terms (1092) with Sultan Kilij
Arslan (1092–1107). When the great Seldjuk empire broke up on the death
of Malik Shah in 1092, Kilij Arslan's share of the inheritance was a part of
Anatolia out of which the Rum-Seldjuk sultanate of Iconium (Rum means
[East-] Rome) was gradually built up. The treaty of 1092 gave Alexius a
respite from Seldjuk attacks and allowed the sultan to consolidate his own
position in Asia Minor.

In Syria, however, Malik Shah's death led to serious disintegration
lasting for more than a decade, by the end of which there had emerged a
system of Seldjuk emirates so delicately balanced that the least alteration
in the political relations of one with another necessarily involved the
reconstruction of the entire system. This explains the incessant variation
in the complicated pattern of Syrian alliances in the first half of the twelfth
century. The newly created crusading states immediately became extra
pieces on the political board.

Meanwhile there had been changes in the West. Gregory VII had died
in 1085 and after the brief pontificate of Victor III, Urban II (1088–99)
had become pope. As a diplomat he was more flexible than Gregory and he
tried to improve relations with Byzantium.[4] In 1089 he sent an embassy
of reconciliation to Alexius and released him from the sentence of
excommunication. Alexius too was conciliatory and so between emperor
and pope friendly relations were established which neither side wished to
endanger by undue emphasis on the theological disagreements. Alexius
was ready to continue the old practice of inserting the pope's name into
the patriarchal lists (the diptychs) if Urban would send a satisfactory
statement of faith within a fixed period of time. Nothing came of it because
Urban was not prepared to do this, but neither of them treated it as vital so
no harmful consequences followed. Urban was quite content that Alexius,
now that he was safe from the assaults of the Normans and on tolerably

good terms with the pope, should break off the negotiations with the Emperor Henry IV which he had earlier keenly pursued.

For his part Alexius could now concentrate on re-organizing the Byzantine army which had been declining in standard ever since its overwhelming defeat at Manzikert. One way of doing this was by hiring western mercenaries. One of the reasons he entered into negotiations on Church unity with Urban II may have been his hope of obtaining such men. Western mercenaries were nothing new in Byzantium. In earlier centuries an élite of foreign troops had formed the Varangian Guard at Constantinople. Despite the traditional enmity between the Normans and Greeks there had often been contingents of Norman soldiers in the ranks of the Byzantine army; their fighting spirit was well-known and much feared. Even though Byzantium enjoyed a respite from war after 1092 this did not mean that Alexius could afford to do without mercenaries. Thus when he met Count Robert I of Flanders on a pilgrimage he asked the count if he could supply him with such troops. And when, in March 1095, Urban II held a council at Piacenza to deal generally with Church reform, it was not surprising that envoys from the Byzantine emperor were also present to let it be known how welcome western mercenaries would be. Clearly they exaggerated the dangers facing the empire and so in papal circles men came to hold the opinion that only drastic measures could save Byzantium—and at the same time the Christian Church in the East— measures which might then lead to a reunion of the Churches under the primacy of Rome. Our information on the Council of Piacenza comes from the chronicler Bernold of Constance, and it is today generally accepted as being trustworthy though there was once a good deal of doubt on the subject. The discovery, nearly forty years ago, of a thirteenth-century Byzantine chronicle tended to confirm Bernold's account for although itself written much later, the chronicle appears to contain excerpts from reliable contemporary historians. It also tells us that when Alexius appealed for help at Piacenza he deliberately emphasized the idea of help for Jerusalem because he anticipated that this would prove an effective propaganda slogan in Europe. In reality, of course, his own aims were quite different. He hoped to reconquer Anatolia and a crusade was the last thing he wanted. He had expected some mercenaries, in contingents small enough to be easily controlled, not the huge armies of knights which in fact set out on the first crusade. If he could have foreseen what was about to hit him he would probably have been very reticent indeed. But the keyword, Jerusalem, had been spoken and events now took their course. Little more than six months after the appeal for help at Piacenza, Urban II, at Clermont, called for a crusade.

2

THE ORIGINS OF THE CRUSADES

POPE URBAN II opened the Council of Clermont on 18 November 1095—the moment that has gone down in history as the starting point of the crusades.[5] Since the summer of that year he had been travelling through south and south-east France; at Le Puy on 15 August he issued the summons to the council. Although Urban had made careful preparations for a discussion of the question of a crusade by the Church assembly, there was at first nothing which gave any hint of the extraordinary events which were to follow. The council was attended mostly by French bishops and it dealt mostly with internal Church affairs which particularly concerned the French clergy; with general questions of reform, lay investiture, and simony; as well as with the adultery of the king of France. Also on the agenda was the peace of God, i.e. the prohibition of feuding on certain days and the immunity of certain people, places, and things. The pope's presence meant that the Peace of God movement which had hitherto been organized on a purely regional basis, was now recognized by the papacy and its application was extended to cover the whole Church. Only one of the decrees of the Council dealt with the crusade. It laid down the conditions under which a crusader qualified for a spiritual reward.

The moment which gave the council its special place in history came right at the end on 27 November. On this day the pope was due to make an important speech. So many clerks and laymen gathered to listen to him that the meeting had to be held in a field outside the town. We have four reports of Urban's speech. None of them is unquestionably authentic. Some were written after the turn of the century; and they all differ considerably from one another. None the less it is possible to reconstruct his speech in rough outline, though naturally the actual words are irrecoverable. With Gallic eloquence Urban painted a vivid picture of the supposed oppression of the Christian Churches in the east. The Seldjuks had occupied Asia Minor; the churches and Holy Places had been destroyed and defiled by heathens. Now even Antioch, the city of St. Peter, had been taken. Here then was a noble task for the knights of Christendom whose other activities had been restricted by the Peace of God. In moving words the pope called upon both rich and poor to help their Christian brothers in the east. In this way peace might be restored to Christendom; there would be an end to the fratricidal wars in Europe, to the oppression of widows and orphans, and to the threats made against churches and abbeys by a rapacious nobility. In denouncing what was, in effect, a state of civil war, the pope (according to Robert the Monk's version of his speech) explained it in terms of the widespread poverty and malnutrition which resulted from inadequate cultivation of the soil.

The success of this appeal was extraordinary. *Deus lo volt*—God wills it—was the cry which went up from the listening crowd. Bishop Adhemar of Le Puy, who had undoubtedly known of the pope's plans for some time, was the first to take the cross. Many of those present followed his example. Garments were cut up into the shape of crosses which each of them attached to his shoulder in imitation of Christ (Matthew 10:38). On 1 December messengers came from the powerful count of Toulouse, Raymond IV of St. Gilles, announcing their lord's readiness to take part in the crusade. Since Raymond must have sent his messengers before he could have heard any news of Urban's speech, it is clear that he had advance knowledge of the pope's intentions. The enthusiasm spread far beyond Clermont. Urban remained in France for several months longer and continued to preach the crusade, at Limoges for example. He also sent out written appeals. Three of these, to the Flemings, the Bolognese, and the monks of Vallombrosa, are still extant today. The bishops played their part in the crusading movement and sent preachers out among the people. The response was enormous, especially in south France but also in the Mâconnais, in Lorraine, in the western parts of the Empire, in Champagne, Normandy, and Flanders. Everywhere warriors and men of peace alike were ready to go on the journey to Jerusalem, certainly in far greater numbers than Urban could possibly have foreseen.

The success of the Clermont appeal has still not been fully explained and probably never can be. Nor will any definitive interpretation be offered here; after all, the reasons for taking the cross varied considerably from one individual to another. All one can do is to examine a whole range of spiritual and worldly motives of different kinds which coalesced not only to produce the spark of that unique and spontaneous success at Clermont but also to light a fire which burned for two hundred years.

Originally the object of the crusade was to help the Christian Churches in the East. However unnecessary such help may, in fact, have been, it was in these terms that Urban is supposed to have spoken at Clermont. But very soon men had a more definite object in mind: to free the Holy Land and, above all, Jerusalem, the Sepulchre of Christ, from the yoke of heathen dominion. It seems that Urban himself had not used the word Jerusalem at Clermont. At any rate it is not mentioned by Fulcher of Chartres whose report of the speech is the one closest to the event. Only in the later versions does Urban make an impassioned appeal for the liberation of Jerusalem. But there is still better evidence of this in the letters which Urban himself wrote. The accounts of the Clermont speech in the chronicles are too much coloured by the tendency of the authors to show off their own rhetorical skills. In the letter sent to the Flemings late in 1095 the pope still speaks mainly of the liberation of the Eastern Churches; Jerusalem is mentioned only in passing. In the letter sent to Bologna in September 1096, however, Jerusalem has quite explicitly become the goal. On the other hand both the second canon of the Council of Clermont and the letter to Vallombrosa of October 1096 refer, in very similar terms, to the 'march to Jerusalem to free the Church of God'. Erdmann hoped to resolve the difficulty by making a distinction between the object of the war, the liberation of the Eastern Churches, and the goal of the march, Jerusalem. It is, perhaps, an oversubtle interpretation. Jerusalem cannot have been used merely as a lure; the name was too potent and would inevitably have pulled the whole enterprise in this one direction. It is rather more likely in view of the evident lack of over-all planning that Urban had not in fact made much of Jerusalem while at Clermont but that during the course of the next year he gave in to public opinion which needed and created a concrete goal.

In contrast to the opinion expressed here, H. E. J. Cowdrey, in a very impressive study, saw things differently and argued on the basis of various previously unnoticed sources, especially the *Fragmentum historiae Andegavensis* of February 1096 and some charters, that Jerusalem had a central role in Urban's crusading ideas. He believes that for the pope Jerusalem was the centre of the Eastern Church he wished to liberate and that therefore its conquest was a necessity. While admitting that Cowdrey might be correct, I would observe that one should not lose sight of the danger that the pope, in pushing for a conquest of Jerusalem, might create a new rival for Rome (Jerusalem) instead of eliminating an old one (Constantinople). I should also point out that there is no evidence that immediately after the Council of Clermont men talked exclusively of Jerusalem rather than of Jerusalem in the context of the Eastern Churches. Both the second canon of the Council of Clermont and Urban's letter to the Flemings—and these are the only two sources which date from 1095— refer to Jerusalem only in a wider context. So also does the *Fragmentum* when it urges people to go there to subdue the race of the heathen 'who had seized that city and all the land of the Christians up as far as Constantinople'. It should also be remembered that the same pope, who, according to Cowdrey, placed Jerusalem at the heart of his notion of the crusade, spoke not one word about Jerusalem in a letter written in May 1098, when the crusade had come to a halt outside Antioch. Instead he declared that it was the task of the moment to fight the Turks in Asia and the Moors in Europe (*in Asia Turcos, in Europa Mauros*). Cowdrey's charter evidence is impressive and as a rule these charters speak of the march to Jerusalem. But that public opinion in 1096 saw things in these terms is not in dispute. And even in the charters there is no uniform terminology. From the Auvergne, where the Council of Clermont took place, a charter for the abbey of Sauxillanges refers unmistakably to the First Crusade but speaks an entirely different language: 'When the persecution of the barbarians rose up to destroy the liberty of the Eastern Church, it came about that the entire strength and faith of the western peoples hastened to assist the destroyed religion at the exhortation of the pope'. But though I still hold to the view that it was the people and not the pope who brought about the concentration on Jerusalem itself, it is evident that this is an obscure area where different interpretations, like Cowdrey's, are perfectly possible.[6]

Even the mere sound of the name Jerusalem must have had a glittering and magical splendour for the men of the eleventh century which we are no longer capable of feeling.[7] It was a keyword which produced particular psychological reactions and conjured up particular eschatological notions. Men thought, of course, of the town in Palestine where Jesus Christ had suffered, died, been buried, and then had risen again. But, more than this, they saw in their minds' eye the heavenly city of Jerusalem with its gates of sapphire, its walls and squares bright with precious stones—as it had been described in the Book of Revelation (21 : 10ff.) and Tobias (13 : 21f.). It was the centre of a spiritual world just as the earthly Jerusalem was, in the words of Ezekiel (5 : 5) 'in the midst of the nations and countries'. It was a meeting place for those who had been scattered, the goal of the great pilgrimage of peoples (Tobias 13 : 14; Isaiah 2 : 2), where God resides among his people; the place at the end of time to which the elect ascend; the resting place of the righteous; city of paradise and of the tree of life which heals all men.

Since a good proportion of the crusaders would not have been capable of distinguishing between the earthly and the heavenly Jerusalem such images must have had a powerful effect upon them. They believed that they were marching directly to the city of eternal bliss. Above all it was the *pauperes*, the landless poor, whose apocalyptic and eschatological piety was crystallized in the vision of Jerusalem. The increasingly millenarian outlook of the masses was studied by Alphandéry who, in the course of his investigations, contributed many original and noteworthy ideas to the problem of the origins of the crusades, though he was probably inclined to exaggerate the importance of such eschatological influences. These influences, discernible chiefly in the form of visions, were not equally present throughout the crusade. They appear both before and during the departure but not again in any significant number until after the capture of Antioch in 1098. Between 1096 and 1098 there are few traces of this kind of thing. This suggests that the masses came under the spell of eschatological ideas only in certain situations and not while the crusade was advancing smoothly. Some visions were clearly induced and exploited by the leaders in order to raise morale at critical moments. The most remarkable example of this is the discovery of the Holy Lance (see below, p. 52). But there are also clear signs of an eschatological outlook right at the start, especially when the poor were beginning their march without waiting for the official crusade. The 'signs'—a plague of locusts, a rain of stars from heaven—are apocalyptic in character (cf. Revelation 9: 3; 6: 13). Baudri of Dol tells us that this apocalyptic atmosphere was not created by the official preaching organized by the bishops. Instead it was spontaneously disseminated through a process of mutual, sermon-like exhortations to which the *pauperes* responded all the more readily since the bad harvests of the years before 1096 made it easy to leave home and fields in order to follow the path to salvation, the road to a better future—a future which the theologically uneducated masses, filled with dim, vague, and incoherent eschatological dreams, probably pictured in an entirely material fashion. Some of the *pauperes* certainly believed that they were of the elect, believed that the words of Psalm 147 referred to them: 'The lord doth build up Jerusalem; he gathereth together the outcasts of Israel.' Believing this they had no hesitation about occasionally bringing pressure to bear on the commanders of the crusade; on the other hand leaders like Raymond of Toulouse reckoned with such feelings and turned them to their own purposes. It would be wrong to impute apocalyptic and eschatological motives only to the *pauperes* and deny them to the knights who, according to Alphandéry, were more strongly driven by the idea of a holy war in the service of the Church.[8] But the effectiveness of eschatological ideas should, in any event, not be overestimated. The evidence comes from chroniclers who were themselves actively creating a doctrine of the crusade and who were writing after the event, some of them a long time after. There is a good deal more to the crusade than this. After all, a great many pilgrimages to Jerusalem were made in the year 1033, the millennium of Christ's passion. According to Ralph Glaber's account they too were preceded by supernatural signs and were entirely eschatological in spirit, seeming to proclaim the coming of Antichrist which itself precedes the Parousia, the second coming of Christ (2 Thessalonians 2: 3–12). Yet these pilgrimages did not become a crusade. Above all there was nothing like the all-embracing mass movement of 1095–6. In the final analysis what was decisive was not millenarian thought but the arming of the pilgrimage and the idea of a reward which was latent in the crusading indulgence.

Counting for just as much as the images conjured up by a child-like, mystical faith was the long tradition of pilgrimage to Jerusalem.[9] As early as 333 a pilgrim from Bordeaux reached Palestine; and not much later a Gallic noblewoman named Egeria visited the Holy Places leaving to posterity a report which is as important a monument of a Latin changing from ancient to medieval as it is for the topography of the *loca sancta*. In 386 Saint Jerome settled in Bethlehem; half a century later the Empress Eudocia went into retreat at Jerusalem. Monasteries and hospices were built to receive the travellers who, following the new fashion—as it can fairly be called—came to Palestine. The stream of pilgrims never dried up, not even after the Arab conquest of the Holy Land in the seventh century. The growing east–west trade in relics played some part in awakening and sustaining interest in the Holy Places, but more important was the gradual development of the penitential pilgrimage. This was imposed as a canonical punishment and for capital crimes like fratricide it could be for a period of up to seven years and to all the great centres: Rome, San Michele at Monte Gargano, Santiago di Compostella and, above all, Jerusalem and Bethlehem. With the belief that they were effective ways to salvation the popularity of pilgrimages grew rapidly from the tenth century onwards. Saint John of Parma journeyed no less than six times to the Holy Land—given the conditions of travel at the time an astonishing achievement. Men of violent passions like Fulk Nerra, Count of Anjou, or Robert the Devil, Count of Normandy, went on pilgrimages to Jerusalem when their consciences plagued them on account of the crimes they had committed against church and monastery, so sometimes they had to go more than once. Returning from one of these pilgrimages Fulk founded the abbey of Beaulieu near Loches and gave it as its chief relic a piece of stone which he was said to have bitten off the Holy Sepulchre while kneeling before it in ecstatic prayer. The new Cluniac order, gaining all the time in prestige and influence, used its far-flung net of contacts and its genius for organization both to urge men to go on pilgrimages and to improve facilities for those who did. For many pilgrims in the eleventh century the journey to Jerusalem took on a still deeper religious meaning; according to Ralph Glaber, himself a Cluniac monk, it was looked upon as the climax of a man's religious life, as his final journey. Once he had reached the Holy Places he would remain there until he died.

It is clear that in the middle of the eleventh century the difficulties facing pilgrims began to increase. In part this was a result of the Seldjuk invasions which made things harder for travellers on the road through Anatolia—a popular route because it permitted a visit to Constantinople. But it was also a consequence of the growing number of pilgrims, for this worried the Muslim authorities in Asia Minor and Palestine, just as the Greeks in south Italy looked sceptically upon the groups of Norman 'pilgrims' who were all too easily persuaded to settle there for good. It has been suggested that the Muslims may have had a commercial interest in promoting pilgrimages but, except perhaps in Jerusalem itself, the income from this source cannot have been very significant—poverty was, after all, one of the ideals of the pilgrim. So there was little or no incentive for them to make the journey any easier. Conditions were, of course, nothing like as bad as they had been during the persecution of the Christians under the mad caliph, Hakim, who, in 1009, had had the Church of the Holy Sepulchre in Jerusalem destroyed; but neither were they as favourable as they had been during the great days of the Byzantine Empire or in the time of Charlemagne who had himself taken a keen interest in the pilgrimage to Palestine. Yet despite the occasional trouble the number of pilgrims grew steadily. In 1064–5 Bishop Gunther of Bamberg led a party over 7,000 strong into the Holy Land. Near Ramleh in Palestine they were suddenly attacked by Muslims and for several days they had to fight a defensive battle. It is not easy to explain how they managed this since pilgrims were always unarmed.

Here we have reached the critical point of difference between crusader and pilgrim. The crusader carried weapons. A crusade was a pilgrimage, but an armed pilgrimage which was granted special privileges by the Church and which was held to be specially meritorious. The crusade was a logical extension of the pilgrimage. It would never have occurred to anyone to march out to conquer the Holy Land if men had not made pilgrimages there for century after century. The constant stream of pilgrims inevitably nourished the idea that the Sepulchre of Christ ought to be in Christian hands, not in order to solve the practical difficulties which faced pilgrims, but because gradually the knowledge that the Holy Places, the patrimony of Christ, were possessed by heathens became more and more unbearable. If the link between pilgrimage and crusade is obvious, the credit for bringing it about belongs to Urban II. Although historians today are less inclined to argue that the crusades were caused by increasing difficulties in the way of pilgrims, it still remains true that pilgrimages were of decisive importance in the rise of the crusading movement. In Erdmann's words, Urban 'took the popular but, in practical terms, unfruitful idea of pilgrimage and used it to fertilize the war upon the heathen'. It is significant that contemporaries were at first unable to distinguish clearly between the two things. Not until the mid-thirteenth century was there a Latin word for 'crusade' and even then it was seldom used. (The English word crusade, like the German word *Kreuzzug*, was only invented in the eighteenth century.) In the Middle Ages men almost always used circumlocutions like *expeditio, iter in terram sanctam* (journey into the Holy Land) and—especially early in the crusading period— *peregrinatio*, the technical term for pilgrimage. The line between crusade and pilgrimage was obviously a blurred one.

Naturally the idea of an armed pilgrimage appealed above all to the knightly classes. As Erdmann has shown, thanks to the influence of the Church reformers they had gradually been drawn to the idea of a holy war, the battle for the Church against the heathen. Faced by the problem of harmonizing an inevitable evil with the peaceful and non-violent teaching of Christ, the attitude of the Church to war was understandably a delicate one. In the Byzantine world theologians had unambiguously condemned war but in practice their condemnation had little effect. In the Latin West, men were not ready for so radical and ineffective a point of view. Throughout the Middle Ages, St. Augustine's doctrine of the just war, *bellum justum*, remained authoritative.[10] Only in a just cause was war permissible; only when fought to defend or to recover a rightful possession. Clearly the second of these justifications left plenty of room for a generous interpretation of political circumstances.

The unceasing onslaughts of the pagans on the whole of Christian Europe in the ninth and tenth centuries gave obvious importance to the concept of a defensive war. Armies and raiding parties of Vikings, Magyars, and Arabs swept into Christian territory and under this pressure the population had to endure the hardest time of the Middle Ages in the years following the collapse of the Carolingian Empire. Since the wealth of churches and monasteries made them obvious targets for plunder-hungry invaders, it was only natural that the Church should support what was undoubtedly a clear-cut case of a war of defence. As all these invaders were heathens—for not until after 911 when they settled in Normandy and became a little less aggressive did the Vikings become Christians—this was to be an important stage in the development of crusading thought. The idea of the *bellum justum* became closely associated with war against the heathen. In the ninth century Popes Leo IV and John VIII promised eternal life to all those who fell in battle against either the Arabs or the Vikings. Later on, crusaders received the same assurance. None the less it would be a mistake to see these promises as early symptoms of the crusading idea. The two popes had been influenced by a dictum of the famous sixth-century Spanish bishop, Isidore of Seville: 'men whose wisdom and courage make them worthy of heaven are called heroes'. The importance of these papal promises lies in their emphatic support of the war against the heathen. This war itself was a royal and, in particular, an imperial duty. It had always been the emperor's special task to preserve peace within the Church and to further the spread of Christianity abroad. In time men went over from defence to attack but nearly always they continued to look upon it as a just war in St. Augustine's sense, a war fought to recover what was rightfully theirs. It was always possible to throw the blame for war on the other side and build up a plausible *casus belli* for oneself. It is from this point of view that medieval chroniclers, popes, and preachers must be judged when, and especially after the third crusade, they time and again refer to the Holy Land as the 'patrimony' of the Lord, which belongs to Christendom and which must be defended or reconquered. For this phrase alone was enough to justify the crusades.

The Church's attitude to war was further influenced by the Peace of God movement. In its beginnings this movement had been essentially a self-defence mechanism on the part of the Church. The disintegration of the Carolingian Empire had brought with it a decline in the authority of the state and a general decline of public morals. Everywhere in the tenth century the warrior class, composed of men who were gradually coming to be called knights, was patently brutalized. Private property, especially

Church property, was attacked just as greedily as it ever had been by Vikings or Magyars. The state could do very little about this unhappy state of affairs and it became increasingly difficult to see any sign whatsoever of public order or security. Though it was primarily concern for its own property which persuaded the Church to step in at this point, it is none the less impossible to overlook the beneficial consequences for the whole fabric of society. In the early regional peace agreements, for which there is a good deal of evidence from the end of the tenth century onwards, it was usual for the local nobility to swear to observe the immunity of the clergy, unarmed persons, and ecclesiastical property. Then, from about 1040, it became increasingly the practice to issue decrees prohibiting feuding on certain days; the final stage was to try to abolish the feud altogether and replace it with arbitration. Credit for promoting this movement belongs chiefly to men associated with Cluniac reform. At Cluny, not far from Mâcon in Burgundy, a monastery was founded in 910 which under some vigorous abbots rose to be one of the most important monastic communities in the West. From this centre radiated a reform movement with the primary purpose of achieving a stricter and more profound observance of the Benedictine Rule as well as a liberation of the monastery from external aristocratic influence. But at the same time the outside world was by no means ignored. Efforts were made to bring about a certain spiritualization, a deepening of the layman's religious life so that he was more closely bound to those forces in the Church which, as the reformers saw it, regulated the moral order. In particular these efforts were aimed at the much brutalized knightly classes, and the Peace of God was just one of the means used to get at this group. Yet all this meant that the Church had made a decisive move towards war, indeed towards active participation in war, because it was simply not enough to persuade the nobility to swear peace-oaths; some way of forcing men to keep the peace had to be devised and, if necessary, put into practice. So, in order to punish disturbers of the peace, the Church became involved in organizing and directing military campaigns.

Ecclesiastical wars of this kind—and later, in another context, they were to become more common—were considered to be 'holy wars' fought in the service of an approving Church. But on this question Augustine's teaching presented difficulties of interpretation and so the views of individual clerics differed considerably; by the end of the tenth century the whole doctrine was in a state of flux. In the eleventh century support for this concept of holy war came from the reformers, both those who were chiefly concerned for the monasteries and those who, under papal leadership, were trying to improve the condition of the whole Church. In part doubtless the reformers recognized that in the 'holy war' the Church possessed a valuable political weapon. The same men that played such a decisive part in the transformation of the warrior class into a knightly order were also involved in taking the responsibility for holy war out of the hands of the king who previously had been held to be alone responsible for war, and transferring it on to the shoulders of the knightly class as a whole. This development was an essential pre-condition for the growth of the crusading idea.

But it has been suggested that not only the reform papacy looked favourably upon the idea of a holy war. Two popes from the days before the period of Church reform have even been credited with plans for real crusades.[11] Among the letters of Gerbert of Aurillac, later Pope Sylvester II (993–1003), there is one he wrote before he became pope. Although there has been much argument about the genuiness of this document, it is difficult to reject it altogether. In it some historians believed they could see Gerbert calling for armed help for the Church of Jerusalem. But Erdmann has shown that in fact Gerbert was only concerned to raise alms. It is true that the thought of military intervention did cross his mind but only to be dismissed at once as impracticable. An encyclical published by Sergius IV (1009–12), however, seemed to be more significant. In this the pope really did appear to be calling for some kind of crusade. He had heard the news of the destruction of the Church of the Holy Sepulchre in Jerusalem by Caliph Hakim (1009) and he declared his intention of commanding a fleet which would sail to Syria and there defeat the Muslims and rebuild the Sepulchre. At the beginning of this encyclical he referred clearly to the tradition of pilgrimage to Jerusalem. It would have been hard to overestimate the importance of this document for the growth of the crusading idea, had it not, some twenty-five years ago, been proved to be a forgery. In a fine piece of research Gieysztor demonstrated that it had been written in 1096, not long after the Council of Clermont, at the monastery of St. Pierre de Moissac near Toulouse. In other words this 'encyclical' belongs to the class of documents known as *Excitatoria* of which several others, in letter form, are still extant today. They were written simply as propaganda to drum up support for the crusade.

In fact it was not until the period of reform in the second half of the eleventh century that the papacy was anything like powerful enough to think seriously of a military expedition to the East. The more active policies of the popes of this period also involved them in a new attitude to war. In 1053 Leo IX (1048–54) one of the first reforming popes, took personal command of a campaign in south Italy against the Normans who behaved in much the same way as the heathens and were therefore treated in a similar fashion. To the Germans who took part in the campaign the pope offered exemption from punishment for their crimes and remission of penance. This came nearer the promise of 1095 than those made by Leo IV and John VIII. Then Pope Nicholas II (1058–61) tried to solve the Norman problem by allying with their leaders, Richard of Capua and Robert Guiscard, at Melfi in 1059. The two Norman princes agreed to be

enfeoffed with their possessions by the pope. Thus they became vassals of
the Church and as such, like all vassals, they had the duty of doing military
service for their lord, though in this case the duty was still limited to
undertakings which could be reconciled with the teachings of the Church.
So now the Church had a feudal military force available for the defence of
the papal states, a force which could be used for the purposes of holy war.
For their part the Normans recognized the usefulness of a holy war just as
much as the churchmen did. Robert Guiscard carried out his conquest of
northern Sicily (1061–72) very much in the style of a religiously motivated
holy war, a war against the heathen. He had announced his intention of
doing this in his oath at Melfi in 1059 and had thus obtained the approval
of the Church for the enterprise. Erdmann believed that this war for the
conquest of Sicily had been a kind of crusade, but in fact one essential
ingredient of a crusade was missing. There is no evidence for active papal
participation though it is difficult to believe that the popes did not connive
at it.

Even more than these Norman wars, the fight against the Muslims in
Spain has often been described in terms appropriate to a crusade.[12] In
particular, the conquest of Barbastro in 1064, in which many Frenchmen
took part, has been elevated to the status of a 'proto-crusade'. But here too
the same essential element, active papal co-operation, seems to be missing.
Alexander II's approval of, and support for this war was limited to
granting a kind of indulgence to all participants. The mere fact that the
war against the Muslims in Spain was believed to be meritorious and thus
attracted a certain number of French knights does not make it a crusade.
War against the heathen was, in general, felt to be meritorious and the old
Church doctrine that a soldier had to do penance even when he killed
during the course of a just war in the service of a just prince was fast
disappearing. What happened in Spain was, in fact, a normal holy war, and
here the war against the heathen fitted into a long tradition of resistance to
Islam and as part of the European pattern of resistance it naturally played
an important part in the origins of the crusades. It helped to keep the idea
of fighting the heathen in the forefront of men's minds, above all in
France, where the Spanish campaigns awoke a very strong response.
Obviously there was a connection, however tenuous, between resistance to
the Arabs on the one hand and the crusades on the other. Nevertheless the
war in Spain was not a crusade. Later it became a substitute for a crusade;
French knights, chary of the difficult journey to Jerusalem, could instead
fight Islam in Spain. The popes promoted this, recognizing it as the
equivalent of a crusade. But this cannot hide the fact that these Spanish
'proto-crusades' were actually just holy wars. And not until the pontificate
of Urban II can we see the influence of Spain on the developing concept of
the crusade. These considerations also seem to apply to the naval
expedition of the Pisans and Genoese to Mahdia in Tunisia (1087). The

Pisans combined it with a pilgrimage to Rome and therefore many of them still wore the pilgrim's scrip in Africa. But this was coincidental and Erdmann went too far in asserting that the campaign had been 'conducted entirely as a crusade'. However, this campaign may have alerted Urban to the possibility of arming pilgrimages.

When making his own crusading plans Urban could look back to his predecessor, Gregory VII, after whom this whole period has been called the Gregorian Age. Gregory was one of the most energetic and pugnacious men ever to sit on the throne of St. Peter. For him it was no longer just a question of the freedom of the Church from secular lordship. He proclaimed the overlordship of the pope. This policy led inevitably to the struggles of the Investiture Contest. Both sides used polemical writings as war propaganda and, given the bitterness with which they waged the struggle, it was pretty well inevitable that they would in some way or another become involved with the question of holy war—especially since Gregory VII paid a great deal of attention to the knightly classes and tried to win them over to fight in the service of the Church. To do this he used the old concept of a soldiery of Christ, *militia Christi*. Previously this had been taken to mean the clergy who fought with the weapons of peace. Under Gregory it became a 'new model army', the *militia sancti Petri*, the knights of St. Peter, and retained little of the old peaceful content. The knights of St. Peter were the armed soldiers of the church. One of the most convinced Gregorians, Bishop Bonizo of Sutri, was, in his book *De vita christiana* (c. 1090–5), the first writer to compile a catalogue of the duties of a Christian knight. With this work the Church had finally arrived at a new attitude to war. The knights, as a class, had acquired their own professional ethos—an ethos firmly rooted in the Church's conception of the world—with its visible liturgical expression in the ceremony of dubbing. It is important to realize that on the eve of the crusades there existed a fully developed class of knights, sharing a moral code which transcended political frontiers and which enabled them to undertake common enterprises.

Bonizo, however, expressly disavowed the idea of fighting the heathen. They no longer posed an immediate threat and in the heat of the Investiture Contest it was common for other considerations to assume greater importance in the Church's theory of war. Instead of war against the heathen, men thought in terms—once again they were essentially St. Augustine's terms—of war against heretics and schismatics. Without going into details it is possible to distinguish roughly between the Gregorians who were in favour of an aggressive war against heretics and the supporters of the emperor who opposed it.

Even so the idea of war against the heathen was still far from being dead. Ivo of Chartres, a man who looked for a compromise solution to the Investiture Contest, continued to propound it. And during the whole of the year 1074 no less a person than Gregory VII cherished the plan of an expedition to the East. He wanted to lead it himself and in this way help to defend the Christian empire of Byzantium against the advancing heathens. It is impossible to say whether Gregory wanted to go to Jerusalem itself, but Our Lord's Sepulchre was mentioned—the words which later were to be so effective had been spoken. We know about the plan from the references to it in Gregory's letters, but how he came to devise it remains a mystery. Occasionally his intentions were clothed in such adventurous and fantastic terms that it is difficult to see clearly just what lay behind it all. Certainly the plight of the Byzantine Empire was desperate enough to warrant such intervention. The Greek army had been annihilated by the Seldjuks at the battle of Manzikert in 1071 and, as a result, Anatolia lay open to the Turcoman attacks. At the same time the Petchenegs were pressing forward in the Balkans; in south Italy Bari fell to the Normans. Moreover Gregory VII, like Urban II and many later popes, hoped to mend the schism of 1054 and it is quite possible that some idea of reuniting the Churches lay behind the plan of 1074. In fact, his plan was quite impracticable. With the Investiture Contest breaking out the pope could not leave and there was no hope of German co-operation. Besides this, the Normans were at odds with Byzantium and Gregory was urging the French nobility to take action against their king in support of the Church's policy. None the less Gregory's plan is important in as much as here, for the first time, we can see the idea of a papally directed military operation in the Middle East. In broad terms, what Urban II proposed at Clermont was very similar to what Gregory VII had intended, and since in much else Urban was to carry through to completion the plans which Gregory himself had been unable to accomplish, it may well be that the similarity was deliberate. In the event, however, Urban's crusade was not to be an undertaking in the Gregorian manner, 'in the service of St. Peter', as Robinson has suggested. For although Urban bestowed banners of St. Peter on the crusaders and although the official biography of him in the *Liber Pontificalis* emphasizes the leadership of St. Peter in the crusade, none the less, Riley-Smith has clearly demonstrated that for nobles and common folk alike the crusaders were no longer a *militia sancti Petri* but a new style fighting *militia Christi*.[13]

In the historical discussion about the origins of the crusades it seems probable that too much attention has been paid to the eleventh-century developments in the Church's concept of a holy war. Erdmann, in particular, was inclined to give this overriding importance. But one thing at any rate his investigations have shown beyond all question: a crusade was possible only after the Church had prepared the ground for it by working out a theory of holy war and by creating a class of Christian knights.

Despite everything that has been said about pilgrimages and holy war, it would be wrong to hope to explain the big part played in the crusade by the knights only in terms of religion, group psychology, and a professional ethos. Dry economic and social factors were also significant, more so indeed than is commonly allowed today. Frequently specialists have tended to ignore this side of the problem, important though it clearly is. Instead a great deal has been said about the knight's love of adventure and his lust for booty. In the East he had the chance of making a quick fortune and of rising to a much higher position than he could ever have hoped for in his native country. The Norman Conquest of England had shown what could be done. Doubtless some of the leaders of the First Crusade thought in such terms, especially the Normans from south Italy, Tancred and Bohemund of Taranto, and perhaps Robert of Normandy as well. After all, at Clermont Urban himself had promised that all those who went on crusade would enjoy undisturbed possession of the lands they conquered.

Love of adventure, lust for booty—these are characteristics of individuals. But thanks to the work of Duby and Herlihy we know of economic and social problems which touched the knightly class as a whole and taught it to look upon the crusade as a way out.[14] Herlihy has argued that there was a crisis in the agrarian economy of south France and Italy beginning in about 850 and becoming steadily worse until its climax was reached in about 1000. For the years after 1000 we have vivid chronicle descriptions of recurring famines which can be explained in terms of the failure of agricultural production to keep pace with the rising population. The still prevalent Carolingian custom of dividing an inheritance between all the heirs tended to hinder efforts to increase production. After 1000 the position began to improve, slowly at first, but then with gathering momentum. This was achieved mainly by doing away with the custom of splitting up the land into ever smaller holdings. There was no relaxation of population pressure. The Church and the nobility began to buy out small landholders in order to build up efficient economic units. Care was taken to ensure that land, once gathered together, should not again be dispersed. The knightly classes—the crusading classes par excellence—did this in various ways. In north France they developed the system of primogeniture, the right of the eldest son to succeed to the inheritance. Younger sons had to look after themselves, whether by entering the Church or by going in for a military career. Obviously the crusade acted as a kind of safety valve for a knightly class which was constantly growing in numbers. It is within this context that we must see an individual's love of adventure or hunger for loot.

In Italy and in France south of the Loire, above all in Burgundy, fragmentation of land was avoided by various forms of shared possession. We are particularly well informed about conditions in the Mâconnais, where there was a very strong tie binding the individual to the family. Here allodial land i.e. land which was freely owned, was almost always held in common by the members of the family. This was a legal form known as *frérêche (fraternitia)*. It usually remained effective up until the second generation and prevented the splitting up of allods. Control of an inheritance passed to the brothers in common, or sometimes it might be shared with uncles, nephews, and even legal persons. Even if the individual's stake in the whole was only a small one, the community remained rich enough to equip one or two mounted knights. In this way the family's social status was preserved and at the same time provision was made for the uninterrupted administration of the estate by those who stayed at home. But this was an institution which worked only when the individual submitted to a tight discipline—the control exercised by the head of the family, a control which seems to have been extraordinarily strict at the end of the eleventh century. This was particularly so in matters of marriage, since, for economic reasons, the success of the *frérêche* depended upon an upper limit to the number of share-holders being enforced. Against the tide of a generally rising population the number of children had to be kept roughly constant. At that time there was only one really effective way of doing this: by a deliberate restriction of marriage. If, despite this, there were still too many potential heirs, some of them would have to be provided for in monasteries or in cathedral chapters. It is in fact possible to trace the outlines of such policies being pursued by the families of the Mâconnais.

Thus the maintenance of the family's economic and social position, in other words its standard of living, involved considerable sacrifices on the part of the individual. Men of an independent outlook may well have been frustrated by such strict family authority; not all were prepared to bow to the harsh requirements of the community, to renounce marriage even. One way out was to enter the Church but that was to exchange one community for another. The other great safety valve of the twelfth century, the crusade, offered a real chance of escaping from the tutelage of the *frérêche*, a real chance for the individual to become independent. But if there were some men who went on crusade in order to break away from the forced community of the family and to make a freer life for themselves, there were also others who chose to go in order to serve the best interests of the family, particularly in a situation where there were too many heirs and where fragmentation seemed inevitable unless some of them left home. An example of this occurred in the Mâconnais family of La Hongre. In 1096 it consisted of five men. Two of them were monks; two went to Jerusalem and did not return. This left Humbert who remained behind as the sole heir of their allodial possessions. In 1147 one of Humbert's grandsons went on the Second Crusade, leaving the whole inheritance to his brother. Thus the La Hongre family was still well-off at the beginning of the thirteenth century when others of their class were already beginning to feel the pinch of new economic developments. It is also worth noting that the early legislation of the crusader kingdom of Jerusalem was clearly appropriate to the needs of men with strong family ties like those of the *frérêche*. The estates held by the knightly families of Jerusalem could be inherited not only by daughters but also by collateral relatives. Not until *c*.1150 was the right to succeed limited to direct descendants. The earlier custom was clearly designed to persuade knights to settle down in the Holy Land; thus it had to accept the requirements of the *frérêche*. If the crusader died then the family back home in Europe could choose another member to take over the Palestinian inheritance, in this way further easing conditions within the *frérêche* itself. It is not accidental that the Mâconnais has bulked large in this discussion. In this region Urban II's appeal met with a notable response. We know the names of many crusaders who came from this part of Europe in the first half of the twelfth century. This is not just the result of chance survival of evidence. It reflects clearly the social and economic situation of a class which looked upon the crusade as a way of solving its material problems or—to say the very least—which was, owing to this situation, all the more ready to consider going on a crusade. Riley-Smith has recently expressed doubts about taking the cross in the interests of the family. Instead he has justly pointed to the importance of vassalic loyalty as a motive for settling in the East, a motive which must also have applied to taking the cross. However, restricting the number of marriages is a drastic way to safeguard a family's economic position, and in situations where only the eldest son and heir was allowed to marry—as was also the case, so Duby has more recently argued, among the aristocracy of northern France—it is natural to assume that younger sons would make use of every available opportunity, the crusade included, to ease their lot. In any event we should not overlook those crusaders, particularly numerous in the count of Toulouse's contingent, who were not tied as vassals to one of the leaders of the crusade.

One more motive for taking the cross remains to be considered; and this one was to put all the others in the shade. It was the concept of a reward in the form of the crusading indulgence.[15] In modern Roman Catholic doctrine the indulgence comes at the end of a clear process of remission of sins. First the penitent sinner must confess and receive absolution so that the guilt of the sin is remitted and instead of suffering eternal punishment he will have to suffer only the temporal penalties due to sin. (It is important to note that these penalties may take place either in this world or the next and will include purgatory.) Then in return for indulgence-earning works the Church may grant him remission of all or part of the penalty due to sin, depending on whether the indulgence is a plenary one or not. This is a judicial act of grace based on the authority of the Church's power of the keys and is entirely separate from the sacrament of penance. The indulgence would affect both the canonical punishment imposed by the Church—the penitential punishment— and the temporal punishment imposed by God, since the Church could offer God a substitute penance from the 'Treasury of Merits'—an inexhaustible reservoir of merits accumulated by Christ and added to by the saints on a scale far in excess of what they themselves needed. Undoubtedly then the indulgence has a transcendental effect before God (*in foro Dei*). Where the theologians disagree with one another is on the question of whether one can absolutely guarantee that this judicial act will have a positive result *in foro Dei* or whether it runs up against the problem of God's freedom. In this case the positive result is only indirectly and morally assured in as much as the Church guarantees that the offer of a substitute penance is sufficient to discharge the whole of the punishment due, i.e. the sinner could not have achieved any better result even if he had himself done full penance. But when considering early indulgences, especially the first crusading indulgences, it is vital to remember that this logical doctrine was a later construction designed to give theological authority to customs which, in practice, already existed.

Not until after the First Crusade did the theologians of the twelfth century, first among them Hugh of St. Victor, work out—in practical, if not yet in formal terms—the distinction between the guilt of sin and the punishment due to sin which is crucial to the theory of indulgences. And not until *c.*1230 was the important doctrine of the 'Treasury of Merits', which provided the equivalent substitute necessary if punishment were to be remitted, formulated by Hugh of St. Cher. The detailed problems of the precise nature of an indulgence and the justification for it were hotly disputed in the twelfth and thirteenth centuries. Even St. Thomas Aquinas was clearly hard put to it to explain the indulgence because he began his proof of it by producing a classic logical fallacy (*petitio principii*): 'Everyone agrees that indulgences are effective because it would be godless to say that the Church does anything in vain.' Where even theologians found much obscure, there was little chance of popular opinion being well-informed. Any discussion of the crusades must take this point more fully into consideration than has hitherto been customary. In assessing the effect of the crusading indulgence what matters is what people understood or believed they understood by it, not what it actually was. And it is worth noting that the debate about indulgences which started *c.*1130 was sparked off by the fact that they were being abused. As long as the abuses were not too blatant, people looked upon the indulgence as an acceptable innovation without bothering too much about the theology of the matter. We must always remember that the publicizing of the first crusading indulgence took place in an atmosphere which was free of the limitations imposed either by an official Church pronouncement or by a proper theological debate. The only way the new elements could be defined was by comparing them with earlier penitential practices.

The indulgence must, in fact, be seen as a development of the Church's earlier penitential discipline. This was originally divided into three stages: confession, satisfaction, and reconciliation (i.e. being readmitted to communion). Satisfaction was looked upon as the element which earned extinction of sins and thus made the reconciliation possible. At this time no distinction would have been made between remission of guilt and remission of punishment. In principle, the penance had to be equivalent to the sin committed. One had to pay, as it were, pound for pound. But obviously it was only a matter of chance whether or not a precisely equivalent penance was found; thus in addition there had to be the temporal penalties due to sin which, being imposed by God, could measure exactly any guilt that was still remaining. Since God's temporal punishment was feared far more than any earthly penance, a penitential system of draconic severity was developed on the theory that the harsher the penance in this world, the smaller would be the settlement in the next. The fact that up until the sixth century only serious offences were subject to the penance of the Church helped to establish the severity of penitential practice. Yet when, for reasons which cannot be gone into here, this changed so that penance had to be done for venial sins as well, the old system at first remained in force. But now harsh tasks and long penances during which the sinner remained excluded from the sacraments were no longer always appropriate, so inevitably there developed a trend towards a milder and a more differentiated system of punishment. At first this was done by the use of commutation and redemption, i.e. one form of punishment was exchanged for another which theoretically was still equivalent to the sin committed. Thus if it were shorter, it was also supposed to be harder; but in practice it tended to be more lenient. Lists of the penalties due to various sins were drawn up tariff-fashion in the 'Penitentials', together with the appropriate redemptions. In these redemptions we have one of the main roots of the crusading indulgence. In the eleventh century the system became still milder when it became customary to allow reconciliation to take place as soon as a man had begun his penance, though of course he still had to complete it. Thus long-term excommunication—one of the most feared consequences of sin—was in effect abolished. This change also meant the end of the old custom of total reconciliation. Its place was taken by an absolution granted immediately after confession. This involved reconciliation with God and the Church, i.e. forgiveness of the guilt of sin, but it did not mean full remission of the punishment due to sin. Nevertheless absolution went further than redemption and thus came closer to the indulgence in that the Church made a powerful plea for pardon; so a transcendental effect was at least intended. This was still not a judicial act, however, nor was it a remission of punishment granted independently of the sacrament of penance. But from here it was only a short step to the indulgence, i.e. to a more clearly

defined and more certainly effective remission of the penance imposed by
the Church. By an act of grace allowance was made for the transcendental
effect *in foro Dei* of the Church's plea. This then made it possible to curtail
the penance imposed by the Church. According to Poschmann, one of the
leading Catholic experts on the subject, 'the indulgence was no longer just
a part-payment on the time after death, it was also a most welcome relief
during this earthly life'. The special feature of the indulgence was that the
ideal of equivalence was no longer adhered to in practice. Later on the
doctrine of the 'Treasury of Merits' was developed in order to justify this
practice.

It is revealing that the idea of indulgence only became really effective
when it was linked with the pilgrimage to Jerusalem. Papal pronouncements rather similar to indulgences were occasionally made before the
crusades, but these were, in fact, usually absolutions. Alexander II, for
example, promised a remission of penance to the soldiers who had joined
the Barbastro expedition of 1063. In addition he also offered them the
remissio peccatorum, the remission of the temporal penalties due to sin. It
has been argued that the pope's letter is a forgery, but in fact it is a
perfectly genuine plenary indulgence. Yet for various reasons it had very
little effect. For one thing, it was addressed to a much smaller group than
was the crusading indulgence of 1095. Alexander's offer applied only to
those who had already decided to take part in the Spanish campaign; and
he left it open whether he would extend the terms of the indulgence to
include those who joined later. Furthermore normal penitential practice
was adhered to in that a penance had first to be imposed, at least formally,
before it could be considered as cancelled by the indulgence. Finally a
campaign in Spain did not have the same mass-appeal as an expedition to
the Holy Land. This example shows clearly why the full effects of the
indulgence were felt only when it became linked with the pilgrimage to
Jerusalem.

In this context it was important that the penitential journey to
Jerusalem was thought to be especially meritorious and salutary. In theory
the Church had always taken the view that movement from one place to
another did not bring a man any nearer to God; but it was impossible to
extinguish the popular belief in the value of a pilgrimage to Jerusalem. Its
popularity was assured from the moment when the reconciliation with the
Church was moved forward to the beginning of the work of penance, in
this case the pilgrimage. This applied, of course, to any penitential
pilgrimage; what gave Jerusalem its special significance was the tradition
of the Holy Places. There is evidence from as early as the eighth century
for the belief that remission of sins could be earned by a visit to the Church
of the Holy Sepulchre. But those who shared this belief in the value of
pilgrimages were denounced at the Council of Chalons in 813. The
Council was relying on the authority of Jerome who had said that it was not

seeing Jerusalem that was praiseworthy, but living a good life there. Indeed, in Jerome's eyes, even this had no special purifying value. He wrote that he had gone to Palestine in order to understand the Bible better, not to obtain spiritual advantages. But since the Council quoted only Jerome's first statement and not his commentary on it, it was possible to believe that both Jerome and the Council were prepared to concede an indirect purifying value to the journey to Jerusalem—i.e. when it led to a long period of residence there. Later on the Church quite patently failed to combat the belief that the pilgrimage to Jerusalem was worth an indulgence. Indeed it formally granted partial indulgences for it, like the year's indulgence allowed by Alexander III. This was during the heyday of the crusades, when the crusader was granted an unlimited plenary indulgence; understandably the peaceful pilgrim obtained just a partial indulgence.

There are some good reasons for assuming that in the pre-crusade period pilgrimages to Jerusalem were valued more highly and that those who undertook them received promises rather in the style of indulgences. The first official pronouncement on this point was made by Urban II. In 1089 he revived the archbishopric of Tarragona and ordered the Catalan nobility and clergy to help with the rebuilding of the town. He then added that those who, in a spirit of piety and penitence, were intending to go to Jerusalem should be advised to devote to the rebuilding of the church of Tarragona the money they would have spent on a pilgrimage. In this way the town would become celebrated as a bulwark of Christendom against the Saracens. Everyone who followed this advice should be granted the same indulgence as he would have obtained had he gone to Jerusalem. (Then, as now, the word 'indulgence' could be used both in a precise, technical sense and also with a much more general meaning.) The final sentence of the letter used to be treated with a good deal of scepticism by students of papal diplomatics, but more recently its genuineness has been vindicated. It is no longer possible, however, to ascertain just how comprehensive was the reward for those would-be pilgrims who instead helped to rebuild Tarragona. Certainly there can be no justification for calling it a plenary indulgence.

The importance of the Tarragona appeal for the origins of the crusades is obvious—though only Erdmann has given it the attention it deserves. Here the Christian idea of pilgrimage is linked together with a project intended to promote resistance to the Saracens. Fully six years before the Council of Clermont the pope had already granted an indulgence, indeed a pilgrim's indulgence, for the war against the heathen. It has been objected that whereas the crusade was an offensive enterprise, the rebuilding of Tarragona was defensive in character. But this objection cannot be sustained. When Urban returned to the same theme at some date between 1096 and 1099 he suggested to some Catalan counts that they should help with the work at Tarragona in order to obtain *remissio peccatorum* (remission of sins). He argued that since the knights of other lands had unanimously decided to help the Church in Asia and to free their brothers from the Saracen yoke, it was only right that they in their turn should help the Church in Catalonia against the attacks of the Saracens there. The pope then offered to all who fell in the defence of Tarragona the same indulgence that he had granted to the crusaders. It is true that in this letter we hear only of a reward for those who were killed, but Tarragona could not be rebuilt by candidates for martyrdom alone. The majority of those who were willing to fight wanted to obtain an indulgence and return home alive. It was this majority that Urban had to persuade to go to Tarragona. So clearly those who came through the defence of Tarragona must have been granted the same indulgence as those who survived a crusade. If this were not so it would have been irresponsible to prevent Spaniards from going on crusade to Jerusalem. Urban's attitude to the rebuilding of Tarragona had not changed. In 1089 he had seen it as the equivalent of a pilgrimage; later as the equivalent of a crusade. The fact that for one and the same task he at first promised a pilgrim's reward and then a crusader's indulgence tells us a good deal about his way of thinking. For him the crusade was an extension of the pilgrimage.

Erdmann approached these facts in a rather different way. He believed that the idea of a christian and knightly holy war was in the forefront of Urban's mind and that the pilgrimage was merely incidental. The reverse seems more likely to be true and to fit better into the logic of things. It is easy to arm a pilgrimage and pursue entirely new ends while preserving the old forms; but it is difficult to force a warrior into the peaceful form of the pilgrimage, no matter how holy the cause for which he fights. As Erdmann saw, from the Church's point of view the decisive event at Clermont was not the indulgence but the militarization of the pilgrimage and the ecclesiastical approval given to this process. The crusader was a kind of superior pilgrim, a pilgrim with the honour of bearing arms. He stood one step higher than the peaceful pilgrim but the difference between them was only one of degree. This is how contemporaries looked at it. The crusader's sword was blessed, but so were his staff and his scrip—the traditional attributes of the pilgrim. A hundred years later Frederick Barbarossa and the kings of France and England received the staff and scrip before they set out on crusade. It is true, as Erdmann pointed out, that on crusade the expression 'soldier of Christ' came to mean 'crusader' while the word 'pilgrim' dropped into the background. This observation undoubtedly played a considerable part in Erdmann's thesis that the pilgrimage was a minor factor in the origins of the crusade. But here so much depends on what kind of source material is used. Erdmann relied on chronicles and crusaders' letters. The chronicles are, however, poor evidence. Most of them were written after the capture of Jerusalem by churchmen who were working on the development of a doctrine of the crusade. But even in the anonymous chronicle known as *Gesta Francorum* we find the expression *Christi milites peregrini*, 'pilgrim knights of Christ'. More valuable testimony, however, is provided by the charters of men who borrowed money from the Church in order to cover their crusading expenses. When they say anything about the purpose of the crusades, it is in phrases taken almost entirely from the world of the pilgrim. Only rarely does the idea of fighting the heathen appear. The unknown author of the *Gesta Francorum* wrote of the people of Macedonia: 'They did not believe that we were pilgims but thought that we had come to devastate their land and kill them.' It was in the crusading army itself that the conceptual change from armed pilgrim to soldier for the faith took place. But in 1096 when the march began it seemed—apart from its eschatological aspects— to belong entirely to the traditional world of the pilgrimage to Jerusalem.

This is how Urban II must have seen it. The two Tarragona appeals show clearly that his idea of the crusade was based on the pilgrimage. It was in this way that the wars in Spain contributed to the origins of the crusades. Not that Spain had seen any striking success of the kind that might have been likely to persuade Urban to apply more widely the combination of pilgrimage and war against the heathen. Despite the papal promise of a spiritual reward and the financial contribution made by the count of Barcelona, the Tarragona appeal of 1089 achieved little. This lack of success indeed only serves to show that a pilgrimage was more attractive than the war in Spain. But what had failed in Spain might work if the combination of war against the heathen with the idea of a reward were transferred to the Christian East, the main goal of pilgrims. It is clear that the idea of making a pilgrimage there was far more potent than the idea of fighting the heathens in Spain. This is demonstrated by the fact that the pope could not even persuade the count of Barcelona to stay in Spain though as the local lord he was more involved than anyone in the rebuilding of Tarragona. He died in 1096 in the Holy Land. A watchful observer can hardly have failed to see that the pilgrimage motif would be of great help in organizing a military expedition to the East.

Although Erdmann drew attention to the Tarragona appeals he also explicitly denied that Urban II had any interest in the idea of pilgrimage except as crusade propaganda. But in fact the pope's few crusade letters tell us nothing about his attitude to pilgrimages. Neither does his speech at Clermont; in none of the versions is there even a passing reference to pilgrimages though practically every possible motive, religious, economic, and social, is touched upon somewhere. This is all the more remarkable since at Clermont Urban must have used the arguments which he judged would have the gratest effect on his audience. Yet, if we can believe the chroniclers who unanimously omit any reference to the subject, the pilgrimage was not one of these arguments—and this despite the fact that

Urban had already closely concerned himself with the problems of the pilgrimage when dealing with the Spanish campaigns. For him then it cannot have been a propaganda device. But it was one of the basic roots of his concept of the crusade. Later on indeed the idea of arming the pilgrim was permanently taken over by the crusade propagandists when it had become obvious just how effective an idea it was. The false crusading encyclical of Sergius IV which was fabricated at this time is clear proof of this.

Even more important in the eyes of the general public was the indulgence, especially once it had been linked with the enormously popular pilgrimage idea. Basically there was nothing new about the 'indulgence' of Clermont. What the council decreed was, of course, a judicial act, but it was something thoroughly traditional—not a plenary indulgence in the modern sense. It laid down, in precise and unambiguous words, that whoever took the cross for reasons of religion alone, would be freed from all penances imposed by the Church.* Exactly this is repeated in Urban's letter of September 1096 to Bologna. I cannot agree with the view generally accepted until twenty years ago that this was a plenary indulgence since nowhere does the council even hint that its decree would have a transcendental effect. It granted nothing more than a redemption or absolution i.e. the remission of the canonical penances by means of a kind of redemption, that is to say by going on crusade, a penitential task which was the equivalent of a full remission. It is impossible to see how this can somehow be regarded as less of an absolution than the remission of sins granted in 1079 by Gregory VII to the English. This is formulated very much more, indeed almost precisely, in the terms of an indulgence. Yet, despite the difficulties, theologians regard this as an absolution. The fact is that interpretation of the Clermont decree has been too much influenced by what developed later, and too little by the actual text. So far as I know, Poschmann has been the only one to realize this when he writes that at first indulgences were plenary only in the sense that they meant the remission of the entire penance (*remissio iniunctae poenitentiae*); they did not yet mean the full remission of all the temporal penalties due to sin in the next world. But against this interpretation there is the existence of the customary formula *remissio peccatorum* which, although it does not appear in the council's decree, had always been used to mean the remission of temporal penalties including those of the next world. It really is impossible to see why an expression more precise than *remissio peccatorum* could not have been found if no more than the *remissio poenitentiae* was intended. The formula itself does date back to the time when the single process of

---

*Quicumque pro sola devotione, non pro honoris vel pecuniae adeptione, ad liberandam ecclesiam Dei Ierusalem profectus fuerit, iter illud pro omni poenitentia reputetur.

canonical satisfaction redeemed simultaneously both guilt and punishment. But it was not used in papal letters until the second half of the eleventh century and it inevitably became more and more ambiguous as the distinction between guilt and punishment was developed. Poschmann's argument becomes circular when he tries to solve the problem by making the unproven assertion that at that time *remissio peccatorum* meant only the remission of penance. There is, however, no need to see in this argument an attempt to refute earlier Protestant polemic against indulgences, some of it in a very coarse style, which had tended to concentrate heavily on the *remissio peccatorum* formula. Poschmann is simply trying to reconcile what is, for him, irreconcilable—the Council's decree and the customary papal formula. But in fact they are irreconcilable only in the context of a preconceived and until the 1960s generally accepted opinion: that the Council of Clermont proclaimed a genuine plenary indulgence.

At Clermont words were chosen with precision and all that was actually offered was the full remission of the earthly penances imposed by the Church. Preachers then went out and preached something else, the *remissio peccatorum* which literally means the remission of sins and in theology refers to the remission of the temporal penalties due to sin, though not until the time of Huguccio (d. 1210) was this definition clearly established. Popular crusading propaganda at once went unhesitatingly far beyond the more limited formula used at the Council. None of the contemporary chroniclers reproduce the official doctrine in their decriptions of the Council. Orderic Vitalis was one of the very few people to mention the remission of penance and, even in his view, the remission of the penalties due to sin—never in fact referred to at Clermont—was more important. Erdmann misses the heart of the matter when he says that in the eyes of the world it was a meaningless distinction and that here we see the effect of the popular belief that to go on a crusade was to obtain forgiveness of sins. But, in fact, the men who tell us about the remission of the penalties due to sin were trained in theology and well able to make the distinction. Yet none of them utters a word of criticism or explanation. Clearly the Clermont decree had been pushed into the background by the crusade propagandists. It looks very much indeed as though the preachers explained the distinction—and then pointed out the advantages of the remission of the penalties due to sin (or perhaps simply the remission of sins, cf. pp. 33f.) which was now supposed to have been granted at the Council. From now on the dominant note in the crusade publicity was the idea of a reward—and moreover a special reward which could be obtained only by taking the cross. Although there is very little evidence for the First Crusade, here at any rate we are entitled to draw on what we know of the later crusades.

Up to a point the extended meaning given to the Clermont decree can be described as a misunderstanding. More was promised than could, according to the strict doctrine of the Church, be given. But it must be remembered that the preachers were working, so to speak, in a vacuum. It would have been no use them looking for guidance from the official teaching of the Church or from theological literature because at that date there was still no theory of indulgences. For this reason there is no force in the assertion made by early Protestant critics of the system of indulgences, that the popes had here created for themselves a superbly manipulated 'instrument for the production of unconditional devotion' (T. Brieger, 1901). It is true that in the thirteenth century the crusading indulgence was used for political purposes; none the less it was not a papal invention. Yet there is no way of explaining the success of the crusade propaganda in 1095–6 except as a consequence of this extension of meaning to include a transcendental effect, for, after all, the substitute—the crusade—was in many cases harder than the penance it replaced. It seems likely then that the full crusading indulgence was produced neither by the pope nor by the official Church; rather it was 'manufactured' by preachers who expanded on the Clermont decree. In other words it emerged in response to the needs of the people and the requirements of the crusade. This much seems clear from the biting criticism to which the indulgence became subjected from *c*.1130. Peter Abelard was the first in the field. In his fierce attack he pointed out that the Church had always held firm to the theory of equivalent penance (indeed if this had been given up the development of the doctrine of the Treasury of Merits would have been pointless). But in an indulgence there could be no equivalence—not, at any rate, until men had learned of the existence of the Treasury of Merits. In Abelard's day the bishops who dispensed indulgences relied upon their power of the keys (John 20:23), but the French theologian was entirely within the bounds of traditional learning when he dismissed this as insufficient (Poschmann). Until the Treasury of Merits had been defined, the Church was, strictly speaking, in no position to remit the temporal penalties due to sin because it was unable to preserve the equivalence of the penance. Yet it is indisputable that indulgences were dispensed. It seems clear that a practice which originated outside Rome had been brought within the Church, and only later was the theory of it all worked out. Public pressure in its favour meant that the practice could not be eradicated, but it was not easy to justify and there is an air of helplessness about the attempts to do so made by twelfth-century theologians. Even Peter Cantor (d. 1197), writing after indulgences had been dispensed and discussed for a hundred years, and the first theologian to try to see something of positive value in the indulgence, still looked upon it essentially in terms of the long-familiar redemption. Nor have modern theologians tried, even hypothetically, to work out a flawless justification for the system of indulgences which would have held good even at a time when the Treasury of Merits was still unknown. They cannot do it—even only hypothetically—without being forced either to label the Treasury of Merits as not absolutely necessary or to explain it as the (still unrecognized) basis of the Church's official intercession for the remission by God of the temporal penalties due to sin.

It seems then that right at the start of the crusading movement control had slipped out of the hands of the curia. We have already seen how men disregarded papal schemes and chose Jerusalem as their own goal; and we shall see how the pope's plans for organizing the campaign were, in part, overtaken by events. Something similar had happened in the case of the indulgence. Urban's expressions of opinion on this subject are ambiguous. In the letter to the Flemings written at the end of 1095 he himself spoke of *remissio peccatorum*, i.e. remission of the penalties due to sin. But in his letter to the Bolognese he used the more limited formula of the remission of penance. The letter to Vallombrosa does not mention the indulgence at all. Of course the first letter was intended to recruit crusaders, while the second and third were meant to prevent ecclesiastics from going. At all events the curia did not hinder the popular interpretation of the Clermont decree. Indeed in later years it became necessary for popes to make this interpretation their own. This development begins with Eugenius III who, on his own admission, looked back to the chronicle accounts, not to Urban's privileges, when he proclaimed an indulgence at the start of the Second Crusade. Not surprisingly this brought the *remissio peccatorum* into prominence.

Some popes like Gregory VIII tried to put the clock back. They avoided the highly ambiguous expression *remissio peccatorum* and only offered a remission of penance, as the Council of Clermont had done. But the process had gone too far to be halted now and in the crusade decree of the Fourth Lateran Council of 1215 it reached its conclusion. From then on this decree formed the basis of the papal theory of the crusades. To all men who, in person and at their own expense, went on a crusade it promised full forgiveness of all those sins which, with a contrite heart, they had truly confessed. The confusion was now complete, for this seems to have meant a full remission of the sins themselves, a complete discharge obtained through the Church by means of an extra-sacramental work of penance. It cannot possibly be referring only to the penalties due to sin for only sins can be confessed, not penalties. This is where the doctrine formulated by Huguccio and finalized by Aquinas came in. According to this doctrine there were two senses in which sins could be forgiven. Firstly the guilt, through confession, and secondly the punishment. But how could the preachers of the crusade have explained this? They were 'fishers of men'— as one of them referring to Matthew 4: 19, called himself—and they hoped to make a good catch from an audience which consisted largely of illiterates. It was not the place for subtle and still not definitively accepted distinctions. It was not the time to be more papal than the pope who, after all, had said remission of sins even though he may have meant no more than the remission of the penalties due to sin. In any event there is no evidence that the preachers tried to give special emphasis to the narrower concept. On the contrary when Abbot Martin of Pairis preached the Fourth Crusade at Basle at the beginning of the thirteenth century the concluding words of his sermon were as follows: 'But if you ask, what more certain reward from God may you hope for in return for such efforts, then I promise categorically that each of you who takes the cross and confesses truly will be entirely cleansed of all his sins.' What listener, if he were not trained in theology, could have heard this and not believed that he was meant to look forward to a complete remission of sins, both the guilt and the punishment?

Favoured by the extended interpretation of the Clermont decree, the reward motif, along with some other themes, played an important propaganda role throughout the whole period of the crusades. None of the preachers felt able to do without it. They used clearly drawn images and had no hesitation in calling a spade a spade. The believer was offered a spiritual bargain and he would have been a fool to refuse. Particularly effective was the picture of the 'shrewd businessman' which was first drawn in a propaganda letter written by St. Bernard of Clairvaux, in which the transcendental effect of the indulgence was most strongly emphasized.

O mighty soldier, O man of war, you now have a cause for which you can fight without endangering your soul; a cause in which to win is glorious and for which to die is but gain. Or are you a shrewd businessman, a man quick to see the profits of this world? If you are, I can offer you a splendid bargain. Do not miss this opportunity. Take the sign of the cross. At once you will have indulgence for all the sins which you confess with a contrite heart. It does not cost you much to buy and if you wear it with humility you will find that it is worth the kingdom of heaven.

It could hardly have been said more clearly than this and it could not have failed to make an impact. The same metaphor reappears in an early twelfth-century poem in the collection known as the Carmina Burana:

> The clever merchant will be there
> Who wants to purchase life . . .
> The last will be first
> And the first last
> The summoning is different
> But the payment (*remuneratio*) the same
> For to all workers (i.e. crusaders)
> The penny of life will be given.

A French crusading song of the same period runs:

> I have heard it said by way of advice
> That it costs gold to clinch a good deal.

The man is thoughtless
Who sees the good and takes the bad.
Do you know what God has promised them
Who will take the Cross?
By God! He has promised to reward them well
Paradise for evermore.
He who knows how to make a profit
Is a fool if he waits till tomorrow.

In these lines not only can we hear the voice of the persuader; we can also sense the mood of the persuaded. Towards the end of the century the Provençal poet Aimeric de Belonoi wrote:

For the march means hope
For possessions and joy and thanks
And for diligence and honour
And for deliverance from sin.

At about the same time Heinrich von Rugge, referring to the crusade, wrote:

All my thoughts are fixed on a better reward.

From the early thirteenth century there have survived the crusade sermons of James of Vitry. In one of them he tells a story which does not have to be true but which must have been possible otherwise he would not have used it. It illustrates the frame of mind of his audience. A wife kept her husband indoors so that he would not be able to listen to the preaching of a crusade. But through a window he managed to hear what was said. As soon as he learned that by taking the cross a man could regain as much remission as otherwise would require fasting and wearing a penitential belt for sixty years and that he would most certainly escape purgatory and hell, he immediately jumped clean through the window in order to take the cross himself.

It would, of course, be wrong to assert that the crusade propagandists avoided a more spiritual approach and worked only in such blatantly commerical terms. Nevertheless a great deal was done by such methods; we should remember that it was an age which witnessed a tremendous boom in long-distance trade. St. Bernard, though he used the vocabulary of merchants, did, of course, also say very different things (see pp. 96f.), but he too did not want to renounce this effective propaganda theme.

It is perhaps better to put aside the question of whether or not the Church gave the impression that a complete remission of sin, both guilt and punishment, was possible through the indulgence and therefore through a procedure outside the Church's sacrament of penance. It is certainly possible that sometimes contemporaries did so interpret the Church's ambiguous terminology. But in any case the difference between remission of penance and remission of the temporal punishment due to sin, a difference which existed in the Church's traditional doctrine of indulgences, was of itself quite enough to explain the success of Clermont. There had been nothing new about being able to obtain remission of penance by going to fight the heathen. But that the penalties due to sin could be remitted simply as a result of taking the cross—as the crusade propagandists suggested—this was an unheard of innovation. Previously both the reconciliation granted at the start of the penance and the redeeming commutation had affected only the penances and had had no transcendental effect upon the penalties due to sin. It was indeed hoped that absolution would have such an effect, but it could certainly not be guaranteed. The indulgence on the other hand availed before God in a certain and in a quantitatively measurable fashion so that both the temporal penalties due to sin and the earthly penances were remitted and, in the case of a plenary indulgence, fully cancelled. Only Alexander II had promised as much as this for the war against the heathen and his promise, being addressed only to a small group, had met with little response. It was when linked with the universally popular idea of pilgrimage to Jerusalem that the explosive force of the crusading indulgence was revealed. Ekkehard of Aura spoke of 'a new way of penance' now being opened up. Here lies the secret of the astonishing success of Urban's summons, a success which astonished the Church as much as anyone else. Imagine a knight in the south of France, living with his kinsmen in the socially and economically unsatisfactory institution of the *frérêche*. His feuds and the 'upper class' form of highway robbery which often enough went with them, were prohibited by the Peace of God. Suddenly he was offered the chance of going on a pilgrimage—in any event the wish of many men. This pilgrimage was supervised by the Church; it was moreover an armed pilgrimage during which he could fulfil his knightly function by taking part in battle. There would be opportunities for winning plunder. Above all there was the entirely new offer of a full remission of all the temporal penalties due to sin, especially of those to be suffered in purgatory. The absolution given in the sacrament of penance took from him the guilt; taking the cross meant the cancellation of all the punishment even before he set out to perform the task imposed. Not to accept such an offer, not—at the very least—to take it seriously, would indeed have been mad. The 'shrewd businessman' seized his chance. And who did not want to be numbered among the shrewd?

Taking the cross in these circumstances was, of course, an act of faith just as much as an act of naive trust in the promises made by Church publicists. Naturally not all crusaders were moved by piety. In the Middle Ages too there were sceptics and the motives for going on crusade were many, various, and tangled, often social and economic in character. But the offer of indulgence must have had an irresistible attraction for those who did not doubt the Church's teaching, who believed in the reality of the penalties due to sin, or at least accepted the possibility of their existence. Such believers must have made up a great part of those who went on the First Crusade—whatever proportion of the total population of Europe they may have been. And, of course, the crusaders of 1095 could not have guessed that the offer which they were accepting was in reality much more limited than the one promised them by the 'fishers of men'.

3

THE FIRST CRUSADE, 1096–1099

THE preaching of the crusade was by no means finished when the promise of a spiritual reward was made.[16] It was still necessary to endow the enterprise with a legal form which was appropriate to the kind of participants whom it was intended to attract. That the kings of Europe would take part was entirely out of the question. So Urban thought in terms of an army of knights under the control of the Church, for there was no other higher authority which could have taken command. While still at Clermont he nominated Adhemar, Bishop of Le Puy, as his legate, and later he decribed him openly as the leader of the crusade. How far Urban had originally envisaged Adhemar as a political, as well as a religious leader, has been much debated, but the political side of his functions should not be exaggerated. The military commander was probably to be Count Raymond IV of Toulouse, with whom Urban had discussed the project even before the Council met at Clermont.

All knights who swore to go on crusade were admitted to the ranks of the crusaders in a symbolic ceremony. Referring to the words of St. Matthew's Gospel about those who would follow Christ (Matthew 16:24), Urban, at Clermont, distributed cloth crosses to all those who were prepared to go, and they then sewed them on to the shoulders of their surcoats. The cross was to be the badge of every crusader on every crusade. As a symbol it had a double significance. First, it was a sign of God's protection, a sign that the wearer belonged to a special community, the sign of a pilgrim with the privilege of bearing arms. Second, it was a legal symbol, vouching for worldly privileges, for the Church issued far-reaching ordinances in favour of the crusader. The Peace of God and the Church's protection were extended to cover his belongings. During the period of his absence on crusade his privileges went, in theory, still further. His possessions were released from the controlling authority of the state: no taxes could be collected. He was normally granted a moratorium on his debts, especially since he might well have to meet considerable expenses in preparing for the journey and have to borrow either from his peers or from the Church. But, in return, anyone who broke the vow, i.e. the oath to take the cross, was excommunicated. Of such central importance was the vow that medieval canon lawyers treated the crusade as an institution of canon law under the heading *De voto*. A. Noth has attempted to prove that neither Urban nor the Council of

Clermont instituted the vow, arguing instead that it developed only gradually in the army of the First Crusade and was taken over by the papacy only under Calixtus II. But Noth's theory has been criticized by Brundage and others. The administration of an oath and the distribution of a cloth cross by the clergy was probably also intended to prevent unwanted elements of no military value from joining the crusade. It looks as though Urban grew nervous of the explosive effect of the crusading ideal on the non-knightly classes. In 1096 he did his utmost to stop the old and the sick from going. Clerks and monks were to travel only with the permission of their superiors. Urban fixed the start for 15 August 1096. It was probably intended that the different contingents should assemble at Constantinople.[17]

For eight months after the Council of Clermont the pope remained in France. He avoided the territory controlled by the Capetian kings of France, but elsewhere he preached the crusade: in Limoges and Angers, perhaps also in Tours and Nîmes. Otherwise he left the preaching to the bishops. This explains why there was little publicity in those areas which had not been represented at Clermont—England, Germany, and south Italy. Apparently men in Germany and south Italy did not hear Urban's call until the crusaders themselves passed through these regions.

Though Urban himself stayed south of the Loire, the crusade was also preached to the north, and not only by the bishops. In Normandy, for example, the abbot of St. Bénigne in Dijon was active. But above all it was the popular evangelists, themselves closely connected with the poverty movement which affected the lower classes, who took over the preaching. Robert d'Arbrissel (*c*.1055-1117), one of the intellectual leaders of this group, which sought to imitate Christ in a life of complete poverty, preached in the Loire valley. But even he was completely overshadowed by the figure of Peter the Hermit.[18] Peter came from Picardy and before the crusade he had probably been active as a preacher in Central France. He did not look very attractive, usually being caked with mud and dirt, as he rode about the countryside on a donkey. Yet he was a man of electrifying eloquence who radiated an unusual power. In the Middle Ages a whole cycle of legends became attached to his name until he was— quite erroneously—given most of the credit for starting the crusades. He is supposed to have carried a letter with him, a letter from heaven, containing the message that the Christians would, if only they dared try it, drive the heathens from the Holy Places. Copies of this letter were actually disseminated. Other reports tell of visions which came to him at the Sepulchre of Christ while he was staying in Jerusalem as a pilgrim. His reputation went before him and must have contributed a good deal to his success. He preached in Berry, in the Orleanais, in Champagne, and Lorraine before going on in April 1096 to Trier and Cologne *en route* for the East. He was followed by a huge army of poor, among whom a knight,

Walter Sans-Avoir, became particularly famous. These 'crusaders' were either badly or not at all armed; above all they lacked the money that was needed for so long a journey. The ecclesiastical authorities proved incapable of stopping them from going, although they had certainly never dreamed of a contingent of crusaders looking like this. Here we can see the immense power which emanated from Urban II's combination of pilgrimage, war against the heathen, and a spiritual reward. The idea gripped men of all classes; it could not be restricted to the knights—as the authorities had doubtless hoped. But when such advantageous offers were made, humbler men had no wish to renounce them.

From the Rhineland these troops, mostly drawn from the lower classes, marched eastwards in various contingents through Hungary and Bulgaria to Constantinople. The first to go was Walter Sans-Avoir whose followers were chiefly Frenchmen. Peter the Hermit meanwhile spent more time preaching the crusade in Cologne. Walter's section reached Byzantium without too much trouble in mid-July 1096. Peter arrived about two weeks later with Lorrainers, Rhinelanders, and south Germans as well as the rest of the Frenchmen. At Nish it became clear that Peter the Hermit was less suitable than the knight Walter as a leader of disorderly troops. Undisciplined behaviour by the crusaders led to sharp clashes with Petcheneg mercenaries in Byzantine service and Peter's men suffered heavy losses. Other contingents, German rather than French in composition, were led by a priest called Gottschalk, a man named Volkmar whose origin is unknown, and by Count Emicho of Leiningen and the viscount of Melun. None of these contingents ever reached Constantinople. Compared with the armies of Walter Sans-Avoir and Peter the Hermit, which had maintained relatively good order, those which followed behaved like hordes of barbarians; as a result they never even set foot on Byzantine territory. In Hungary they occupied themselves with ravaging and looting and there they were all slaughtered. But even before leaving Germany they had managed to acquire a melancholy notoriety. Inflamed by irresponsible preachers and attracted by the wealth of the important Jewish communities of the Rhineland, they had indulged themselves in pogroms on a scale hitherto unprecedented in the Middle Ages. Emicho of Leiningen and his men made a special name for themselves here. The emperor, Henry IV, following the long tradition of the German kings, had taken the Jews under his special protection. In addition they paid large sums of money to the duke of Lower Lorraine in return for his help against the murderous greed of the crusaders. But it was all in vain. Marching downstream (not exactly the most direct route to the East) they plundered and killed the Jews in one Rhineland town after another: Speyer, Worms, Mainz, Trier, and Cologne. Other groups attacked the Jews in Neuss, Xanten, and even Prague. The extant Jewish accounts of these events make grim reading. It was in vain that some of the bishops tried to save them from the bloodthirsty mobs. Frequently the argument that the Jews, as the enemies of Christ, deserved to be punished was merely a feeble attempt to conceal the real motive: greed. It can be assumed that for many crusaders the loot taken from the Jews provided their only means of financing such a journey. But, as it turned out, their newly acquired wealth took them no further than Hungary for there they were all wiped out. Riley-Smith offers a rather different interpretation. In his view the early crusaders lacked an effective image of their true enemy and in the Jews found a convenient substitute ready to hand.[19]

Meanwhile at Constantinople the armies led by Walter and Peter had set up camp outside the city. Peter was given an audience by the emperor, Alexius Comnenus, who gave him rich presents and good advice. He ought to wait for the arrival of other contingents before marching on into Asia Minor. Peter was ready to do this but his followers were impatient. They became more and more restless and began to plunder the suburbs until finally the Byzantines too advised him to cross the Bosporus. On 6 August 1096 they were taken across and then they marched through Nicomedia to Civetot where there was an army camp which had once been used for English mercenaries in Byzantine pay but which now lay empty. They had now reached the frontier of the region controlled by the Turks and could not resist making forays into it. A French raiding party carried off rich booty from the neighbourhood of Nicaea. Some Germans, in trying to follow this example, were trapped by the Turks at Xerigordon. When the main army set out to try to help them it was routed by the Turks on 21 October 1096. A bare handful of survivors managed to return to Constantinople where Peter the Hermit had been for some time, having left the camp earlier in order to negotiate with the emperor. This meant that he was later able to accompany the knightly armies. The People's Crusade was over. It had ended in disaster and had achieved nothing. Worse, it had made an unfavourable impression on the Byzantine people and authorities. From now on the Byzantines looked sceptically upon crusaders—upon the allies whom they themselves had called for. The prospects for co-operation between Byzantium and the crusaders had been dimmed right at the start by the shadow of mutual distrust.

The only hope for a successful crusade lay with the knightly armies. Their expedition will be described here in some detail in order to illustrate the difficulties facing all crusades. One of the first to depart was Godfrey de Bouillon (d. 1100). With a great following of Lorrainers, north Frenchmen, and Germans, he set out in mid-August 1096, at the time appointed. He was a member of the family of the counts of Boulogne; in 1087 he had been appointed duke of Lower Lorraine by Henry IV, but he was unable to make much of this position and it is possible that he saw the crusade as a chance of achieving higher things. We know nothing for certain about the reasons which led him to take the cross. Certain sources report that he sold his allodial possessions, even his castle of Bouillon, and this has led historians to speculate that he burned his boats and had no intention of returning home. A closer look reveals, however, that of his family lands he sold only Stenay and Mousay (between Verdun and Sedan) to the bishop of Verdun with whom he had long quarrelled over these villages. He also returned to the bishop, as part of this settlement, the county of Verdun, which he had held as a fief and which the bishop now promised to bestow on Godfrey's brother Baldwin. On the other hand, he only mortgaged to the bishop of Liège his principal possession, the 'Pays de Bouillon' (east of Sedan in Belgium), expressly reserving to himself and his heirs a right of recovery or redemption. What is even more revealing, he never relinquished his duchy but remained strictly within the law in requesting the Emperor's permission to leave the Empire. Thus it was not until after Godfrey's death that the Emperor appointed a new duke for Lower Lorraine (1101). As first ruler of Jerusalem Godfrey was to become the focal point of legends which turned him into the ideal crusader. This process was begun soon after the First Crusade by Albert of Aix who made Godfrey the hero of his chronicle. If he were not quite so pure in heart and spirit as medieval legend made him out to be, neither was he the thorough mediocrity described by nineteenth-century historians. He was rich enough to be accompanied by a considerable retinue of vassals and knights, among whom the Lorrainers were the most influential both during and after the crusade. His brother, Baldwin of Boulogne, and another relative, Baldwin of Bourcq, were the outstanding members of this group. His brother, who was to succeed him in Jerusalem, had originally been intended for a clerical career but had abandoned this at some date between 1076 and 1086. Since the paternal as well as the maternal inheritance had already been divided among his two brothers by 1076, Baldwin was then in straitened circumstances and tried to make his fortune by marrying into one of the leading families in Normandy, where he lived in the household of his father-in-law. The prospect of acquiring the county of Verdun caused him to return to Lorraine, but he relinquished his new county almost at once. Although he went on crusade in his brother's retinue, the fact that he took his wife along with him shows that his claim to a Norman inheritance had not been forgotten. Godfrey marched through Hungary and Bulgaria and on to Constantinople via Belgrade, Nish, Sofia, Philippopolis, and Adrianople. Thanks to good discipline and to a treaty with King Colman of Hungary, to whom he gave Baldwin of Boulogne as a hostage, the journey passed off almost without incident. On 23 December 1096 he reached Constantinople where he found that Count Hugh of Vermandois had already arrived. Count Hugh, the brother of the king of France, had set out at about the same time as Godfrey but with his small contingent had preferred to take the sea route.

The Normans of south Italy had never been reluctant to go East. One of their greatest feudal lords was Bohemund of Taranto (d. 1111), the eldest son of Robert Guiscard and now about forty years of age. He was clearly out to obtain more power than he enjoyed in Italy. Guiscard's younger son, Roger Borsa, had succeeded to his father's Italian possessions, while land east of the Adriatic had been assigned to Bohemund. Thus the setback suffered in the Norman–Byzantine War in 1085 had hit Bohemund hard. It was understandable that he should wish to recoup his losses elsewhere. Without doubt he was the most ambitious and most unscrupulous of the crusade leaders. Restless and greedy for power he was a true Norman rather than a true crusader. But he knew well how to use religious ideals for his own ends. When he decided to take the cross—he was besieging Amalfi at the time—he freely distributed cloth crosses to his companions with his own hands. His followers were fewer in number than Godfrey's. Outstanding among them was his young nephew Tancred. He was also accompanied by the unknown knight or cleric who wrote a valuable account of the crusade, the *Gesta Francorum*, which thoroughly idealizes Bohemund. The Normans took ship over the Adriatic and then marched by the land route along the old Via Egnatia to Constantinople. Bohemund maintained strict discipline since he was determined to make a good impression on the Byzantines who looked upon his coming with mixed feelings; they had not forgotten the war with the Normans. For this same reason the inhabitants of the districts through which he passed were not very keen to sell him provisions. Even so he advanced without too much plundering or friction with the Byzantines, though things became worse after Bohemund left the troops under Tancred's command in order to hurry on ahead to Constantinople where he arrived at the beginning of April 1097.

The largest army, made up chiefly of Provençals and Burgundians, assembled in the south of France. Its commander, Count Raymond of Toulouse, was by far the richest of all the crusaders. His vassals alone made up a fine troop. In his company there travelled the papal legate Adhemar of Le Puy. Raymond was a fifty-five-year-old man who, by a combination of great energy, boldness, and cunning, had made himself lord of thirteen counties in Provence and Languedoc. He left them to his son Bertrand, while he himself took his wife with him on the arduous journey during which she bore him a second son. According to William of Malmesbury he swore an oath never to return and in fact he never did see his home again. Among the leaders he stands out as the one least open to imputations of material ambition as his motive for taking the cross,[20] but his character is far from being an open book. The evidence of his chaplain, the chronicler Raymond of Aguilers, has to be treated with caution. His main purpose seems to have been to show that the will of God was expressed in history and he handled his subject-matter accordingly. It is

not known how Raymond's army reached the Balkans, but once there the
count followed the Albanian coast south to Dyrrhachium where he picked
up the Via Egnatia. Because he had not set out until October the army had
to suffer considerably from the severe Balkan winter; but by and large
Raymond managed to keep good discipline. On reaching Byzantine
territory they were provided with a Petcheneg escort. Occasionally trouble
broke out between crusaders and escort. In one skirmish Legate Adhemar
was badly wounded and for a while he had to remain behind at
Thessalonica. The town of Roussa in Thrace was pillaged by the
Provençals. Shortly afterwards Raymond left the army and hurried on to
Constantinople. In his absence the army was very roughly handled by the
Byzantines. It reached Constantinople on 27 April 1097, six days later
than its commander.

The powerful Count Robert II of Flanders (1093–1111) had arrived a
little earlier. He had set out with Duke Robert of Normandy (1093–1106)
and Count Stephen of Blois (1089–1102). Duke Robert had found the
problems of ruling Normandy too much for him and had happily pawned
the duchy to his brother William Rufus of England for 10,000 marks of
silver. Stephen of Blois, son-in-law of William the Conqueror, 'had as
many castles as the year has days' and had little difficulty in financing his
crusade. In his retinue rode Fulcher of Chartres, later chaplain to Baldwin
of Boulogne, and one of the chroniclers of the crusade. Their army also set
out in October. Having crossed the Alps they met Urban II at Lucca. For
some years scholars believed, on the basis of a report in the chronicle of
St.-Pierre-le-Vif at Sens, that at Lucca Urban decided to appoint two
more legates for the crusade. However, Hiestand's as yet unpublished
researches have shown that this view can no longer be maintained.[21] From
Lucca the army marched to south Italy where Duke Robert and Count
Stephen spent the winter months while Robert of Flanders hurried on to
Constantinople. The two others sailed across the Adriatic in April 1097
and reached Constantinople in May without much trouble. The muster of
the troops was now complete.

Alexius had not reckoned with armies of this size but all he could do
now was to make the best of the situation. There could, of course, be no
question of allowing the troops into the city itself. They were quartered in
camps in the suburbs. Only the leaders with a few of their men were
allowed to enter, to gaze upon the riches and relics which filled this great
treasure-house of a city. When he received them, Alexius displayed all the
splendour of the Byzantine court ceremonial. He heaped presents upon
them and we know that Stephen of Blois, for one, was delighted. But none
of this could conceal the fact that the arrival of the crusaders raised
political problems. Alexius could use the fact that he alone controlled the
shipping needed to transport the armies across the Bosporus in order to
bring pressure to bear on the crusaders. On the other hand he could not

leave this for too long otherwise the number of troops outside Constantinople would grow to dangerous proportions. Moreover, he naturally wanted to reach an agreement on what was to be done with the lands which the crusaders would conquer. For Byzantium nothing else would do but that the lands which had once been hers should be restored to her allegiance. On this question Alexius was fortunate that the first contingent to arrive in Constantinople, led by Hugh of Vermandois, was a very small one. Discreetly but unmistakably Alexius restricted the Frenchman's freedom of movement until he was ready to swear that all territories which had belonged to Byzantium before the Turkish invasions would be restored.[22]

Alexius's treatment of Hugh could not be hidden from the other crusaders. The next to arrive, Godfrey de Bouillon, declined several invitations to visit the city. He also refused to swear the oath. Twice Alexius tried to put pressure on him by cutting off the army's food supply. The Lorrainers replied by pillaging the suburbs. On the second occasion, in January 1097, Godfrey even laid siege to the imperial palace of Blachernae. This was more than Alexius was prepared to take and anyway he wanted to see Godfrey in Asia Minor before any more crusaders arrived at Constantinople. So he gave his troops free rein and they soon proved themselves the superior soldiers. Godfrey was now ready, on 20 January, to take the required oath.[23] He and his men were at once shipped across the Bosporus. They marched along the coast of the Sea of Marmora to Pelecanum, a Byzantine army camp. Not much later Bohemund and the Normans reached Constantinople. He was determined to live down his reputation as an old enemy of Byzantium and to make a good impression on Alexius. By mid-April he had sworn the oath and had promised not to keep parts of the empire himself nor to permit others to do so. Possibly he hoped that Alexius would appoint him as commander-in-chief of the imperial troops in Asia. As such he would have been the most powerful of the leaders of the crusade but, in fact, Alexius still distrusted him far too much to agree to any such scheme. The emperor was, however, prepared to supply the crusaders with arms and food.[24]

Hardly had Bohemund's army reached Pelecanum when Raymond of Toulouse arrived at Constantinople. Of all the leaders of the crusade he was the most obstinate in resisting the oath. This was partly because, in Urban's scheme, the Count of Toulouse was to be the military commander of the crusade and Raymond, whose wealth, power, experience in war, and age equipped him to fill such a post, now saw his position threatened— especially if there was anything behind the rumours of Bohemund's demand to be given the post of commanding officer. He declared coolly that he had come east to serve only God. The other leaders, who did not want to see the crusade held up, tried in vain to bring Raymond round. In their talks Bohemund openly took the emperor's side. Finally a compromise was worked out, perhaps with the help of Legate Adhemar of Le Puy. On 26 April Raymond swore a modified oath by which he promised to respect the person and the possessions of the emperor. It probably took a form common in south France and therefore familiar to Raymond; a form which avoided more clearly than the oaths of the others any implication that he was Alexius's vassal. Strangely enough the only one to keep his oath was Raymond who had held out for so long. But perhaps this explains why the others swore so readily. From now on Raymond was on good terms with the emperor; they had their dislike of Bohemund in common. The other princes made no trouble about giving Alexius the promise he wanted and soon they had all reached Pelecanum.

By the end of April 1097 Godfrey and the Normans had already left the camp. Their first objective was Nicaea, the capital of the Seldjuk Sultan, Kilij Arslan. This town, famous as the site of some councils of the early Church, controlled one of the main routes to the east through Anatolia. It was built in a good strategic position on the shore of a lake and was defended by over 200 towers. Godfrey arrived there on 6 May and, although it took a further four weeks before the whole army had assembled, the serious business of the siege began as early as 14 May. Inside the town lay the Seldjuk treasure and Kilij Arslan's family. The sultan himself was away in the east fighting the Danishmends—a Turkish dynasty from east Anatolia who claimed possession of Melitene, a town which, for Kilij Arslan, was the vital gateway to the Seldjuk hinterland in Iraq and Persia. After his experiences with Peter the Hermit's followers he clearly saw no reason to take the crusaders seriously. By the time that he realized the full extent of the danger and hurried back, it was already too late. Unable to enter his own city, he met the crusaders in pitched battle on 21 May. He was defeated and forced to retreat. For the first time the crusaders had proved that if they could catch the Moslems in a pitched battle the tremendous impact of their heavily armed knights could give them victory. But while the lake approaches to Nicaea remained open it was still impossible to take the city. Alexius, who was at Pelecanum organizing supplies, sent ships overland. They were then refloated on the lake and the blockade was completed. Disheartened first by their sultan's retreat and then by this manoeuvre, the garrison surrendered to the Byzantine admiral Butumites. Nicaea was once again part of the Byzantine empire. In view of their oaths the crusaders ought to have expected nothing else. None the less they were disappointed. They were forbidden to enter the city and there could be no question of sacking it. The distrust of the Byzantines grew although Alexius distributed rich presents in order to compensate the crusaders for the plunder of which they felt deprived. But at any rate one obstacle on the way had been removed and this was something to be cheerful about. Stephen of Blois wrote home to his wife

Adelaide: 'unless Antioch proves a stumbling block we hope to be in Jerusalem in five weeks' time'. It was to take them two years. Just to march through Anatolia to Antioch took four months. They had to endure the heat of the summer and a shortage of food and water. The Turks, before retreating to the mountains, had devastated the countryside far and wide. The crusaders did not know the terrain and did not altogether trust their guides. For the first time the disadvantages of not having a single commander-in-chief became clear. The council of princes which acted instead was somewhat ponderous and by no means always unanimous. They left Nicaea on 26 June and headed south-east towards Dorylaeum at which point they would have to choose between several possible routes through Anatolia. They marched in two sections. The first consisted of the Normans of southern Italy and northern France, together with the Flemings and a Byzantine contingent under the command of Taticius; the second of the Provençals and Lorrainers with the troops of Hugh of Vermandois. On 29 June the leading section, in which Bohemund was the dominant personality, came into contact with the army of Kilij Arslan. At dawn on the next day battle was joined. The Turks attacked from all sides. Using their lighter equipment and greater mobility to good effect, they were able to keep out of the way of the ponderous phalanx of heavily armed knights. At the same time they poured in a ceaseless rain of arrows. But they were not strong enough to break into the crusaders' ranks held tightly together by Bohemund. The battle was decided when the Turks were taken by surprise by the arrival of the second section under Godfrey de Bouillon and Raymond of Toulouse, who had been informed of events by a messenger from Bohemund. Adhemar of Le Puy distinguished himself by leading a successful outflanking manoeuvre, although it is not clear whether this had any influence on the outcome of the battle. The sultan fled followed by his panic-stricken army. The Turkish encampment with its magnificent tents and rich booty fell into the hands of the crusaders. The battle had opened the way to Anatolia.

The army, however, avoided the shorter, northern routes even though this meant renouncing well-built Byzantine roads, because to take them would have forced it to go through the central region of Turkish power. Instead the crusaders chose the detour through south-east Anatolia, marching to Philomelium and then along the foot of the Taurus mountains as far as Iconium (Konya). From there they went on to Tyana where the road forked again. It had been a most arduous march. They had enjoyed one short rest—a week at Iconium in mid-August—and then at Heraclea they had to fight their way through against the combined forces of the Danishmends and the emir of Cappadocia. From Tyana the most direct road to Syria led through the Cilician Gates, a steep and narrow pass through the Taurus, then down to Tarsus in the Cilician plain and from there over the Amanus range into the valley of the Orontes in Syria.

Tancred, Baldwin of Boulogne, and Baldwin of Bourcq left the army at Tyana and set out along this route.

For the main army, however, the Cilician Gates posed too many problems. So the other princes decided to follow the road which first took them north-east to Caesarea, the chief city of the Danishmends, and then turned sharply south-east to cross the Anti-Taurus on its way to Marash. One advantage of this route was that the crusaders could hope for support from the local Christian population, above all from the Armenians. In the mid-eleventh century these people had been driven from their home in Armenia by the Byzantines. They settled first in Cappadocia but were then forced by the pressure of the advancing Turks to retire southwards and they now lived in a wide area from Cilicia in the west to beyond the Euphrates in the east. West of the Cilician Gates they were ruled by the Hethoumian dynasty; to the east the Roupenians held sway. Further east there was a group of lesser Armenian princes who recognized Turkish suzerainty. The most important of these was Thoros of Edessa.

At the end of September the army entered Caesarea which the Danishmends had abandoned. From here they marched over the Anti-Taurus; it was a difficult journey made worse by the autumn rains. In mid-October they reached Marash where they were warmly welcomed by the Armenians and could rest for a few days. On 20 October 1097 they fought their way across the Iron Bridge over the Orontes and on 21 October they arrived before the walls of Antioch, the key to North Syria.

Meanwhile Tancred and Baldwin had advanced southwards against the Turkish settlements in the Cilician plain—Armenian control being limited to the mountains. The two of them were almost certainly seeking their own private gain; nevertheless their enterprise did help the crusade. Firstly it meant that the right flank of the main army marching to Antioch was protected. Secondly, the conquest of Cilicia meant that a wedge was driven between the Anatolian and the Syrian Seldjuks, preventing them from joining forces to relieve Antioch. Tancred, with a small party of knights captured Tarsus but was forced to relinquish it to the very much larger forces of Baldwin. Bitterly disappointed Tancred moved off eastwards to Mamistra. Despite his oath Baldwin had no intention of handing over Tarsus to Alexius, especially since there was no Byzantine official anywhere near. He left a Christian garrison in charge and was able to reinforce it with the help of a rich pirate, Guynemer of Boulogne, whose fleet happened to be cruising in those waters. Baldwin then moved on to Mamistra where there was some skirmishing between his men and Tancred's; but they just managed to avert open war. Tancred went south and with help from Guynemer captured the port of Alexandretta. Then he rejoined the main army before Antioch. Baldwin had already met the army while it was still at Marash where his wife had just died. With her Baldwin's hopes of a Norman inheritance vanished. Consequently, after a short conference with his brothers, he headed east again in order to make a more permanent entry into Armenian politics. First he captured the important fortresses of Ravendel and Turbessel which controlled the territory west of the Euphrates. Everywhere the Armenians under Turkish lordship greeted him as a liberator. East of the Euphrates the position of the Armenian Thoros of Edessa was shaky. He had once served the Byzantine Emperor and he was Greek Orthodox by religion. This made him unpopular with his own subjects who were Monophysites belonging to the Armenian Church. Hoping to free himself from Turkish overlordship he invited Baldwin to Edessa. Baldwin wintered west of the Euphrates, then, with a force of only eighty knights, entered Edessa in February 1098. Thoros adopted him as his son using the Armenian ritual whereby both father and son shared the same gown. Baldwin was now heir and co-ruler. But in the next month a conspiracy against Thoros ended with the old ruler being lynched. Baldwin did nothing to help his adoptive father; in fact he probably gave the conspirators his approval. On 10 March he accepted an invitation to be sole ruler of Edessa. As at Tarsus he had no intention of restoring it to the Byzantine emperor. The first crusader state had been founded, the county of Edessa, controlling an area both east and west of the Euphrates, inhabited chiefly by Armenians. It was to act as a north-eastern buffer state protecting the other crusader states further to the south. The new count, his hands full here, thought no more about helping the main army.

During their march through Asia Minor and even more during the coming struggle in Syria and Palestine, the crusaders profited from the state of disarray in Islam. Since the Muslims were unable to grasp what was about to hit them, they saw no reason to abandon their own internal feuds. Medieval Arabic, like medieval Latin, developed no word for 'crusade'. The crusaders they called simply Franks (the First Crusade being predominantly French in character), and the crusader states were the Frankish territories in the Holy Land. That a religious war could serve any purpose other than that of spreading one's own religion was incomprehensible to the Muslims, whose own idea of a holy war, Jihad, was entirely based on this conception. To the Seldjuks the crusade must have looked rather like another Byzantine military expedition, the kind of thing to which they were thoroughly accustomed.

Up to 1095 the dominant political figure in Syria had been Tutush, brother of the great Seldjuk sultan, Malik Shah. He had driven the Fatimids and the Turcomans out of Damascus, Jerusalem, and Acre. His state was a rival to the other Seldjuk powers as well as a useful buffer for them against the Fatimids. In 1086 Tutush added Aleppo to his Palestinian and south Syrian possessions and so Malik Shah judged that the time had come to intervene. He established his own nominees as rulers in Mosul, Aleppo, and Antioch. When Malik Shah died in 1092 the

Seldjuk empire disintegrated. Tutush again tried to extend his dominions and although he was pushed back into Syria by his nephew Berkyaruk, he managed to keep his hold on Aleppo. When he died one of his sons, Ridwan (1095–1113), inherited Aleppo, and the other, Duqaq (1095–1104), obtained Damascus. South Palestine was recovered by the Fatimids who used the opportunity provided by Tutush's death to advance northwards from Egypt. In 1098 they drove the Ortoqids, who had held Jerusalem as a Seldjuk fief, out of the Holy Land. The Shi'ite Fatimids had not the least intention of helping the Sunnite Seldjuks against the crusaders. On the contrary they suggested—though in vain— the formation of an anti-Seldjuk alliance. The growing independence of the minor Armenian principalities added to the confusion. None of the Syrian states was alone powerful enough to stop the Christian army, and so thanks to the disintegration within the Islamic world the crusade was able to reach its goal. For the moment, however, it still stood outside Antioch.

Beautifully situated not far from the sea and on a slope leading down to the fertile valley of the Orontes, Antioch had once been the third city of the Roman Empire. It was no longer quite so splendid but its huge walls and the 400 towers built by Justinian made it practically impregnable. Since 1087 a Seldjuk emir, Yaghi-Siyan, with his Turkish garrison had ruled over a population consisting mainly of Greek and Armenian Christians. Naturally the emir had reason to doubt his subjects' loyalty. When the crusaders arrived at Antioch on 21 October 1097 they decided against trying to take the city by storm, the course advocated by Raymond of Toulouse and one which might have succeeded. Instead, despite the fact that they could not completely encircle Antioch, they decided in favour of a regular siege. This was what Bohemund advised. He hoped to keep Antioch for himself; perhaps Baldwin's success at Edessa strengthened Bohemund's ambition. But the Gate of St. George in the west wall of the city remained open and allowed both supplies to come in and the besieged to come out in sorties against the crusaders, though not in sufficient strength to deal them a decisive blow. Not until mid-November when a Genoese flotilla, bringing reinforcements, sailed into the harbour of St. Symeon, could the besiegers turn to building fortified camps and extend, though not complete, the encirclement of the city. With the winter came food shortage and bitterly cold weather. Stephen of Blois wrote to his wife that he could not understand why anyone in Syria should complain of too much sun. The foraging expeditions were forced to strike further and further afield. At the end of December Bohemund and Robert of Flanders with a large part of the army left the city and advanced up the Orontes valley as far as Shaizar in search of provisions. Here they unexpectedly stumbled upon an army led by Duqaq of Damascus who had at last made up his mind to relieve Antioch. The crusaders won a convincing victory.

Later a half-hearted attempt to relieve the city was made by Ridwan of Aleppo and met a similar end.

Meanwhile the famine in the army grew worse and some of the poor even turned cannibal. Some wild Flemings who had followed Peter the Hermit and were known as 'Tafurs' acquired a considerable reputation for this kind of thing. They always fought in the front line and made the most of any Turks they killed.[25] The Greek patriarch of Jerusalem who had retired to Cyprus was in contact with Adhemar of Le Puy and did his best to help the crusaders, but the supplies he sent were just a drop in the ocean. Likewise, a common war chest established by Raymond of Toulouse (below, p.180) did little to alleviate the situation. In January 1098 men began to desert. Among them was Peter the Hermit, but he was caught and brought back. In February Taticius, the Byzantine general, left the camp. It is hard to know why he did this; and his departure was, of course, exploited by Bohemund in order to stir up anti-Greek resentment. But despite all the difficulties it was at last possible, in March 1098, to complete the blockade. Then in May the situation changed again when it became known that a great warrior, Kerbogha of Mosul (d. 1102), was marching to relieve Antioch. He had obtained additional troops from the Ortoqids who, having been thrown out of Jerusalem, were now ruling in Mesopotamia. The approach of this army put the demoralized crusaders in a terrible position. If Antioch did not fall before Kerbogha arrived the crusade would be all over. It was Bohemund who saved the situation. He had already threatened to leave the army if Antioch were not handed over to him and he now repeated this demand openly. He had established a connection with a captain inside Antioch named Firouz, who was willing to sell the city. Despite the objections raised by Raymond who wanted to remain true to his oath, Bohemund was promised Antioch—if he could take it and so long as the emperor did not come in person to press his claim. Although the fall of the city was now imminent, one of the leading crusaders, Stephen of Blois, decided to leave for home on 2 June. He had probably been responsible for supplies and may well have felt that since Antioch's surrender was certain his task was now completed. On the return journey through Anatolia he met the emperor Alexius who was preparing to advance into Syria in order to safeguard his rights there. In the meantime other deserters had joined up with Stephen and they gave a depressing account of the situation at Antioch with the city now held by the crusaders who were, in their turn, besieged by Kerbogha. They painted so black a picture that Alexius altered his plans and Bohemund's chances of retaining Antioch were thereby much improved. In Europe public opinion turned against Stephen of Blois, accusing him, a little unjustly, of cowardice and desertion. His wife's welcome home was anything but friendly.

On the evening of the day that Stephen left the camp, the crusaders also marched away from Antioch, only to return under cover of night. In the early hours of the morning of 3 June 1098 Firouz admitted Bohemund and his knights into the city. It was not long before the crusaders were in control and had killed all the Turks they could lay their hands on. Yaghi-Siyan was slain while trying to escape. His son managed to reach the citadel which still held out. But the arrival of Kerbogha meant that the crusaders had not gained very much. Once the besiegers they were now themselves besieged in a city suffering from shortage of food.

Fortunately Kerbogha had come too late. He had spent three weeks vainly besieging Edessa and so lost the chance of destroying the crusaders while they were still outside Antioch. On arrival he at once took command of the citadel on the mountain ridge behind the city and from here he constantly harrassed the crusaders besides organizing a complete blockade. Under the pressure of hunger, morale in the Christian army sank rapidly and the number of desertions remained high. Something drastic had to be done if any way out was to be found.[26] Since it was, in any case, a situation which was ripe for religious hysteria and visions of all kinds, use was made of a visionary from Provence, a man of humble origins called Peter Bartholomew. This man informed Count Raymond that St. Andrew had appeared to him on several occasions and had told him that the Holy Lance—with which the Roman centurion had pierced the side of Christ—was buried in the cathedral of St. Peter. Adhemar of Le Puy had his doubts about the story—after all another such lance was in a Constantinople collection. But diggings in the cathedral took place several days later and Peter actually did find a lance on the evening of 14 June. Today it is considered certain that the whole affair was a pious fraud but it is not easy to be certain about the identity of the men behind it. Later on, when it had become common to look upon the lance with scepticism, the Normans blamed the Provençals, but in fact Peter Bartholomew was quite capable, in other circumstances, of having thoroughly pro-Norman visions—especially after it was clear that at least one man from south France, Adhemar of Le Puy, did not have a very high opinion of him. The Normans could just as well have been responsible as could some unidentifiable group of churchmen. In any event, the immediate effects of the discovery were enormous. The army's morale was raised and all were united in the urgent determination to break the blockade and destroy Kerbogha. By now indeed a successful sortie was the only chance. Bohemund—always the central figure in the struggle for Antioch—was particular insistent about this now that rivalries had broken out in Kerbogha's army. The Damascus contingent were offended because Kerbogha had requested help from Aleppo as well. The decisive battle took place on 28 June. Kerbogha did not attack early enough and his attempt to outflank the crusaders was foiled by Bohemund's prudence. It ended when the Turks, led by the Damascus contingent, fled in panic. The plunder was immense and Bohemund was the man of the moment. The citadel too now surrendered to him.

The most urgent problem now was a political one: what should be done with Antioch? On this subject the Normans and Provençals disagreed completely. The crusade came to a halt; in an atmosphere of general distrust no one was prepared to leave the city. In its present state the army could not be expected to march during the heat of the summer, so the starting date was fixed for 1 November. Then an epidemic broke out and the princes scattered to escape it. Bohemund went to Cilicia, Godfrey to Turbessel, and Robert of Normandy to Lattakieh. But Adhemar of Le Puy was struck down by the disease and died on 1 August. He had not been able to play the dominating role originally envisaged by Urban, but among the quarrelling princes he had always stood for compromise and harmony. From now on the conflict between Normans and Provençals grew worse. In September the princes returned to Antioch and dispatched a letter to the pope, informing him of the legate's death and asking him to come to Antioch in person to put himself at the head of the crusade. It was a measure born of desperation, taken in the hope of gaining time when there seemed to be no immediate prospect of reaching an agreement about Antioch. Forays into Muslim territory kept the troops occupied. In October Raymond captured the town of al-Bara and here the first Latin bishop, Peter of Narbonne, was installed, though of course he had to be consecrated by the Greek patriarch of Antioch who had now been restored to his position. This was the first step towards building up a Latin Church which threatened the established rights of the Greek Church. On 5 November the council of princes met again in the cathedral. This time Bohemund was able, by and large, to get his way. He had long had the support of most of the princes and now Raymond too had to yield in face of the restless army's insistent demand that the march be continued. But Raymond had no intention of simply allowing his rival to take over Antioch at once and he agreed only on condition that Bohemund would go with them to Jerusalem. The departure was further delayed, however, by fighting to the south of Antioch and during this period tension between Provençals and Normans mounted. In December Raymond captured Maarat an-Numan, a fortress to the south-east of Antioch, perhaps hoping to use it as a counterweight to the Normans in Antioch. For his part Bohemund began a systematic campaign to discredit the Provençals, in particular by exploiting the doubts about the genuineness of the Holy Lance.

Some time around Christmas a large part of the army offered to recognize Raymond as commander-in-chief if he would lead them on to Jerusalem. Raymond accepted this offer and on 13 January 1099 the march began. Raymond who was now nearly sixty years old left Maarat at the head of his troops, walking barefoot and dressed as a pilgrim. By this finely calculated gesture he reminded his fellow-princes of their crusaders' oaths for it was clear to him that his contingent by itself could achieve little. He offered sums of money to the others to try to persuade them to accept him as their leader: in this way he hoped to strengthen his own position against Bohemund. Tancred and Robert of Normandy were persuaded, but Godfrey and Robert of Flanders would not agree to serve under him. In early January Bohemund had managed to drive the last of the Provençal troops out of Antioch, and despite his promise to join the march to Jerusalem he refused to leave the city. Raymond's army moved south along the eastern slopes of the Nosairi mountains.[27] The advance was free of incident since the local emirs were much too weak to put up any serious resistance and most of them were prepared to pay to avoid being attacked. After the disaster at Antioch the rulers of Damascus, Aleppo, and Mosul preferred to remain passive observers. They certainly saw no reason to help the Fatimids who in 1098 had again advanced into Palestine; indeed the Syrian rulers, as Sunnites, may well have enjoyed seeing Christians move against the Shi'ite Fatimids. North of Tripoli the crusaders returned to the coast, and some small detachments moved northwards capturing a few ports including Maraclea and Tortosa. (The cathedral at Tortosa is one of the finest buildings of the crusading period still standing today.) These successes persuaded Godfrey and Robert of Flanders to change their minds. Even Bohemund joined their march south, but only for form's sake, and after a short while he went back to Antioch where he now ruled unopposed. In the next few years he was able to build up an extensive principality.

Raymond meanwhile had settled down to besiege Arqa, a town to the north-east of Tripoli which he had already marked out as the centre of a Lebanese principality for himself. But despite the arrival of Godfrey and Robert of Flanders the siege proved fruitless and so the army continued its march south along the coast road. The emir of Tripoli bought immunity for himself and for his city. On 19 May the crusaders crossed the Dog River; they were now in Fatimid territory. All the Fatimids' attempts to reach a settlement had failed. Their last offer had been conditional on the crusaders not entering Palestine—it shows how little the Muslims were able to understand what the crusade was all about. The advance continued: Beirut, Sidon, Tyre, Acre, Haifa, and then on to Jaffa where they turned inland. At Ramleh, a Muslim town abandoned by its inhabitants, they installed a Latin bishop and this time, there being no Greek available, he was consecrated by a Latin. The new bishop was to become secular ruler over the nearby village of Lydda—where his cathedral church of St. George contained the tomb of the famous soldier saint—but it is unlikely, despite what William of Tyre tells us, that he also received a lordship at Ramleh. In 1102 this was demonstrably still part of the royal demesne. In the mid 1120s indeed even the bishop's claim to the lordship of Lydda was disputed, though in the end it was generally accepted.[28] On 6 June Tancred occupied Bethlehem and hoisted his banner over the Church of the Nativity. Next day, 7 June, the crusaders' road led them to the summit of a hill from where they could see Jerusalem. Many of them had tears in their eyes for they had waited so long for this moment. They named the hill Montjoie. Three years had passed since the day when Godfrey de Bouillon had set out from Lorraine.

Jerusalem was a well fortified city and the lie of the land meant that it was vulnerable, if at all, only from the north and south-west. The Fatimid governor had taken adequate precautions. He had expelled the Christian inhabitants as being unreliable. He had sufficient food and water and had taken the trouble to make the springs outside the walls unusable. The crusaders, too few in number to be able to invest the city completely, concentrated on the weaker sectors. On 13 June they tried to take Jerusalem by storm but, being insufficiently supplied with scaling ladders and siege engines, they were driven back. Then, quite by chance, six Christian ships sailed into the deserted harbour at Jaffa, bringing urgently needed building materials. Wood was brought from Samaria. But the construction of the wooden castles set on wheels and fitted out with catapults was a slow business. The heat and the water shortage had a bad effect on morale which again sank to a dangerous level. Then it was learnt that the Egyptian army was on the way. Once more a vision came at the critical moment, this time to a priest called Peter Desiderius. He was told that if they held a fast and then a procession round the walls, the city would fall into their hands within nine days—as long as they performed these tasks with sufficient piety. A fast was observed and then, on 8 July, to the astonishment of the besieged, the crusade turned into a barefoot procession of pilgrims which solemnly wound its way round the city. The procession ended on the Mount of Olives where they all listened to the eloquent words of Peter the Hermit and other preachers. The army had recovered its fighting spirit. When three 'castles' were ready, they began the assault during the night of 13–14 July. On 14 July Raymond managed to bring his castle up against the wall in the south-west sector, but he could not capture the wall itself. Godfrey had more success when, on 15 July, he manoeuvred his castle close to the wall near the present Herod's Gate and then made a bridge from the castle to the top of the wall. Litold, a Flemish knight from Tournai, was the first crusader to set foot on the wall. He was followed by Godfrey and the Lorrainers and then Tancred and his men. At this spot a large stone cross was to stand for as long as Jerusalem was held by Christians in memory of the capture of the city by the crusaders. While the Lorrainers opened the gates to their comrades, Tancred rushed ahead into the Temple area, the heart of the city, and seized the Mosque of al-Aqsa. The Fatimid governor who had been directing the defence in the southern sector, now realized that all was lost and withdrew into the Tower of David, a massive citadel near the western Jaffa Gate. In return for being allowed to retire safely to Ascalon he surrendered this to Raymond who thus obtained a strategically important strongpoint. The governor and his retinue were the only Muslims to escape alive. The intoxication of victory, religious fanaticism, and the memory of hardships bottled up for three years exploded in a horrifying bloodbath in which the crusaders hacked down everyone, irrespective of race or religion, who was unfortunate enough to come within reach of their swords. They waded, ankle-deep in blood, through streets covered with bodies. The Lorrainers were relatively restrained; at least they refrained from raping Jewish women. When the frenzy of killing was over the first task was to dispose of the corpses. The precious Jewish library (eight Torah rolls and three hundred and thirty manuscripts) escaped destruction and was sold, at a high price, to the Jewish community at Ascalon. The Muslim world was profoundly shocked by this Christian barbarity; it was a long time before the memory of this massacre began to fade. The crusade, however, had reached its goal. The Sepulchre of Christ was again in Christian hands. But for how long? The Egyptian army was coming closer.

After the sanitary problem of the corpses had been dealt with, the leaders of the crusade, both clerics and laymen, met to decide what was to be done next. The curious fact now became clear that they had left Europe without any idea of what to do with Jerusalem once they had captured it. Nor, apparently, had anything been worked out during the long march. It was generally accepted, however, that an ecclesiastical and a secular system of government had to be devised if they wanted to keep what they had won. The churchmen, headed by Bishop Arnulf of Marturano, demanded that the first step, before going on to secular affairs, should be the election of a patriarch.[29] But this had to be postponed when it was found that the clergy from Lorraine and Provence would not accept the only candidate, Robert of Normandy's chaplain Arnulf of Chocques (also erroneously called of Rohes). The claims of the Greek patriarch were ignored. The crusaders believed him to be in Cyprus though in fact he had died a few days before they entered Jerusalem. There were only two serious candidates for the throne. Raymond of Toulouse and Godfrey de Bouillon. The other leaders either intended to return home or lacked the necessary authority. The crown was first offered to Raymond but he refused it with the words that he did not wish to be king in Christ's holy city. He realized that the offer had been made half-heartedly and he hoped, by this cunning reply, to prevent Godfrey from accepting it. Godfrey was popular with the whole army and had managed, on the whole, to keep out of the unedifying quarrels of the princes. On the other hand it was clear that he lacked the personality of a Bohemund or a Raymond. But he was clever enough—or perhaps his advisers were—to find a solution to the immediate problem. He outmanoeuvred Raymond by refusing to be king but agreeing to be ruler. This also had the advantage of leaving open for the moment the critical question of the relationship between the lay ruler and the Church, so avoiding a clash with the clergy. Among the latter there was in any case no commanding personality with enough authority to found a new kingdom by crowning a king.[30] Godfrey then tricked Raymond into handing over the Tower of David, the military key to Jerusalem. In a rage, Raymond left the city and went on a pilgrimage to Jericho and the Jordan. His absence simplified the problem of choosing a patriarch. The Norman Arnulf was elected, despite the fact that he was illegitimate and not even a subdeacon and therefore, in canon law, not eligible. For this reason he was not consecrated and had at best the position of a bishop elect. But perhaps he was no more than the leader of the Jerusalem Church in an unclear legal position. During the siege of Arqa he had finally demolished all belief in the Holy Lance and he now strengthened his own position by looking for and finding the True Cross—a relic powerful enough to supplant the 'Provençal' lance.

Despite all this tension, both Raymond and Robert of Normandy, whom Godfrey had somehow managed to offend, responded loyally to the new ruler's request for help against the Egyptian army. On 12 August 1099 battle was joined on level ground near the Egyptian harbour-fortress of Ascalon. The Egyptians were taken by surprise while still in their camp and were completely defeated. Their commander, the vizier al-Afdal (1094–1121) fled back to Egypt. On 13 August the victorious army returned in triumph to Jerusalem. The success of the crusade was now assured. The regaining of the Holy Land was an astonishing achievement. The rejoicing in Christendom was fully justified.

4

THE CRUSADER STATES, 1099–1146

THE Bible had promised a land flowing with milk and honey but the crusaders found that they had conquered an economically depressed area with a geographical structure that tended to force people to settle in isolated groups and to favour the development of small or very small states.[31] At the time of their greatest extent the crusader states stretched from the Gulf of Alexandretta to the Gulf of Akaba in the Red Sea. Excluding the eastern outpost at Edessa which by that time had been lost again, they covered an area about 500 miles long and anything up to 100 miles wide. Throughout the whole of this region the main geographical features are very similar. Going from west to east there is a coastal plain rising gradually up to a high range of limestone mountains; then a steep drop into a depression which in turn opens out into a fertile cultivated plateau, though in places a second mountain range, the Anti-Lebanon, has to be surmounted. This plateau then merges into a treeless steppe country. In the south the coastal plain is wider and separated from the sea by a belt of sand dunes. The principal mountain ranges are the Nosairi and Lebanon Mountains (up to 3000 metres high) in the north; the Anti-Lebanon and Mount Hermon (up to 2700 metres) in the centre; and the Palestinian highlands (Hebron is over 1000 metres above sea-level) in the south. The depression is formed by the Syrian rift valley with the Orontes in the north; it continues as the Leontes valley running between the mountains of Lebanon and the Anti-Lebanon and then as the valley of the Jordan and the Dead Sea (919 square kilometres in area; in places more than 396 metres below sea-level; salt content up to 22 per cent). The three main crossing points on the Jordan were Jacob's Ford north of the Sea of Galilee and, to the south, the Pont de Senabra and the Pont de Judaire. South of the Dead Sea the hills merge into the gently undulating plateau of the inhospitable Negev Desert. Apart from the coastal plain the whole region is rather infertile and becomes increasingly so as one moves south from Galilee. The Palestinian highlands are particularly rocky and lacking in water. There are few good east–west routes. The only good road to the Jordan runs from the much fought-over plain of Acre. East of the Jordan the crusaders penetrated temporarily into the Terre de Suète (from Arabic as-sawad meaning 'black country') a fertile plain east of the Sea of Galilee covered with soil of dark basaltic detritus, and into the volcanic hill regions of Moab and Edom through which strategically and economically important lines of communication ran from south Syria to Egypt. The climate is characterized by very hot, dry summers and by abundant cool winter rain, with occasional snowfalls even outside the high mountainous areas. The temperature figures for Jerusalem are as follows: in July and August an average temperature of *c*. 25° C. (77° F.) with daily maxima of *c*. 35° C. (95° F.), sometimes going up to 40° C. (104° F.) at midday; average temperatures in January and February 8° C. (46° F.), going down to −5° C. (23° F.) in the early hours of the morning. At Jericho summer temperatures can rise as high as 50° C. (122° F.). Additional hazards were earthquakes (in 1114, 1170, and 1185) and plagues of mice (1120–4, 1127) and of locusts 1114, 1117, 1120) which decimated the herds and destroyed the vegetation. So far as climate and the rural economy were concerned, both Provençals and south Italians had been better off at home.

Early in September 1099 most of the crusaders left Jerusalem. Robert of Flanders, Robert of Normandy, Baldwin of Bourcq, and Raymond of Toulouse marched north with their troops; the two Roberts were on their way home. Only Godfrey de Bouillon and Tancred remained in Jerusalem. With them were only some 300 knights and 2,000 foot soldiers.[32] Originally Godfrey's lordship consisted of no more than Jerusalem, the port of Jaffa, and some towns, Lydda, Ramleh, Bethlehem, and St. Abraham (Hebron) which he fortified strongly. The countryside was inhabited by hostile Muslims who at first—while Frankish power still seemed precarious—refused to co-operate with their new lords. Even the population of Jerusalem felt insecure because the city walls were still badly damaged and only the offer of considerable material advantages persuaded them to stay. According to the *Assise de l'an et jour* anyone who left intending to come back later when and if things had settled down, would forfeit his possessions to the person who, in the meantime, had held them for a year and a day. Only gradually was Godfrey able to extend his influence over the rural areas of Judaea and Samaria. Tancred moved further north to Galilee and carved out a lordship for himself. It was originally made up of Tiberias, Nazareth, and Beisan; later Haifa and the Terre de Suète together with the area which lay between them were added. Tancred held this region, the lordship of Tiberias, as a fief of Godfrey; gradually it evolved into the principality of Galilee. In time Godfrey's territory developed into a compact Christian state separating the coastal region which was still controlled by the Fatimids from the Muslim interior of the Hauran and Transjordan. The geography of the region required that the crusaders should try to push back the Muslims in the south and east until the desert had been reached. This could then serve as a *cordon sanitaire* between the Christians and the Muslims, with the latter being confined to Egypt and Mesopotamia. In order to achieve this the crusaders had first of all to capture Aleppo and Damascus. But in fact they failed to do this and had to be satisfied with a series of treaties made in 1108–10 which created a no man's land in northern Transjordan in the biblical region of Gilead between the rivers Yabbok (Zerqa) and Yarmuk, in the Terre de Suète, and in the Lebanese plain of Beqaa between the mountains of Lebanon and Anti-Lebanon, as well as on the fringes of the Hauran. In these areas the revenues were shared with Damascus and both sides were able to use the extensive pastures and the granary on the Golan.

Raymond of Toulouse meanwhile, once Godfrey had prevented him from building up a lordship in south-west Palestine, had also gone north. He found his old rival Bohemund engaged in besieging Lattakieh, a Byzantine port south of Antioch which Bohemund had feared might be used as a bridgehead if Alexius decided to invade Antioch. Raymond forced him to raise the siege. Bohemund had been receiving naval support from a Pisan fleet commanded by Daimbert, the archbishop of Pisa. It was a sign that a new force was entering the politics of Syria and Palestine. The two great sea powers in the eastern Mediterranean were Byzantium and Egypt. The crusader states never owned a fleet worth mentioning. But without a fleet the Egyptians could not be driven out of the harbour towns and without the possession of the fertile coastal plain and the economically valuable ports, the Frankish states would never flourish. The Byzantines generally needed their fleet for their own affairs so the Italian maritime towns stepped into the breach. Being realists they had originally looked upon the crusade with great scepticism. Only when, against all their calculations, it succeeded did they come round to giving official support to the crusaders' cause. But in return for their help they always demanded and received a high price. The privileges which they secured, often by pure blackmail, seriously impaired the legal integrity of the state and became a permanent burden on its financial resources.

The Pisans were the first to sense that a great opportunity had come. They equipped a fleet which Archbishop Daimbert was then able to use to further his own private ends in Outremer. Like Bohemund he was suspicious of the Greeks so he and the prince of Antioch were natural allies. After the abandonment of the siege of Lattakieh they travelled to Jerusalem where they spent Christmas 1099 together with Baldwin of Edessa who had joined them on the way. Bohemund and Baldwin had at last fulfilled their vow to make a pilgrimage to Jerusalem. But they had political considerations in mind as well. Godfrey needed their knights just as urgently as he needed Daimbert's fleet, and was in no position to resist their demands. The Norman Arnulf was removed from his position as leader of the Church of Jerusalem and Daimbert was created the first Latin patriarch in his stead (1099–1102). Then Godfrey had to submit to being invested in his lordship by Daimbert. Bohemund in his turn was ready to hold Antioch as a fief of the patriarch. Baldwin of Edessa did not follow this example. For Bohemund such an investiture offered only advantages. While Daimbert remained in Jerusalem his *de facto* influence in Antioch was small, while Bohemund, as vassal of the Latin patriarch, could at last claim that he had some right to Antioch which previously he had held unlawfully and against the terms of the oath he had sworn to Alexius.

It was once generally accepted by historians that Daimbert's actions were an expression of the theocratic nature of the Church's claims in the East. But there is, in fact, very little to support this view (see pp. 56f., n. 29). It is most unlikely that Daimbert's actions were in accordance with Urban's intentions. The pope would hardly have planned to deal with the question of the relationship between the Latin and Greek Churches in Daimbert's crass manner. Daimbert, however, who had originally obtained the archbishopric of Pisa as an Imperial appointee but was now a Gregorian reformer, displayed the excess of doctrinaire zeal so typical of the recent convert. The rights of the patriarch of Antioch had been infringed not only by the investiture of Bohemund but also by Daimbert's consecration of four Latin bishops and archbishops in Bohemund's principality: Tarsus, Artah, Mamistra, and Edessa. These infringements and Bohemund's hostile attitude forced Patriarch John of Antioch to take refuge in Constantinople. The result was a schism since Bohemund immediately installed a Latin patriarch, Bernard of Valence (1100–35). For a while Daimbert even refused to allow the Greeks to hold services in the Church of the Holy Sepulchre in Jerusalem. What happened there at Christmas 1099 was simply a normal ecclesiastical consecration, though it was being interpreted as the formal grant of Jerusalem as a fief as early as the twelfth century, and was perhaps already referred to as such by Daimbert himself in his letter to Bohemund (see below, n. 33). But Godfrey would have found this unacceptable. As Prawer suggests, he only seems to have been prepared to let the patriarch have an ecclesiastical seignory, like Lydda, but grander and based on that quarter of Jerusalem which had belonged to the patriarchs ever since the Fatimids, for reasons of security, had forced all the Christian population into one section of the city. Daimbert too seems at least to have started out with less ambitious plans. In a letter written before his arrival in Jerusalem, he gave Godfrey the rarely found title of *Sancti Sepulchri advocatus* and, in Hiestand's view, this is how he thought of him: as Defender of the Holy Sepulchre. But he did not remain content with his quarter of Jerusalem. He used his wealth and power in a campaign of blackmail which forced Godfrey to concede first a quarter of Jaffa, then the citadel of Jerusalem, and finally the whole city and the rest of Jaffa, leaving Godfrey with no more than a life interest in them.

This agreement at least had the advantage of giving Godfrey time to extend his rule over the coastal plain. Several minor emirs, as well as some of the Transjordan sheikhs, were in fact ready to pay him tribute. Daimbert's stranglehold was weakened when the Pisan fleet sailed home.

Then in June 1100 a Venetian fleet arrived at Jaffa. Godfrey welcomed it warmly for he saw a chance of further loosening the patriarch's grip. While he was still negotiating with the Venetians he became seriously ill; none the less a treaty was arranged. The Venetians were to be allowed to trade freely throughout the state, to hold a market in every town and were to receive a third of every town they helped to capture. In return they would help him until 15 August. The colossal price which Godfrey was prepared to pay for some temporary assistance shows how anxious he was to create a counterweight to Daimbert. But he himself did not live to enjoy the changing situation. On 18 July he died. As the first Christian ruler of Jerusalem he was found a worthy resting place on the hill of Golgotha, the place of the crucifixion.

Daimbert made one fatal mistake. He left Jerusalem shortly before Godfrey died. Had he been there he would possibly have been able to see that the terms of his agreement with Godfrey were carried out. In that event there might never have been a kingdom of Jerusalem. But now when this Lorrainese state was in danger of being turned into a Pisan one, a group of Lorrainers, Godfrey's household officials, seized control of the city and thus ensured the continuity of the Lorraine dynasty. Acting in accordance with customs of their homeland they summoned Godfrey's nearest relative, his brother Baldwin of Edessa, to take over the inheritance. There was, in other words, no question of a free election of a new ruler. Later the 'election' of Godfrey was to be used as a precedent to justify the development of a system of election by the barons, though in fact Godfrey had been chosen by his peers and battle-companions, not by the barons of Jerusalem. In the course of time two parallel constitutional procedures came to be evolved. One emphasized the electoral rights of the barons and looked back to Godfrey; the other emphasized hereditary rights and looked back to the succession of Baldwin.

Daimbert tried to block Baldwin's succession by writing to Bohemund and asking him to prevent Baldwin from reaching Jerusalem. The letter never reached the prince of Antioch.[33] In August 1100 Bohemund, still ignorant of events in Jerusalem, had marched north to consolidate his hold on his border regions. He had been ambushed and was now held prisoner by the Danishmend emir. Baldwin of Edessa intervened to save Antioch and then, in October, having left Edessa to be administered by his cousin Baldwin of Bourcq (1100–18), he set out on an arduous march to Jerusalem where he arrived in November. Daimbert now recognized that there was no chance of his plans succeeding. The best he could hope for was to remain patriarch so towards Christmas he came to terms. On 25 December 1100 he crowned Baldwin king. The ceremony took place, not in the centre of the kingdom's religious life, the Church of the Holy Sepulchre, but in the Church of the Nativity at Bethlehem. A point of debate, whether it was fitting to wear a royal crown in a city where Jesus had worn the Crown of Thorns, was thus avoided. In his coronation oath Baldwin promised to serve the Holy Sepulchre and to rule the Church and people of Jerusalem justly and in peace. His successors were to swear to protect the patriarch—but this was not mentioned in Baldwin's oath. Instead of being vassals of the patriarch, as Daimbert at one point seems to have claimed they were, the rulers of Jerusalem were once again the protectors and defenders of the Holy Sepulchre. Baldwin's insistence upon the royal title completed the process of freeing the newly created state from the threat of patriarchal overlordship. From now on the patriarch was no more than the kingdom's *seigneur espirituel.*

Baldwin I had originally been destined for the Church and he was correspondingly well-educated. Moreover, as he had demonstrated when he founded the county of Edessa, he was made of sterner stuff than his brother. Once Daimbert had crowned him he had no further use for him. With the assistance of a new papal legate, Maurice of Porto, he had him suspended. (Maurice had come to the Holy Land with a fleet from Genoa, the last of the three great maritime republics of Italy to extend its sphere of operations to Outremer.) For a short while in 1102 Daimbert was able to regain the patriarchal throne thanks to the support he received from Tancred who had exchanged the lordship of Tiberias for the regency of Antioch during the absence of the captive Bohemund. But then he was finally deposed and once again forced to go into exile in Antioch. He appealed to the pope on the grounds that he had been unlawfully expelled by Baldwin and was, in fact, able to convince Paschal II of the truth of this version although as far as canon law went he had been validly deposed, for serious offences, by a synod held by a papal legate. Paschal ordered his reinstatement and a new conflict with the king was avoided only because Daimbert died before he could return (1106). The pope's judgement must be seen in the light of the contemporary Gregorian demand for the *libertas ecclesiae.* He would not and could not allow the king to rule the Church in so direct a fashion. But the fact that even the ambitious Daimbert had to appeal to the pope, that since 1099 papal legates had three times intervened in church affairs in Jerusalem, suspending or deposing patriarchs, shows that the Church of Jerusalem, in contrast to that of Antioch, was clearly subject to papal authority and was firmly integrated into the Roman system. From now on the patriarch was nothing more than a metropolitan in a particularly venerable city with a particularly venerable title. The unhappy quarrel between the patriarchs of Jerusalem and Antioch over the distribution of suffragan bishoprics (see below, p. 76f.) only served to confirm the pope in his role as lord and judge superior to the contending parties.

In the West the success of the First Crusade had been greeted with universal jubilation. The election of a new pope in 1099 in no way interrupted the work of preaching the crusade. This was directed particularly at those men who had abandoned the crusade before it captured Jerusalem and who therefore had failed to fulfil their vows. But many others stepped forward to take the cross for the first time, moved both by the news of victory and by the requests for reinforcements which came from Outremer.[34] The preaching had its biggest success in Lombardy where a large army mustered under the command of Archbishop Anselm of Milan. In the south of France the powerful duke of Aquitaine, William IX—one of the earliest troubadours—took the cross. In the north, Stephen of Blois and Hugh of Vermandois were ready to march for the second time; both submitted to growing public and private pressure that they should fulfil their vows. Count William II of Nevers and Auxerre, Duke Otto of Burgundy, and Count Stephen of Burgundy set out from eastern France. Among the clergy to take the cross were the bishops of Paris, Laon, and Soissons, and the archbishop of Besançon. In Germany crusading enthusiasm affected Bavaria and Austria in particular. Old Welf IV, duke of Bavaria, and many of his lords took the cross. He was accompanied by Ida, the widow of Margrave Luitpold II of Austria, and by Archbishop Thiemo of Salzburg, Bishop Ulrich of Passau, the abbot of Admont, and the chronicler Ekkehard of Aura.

The first to go were the Lombards. They set off in autumn 1100 and reached Constantinople early in the next year. During the course of the summer the other contingents arrived. But the Lombards pushed on without waiting for their fellow-crusaders. They crossed the Bosporus after Easter and marched to Nicomedia where Stephen of Blois and the Burgundians caught up with them. Here too they were joined by Raymond of Toulouse, recently arrived from Lattakieh. In vain the experienced crusaders tried to dissuade the Lombards from their plan of invading north Anatolia in order to rescue Bohemund from his prison at Niksar in Pontus. On the march through north Anatolia the army suffered badly from lack of provisions. Their route is difficult to reconstruct but it ended in mid-July near Mersivan, east of the River Halys, where the crusaders were met by a Turkish army composed of contingents sent by Sultan Kilij Arslan, the Danishmends, and Ridwan of Aleppo. The battle lasted several days and ended with the complete destruction of the Lombard army. Only a few survived to find their way back to Constantinople, among them the counts of Toulouse, Blois, and Burgundy and the archbishop of Milan.

The army led by Count William of Nevers had no better luck. It also marched towards north Anatolia but then turned south at Ankara, only to be destroyed at Heraclea. William himself managed to find his way to Antioch. The Aquitanians and the Bavarians meanwhile had fought their way through the Balkans to Constantinople. There they had to swear the same oath that the first crusaders had sworn; and from there they took the same road that the first crusaders had taken. At Heraclea they too met their fate. In September 1101 they fell into a Turkish ambush and were completely defeated. Ida of Austria and Thiemo of Salzburg were imprisoned or murdered. The legends which sprang up around them contain motifs which were to become commonplace in the romantic literature of the crusades. According to the legend Ida married a Saracen emir and became the mother of Zengi the great enemy of the Christians. While he was in prison Thiemo was supposed to have been put to work repairing a Muslim idol. Suddenly the idol began to speak in a blasphemous fashion and, as a result, Thiemo had to suffer a martyr's death. The dukes of Aquitaine and Bavaria with a few followers got through to Antioch where they were soon joined by those who had earlier escaped back to Constantinople. From Antioch this pitifully small band marched on to Jerusalem. The crusade had failed. For the moment the West was not ready to despatch another big army. A penitential crusade by which the emperor, Henry IV, hoped to have his excommunication lifted and in preparation for which he issued the *Reichslandfriede* of 1103, never got beyond the planning stage as a result of the hard lines still being taken in the Investiture Contest and the rebellion of the emperor's own son.

Meanwhile in Antioch the warlike Tancred was trying to extend the frontiers of his state in all directions. In 1101 he reconquered Cilicia from the Byzantines; then he moved south to Lattakieh which finally capitulated in 1103 after a long siege. But despite all his efforts he could not prevent Raymond of Toulouse and his Provençal followers from occupying the port of Tortosa, south of Lattakieh, and then settling down to besiege Tripoli. Ever since the First Crusade Raymond had had his eyes on this city and now he intended not to rest until he had captured it and made it the centre of a principality of his own. This state would form a link between the Normans in Antioch to the north and the Lorrainers in Jerusalem to the south and was intended to ensure that Raymond had the power to cope with his Norman rivals. By building a massive castle on Mount Pilgrim Raymond was able to control the land approaches to Tripoli. He did not live to see the surrender of the city but a charter of 1103 in which he already took the title of count of Tripoli admits of no doubt about his plans.

In 1103, on payment of a large ransom, Bohemund of Antioch was freed. The money was raised by the efforts of Baldwin of Bourcq who had gradually come to realize that Tancred was too powerful a neighbour for comfort. But even after Bohemund had once again taken the reins of government into his own hands Tancred remained in Antioch. He could have returned to his old lordship, Tiberias, but declined to do so, possibly remembering his old rivalry with King Baldwin I. Bohemund immediately launched an offensive against Ridwan of Aleppo. In this he was supported by Baldwin of Bourcq and Joscelin of Courtenay. Joscelin had arrived in the Holy Land in 1101 and had been enfeoffed with Turbessel by Baldwin. This made him the most important vassal of the count of Edessa west of the Euphrates. In 1104 they planned to capture Harran, the great fortress south-east of Edessa. The idea was good. Harran was the gateway to Mosul where the death of the powerful Kerbogha (1102) had been followed by bitter quarrels between the new atabeg (i.e. regent) and his Muslim neighbours. The possession of Harran would have effectively thrust a wedge between the three Seldjuk centres, Anatolia, Iraq, and Syria. In particular, Aleppo and Damascus would have been cut off from their fellow-believers in central Asia. Even in these circumstances, however, the ruler of Damascus was not prepared to go to war against the Franks for, in his eyes, Antioch and Edessa were valuable buffer-states against Aleppo and Mosul. Taking a wider perspective this was an outlook which meant that Muslim opportunities were being frittered away. Indeed, precisely this point was made in the course of a penetrating analysis of the situation by the Damascus philologist as-Sulami. In a treatise written in 1105 he called for a halt to internal Muslim quarrels on the grounds that resistance to the Franks would be effective only if it were organized before they had a chance to establish themselves. As it happened, however, even without Damascus the Frankish army was cut to pieces on the banks of the River Balikh not far from Harran (1104). Baldwin of Bourcq and Joscelin of Courtenay were captured, leaving Tancred happily in possession of the regency of Edessa. The defeat had other far-reaching political consequences though the importance of these was not immediately apparent. Together with the failure of the crusade of 1101 it destroyed the legend of the invincibility of the crusaders. The failure to split the Seldjuks meant that Edessa's position as an eastern outpost of Christendom was increasingly vulnerable. The newly founded county survived for as long as forty years only because of the lack of unity among the Muslims.

Byzantium took advantage of the defeat at Harran to reconquer Cilicia from Antioch and to reoccupy parts of Lattakieh—the harbour and the lower town. Bohemund, desperately concerned about the future of his principality once again handed the regency over to Tancred and returned to Europe. He went first to his own lands in Apulia and then on to Rome and France where he used all the means at his disposal—money and propaganda—to raise an army to fight Byzantium. He enhanced the standing of his family by skilfully arranging advantageous marriages for himself and for his nephew Tancred. In 1107 he sailed across the Adriatic and laid siege to the great coastal fortress of Dyrrhachium.[35] But it was a hopeless enterprise. Bohemund had no fleet of his own and Byzantium was now stronger than at the time of the last Norman war. A year later (1108) he had to submit to the terms dictated by his old opponent, Alexius, in the Treaty of Devol. He promised to hold the principality of Antioch (less Cicilia and Lattakieh) as a fief of the emperor and to restore the Greek patriarch. As compensation Alexius would allow him to keep any lands he could conquer from Aleppo. This treaty, if carried out, would have meant the end of Tancred's power in Syria, so, not surprisingly, Bohemund never dared to show his face in Outremer again. He returned to Apulia where, in 1111, he died, a forgotten man. With him there vanished the most restless, ambitious, and unscrupulous—and also the cleverest—of the leaders of the First Crusade. In 1108 Tancred finally took over in Antioch, formally as regent for Bohemund, in fact as an independent ruler. Naturally he had no intention of executing the terms of the Treaty of Devol. Instead he devoted the rest of his life to the extension of Antioch. In the north he drove the Byzantines out of East Cilicia for good; in the south he expelled them from Lattakieh and captured Jabala, Buluniyas, and Marqab from the Muslims. Marqab (in Latin Margat) was to become one of the great crusader castles. As regent of both Antioch and Edessa, Tancred was the most powerful man in Syria and Alexius Comnenus (d. 1118) was too busy fighting the Seldjuks of Anatolia to try to enforce the Treaty of Devol.

When Baldwin of Bourcq and Joscelin of Courtenay regained their freedom in 1108 a quarrel at once broke out between them and Tancred: Tancred was reluctant to hand back Edessa. For the last four years he had been regent there and had been able to appoint a relative, Richard of the Principate (1104–8), to rule it for him. At first he gave way to Baldwin's and Joscelin's remonstrances but then a series of armed clashes occurred as a result of which the first alliance between Franks and Syrians was formed. To the Muslims there was nothing peculiar about such an alliance because they did not yet look upon the crusaders as enemies in a holy war. But on the Christian side a true crusader must have been shocked, for there can hardly have been anything so opposed to crusading ideas as a civil war between Christians in which both sides called in Muslim allies. It is very evident that the Syrian barons had moved a long way from the spirit of the crusade. On one side was Tancred supported by Aleppo; on the other, Baldwin, Joscelin, and Mosul. In the end, although Tancred was victorious in battle, Baldwin kept Edessa. But for reasons which are now obscure he made radical changes in his internal policy. Previously he had shown favour to the Armenian inhabitants of Edessa; now he drove many of them out of the land. There might well have been further fighting between Tancred and Baldwin had not the attention of all the participants been drawn to the question of the succession to Tripoli.

The old count, Raymond of Toulouse, had died outside the walls of Tripoli on 28 February 1105. He had been one of the outstanding figures of the First Crusade, indeed the humbler folk, the *pauperes*, regarded him as its real leader. Certainly he was the only man with the personality to stand up to Bohemund. Contemporary chronicles, Norman propaganda, and modern histories have not always been fair to him. Only in recent years, thanks to the work of J. H. and L. L. Hill, have his achievements been given their due. When contemporaries described him as the most illustrious prince of Christian chivalry they were hardly exaggerating. What complicated the succession to Tripoli was the fact that Alfonso-Jordan, Raymond's only son in Outremer, was still a child. The Provençal soldiers therefore chose his cousin, William-Jordan, as their commander. Back in Toulouse the barons who, in Raymond's absence, had been ruled by his eldest son, Bertrand, now refused to recognize him as Raymond's heir and instead had young Alfonso-Jordan brought home from Syria. So Bertrand decided to seek his fortune in the East. In 1108 he arrived at Mount Pilgrim and at once he and William-Jordan became entangled in arguments about the inheritance. When William recognized Tancred of Antioch as his lord, Bertrand asked King Baldwin I to act as arbitrator. Baldwin I answered the appeal and in July 1109 he held a meeting of all the princes outside the walls of Tripoli. Tancred and William faced by a united front—Baldwin I, Baldwin of Bourcq, Joscelin of Courtenay, and Bertrand—were forced to accept a compromise. Tancred had to renounce his claims to Edessa. By way of compensation he was to receive his Galilean lands back should Bohemund ever return to Antioch. This was most unlikely, however, so Tancred suffered no real loss of face. Raymond's lordship was divided between the two claimants, each of whom became the vassal of his chief ally. This agreement restored the harmony so essential to the Christians in Outremer, and at once the princes, with help from Genoese and Provençal fleets, settled down to besiege Tripoli in earnest. On 12 July 1109 the city capitulated. This was a bitter blow for Damascus. Until Raymond laid siege to it, Tripoli had been its port, just as Lattakieh had been the port of Aleppo, and Tortosa, at least according to the geographer Idrisi, the port of Homs. Since the port of Beirut only began to be developed in the 1220s—and not until the end of the 19th century was there a good Beirut–Damascus road—this meant that the maritime trade of Damascus now shifted much further south to Tyre and later also to Acre. But with the conquest of Tripoli the last crusader state was finally established. Its division into two was short-lived. Shortly after the capture of Tripoli William-Jordan died of an arrow wound. The whole county was taken over by Bertrand and became a fief of the kingdom of Jerusalem.[36]

The settlement made by the princes at Tripoli in 1109 was a climax in the career of King Baldwin I. It revealed him in a truly royal light, chief arbiter of all the Christian princes of Outremer, to whose judgement even the formally independent Tancred of Antioch had to submit. Baldwin had reached this position as a result of his energetic extension of the kingdom. In 1101 he had captured the coastal towns of Arsuf and Caesarea. In return for their help he had been forced to concede to the Genoese one third of the booty (the chief trophy was the octagonal Roman green glass vessel now in the cathedral treasury at Genoa and known as the *Sacro Catino*) and a quarter in all conquered towns. But Ascalon remained in Egyptian hands, a serious thorn in his flesh. It was an ideal base for Fatimid expeditions into Palestine and was in fact used as such by big Egyptian armies in 1101, 1102, and 1105. Only after fierce fighting in the Ramleh area—in which the Franks by no means always had the best of it—were these invasions beaten back. In one of these battles that tireless crusader, Stephen of Blois, met his death. During these years Baldwin was fortunate not to be attacked from the rear as well, but Damascus feared Fatimid imperialism just as much as he did and so made no move against him. After 1105 the Fatimids made no more serious attempts to reconquer Palestine; Baldwin had forced them to recognize that the Christian kingdom would not vanish overnight. Nevertheless the latent threat from Ascalon still remained. Baldwin once again turned his attention to the coast. He had already, in May 1104, captured Acre with the help of a Genoese fleet. By the mid-twelfth century the Genoese were claiming not only that they had received a royal charter of reward but also that there had once been an inscription in the Church of the Holy Sepulchre relating, in letters of gold, how Baldwin had granted them extensive privileges in Acre. In fact neither the charter nor the inscription ever existed—until, that is to say, the charter was forged, probably for use in litigation in the papal court, and until, in 1192, Conrad of Montferrat was persuaded to 'restore' the long-lost inscription.[37] With the conquest of Acre, however, the kingdom at last had the use of a large, safe harbour and one which was relatively unaffected by the weather; in all these respects Acre, which quickly became the economic centre of the kingdom, was far superior to the open roads of Jaffa. This, however, was a development Damascus, dependent on its trading connections with the Palestinian coast, could not afford merely to sit and watch. It began to give indirect help to the Egyptian governors of the coastal towns by involving Baldwin in a series of minor engagements in the Hauran (south Syria) and Galilee where the lord of Tiberias had built several castles to control the caravan routes to and from Damascus. Not until 1108 could Baldwin secure a truce in this region (see above, p. 59f.) and even then Damascus continued to support the Egyptians on the coast. In that year an attempted siege of Sidon failed and in the next (1109) Baldwin had to march north in order to restore peace between the quarrelling princes of Syria. Sidon and Beirut held out until 1110, succumbing only when Baldwin received vigorous help from a Norwegian fleet under the command of King Sigurd.

The Franks now controlled all the harbours on the coast of Syria and Palestine with the exception of Ascalon and Tyre. This meant that the balance of forces in this part of the world was upset and Damascus felt seriously threatened. So its atabeg, Toghtekin (1095–1128) allied with the new ruler of Mosul, Mawdud (1108–13). Under the auspices of the

Seldjuk sultan, Mohammad ibn Malik-Shah, Mawdud was trying to organize a great Muslim coalition to sweep the Franks out of Asia. A penetrating analysis of the situation by Prawer has shown that up until 1115, and indeed as late as 1119, the sultan's support for this project was dominated by a conflict of interests between two power blocs, the Arabo–Syrian and the Turco–Seldjuk. The Seldjuk sultans themselves were more interested in Persia than in the territories west of Mosul, but public opinion, skilfully moulded by refugees from Syria and Palestine, forced the sultan to intervene in order to avoid losing prestige with the Muslims. In this pressure exerted by public opinion we can detect the beginnings of a characteristic aspect of the struggle between Franks and Muslims which was to become more marked in the course of time and was to culminate in the holy war. Mawdud's first campaigns in 1110 and 1111 were indecisive because the Franks were united under Baldwin I while the Muslim league was not as firm as it seemed. But no sooner had the threat receded for a moment than the Franks split into two camps. Baldwin of Bourcq found that Joscelin of Courtenay had become more powerful than he altogether liked, so he took him prisoner and forced him to hand over the lordship of Turbessel. Joscelin therefore entered the service of King Baldwin and was given Tiberias which no longer had to be kept available for Tancred now that Bohemund had died in Apulia in 1111, leaving a son who was still a minor and in whose name Tancred could continue to rule Antioch. When Tancred himself died in December 1112 the regency was taken over by his nephew, Roger of the Principate (1112–19). Thanks to Tancred's indefatigable zest for war Antioch was now a strong state. It was an extraordinary achievement for a man who, like Baldwin I, had once been a penniless adventurer. Bertrand of Tripoli also died in 1112 and was succeeded by his young son Pons (1112–37). Pons finally broke with the traditional anti-Norman policy of the Provençals. Symbolic of this change was his marriage to Tancred's widow. Another marriage, between Roger of Antioch and Baldwin of Bourcq's sister, completed the process of reconciliation in the Frankish north. Perhaps it was because of this that the Byzantine Emperor no longer continued with the plans for a campaign against Antioch which he had pursued between 1110 and 1112 and for which he had obtained the benevolent neutrality of Pisa.[38]

When, in 1113, Baldwin I broke the truce with Damascus, Mawdud took the opportunity to launch another assault. This time he directed his forces not against Syria but, in alliance with Toghtekin of Damascus, against Palestine. He beat Baldwin's army in a battle fought to the west of the Sea of Galilee and occupied the surrounding countryside. But most of the towns held out against him and in September the approach of another Christian army, strengthened by contingents from the northern principalities, forced him to retreat to Damascus. Here, in October, this outstanding and energetic Muslim soldier was murdered by an Assassin—

much to the relief of the Franks and Toghtekin himself, who had learned to fear Mawdud and had no wish to see Jerusalem completely extinguished. For this reason he was suspected by the sultan of Baghdad of being responsible for Mawdud's murder and so in 1114 he judged it wise to patch up another truce with Baldwin. The outlook for the Franks had been further improved by the anarchy in Aleppo which followed the death of its ruler, Ridwan, in 1113. But this did not prevent the Seldjuk sultan from continuing to organize the war against the Franks, commissioning first Aqsonqor il-Bursuqi, whom he appointed atabeg of Mosul (1113–26), and then Bursuq ibn Bursuq (d. 1116) to carry out his policy. Bursuq was an outsider, a Persian, and all the powers of Syria united against him. The Franks allied with both Aleppo and Damascus and in September 1115 they defeated Bursuq in battle at Tel-Danith, south-west of Aleppo. The Muslim–Frankish coalition soon collapsed in its turn because it was now the Franks who seemed to be too strong. None the less Tel-Danith had put an end to the efforts of the Seldjuk sultans to reconquer Syria.

Although from 1109 to 1115 Baldwin I had been almost continuously involved with affairs in north Syria, he was well aware of the need to secure his southern border. To this end he pushed forward into the Negev desert in 1115 and there, south of the Dead Sea where it could control the road to Akaba, he built the great castle of Montreal (Shobak in Arabic). In the following year he occupied Akaba (Aila). He now had a base on the Red Sea and he protected it by fortifying the off-shore island of Graye. His policy in the Transjordan was limited to a loose supervision of the Bedouin tribes there, backed up by occasional punitive expeditions. In 1117 the problem of the king's marriage, which had scandalized all Christendom, was finally settled.[39] He had made a second marriage with an Armenian in Edessa. Before 1108 he rid himself of her by forcing her to enter a nunnery, on the threadbare excuse that while in captivity she was supposed to have had sexual relations with Muslims. Not long afterwards she escaped from her Jerusalem convent and fled to Constantinople where she had relatives. In 1113 the king had then married Adelaide, the widow of Roger of Sicily. To Baldwin she was desirable on account of her dowry which he badly needed and because she represented the Sicilian alliance which could bring him a fleet. She was able to secure Baldwin's promise that if they had no children then the heir to Jerusalem would be her own son from her first marriage, Count Roger II of Sicily. It was not likely that they would have children, not only on account of Adelaide's age but also because, to all appearances, the king was homosexual. This could easily have spelt the end of the Lorraine dynasty, but Baldwin ruled his vassals with a rod of iron and, though they grumbled about the explosive succession clause as well as about the fact that they had barely been consulted, they could do little but agree. The marriage, however, was bigamous because Baldwin's second wife was still alive—a fact which could not be altered even by spreading the slander that she was living the life of a common prostitute. In the winter of 1116–17 the king fell seriously ill and the Sicilian succession appeared to be close at hand. At this point the opposition which, at papal insistence, was supported by the patriarch, forced the king to repudiate Adelaide in a public synod, and in the spring of 1117 she returned to Sicily. This was a grave mistake in foreign policy. The Sicilian court was deeply insulted and for a long time afterwards would do nothing to help the Kingdom of Jerusalem. It was also the king's first serious domestic political setback. If his vassals had entertained hopes that the king, who was at least forty-six years old, would marry again in order, at long last, to produce an heir to the throne, they were disappointed. Baldwin now insisted that he was, after all, the husband of his second wife despite the fact that she was beyond his reach and hopelessly discredited. He lived in celibacy. His vassals had been able to force the annulment of the Sicilian marriage, but they could not force him into a new one.

In 1118 Baldwin invaded Egypt, leading his troops to the banks of the Nile. But there he became seriously ill again. He turned for home and died on 2 April not far from Ascalon. He was buried by the side of his brother Godfrey. He had been a great conqueror and bequeathed to his successor a well-established kingdom and a fine reputation. He had ruled firmly and had made sure that the fiefs held of the crown had not become hereditary. Once he had rid himself of Daimbert of Pisa, he remained on good terms with the Church, especially after 1112 when Arnulf of Chocques (d. 1118) archdeacon of Jerusalem since 1099, eventually achieved his old ambition of being patriarch—though even now Arnulf was unable to enjoy undisputed possession of his office, being temporarily suspended in 1115. Godfrey had not had the time to do more than make a start. Baldwin had conquered the coast, halted the Egyptian and Seldjuk attacks, established a *modus vivendi* with Damascus and added to his territories in the south. He was undoubtedly the real founder of the kingdom of Jerusalem and there was little dispute about his position as the overlord of all the Frankish princes in Outremer.

On the question of who was to succeed him opinions were divided. Some favoured his brother, Count Eustace of Boulogne; others, led by the patriarch and Joscelin of Courtenay, preferred Baldwin of Bourcq who arrived in Jerusalem at the right moment and who had already made a good impression as count of Edessa. Baldwin was chosen, but not without considerable difficulties. Eustace was more closely related to Baldwin I and he had been designated by the dying king. An official embassy was sent to Boulogne to offer him the crown. It was not easy to persuade him to give up his possessions which, in England, were immense. But meanwhile the absence of Eustace's principal supporters—for in the nature of things they had been chosen as ambassadors—made it easy for Baldwin of Bourcq's partisans to push through his candidacy for the throne. At Easter 1118

Baldwin II (1118–31) was consecrated king, though not yet crowned. When the ambassadors who were returning with Eustace, heard in Apulia of the *fait accompli* at Jerusalem, they were so incensed that they urged Eustace to fight for the crown. But since he had not been very enthusiastic about the kingship in the first place he decided to save the kingdom from civil war and returned home. William of Tyre regarded Baldwin II's accession as illegal, but it was this precedent which formed the basis for the opinion frequently heard later on that the nearest relative who was on the spot in the East had a claim to the succession, even though it still needed to be confirmed by an election. Like his predecessor, Baldwin II was a fine soldier, but he was also prepared to give more attention to the internal affairs of the kingdom. He had more self-control than Baldwin I; he was happily married to an Armenian princess, Morphia, and he was extremely pious; indeed he prayed so much that his knees had developed a horny layer of skin. None the less he was a cunning intriguer and somewhat avaricious. The hermit Bernard of Blois publicly accused him of 'dreadful vices'—but without saying precisely what he meant and, in any case, Bernard was a puritanical zealot.

He rewarded Joscelin of Courtenay who had done so much to secure his election by investing him with the county of Edessa (1119–31). Thus Joscelin returned to the principality from which Baldwin had once expelled him. No sooner was this settled than business in north Syria required Baldwin's presence. Roger of Antioch had so much increased Frankish pressure on Aleppo that the citizens had been forced to seek help from the Ortoqid Ilghazi of Mardin. He assumed control of Aleppo (1118–22) and formed an aggresive alliance with Toghtekin of Damascus. Aleppo's central position made it the pivot of the Syrian balance of power system; as such it was the object of a fierce rivalry between the Franks, the Ortoqids, and the rulers of Mosul and Damascus. The scales would tip in favour of the man who controlled Aleppo, particularly after 1118 when Ilghazi took the city out of the Seldjuk empire, just as Toghtekin had made Damascus independent in 1109. In 1119 Ilghazi invaded Antioch. In spite of all the warnings he received, in spite of all the lessons of past experience, Roger decided not to wait for the arrival of reinforcements from Jerusalem and Tripoli. He advanced to meet Ilghazi west of Aleppo with 700 knights and 3,000 foot-soldiers. On 27 June the Franks were encircled and completely beaten. Only two men of baronial rank escaped. Roger himself fell fighting in the midst of his finest knights. Those who were taken prisoner were killed later. This battle, known to the Franks as the *Ager Sanguinis*, the Field of Blood, proved that the Muslims could beat the Franks even without the support of the Seldjuk sultan. The local rulers could do it themselves so long as they remained united.

Luckily for the Franks Ilghazi did not immediately follow up his victory. This enabled Baldwin II, after he had taken over the regency of

Antioch, to push him back. Bohemund's son was still only a boy in Apulia and so until 1126 the government of Antioch lay in the prudent hands of King Baldwin. He redistributed the vacant fiefs and married the widows off to suitable knights in order to create a new fighting force as quickly as possible. The regency was unpopular in Jerusalem, however, because the treaty with Antioch which set it up, failed to take into account the interests of the increasingly self-assertive vassals of Jerusalem. The treaty stipulated that Antioch fiefs had to remain in the families of their former holders even if this meant that they went to collateral heirs. This prevented the Jerusalem nobles from acquiring fiefs in Antioch even though they found themselves obliged to go campaigning in the north for unexpectedly long periods. None the less the quarrel over the king's accession was now over. As feudal lord of Tripoli and Edessa and as regent of Antioch his position in Jerusalem was unshakable. After his return to the kingdom he was finally crowned at Bethlehem in December 1119. Yet it seemed to be a time of permanent crisis. The roads were still unsafe for pilgrims, and the country suffered four years of bad harvests and famine— which may have contributed to the decision to exempt basic victuals from the payment of duty at Jerusalem in 1120 (see below, p. 154). The patriarch wrote begging letters to Compostela. In 1120 the chanter of the Holy Sepulchre sent a fragment of the True Cross to his former church at Paris and discreetly hinted that he would welcome it if he were made a member of the chapter of Notre-Dame. (But perhaps his interest in Paris stemmed from a feeling that he was now out on a limb in Jerusalem; whereas the common life for the canons of the Holy Sepulchre had been instituted in 1114, he was still living in a house of his own seven years later.) Amidst this wide spread pessimism the king paid the Church the political price for its strong support during the period of his accession at what is called the Council of Nablus of 1120, though it was in fact not so much a general council as a meeting of the privy council attended by the most important ecclesiastical and secular office holders. The first three of the twenty-five decrees gave the Church control, hitherto withheld, over ecclesiastical tithes. Since this settled that part of the Investiture Contest which had penetrated even to the eastern Mediterranean, it is appropriate to speak of the Concordat of Nablus. In the remaining decrees penalties for sodomy (i.e. homosexuality), bigamy, adultery, sexual relations with female or male Saracens, theft, and other breaches of the law were, for the first time, laid down. The penalties were draconian but must probably be seen mainly as deterrents. To some extent here, and certainly in other laws, it was assumed that the injured party must initiate proceedings himself and that, in cases where the offender repented, then a milder form of punishment would be provided. In the period of conquest under Baldwin I only the bare minimum of legislation had been issued (see p. 59). Most offences had been punished by each individual judge according to what he felt was appropriate and in line with the custom of his home country. The list drawn up at Nablus is evidence of considerable uncertainty about the law in the absence of any uniform standard; this was now to be dealt with. It is not really evidence of widespread immorality, as Beugnot believed.

Notwithstanding an outward appearance of authority, the weakened position of the king *vis-à-vis* the Church, already indicated by his concession over tithes, is made plain by the fact that at the very heart of the Nablus decrees were precisely those offences which had mattered most in the marriage scandal of Baldwin I: bigamy and homosexuality in his case, sexual relations with Saracens in the case of his second wife (though this was also one of the accusations made in the case of Patriarch Arnulf in 1115). Here the victorious Church lashed out at the pre-Gregorian Baldwin I. At the same council, however, the jurisdiction of the king's court was more precisely defined and the right of self-help was correspondingly limited. Nevertheless, a loss of royal prestige is clear in the secular sphere as well. In June 1120 a section of the nobility used the patriarch as a mouthpiece to express their opposition to a campaign to Antioch. The patriarch at first refused to hand over the relic of the True Cross, without which no army marched out, and strong royal pressure was needed before he gave way.[40] The incident showed just how unpopular Baldwin's regency over Antioch was, for it was clearly the regency to which they objected and not the king's own rule in Jerusalem.

In fact owing to Baldwin II's energetic rule the Frankish pressure on Aleppo was unremitting. The Christians received help from an unexpected quarter. King David II of Georgia became involved in a war with Ilghazi and defeated him in a bloody battle in 1121. Ilghazi died the next year, his power broken. But Balak, his nephew and successor in Aleppo, continued the fight. He captured first Count Joscelin of Edessa and then, as Baldwin II was hurrying to Edessa to make arrangements for the government there, he captured the king himself in April 1123. It says much for Baldwin's powers of organization that no constitutional crisis broke out. In Antioch Patriarch Bernard took over the administration; in Jerusalem the barons chose Eustace Garnier, lord of Sidon and Caesarea, to act as *bailli* (i.e. regent).

Joscelin soon managed to contrive an adventurous escape, but Baldwin II remained in prison until after Balak's death, being released in the summer of 1124 in return for promises which he did not keep. During the king's captivity the regent had dropped his policy of support for northern Syria. But while Baldwin was still in prison the most spectacular event of his reign took place: the capture of Tyre. Much earlier, in 1119, he had sent an appeal for help to Venice. In autumn 1122 a formidable fleet commanded by the doge set sail for the East. The doge had judged his moment well. Pisa and Genoa were at war with one another and unable to spare much time for Outremer. Venetian help was therefore very precious and they could demand a high price for it. In May 1123 they defeated an Egyptian fleet in a battle off the coast of Ascalon; and they were now ready to help capture a port. But only after a bitter debate was it finally decided to attack Tyre instead of Ascalon. The constable and the patriarch of Jerusalem, Gormund (1118–1128), concluded a treaty with the Venetians in which the privileges of the republic were set out in great detail. They were exempted from paying all customs duties; they were allowed to trade freely, using their own weights and measures. The only tax which they would have to pay was the tax on pilgrims. They were to receive 300 besants a year and a third of Tyre. Cases between Venetians and cases in which Venetians were the defendants were to be heard only in their own court at Tyre. The legal integrity of the kingdom had only recently been demonstrated at Nablus. Already, as a result of this treaty, it had been breached and the competence of the king's court had been seriously undermined. This was particularly dangerous since inevitably the same privileges soon had to be granted to all the other maritime towns of Italy and south France.

Following this treaty—which Baldwin II later confirmed—the Franks began a long and determined siege of Tyre. It was a well-fortified city linked to the mainland only by the narrow causeway which Alexander the Great had built in 332 BC. Not until 7 July 1124 when supplies had run out and their position had become hopeless did the garrison surrender on condition that they were allowed to leave the city in peace. The terms of the treaty with Venice were then put into effect. Although the fall of Tyre was a triumph for the Christian cause it was nevertheless to create problems of ecclesiastical organization.[41] Traditionally the archbishopric of Tyre belonged, with all its suffragans, to the patriarchate of Antioch. But at Clermont Urban II had ruled that in the Christian East ecclesiastical boundaries should follow political frontiers; for centuries this had been the practice in the West. Even before the capture of Tyre the position of its suffragan sees had been awkward. The southern sees, Beirut, Sidon, and Acre, lay in the kingdom of Jerusalem and came therefore, according to Urban's ruling, under the authority of the patriarch of Jerusalem. But Tripoli, Tortosa, and Jebail lay in the county of Tripoli which had two feudal overlords, the prince of Antioch and the king of Jerusalem. Antioch was certainly not prepared to renounce old rights and thus arose the long fierce quarrel over the archbishopric of Tyre between the two patriarchs which was anything but helpful to the peaceful growth of the crusader states. In 1110 Paschal II had confirmed Urban's judgement, but later on he became less sure and rather inclined to restore the old boundaries. From then on the papacy remained permanently undecided and so both sides made do without bishops, preferring to keep the disputed sees *sede vacante*. (It is true that in Beirut a bishop was elected in 1112 but possibly he was never consecrated.) But when, in

1122, it became clear that a serious attack on Tyre was a distinct possibility, the patriarch of Jerusalem unilaterally consecrated an archbishop who, however, died before the city was in fact taken. After the capture of Tyre the metropolitan see remained vacant for four years and not until 1128 was the first archbishop consecrated, an Englishman named William (d. *c.*1134; not to be confused with the historian Archbishop William II of Tyre 1175–86). He recognized the authority of Jerusalem and so in turn the patriarch of Antioch began to consecrate bishops for the northern sees. The papal curia was now forced to make up its mind. It decided the case in Jerusalem's favour, and as a result bishops were for the first time ever—as we can see in the case of Acre—appointed to the three southern suffragan sees. Later quarrels between the patriarch of Jerusalem and the archbishop of Tyre led to another, and this time definitive judgement in favour of Jerusalem in 1139. None the less the Tripolitan sees remained subject to Antioch because although in theory the curia upheld the verdict of 1139 up until the thirteenth century, in practice no papal legate ever did anything to subordinate Tripoli to Tyre. The curia tolerated the division of the archbishopric because it was not prepared to risk the whole painfully achieved *modus vivendi* for the sake of the unity of one province. Tyre itself remained permanently attached to Jerusalem. In 1140, a cardinal legate deposed Patriarch Radulph of Antioch because the latter had originally refused to receive the pallium from Rome. This marked the final subjection of the patriarchate to the authority of Rome and the end of these last stirrings of Antiochene independence based on its Petrine associations.

One of the most important events of Baldwin II's reign was the foundation of the Military Orders.[42] A knight from Champagne, Hugh of Payens (d. 1136) was apparently the first to have the idea that it might be pleasing to God if a monk's way of life was combined with fighting against the heathen so as to create a new knightly ideal. He and eight companions swore to Patriarch Gormund that they would be obedient, poor, and chaste; then they took an additional, fourth vow, to offer help and protection to pilgrims on the still dangerous road from Jaffa to Jerusalem. Baldwin II granted them rooms in the royal palace, the so-called *Templum Salomonis* (now the Mosque of al-Aqsa). Thus they became known as the Templars. At first they lived there in poverty like a community of regular canons. Then they aroused the interest of St. Bernard, the influential abbot of Clairvaux, and with his help a rule of their own was approved at the Council of Troyes in 1128. Additional constitutions issued in 1130 by Patriarch Stephen of Jerusalem (1128–30) gave the rule its final form. At about this time the Templars, probably modelling themselves on the Cistercians, began to wear a white tunic. During the pontificate of Eugenius III a red cross was added to make plain the difference between the two orders. A rapid stream of new recruits came in, many of them moved by the eloquence of St. Bernard who was full of praise for the ideal of an order of knighthood dedicated to serving God, an ideal which, in his treatise *In Praise of the New Chivalry* (1128) he contrasted strongly with the banditry of the worldly knight. More conservative minds did not find it easy to accept the combination of two ways of life which had hitherto been considered mutually exclusive. In the days of the Third Crusade the Englishman Walter Map (and before him perhaps the Cistercian abbot Isaac of L'Étoile near Poitiers after 1147) passed pungent criticism upon the Templars focusing in particular on their fighting activities. A quarter of a century later James of Vitry, the bishop of Acre, vigorously rejected such criticism but was careful enough to attribute it exclusively to heretics. The new order was tightly organized under the direction of a Master. It consisted of three classes, the knights, the sergeants who served them, and the chaplains. In the course of the twelfth century the Templars freed themselves from the authority of the patriarch; indeed they cut right through the Church's diocesan structure, for every bishop was bound to consecrate the chaplains without in any way being able to control their entry into the order. By 1139 the formation of the order had been practically completed, twenty-five years earlier than historians once supposed. After 1179, as a consequence of complaints raised by the episcopate during the Third Lateran Council, their general exemption from tithes was reduced to an exemption applying only to the lands they cultivated themselves, i.e. from now on their tenants had to pay tithes. Similarly instead of being entitled to erect their own churches wherever they liked, their authority to do so was restricted to those—usually remote—districts where the existing cure of souls was inadequate. In Europe, though less so in the Holy Land, such districts were becoming increasingly rare. Moreover, when they wanted their chaplains consecrated they were compelled, in the first instance, to approach the diocesan bishop, and only if he refused could they turn to another bishop. By way of compensation they were granted exemption from their diocesan's authority; henceforth he could neither excommunicate them nor place an interdict on their churches and houses. So the Templars came directly under the jurisdiction of the Apostolic See and, in terms of their position within the Church, this was decisive.

In the Christian East the value of the Military Orders was immense for in practice they were the only authority to hold a standing army always in readiness. On the other hand their privileged position meant that they formed a state within a state—a state which often proved to be a troublesome rival to both king and Church. They pursued their own policies and their rights of exemption were such that they constantly threatened to undermine the customary structure of authority. Although they increasingly took over castles, with or without landed estates attached, they could not be integrated into the feudal system because they were expressly forbidden to hold anything in fee from anyone. This prohibition applied to the Templars after 1139, the Knights of St. John after 1186, and the Teutonic Knights after 1220. Their special position in Outremer was enhanced by the fact that they received rich gifts of land in every part of Western Europe and on the basis of this wealth they soon developed into an international organization of great importance in the world of finance.

The Hospitallers, also known as Knights of St. John, profited from the rise of the Templars. In about 1080 some merchants from Amalfi had founded a Christian hostel on the model of older establishments. It was situated near the Amalfitan Benedictine monastery of St. Maria Latina in Jerusalem and dedicated to St. John the Baptist (probably not to St. John the Almsgiver, as was believed until recently). It was probably originally a community of laymen who even before the First Crusade had extricated themselves from the control of the monastery and then developed into an autonomous body corporate, recognized as such by the pope in 1113. It was more difficult to escape the supervision of the Patriarch of Jerusalem, especially since the Holy Sepulchre and the Hospital of St. John had jointly solicited donations in Europe and inevitably these now proved difficult to separate. Originally the Hospitallers' role had been a purely charitable one and indeed this side of their activities was to remain important throughout their history. But as early as 1136 they accepted responsibility for land settlement and frontier defence when they received the castle and adjoining territory of Beth Gibelin near Ascalon. From the early 1140s on there was a wave of such take-overs in the County of Tripoli. However, the actual military functions were exercised at first (after *c.* 1140) by paid knights, who also had the task of protecting pilgrims on the roads. Before 1153 the Hospitallers were organized into an order living according to a rule based on that of St. Augustine and this internal development, though it had not been a smooth one—there had been considerable setbacks, particularly in the sphere of relationships with diocesan bishops—was given external recognition by the grant of a papal privilege in 1154.

The order's militarization which, as early as 1168, enabled it to promise to the king 500 knights and 500 Turcopoles (light cavalry), was a gradual development which in 1179 was finally completed by the pope when he transferred the tasks previously carried out by the paid knights to the Hospitallers themselves. A merchants' foundation had become an exclusive knightly order devoted, like the Templars, to the war against the infidel. Though the course of this development cannot be traced in detail, it is surely probable that it was initiated, or at least accelerated, by paid knights choosing to join the order while still wishing to carry on with their former duties. In any event soon after 1170 there was a grave crisis in the order and it was clearly the take-over of castles, i.e. an integral aspect of the militarization, that the conservative opposition found objectionable. Obviously they were more intent on the traditional tasks of caring for the sick and the poor. It is possible that they placed too much emphasis on the considerable financial problem which these take-overs caused in order to conceal their basic aversion to the process of militarization. The clock could not be turned back, but at least the opposition gained a partial victory by requiring a hitherto autocratic master to obtain the approval of the chapter of the order before making important decisions—and here the question of castles was expressly included. Not until 1259 was the battle dress of the Hospitallers (a red tunic with a white, eight-pointed cross) finally settled. Inevitably the Templars and the Hospitallers became, in the end, bitter rivals, but at first the advantages of their foundation far outweighed the disadvantages.

Another knightly order was that of St. Lazarus which enabled leprous (but also healthy) knights to engage in the war against the infidel. The sources on these leper knights are so scarce that the internal development of their order remains largely obscure. Although the corporation can be shown to have existed by 1142, not until 1244 is there any evidence of its participation in warfare. A turning point in the order's history came in 1253 when the pope approved a change in the statutes permitting the future election of healthy members of the order to the office of master on the grounds that so many actual lepers were being killed in action. This order never seems to have achieved diocesan exemption. A Spanish knightly order which in c.1177 established a house on the *Mons Gaudii* (Montjoie) north of Jerusalem enjoyed only an ephemeral history in the Holy Land.

We must now return to the history of the crusader states. In 1124 Baldwin had been released from captivity and at once he carried the war to Aqsonqor il-Bursuqi who, in 1125, had taken over control in Aleppo in addition to Mosul. This had upset the balance of forces in Syria. Previously Damascus had been balanced by Jerusalem, Aleppo by Antioch, and the lesser emirates in the valley of the Upper Orontes by Tripoli. But now there had arisen a larger state with a centre at Aleppo which was relatively distant from the Seldjuk bases of power and which thus had a chance of developing into a principality independent of Baghdad. This inevitably meant a shift away from the previous distribution of forces and it was, in fact, only with reluctance that Aleppo had exchanged its former independence for the greater security contained in the union with Mosul.

In May 1125 Baldwin II inflicted a heavy defeat on the troops of il-Bursuqi at Azaz in north Syria. In the next year he was at last relieved of the responsibility for Antioch. Bohemund II (1126–30), the son of Antioch's founder, arrived from Apulia to take over his inheritance. It would be his task to conquer Aleppo, a task which seemed quite possible in view of the incredibly chaotic state of the emirate following the murder of the atabeg in November 1126. In fact it was to be the last chance of capturing Aleppo but Bohemund II let it slip. He was already involved in the customary civil war with the count of Edessa, Joscelin. During 1127 and 1128 Imad ad-Din Zengi (d. 1146) rose to be ruler of Mosul and Aleppo. From then on it was too late. In Zengi the Franks had met a most dangerous opponent.

In 1128 the powerful ruler of Damascus, Toghtekin, died. Baldwin II, hoping to exploit the situation, tried to capture Damascus but the attempt failed. Two years later Bohemund II fell in battle in Cilicia. His only child was a two-year-old daughter, Constance; once again the king was forced to assume the burden of government in Antioch, though not before his own daughter Alice, Bohemund's widow, had attempted to seize power for herself. Despite the disgraceful lengths to which she was prepared to go her coup failed. But the years and the effects of two periods of imprisonment had begun to leave their mark on Baldwin. On 21 August 1131 after a fairly long illness he died. On his deathbed he was received into the community of canons attached to the Church of the Holy Sepulchre where, in the Golgotha chapel, he found his last resting place. The count of Edessa, his comrade-in-arms for thirty years, died shortly afterwards. Owing to a serious injury he had been forced to entrust the defence of Edessa to his son Joscelin II (1131-50; d. 1159). But his son refused to accept the responsibility on the grounds that Edessa's army was too weak to stand against the invading Muslims. This made the old warrior so angry that he struggled out of bed once more and had himself carried on a litter to meet the enemy forces. When they heard that he was coming they dispersed. Content, but exhausted by the effort, Count Joscelin I, still in his litter, died by the roadside.

With the deaths of Baldwin of Bourcq and Joscelin of Courtenay the last two members of the first generation of crusaders had gone. Imperceptibly but steadily a new community was emerging, composed of the younger generation and newly arrived settlers. They looked upon Outremer as their home and developed their own sense of political identity. In 1127 the chronicler Fulcher of Chartres, now in Jerusalem, wrote the following famous words:

We who had been Occidentals have become Orientals; the man who had been a Roman or a Frank has here become a Galileean or a Palestinian; and the man who used to live in Reims or Chartres now finds himself a citizen of Tyre or Acre. We have already forgotten the places where we were born; already many of us know them not, or at any rate, no longer hear them spoken of. Some among us already possess in this country houses and servants which belong to them as a hereditary right. Another has married a wife who is not his compatriot—a Syrian or an Armenian woman perhaps, or even a Saracen who has received the grace of baptism. . . He who was once a stranger here is now a native. Every day our dependants and our relatives follow us, leaving behind, unwillingly perhaps, all their belongings. For he who was poor there now finds that God has made him rich here. He who had little money now possesses countless besants [gold pieces]. He who did not hold even a village over there now enjoys a town which God had given him. Why should anyone return to the West who has found an Orient like this?

No word here of chivalry or the spirit of the crusader. At a time when Bernard of Clairvaux in his treatise in praise of the Templars added a new element to the knightly crusading ideal, Fulcher of Chartres was giving eloquent expression to the self-confidence of a 'middle class' community of settlers. It was not easy to unite the two worlds; indeed often enough they were to stand in opposition to one another.

   The succession to Baldwin II had been arranged while he was still alive.[43] Because he had no sons, his eldest daughter Melisende was to succeed him. This meant that agnatic succession, in which only men related through men had any claims, was replaced by cognatic succession, in which all blood relatives inherited, daughters included. Given the lack of an agnatic heir at the time, it remains open to doubt whether the decision was seen then as a matter of principle, but it became a precedent for the future. A husband was needed for Melisende, however, to assist her in government, to assume the king's role in war and, of course, to beget an heir. In the autumn of 1127 an embassy was sent to France to offer Melisende's hand in marriage to the powerful Count Fulk V of Anjou. As an inducement, or perhaps in order to make female succession more palatable to the nobility, he was promised that he would not be a mere prince consort but would become co-ruler with his wife in a system of joint rule. The negotiations were difficult and long-drawn-out because a shadow was still cast over Melisende's hereditary right by the illegal fashion in which her father had gained the crown. Jerusalem therefore got the pope to confirm in express terms the legitimacy of Baldwin II's rule in 1128. But the breakthrough in the negotiations did not come until 1129 after Melisende had been formally appointed as heiress of the kingdom (*haeres regni*). This must have been done at Fulk's instigation. He was well acquainted with Henry I of England's designation of his daughter, the Empress Matilda, as his heir in January 1127 and it was this 'English model' which Fulk then transmitted to the East.

   In 1129 Fulk arrived in the Holy Land and the marriage was celebrated at once. He assisted Baldwin II in government during the remainder of the king's life. On his deathbed the king made his intentions once more absolutely plain. He designated not only his daughter and son-in-law to succeed him but also their two-year-old son Baldwin III. He thereby established the joint rule of three persons—although, obviously, in Baldwin III's case this meant only the establishment of his right to rule when he came of age. On 14 September 1131 Fulk and his consort were crowned, this time not in Bethlehem, but in the Church of the Holy

Sepulchre in Jerusalem where the tremendous building programme undertaken by the crusaders was still under way. Fulk's reign was to witness its completion though the church was not to be consecrated until 15 July 1149. All future coronations up to 1186 were to take place here. The connection with Fulk (1131–43) considerably enhanced the prestige of the Jerusalem dynasty. Now about forty years of age, he enjoyed the confidence of both the pope and the king of France, while his son, Geoffrey Plantagenet, had married the Emperor Henry V's widow, Matilda, the only daughter of Henry I of England, thus founding the house of Plantagenet which was to rule an immense empire: England, Normandy, and the Angevin family lands. With the accession of Fulk to the throne of Jerusalem, England began at last to show some real interest in the well-being of the crusader states.

Immediately after his coronation he had to go north, just as his predecessor had done, in order to deal with the affairs of Antioch. His sister-in-law, the dowager princess Alice, had again tried to seize power, this time supported by the counts of Tripoli and Edessa, both of whom hoped to throw off the overlordship of Jerusalem. This forced Fulk to take the sea route to Antioch. Once there he took over the regency. He then defeated the rebel count of Tripoli in battle at Chastel Rouge and brought about an enforced reconciliation.

During this same period the kingdom was, for the first time in its history, disturbed by internal revolt. Roman of Le Puy who had been granted a large fief in Oultrejourdain (Transjordan) by Baldwin II, quarrelled with King Fulk. His fief was confiscated and given to Pagan, the king's butler. This revolt should probably be dated to the latter part of the reign of Baldwin II, as Richard has suggested, but in that case Roman must have rebelled a second time for he was undoubtedly deeply involved in the very much more dangerous rebellion led by Hugh of Le Puiset, the powerful count of Jaffa, a great crown fief carved out of the royal demesne between 1108 and 1110.[44] Hitherto Hugh's rebellion has been dated to 1132. This is certainly wrong. 1133 is the earliest possible date and the latter part of 1134 the most probable. Rumour spoke of an affair between Melisende and Hugh and explained the clash between the king and the count in terms of Fulk's jealousy. But William of Tyre, although he repeats these rumours, also says that he does not know what the true cause of the dispute was. Fulk tried to rid himself of Hugh by having him brought to trial before the Haute Cour, the king's feudal council. Hugh had been accused of high treason by his stepson, Walter of Caesarea, and a judicial duel was arranged. Hugh failed to turn up and, as a result, must have been sentenced to the normal punishment for felony—forfeiture of all his fiefs—since only a verdict as drastic as this can explain his despairing and foolish reaction. He retreated to his fortified town of Jaffa and went so far as to bring in Egyptian auxiliaries from Ascalon. Now he really had committed blatant treason and his own vassals turned against him. Caught in an untenable position he had no option but to make his submission. He was banished for three years with the assurance that, at the end of that time, he would recover his fiefs. But before he left the kingdom he was badly wounded when he was the victim of an assassination attempt for which public opinion held the king responsible. Hugh recovered from his wound only to die in exile.

Many aspects of this rebellion have been overlooked by previous historians. Clearly Hugh had enjoyed the support of a considerable section of the nobility. His vassals seem to have been convinced that his cause was just for they stood by him until he committed the fatal error of making an alliance with the Saracens. The final punishment was unusually lenient— certainly more lenient than the earlier sentence passed on him, even though, in the meantime, his offence had become more heinous. This leniency was the result of mediation by influential people who felt that the very existence of the kingdom was at stake and who cited Matthew 12:25 in support of their arguments: 'Every kingdom divided against itself is brought to desolation.' Although Hugh had obviously gone too far to escape punishment altogether he still had supporters among the clergy and nobility who were able to force Fulk to acquiesce in a sentence which was much less severe than the king would have liked. The attempt on Hugh's life led to unrest in Jerusalem where the populace took the count's side. It is plain that the rebellion had been bound up with the political interests of Queen Melisende since her anger remained unabated for many months after the rebellion itself had been put down. The fact that she could afford to remain angry suggests that it was not her alleged liaison with Count Hugh that was at the root of the trouble. Her continued anger reveals moreover that Fulk had been the victor in appearance only. The royal marriage now went through a period of serious crisis. The queen's anger was such that it was unsafe for those nobles who were close to the king to appear in public and even Fulk himself went in fear of his life. Once more mediation was called for and was, in fact, finally successful in assuaging the queen's anger. But William of Tyre says that from this time onwards Fulk—whom he portrays as an energetic warrior with an unusually bad memory—became so uxorious that even in trivial matters he did nothing without his wife's consent. It is here that we have the key to the whole affair—an affair which had obviously shaken the kingdom much more severely than is suggested in William of Tyre's account. It seems that Fulk had begun his reign by trying to act as sole ruler, thereby not only infringing Melisende's political interests but also antagonizing that section of the nobility which wished to ensure that Baldwin II's last wishes were respected. It was certainly not just a matter of chance that in those years Fulk had himself referred to as *haeres regni* (a unique form) in a charter published by Rudolf Hiestand. The reasoning which lay behind this emphasis on his right is revealed in the succession dispute and the division of power which followed. Against Fulk there was ranged a very considerable party which, led by Hugh of Jaffa, stood for the execution of Baldwin II's testament, for the rights of Melisende, for the cognatic principle and, in general, for the rights of the legitimate dynasty. This party proved strong enough to force Fulk to accept joint rule with Melisende though in return they had to sacrifice the count of Jaffa—but Hugh's position had, in any event, become hopeless. This allowed Fulk to save face and appear before the world as the victor. But the real winners were the principle of cognatic succession and Melisende, a woman of extraordinary vigour and—like her sister Alice of Antioch—of driving ambition.

These profound disputes over the right form of government, disputes which must have troubled the kingdom for some time before the open outbreak of Hugh's rebellion, were not the only things which Fulk had to worry about. Once again he was forced to go north to meet a threatened Muslim invasion of Antioch. It was high time that the principality had a prince of its own and in 1133 Fulk decided in favour of Raymond of Poitiers (1136–49), the thirty-four-year-old son of Duke William IX of Aquitaine. But it took Raymond three years to reach Antioch. King Roger II of Sicily, being a kinsman of the Norman princes of Antioch, believed that he had a claim on their inheritance, and this forced Raymond to disguise himself in order to escape from Apulia. During these years Fulk was fully occupied in the south so yet again the dowager princess Alice tried to take advantage of the situation. In 1135 she left her own estates at Lattakieh and appeared in Antioch. There she bolstered up her insecure rule by an alliance with the uncanonically elected patriarch Radulph of Domfront (1135–40). Just as, on an earlier occasion, she had flirted with the idea of being protected by Zengi of Mosul, so now she had no hesitation about offering the hand of her nine-year-old daughter Constance to a Byzantine prince, Manuel Comnenus, though in fact she had already been promised to Raymond of Poitiers. The plan implied Byzantine overlordship and was impossible to carry out in face of opposition from the barons and the patriarch who had no intention of yielding his place to a Greek Orthodox rival. Radulph went over to Raymond's side and in 1136, soon after Raymond's arrival, he married him to Constance. In return Raymond is supposed to have recognized the patriarch as his feudal suzerain. Alice had been outmanoeuvred by an elaborate trick—she had been persuaded that Radulph was going to marry her to Raymond—and in resignation she withdrew to Lattakieh where she spent the rest of her days. Raymond immediately became involved in a war with the Armenians of Cilicia which dragged on until settled by the intervention of Byzantium. As a consequence of Raymond's arrival the Norman elements in Antioch were finally ousted by French influence. One indication of this change is the fact that the *Chanson des Chétifs*, an epic poem in Old French, was written at Raymond's court shortly before 1149. It was based largely on memories of the 1101 crusade, the crusade which failed. This remains as the only surviving piece of evidence for the contribution to vernacular poetry which was made by the crusader states.

Zengi meanwhile had been assiduously preaching holy war ever since his accession to power in Mosul and Aleppo. But the chief object of his ambition was in fact a Muslim state, Damascus. Indeed Prawer believes that it was only the Mosul historians, writing after Zengi's death, who retrospectively applied the concept of the *jihad* to the period of the struggle for Aleppo. The Damascus chroniclers were understandably more reserved and did not celebrate Zengi as the protagonist of the holy war until after he had captured Edessa in 1144. Zengi's first attempts to conquer Damascus, in 1130 and 1135, failed; he was all too often caught up in the long-lasting succession dispute in Iraq which followed the death of Sultan Mahmud in 1131. In 1134 indeed Damascus was able to launch an invasion of Galilee and King Fulk was hard put to it to hold his own. Three years later the Damascenes attacked the county of Tripoli. In the struggle which followed Count Pons lost his life and was succeeded by his son Raymond II (1137–52). This aggressive Damascene policy was not at all to Zengi's liking so he moved from Iraq to Syria. A brief, if unsuccessful, siege of Homs clearly warned Damascus that he meant business, though he had to agree to a truce when a Frankish army approached. Instead of Homs, he now besieged the Franks in the castle of Montferrand (Barin) in the valley of the Upper Orontes. Fulk led his army to the relief of Montferrand but was defeated in battle and had to take refuge in the castle where he himself became the besieged. In July 1137 he and Zengi came to terms. Montferrand was surrendered to the Muslims and the Franks were allowed to go free. In making these terms Fulk had been unaware that the united contingents of Jerusalem, Edessa, and Antioch were marching to his relief, while for his part Zengi had known that the Byzantine emperor John II Comnenus was on his way to Syria and had feared that he might besiege Aleppo. The Frankish intervention dealt with, Zengi once more turned his attention to Homs. Here, in spring 1138, he was surprised by the news of a Byzantine attack.

At the beginning of his reign Emperor John II (1118–43) had been compelled to neglect Syrian affairs. He had other wars on his hands: against Venice, the Petchenegs, and the Danishmends of eastern Anatolia. Not until 1137 did he find time to intervene. His main aim was to restore Byzantine authority over Antioch and North Syria, but he also wished to help the Franks against the menacing power of Zengi. The apparent contradiction of these motives is explained by the fact that if Byzantium wanted to realize its theoretical claims to North Syria it had to spread its protective wings over all the crusader states. It could not afford to destroy them; at most they could be reduced to the level of vassal states. Moreover as head of the Orthodox Church the emperor was duty bound to protect his fellow believers from the perils of Muslim dominion—even though conditions for them were in fact sometimes worse under the Latins than they had been under the Muslims, when, as *dhimmis*, they had been permitted to enjoy the status of a protected minority. But in the eyes of the Orthodox Church rule by the Latins was unquestionably to be preferred to rule by the Muslims.

The emperor's march through Cilicia turned into a triumphal procession and by the end of August 1137 he stood before the walls of Antioch. A few days later the city capitulated. King Fulk had not been prepared to support Raymond of Antioch against Byzantium. Though the emperor's arrival created political problems for him too, Fulk was quick to see that here was help against Zengi. Thus he agreed to the terms which Raymond was forced to accept. The prince of Antioch did homage to the emperor and the imperial standard was hoisted over the citadel. In return John refrained, for the moment, from entering the city. Nevertheless Raymond had to promise that if John could conquer Aleppo, Shaizar, and Homs he would accept them as a new principality and hand back Antioch to the emperor. This agreement was based on the Treaty of Devol of 1108 (see above p. 66f.). John spent the following winter in Cilicia. Then in March 1138, with support from Antioch and Edessa, he launched an offensive against Zengi. But a surprise attack on Aleppo failed, and when John moved on to besiege Shaizar, the town which controlled the middle Orontes, the Franks refused to give him proper assistance. They feared that if Shaizar fell then they might have to think seriously about carrying out the terms of the treaty of the previous year. Angrily John returned to Antioch and this time he made a ceremonial entry into the city. But before the main imperial army had arrived back at Antioch, Joscelin II of Edessa ingeniously engineered a city riot which forced John to leave.

The emperor spent the next few years in Anatolia fully occupied with a war against the Danishmends. Raymond of Antioch spent the time intriguing, in the end successfully, to rid himself of the ambitious patriarch Radulph. Zengi meanwhile had returned to his unfinished business with Damascus. In 1139 he besieged the city so closely that the ruler of Damascus was forced to appeal for help to Jerusalem. Fulk and his barons had no hesitation in concluding an alliance. Indeed the alliance was popular even with the citizens of Damascus who had learned to fear Zengi as a ruthless and brutal conqueror and who saw that as a result of the alliance Frankish pressure on the Hauran, the agricultural hinterland of their city, would be eased. For this reason in 1140 Damascus even helped the Franks to recapture Banyas, a town which controlled the road from Galilee to Damascus and from which, if he had held it, Zengi would have been able to threaten both Jerusalem and Damascus. Zengi was forced to retreat and for the next five years he had his hands full in Iraq. During this period the alliance of Jerusalem and Damascus remained intact. Fulk used all his diplomatic skill to prevent the escalation of local border clashes. During this breathing space he gathered up again the threads of the policy of strengthening the defences of the southern frontier which had been begun by Baldwin I. Just as Baldwin had built a *Gegenburg*, Scandelion, to blockade Tyre in 1117, so between 1136 and 1142, Fulk constructed a ring of fortresses around Ascalon, at Ibelin, Blanchegarde, and Beth Gibelin.[45] This made it difficult for the Egyptians to raid the kingdom and at the same time enabled the Franks to devastate the countryside around Ascalon. Moreover the protection afforded by these castles permitted the cultivation of the land, the settlement of Frankish farmers, and an altogether more intensive exploitation of the region. The castles themselves were granted to the Hospitallers and to loyal vassals. They became the centres of important lordships and powerful dynasties, notably the Ibelins, one of the best-known families of Outremer, whose rise to fame really began when Barisan the Old was appointed castellan of Ibelin. He had previously been the constable of Count Hugh of Jaffa. During the latter's revolt he had, in the end, led the count's vassals into the camp of the king who now rewarded him with Ibelin. From now until the fall of the kingdom, and then in Cyprus, the Ibelins—a family whose origins are probably to be found in Italy rather than in France—were always to be found near the centre of the stage.[46] Baldwin of Ramleh had been rewarded still earlier. Originally the royal castellan at Ramleh, by 1120 he was already in a semi-seignorial position, though theoretically a vassal of the count of Jaffa. After Hugh's downfall he formally obtained the position of lord of Ramleh. (And this helped to clarify the seignorial status of the bishop in neighbouring Lydda.) In the Transjordan, Pagan the Butler, with Fulk's approval, was pursuing a similar policy. He encouraged agriculture and in 1142 he further protected the trade route between the Dead Sea and the Red Sea by building at Moab a great castle known as Kerak or *Petra Deserti*, the Stone of the Desert. The lord of Transjordan now controlled the Bedouin sheep farmers as well as agriculture on the high plateau east of Kerak, and the saltpans of the Dead Sea. He had joined the ranks of the great barons. Further north the castle of Belvoir (built 1140) protected the Jordan Valley road and the Pont de Judaire; Safed (built 1102; cf. below, p. 154) controlled the road between Acre and Damascus and Jacob's Ford over the Jordan; Toron (*c.*1105) and Subeibe (*c.*1130) controlled the road between Tyre and Damascus; Beaufort (occupied in 1139) dominated the valley of the Leontes and the approaches to Sidon.

Krak des Chevaliers, the mightiest fortress of the Hospitallers, guarded the north-east flank of Tripoli. It was temporarily occupied by the crusaders in 1099 and permanently in 1110. In 1144 the count of Tripoli gave it to the Hospitallers who from there controlled not only important roads running from Hama and Homs to the coast but also the extremely fertile plain known as La Boquée at the foot of the castle. The Hospitallers also shared with the Muslims the valuable fishing rights in the Lake of Homs visible in the far distance which, in times of war, was an important rallying point for Muslim invaders. In 1212 Willibrand of Oldenburg, although he did not see the castle, was told that in peace time it had a garrison of 2,000 soldiers, perhaps a slight exaggeration when compared to Safed (below, p. 154), but in 1255 only sixty of them were knights. The castellan of Krak des Chevaliers was among the more important officials of the Order in the East. In 1163 Nur ed-Din came to lay siege to Krak des Chevaliers and was routed in the plain of La Boquée by a force composed of Welsh (an early example of British involvement in Outremer), Byzantine, and Poitevin contingents. The last included Hugh le Brun of Lusignan whose family was to rise to the kingship of Jerusalem and Cyprus. The battle is said to be depicted in a famous fresco in the Templar chapel at Cressac in the Charente and, although there is no positive evidence for this interpretation, one would like to believe that this is so, particularly because William of Tyre tells us that Gilbert de Lacy, commander of the Templars in those parts and formerly lord of Ludlow in Shropshire, was one of the leaders of this *chevauchée*. Krak des Chevaliers became the centre of a virtually independent frontier march, protecting the county of Tripoli against Hama and Homs and sharing in the defence of the county against the Assassins with the lords of Maraclea and the Knights Templars who created for themselves a similar but smaller independent territory stretching from Tortosa to Chastel Blanc (Safita) with its magnificent donjon considered by T. E. Lawrence to be the finest of all crusader towers. Except for Maraclea, the common frontier between the county of Tripoli and the Muslims thus shrank to a small strip of mountainous region between Gibelacar and Le Moinetre, although this meant that the north of the county, again with the exception of Maraclea, had slipped from the control of the counts to that of the Military Orders.

At Tortosa, as has been conclusively shown by Riley-Smith, the enormous citadel in the north-west of the episcopal city was built by the Templars after 1152. On the landward side it was protected by a double ring of walls with two moats. The inner wall, in one place still rising today to its full height of 25 metres, was reinforced by no less than nine towers. The donjon was originally placed behind the single sea wall and was later brought into line with it by additions. The scarps on the landward sides of the donjon are missing on the sea front. Instead there are three doors giving direct access to the sea. This and other features seem to indicate that ships could be loaded and unloaded from the donjon itself.

In the north the mighty castle of Sahyun (first third of the twelfth century) is one of the most impressive crusader castles. Situated 33 kilometres east of Lattakieh at an altitude of 439 metres above sea-level and commanding a fine view of the distant Mediterranean it is sited on a rocky spur formed by two deep valleys, thus resembling a long isosceles triangle of about 740 metres. The whole fortress covers slightly over 5 hectares (about 12.2 acres). It is built on two levels with a *Cour Basse* facing west, a Byzantine fortress in the centre, and the crusader fortress proper in the east with its massive donjon, built from carefully chiselled stone slabs and with walls more than 5 metres thick. But the most prominent feature of the eastern front is the slender needle-like pillar which at one time supported the drawbridge. It had been left standing when the ditch was dug by hand into the living rock. Measuring 128 metres in length, 18 metres in width, and 26 metres in depth, the ditch is, as Smail called it, 'a truly stupendous work'. In order to reach up to the drawbridge the rock needle had to be capped with masonry. From the bottom of the ditch to the top of the donjon the height is no less than 51 metres. Though Huygens pointed out certain structural weaknesses in the defence of the eastern side, it is by any standards one of the most impressive of medieval castles, comparable in the east only to Kerak in Jordan but bigger. Yet Sahyun is an enigma. It is generally said to have controlled the road from Lattakieh to the Orontes River, from where routes ran north to Antioch, east to Aleppo, and south to Apamea. But, in fact, as Saadé pointed out and as a visit to the place makes plain, Sahyun does not protect any route at all. The principal road from Lattakieh to Aleppo which has not changed its course since ancient times was certainly out of the reach of the castle. And even though the lord of Sahyun was one of the great feudatories of the principality of Antioch—probably also lord of Zerdana, some 75 kilometres away to the east of the Orontes,—one cannot help wondering where the money to build this gigantic fortress came from, since the resources of the highly fertile mid-Orontes valley were controlled from other castles, Choghour Bakas and Bourzey.

Life in these castles, except perhaps in the very largest ones, must have been full of hardships. The fort of Le Moinetre which guarded a pass in the Lebanon mountains and from where the distribution of revenues in the northern Beqaa Plain was supervised (see above, p. 60) stood at an altitude of 1260 metres and was under snow for several months during the year. The cave fortress of Cave de Suète (Habis Jaldak south of the Yarmuk River), from where the Franks controlled their advanced positions in the Terre de Suète, had been dug three storeys deep into a semi-circular wall of rock. Into these caverns the light of the sun scarcely penetrated and during the rainy season they were almost completely shut in by solid curtains of water falling from the rocks above. The only desirable feature was the superb view (at least in the dry season!), just as it was also in the cave fortress of Cave de Tyron further north. But the advantage of cave fortresses was that they cost almost nothing to build. Moreover, at times of a siege they tied up a lot of the enemy's troops both above them and in the valley below, while they could be held by a very tiny garrison. The only entrance was by way of a narrow mule-track which, for a length of 9 metres at the Cave de Tyron shrank to a gallery only three feet wide and three feet high with a vertical drop of nearly 300 metres on one side. William of Tyre vividly describes how the Franks during the reconquest of the Cave de Suète in 1182 found no other way to direct their attack than to dig shafts through the rocks from above for more than three weeks in day and night shifts until the Muslims, enervated by the continuous hammering, capitulated. This is another example illustrating the importance of the non-mounted soldier in medieval warfare recently emphasized by Gillingham. While Fulk built castles, his wife Melisende favoured monasteries and houses of canons, in particular the *Templum Domini* in Jerusalem and the double monastery (housing both nuns and monks) of Bethany which she lavishly endowed with Jericho in order to provide, in extravagant fashion, for her sister Joveta.

Then in 1142 John II Comnenus once again marched through Anatolia and Cilicia into Syria. This time Raymond of Antioch, taking shelter behind the very real hostility of his vassals to the claims of Byzantium, refused to repeat his submission of 1137. Now, for the first time in the period of the crusades, we can observe a theory which was becoming more and more prevalent and which conceived of the crusader states as the special responsibility of all Christendom. The consequence of this was that European rulers exercised some measure of rulership when they were present in the Holy Land. In this particular case this right of intervention was still limited to the universal powers because the bishop of Jabala rejected the Byzantine claims not only in the name of the vassals but also in the names of the pope and the 'emperor', i.e. the German king Conrad III.[47] The season was too far advanced for war, so John returned to his winter quarters in Cilicia. There he made plans which imply that he was even intending to restore Byzantine authority over Palestine though this had been lost to the Arabs as long ago as 638. By skilful diplomatic manoeuvring Fulk was able to persuade John to postpone an armed 'pilgrimage' to Jerusalem. But Antioch was saved only by a hunting accident in which John received injuries from which he died in April 1143 just before the time arranged for another invasion of Syria. Some months later a second hunting accident caused the death of Fulk (10 or 13 November 1143). He had ruled by virtue of his marriage to Melisende and since their eldest son, Baldwin, was only thirteen years old, she now took over the government. For the first time we hear nothing of an election. The joint rule established by Baldwin II continued to function smoothly, now in the names of mother and son only. It is true that Melisende was regent for her son, who was still a minor, but as well as this she also had her own share, territorially undefined, in the kingdom, and therefore, as William of Tyre's explicit phrases make clear, she ruled by hereditary right.

Consequently, she was crowned again when Baldwin III received the crown for the first time on Christmas Day 1143.

With the emperor of Byzantium dead and neither Melisende nor her son in any position to intervene in the affairs of North Syria, Zengi had an opportunity which was far too good to miss. He invaded the county of Edessa. The city itself was inadequately defended and Joscelin II was unable to march to its relief. On Christmas Eve 1144, after a siege of four weeks, Zengi broke into the city. As Prawer has rightly emphasized, it was not just on account of the feeble personality of its ruler that Edessa succumbed so easily. The demographic and economic conditions in the county were also significant. The high proportion of Syrians and Armenians in the population inevitably meant that these two elements were represented in the army. But the Syrians were poor soldiers and both groups, moreover, suffered from the decline in the economic situation which was caused by the frequent Turkish raids into this crusader outpost. Thus it is not hard to see why the city of Edessa failed to resist for long.

Joscelin, from a new capital at Turbessel, managed to hold the line of the Euphrates until 1150. But he was then captured and died in prison in 1159. His widow, recognizing the hopelessness of her position sold the six strongpoints she still held between the Orontes and the Euphrates to Byzantium, but even the empire could not hold them for as long as a year. The first crusader state to be founded was also the first to go. Antioch was now robbed of its outer defence works to the north-east. Zengi, however, did not live to witness these later triumphs. He was murdered in 1146. In Mosul he was succeeded by his eldest son, Saif ed-Din Ghazi; the second son, Nur ed-Din (1146–74) took over in Aleppo. He was to ensure that the death of Zengi brought no relief for the Franks.

5

THE SECOND CRUSADE, 1145–1149

THE news of the fall of Edessa caused a considerable stir in the West, but though it saddened men it did not immediately spur them on to a spontaneous crusade.[48] A Frankish embassy led by Bishop Hugh of Jabala arrived at the papal curia at Viterbo shortly after Eugenius III (1145–53) had ascended the pontifical throne. A little later on an Armenian delegation appeared. Eugenius listened receptively to their pleas and on 1 December 1145 he issued the first crusading bull, known from its opening words as *Quantum praedecessores*. But at first it met with no response at all. Indeed although it was addressed to the king and nobility of France, there is no evidence to show that it was, as yet, promulgated there. Eugenius's plan, however, clashed with certain ideas which King Louis VII (1137–80) himself developed, though it is not clear whether or not he knew of the papal bull when he formulated them. They were in any case not acceptable to the Church. The king held court at Bourges at Christmas 1145 and there he declared that he was planning to lead an expedition to the East. Various motives were attributed to him by contemporaries. But Louis was probably thinking in terms of a purely French armed pilgrimage which might also be of some assistance to the Holy Land rather than a crusade in the style of 1095. Thus at Bourges, after describing the plight of the crusader states, Bishop Godfrey of Langres called upon the nobles to fight for God at the side of their king; no mention was made of the pope, of the indulgence, or even of the papal bull. The appeal met with a cold response; the nobles were just not interested. When even his own chief counsellor, Abbot Suger of St. Denis, spoke against the scheme, Louis VII had no choice but to postpone a decision until Easter 1146 and, meanwhile, to lay the whole matter before Abbot Bernard of Clairvaux.

Unquestionably Bernard (1115–53) was at that time the most distinguished figure in the intellectual and political life of the West. It was he who had given impetus to the new Cistercian order which aimed at achieving a stricter observance of the Benedictine Rule. He had been one of the leading Church politicians ever since his tireless struggle to end the schism of 1130 between Innocent II and Anacletus II. On the question of the crusade his advice was sought as though he were a 'divine oracle' as one of the chroniclers put it. Bernard was probably well aware that the clash between the king's plan and the pope's wishes created a delicate political problem—a problem which was to play a considerable role in the later history of the crusades. Even if Louis VII had only planned an armed pilgrimage this inevitably came to be looked upon as a crusade in the light of the pope's crusading bull which had, after all, been issued earlier. Should the French authorities have argued that the bull had not been discussed at Bourges and that the king acted on his own initiative, this might have given rise to the opinion that a king could summon and carry through a crusade independently of the Church. For this reason the question of how much influence the pope's bull had on the assembly at Bourges was bitterly debated in the last century—and all too often debated in the polemical and anachronistic terms common to nineteenth-century nationalism or religious feeling. The sources simply do not permit a definite answer, though it is perhaps more probable than not that the bull was already known to the king, or at least to Bernard of Clairvaux. The only certain thing is that it was indeed issued on 1 December 1145. This was proved by the researches of Erich Caspar after it had long been obstinately denied by those who wished to give Louis VII the credit for initiating the crusade.[49]

Understandably enough the abbot of Clairvaux was not at all inclined to support an expedition which looked as though it might have been instigated by the king. This would have meant that control over the crusade had been taken out of the hands of the Church. The papacy would have to face a considerable blow to its prestige if it could not maintain its position as overlord of the crusading movement. Bernard therefore tried to give the initiative back to the pope. He declared that he could not consider so important a question without first consulting the pope. The result, early in 1146, was a round of negotiations between the papal and French courts culminating in the reissue of *Quantum praedecessores* (with a slightly amended text) on 1 March 1146. This version was, both in form and content, to be the pattern for all later papal crusading bulls. It was divided into three parts: the narrative, the exhortation, and the privileges (*narratio, exhortatio, privilegia*). Right in the opening phrases the pope—and here doubtless the influence of his teacher, Bernard of Clairvaux, can be discerned—asserted his claim to direct the crusade. He vigorously emphasized the tradition of the Church, appealing to the precedents set by his predecessors and describing the part played by Urban II in setting the First Crusade in motion. There followed a short account of the First Crusade and a description of the fall of Edessa which the pope explained as a punishment for sin (*nostris peccatis exigentibus*). Here Eugenius had hit upon a formula which was to appear time and time again in the writings of preachers and chroniclers. In the *exhortatio* he called upon nobles and magnates to defend, like good sons, the land which their brave fathers had won. As Christians they were summoned to fight for the Church in the East so that they would obtain remission of sins, help to enhance the dignity of Christendom and preserve unblemished their own knightly reputations. Then came a list of privileges headed by the crusading indulgence which, in conformity with the interpretation current as early as 1096, went beyond what had been authorized by the decree at Clermont. At this point Eugenius explicitly referred to the indulgence granted by Urban II but since, as Eugenius himself wrote, he was relying upon chronicle reports and not upon his predecessor's letters, this does not in fact tell us much about Urban's own point of view. The chroniclers had very early gone further than the Clermont decree warranted. The Church's protection for wives, children and possessions of the crusaders was then renewed. The extravagant dress which had been all too common on the First Crusade was forbidden. Crusaders who had to borrow money were exempted from paying interest on it. This, together with the provision which regulated the pawning of land to the Church, meant that the most urgent aspects of the problem of financing the crusade had been dealt with.

Eugenius entrusted Bernard alone with the job of preaching the crusade north of the Alps; in France the bull *Quantum praedecessores* was promulgated only in connection with his preaching. Eugenius III himself did no more than issue a crusading bull in Italy in October 1146. He was unable to leave Italy because of the situation in Rome. He had been driven out of the city and a republic had been set up by Arnold of Brescia. In the German king, Conrad III (1138–52), Eugenius hoped to find an ally who would both enable him to re-enter Rome and support him against the ambitions of Roger II of Sicily who had had himself crowned king (1130–54) after bringing all the Norman lands in Italy under one rule. Thus Eugenius naturally wished to see the preaching of the crusade limited to France and Italy, the countries which had taken part in the First Crusade. The original impulse for the Second Crusade had come from the pope, but it was entirely owing to the eloquence of the abbot of Clairvaux that anything came of that impulse.

At first Bernard adhered to the papal plan of keeping Germany out of the crusade. He began his preaching at the court of Vézelay on 31 March 1146 after the pope's March bull had been read out. The eloquence of the 'honey-tongued teacher' (*doctor mellifluus*) which can still move the modern reader of his literary works and which was acclaimed by all his contemporaries, had its expected effect. The king and a crowd of great nobles took the cross. They decided to allow a year in which to make their preparations. Louis VII used this time to negotiate with the countries through which he intended to march, particularly Germany and Byzantium. He may also have taken a forced loan from some of the churches of France to cover his expenses, but as Constable (below, n. 16) has shown, the evidence for this is by no means compelling, as the measure is attested only at Fleury and Le Puy. In any event this would have been something quite different from a crusading tax.

In the following months Bernard preached unceasingly. His example caused the Cistercians from now on to become the most devoted crusading preachers, and this remained one of their characteristics until, after the crusade against Damietta, they yielded this role to the mendicant orders of Franciscans and Dominicans. By contrast, Bernard had categorically refused earlier on, and did so again now, to permit the personal participation of Cistercians in the crusade. While we do find abbots and bishops from the order on crusade later on, the chapter general time and again handed out punishments for unauthorized participation. Bernard also turned down an offer by the king of Jerusalem to found a Cistercian monastery near Jerusalem and left the fine site to be settled by the Premonstratensians. If Bernard, on his preaching tours, was unable to appear in person he would send envoys to read letters of exhortation, the essential points of which (Letter no. 363) he wrote himself but which his chancery would alter slightly to suit local circumstances before distributing them. Eight different general or individual addresses for this one letter are still extant and other letters must be added. Very characteristic of Bernard's preaching style is the copy of letter no. 363 which was sent to the people of England. There are no cloudy eschatological notions here. For Bernard the crusade was a work of penance. The indulgence, once a means to an end, had become an end in itself. The East, of course, had to be freed from the heathen, but so too the souls of the crusaders had to be freed from sin. For this reason he welcomed the threat to the crusader states as a sign that 'the accepted time, the day of salvation' (cf. 2 Corinthians 6: 2) was at hand. From now on the *acceptabile tempus* motif was an inseparable part of the preaching of crusades. Bernard had a disquieting tendency to take it for granted that his contemporaries were evil-doers who needed to repent. Thus he, more than anyone, emphasized the idea of a spiritual reward.

But Bernard's own words speak more clearly than any analysis. Here therefore some typical passages from his letter to the English are quoted as being representative of all later crusading sermons.

Now is the accepted time, the day of abundant salvation. The earth has been shaken; it trembles because the Lord of heaven has begun to lose his land—the land in which, for more than thirty years, he lived as a man amongst men. . . . But now, on account of our sins, the sacrilegious enemies of the cross have begun to show their faces even there; their swords are wreaking havoc in the promised land. . . . What are you doing, you mighty men of valour? What are you doing, you servants of the cross? Will you throw to the dogs that which is most holy? Will you cast pearls before swine? . . . What are we thinking of, my brethren? Is then the arm of the Lord grown so short that he himself has become powerless to bring salvation and must needs summon us, poor earthly worms that we are, to defend and restore to him his inheritance? Can he not send more than twelve legions of angels . . . and so free his land? Of course there can be no doubt that, should he wish to, he can do this. . . . But I say unto you, the Lord God is testing you. He is looking down upon the sons of men to see if he can find anyone who understands and grieves over what is now happening on earth. . . . See then with what skill he plans your salvation and be amazed. Look, sinners, into the depths of his pity and trust in him . . . He is not trying to bring you down but to raise you up. What is it but a unique and wonderful act of divine generosity when the Almighty God treats murderers, thieves, adulterers, perjurors, and criminals of all kinds as though they were men of righteousness and worthy to be called to his service. Do not hesitate. God is good. . . . He pretends to be in debt so that he can repay those who take up arms on his behalf with the forgiveness of sins and with eternal glory . . . I would call blessed that generation that has the chance to obtain so rich an indulgence, blessed to be alive in this year of jubilee, this year so pleasing to the Lord. . . . O mighty soldier, O man of war, you now have a cause for which you can fight without endangering your soul; a cause in which to win is glorious and for which to die is but gain. . . .

Or are you a shrewd businessman, a man quick to see the profits of this world? If you are, I can offer you a splendid bargain. Do not miss this opportunity. Take the sign of the cross. At once you will have indulgence for all the sins which you confess with a contrite heart. It does not cost you much to buy and if you wear it with humility you will find that it is the kingdom of heaven.

The letter closes with some words of warning. The Jews are not to be persecuted. In other letters Bernard advised men not to leave too soon as Peter the Hermit had done—with terrible consequences for those who followed him. They should wait and then march east in good order. The abbot was an advocate of good order in the Church, of everything being in its proper place within the system. His preaching differed from the preaching of the First Crusade in that he addressed himself not to the whole population but to the knightly classes alone. He relied on their energy and he tried to awake in them the feeling that they had been specially chosen.

The unauthorized activity of a Cistercian monk, Rudolf, caused Bernard a good deal of anxiety. This monk wandered through north France and the Rhineland in the style of one of the popular millenarian preachers of the First Crusade. He had received no dispensation from the decree forbidding monks to preach so he was infringing the preaching monopoly of the secular clergy. Moreover he was damaging Bernard's prestige since the abbot's sermons contained no statements of an eschatological nature. Worst of all was the fact that the inhabitants of the Rhineland towns were once again being inspired to massacre the Jews. In order to bring Rudolf's activities under control, Bernard himself had to go to the Rhineland at the request of the archbishop of Mainz. He dealt severely with the monk and then stayed on in Germany. It was no longer possible to keep the Germans out of the crusade since Rudolf had already filled them with enthusiasm for it. Bernard also had gone further than

Eugenius had originally envisaged as his letter to the English proves. But if a German crusade was to have any success the support of King Conrad III was needed. Bernard and the king met at an assembly at Frankfurt in November 1146. Conrad withstood Bernard's appeal but did agree to another meeting at Speyer at Christmas. Bernard felt that the king's resistance was weakening and inexorably increased the pressure on him. In a tremendous sermon which retained its power even through the words of an interpreter, Bernard brought Conrad to the point of imagining himself at the Last Judgement standing before Christ. Then Bernard, as Christ, asked the king, 'Man, what ought I have done for you that I have not done?' This assault on his feelings was too much for Conrad. He took the cross and his example was followed by countless nobles headed by his nephew, Duke Frederick of Swabia. Germany had been won over to the crusade. The king's decision had been made easier by the settlement of the long and destructive feud between the count of Namur and the archbishop of Trier. One of Bernard's aims in coming to Germany had been to end this feud. On Christmas Eve Conrad's old enemy, Duke Welf VI, had taken the cross though it is unlikely that there had been time for the king to hear of this before he made his own decision. Following the assembly at Speyer a crusading letter was sent to the Bavarians. At an assembly held at Regensburg in February 1147 many of them, including Bishop Otto of Freising, who was to be one of the chroniclers of the crusade, responded to this appeal.

Next month at another meeting of the imperial court at Frankfurt Conrad, who had been in the Holy Land once before in 1125, decided to take the land route through Byzantium and Asia Minor. This was the route hallowed by tradition because it had been taken by Godfrey de Bouillon. To Conrad it seemed particularly suitable because he had a firm alliance with Byzantium sealed by the marriage of his sister-in-law, Bertha of Sulzbach, to the emperor, Manuel I Comnenus (1143–80). Moreover Manuel had enjoyed considerable military success against the Seldjuks of Asia Minor and this suggested that there would be no repetition of the disasters of 1101. In the previous month (February 1147) the French too had decided in favour of the land-route despite the efforts made by their ally, Roger II of Sicily, to persuade them to travel by the sea route from Italy. Roger had suggested that he might then join them on crusade, but Louis realized that in fact the king of Sicily was hoping to secure French support for the anti-Byzantine policy which, in the best Norman tradition, he was pursuing. Even so Manuel had little enthusiasm for the course events had taken. From his point of view the alliance with Conrad had been intended mainly to keep Roger II at bay. This was now out of the question. Since the French were Roger's allies it seemed to the Greeks that the fact that the Germans and French were now taking the same line of march through the Balkans might mean that Conrad had changed sides.

Nor, of course, was the pope overjoyed to learn of Conrad's decision. He had been counting on his help in Italy. But once the crusade had become a general European enterprise there was little that he could or would do to hinder it. None the less the inclusion of Germany meant that right from the start the crusade was saddled with problems which say little for the political insight of Bernard of Clairvaux.

At the Frankfurt assembly of March 1147 the German contingent was weakened when the Saxon princes announced their preference for a crusade of their own against the Wends—Slavs who lived beyond the north-eastern borders of the empire. As early as 1108 a letter had been drafted, probably at Magdeburg, calling upon the people of the western parts of the Empire to go to war against the Slavs. Citing the example of the Frenchmen who had gone to Jerusalem and promising, not, it is true, an indulgence, but at least in general terms the salvation of the soul, the letter went on to ask for settlers. The heathens were evil, it said, but their country was very rich in flesh, fowl, honey, and grain. As an enterprise under royal direction, however, this would be different from a crusade. But at the time nothing came of it; it is even possible that the letter was never sent. In 1147 things developed in a different way. Bernard and the pope approved the Saxon proposal. Although he was not the first to voice such sentiments, it was on this occasion that Bernard, with all the weight which his voice carried, proclaimed, in his letter no. 457, the ill-famed alternative 'Death or Conversion' which, precisely because it was so unambiguous, has found so many whitewashing apologists. More important, however, was the fact that the pope did not take over this formula but, in his bull for the Wendish Crusade, spoke only of conversion. He granted crusaders against the Wends the same spiritual and material privileges as were enjoyed by crusaders to the Holy Land. The pope, however, could hardly do anything else since everything points to the conclusion that Bernard had done this already on his own initiative and without the pope's knowledge—an indication of the extent to which he prejudiced papal leadership of the crusade. But it would, in any case, have been difficult to deny the Saxon request because, Eugenius, at about the same time, allowed Emperor Alfonso VII of Castile to organize a crusade against the Spanish Saracens. Twenty years later from his parish at Lake Plön in Holstein the chronicler Helmold of Bosau saw all three enterprises, in the Holy Land, in Spain, and against the Slavs, as a single whole. This did not prevent him from severely criticizing the Wendish Crusade on the grounds that it seriously embarrassed the policy of peaceful colonization and Christian mission which was being pursued by Count Adolf II of Holstein in Wagria (eastern Holstein) with the aid of the Wendish prince Niklot. At a meeting of the imperial court at Frankfurt, Count Adolf had openly attempted to discredit St. Bernard, though without success, by using a sick boy in order to put his miracle cures to the test. Helmold made the Wendish crusaders wonder, as they were fighting in Mecklenburg, whether, in the end, they were not really engaged in devastating their own land and their own people. From the point of view of crusading ideology such a question was well-nigh blasphemous. The Wendish Crusade became a dangerous precedent. In Spain there was at least a long tradition of war against the heathen going back to the days before the crusades. To this extent Spain was a special case. In Spain, moreover, the enemy was also Islam. But if the example of the Wendish crusade were to be followed then the Holy Land might lose much of the support it so desperately needed, for heathens could be fought in many parts of the world, not just in the Holy Land. And in fact the system of crusades against the Slavs did become increasingly well developed, particularly after the Teutonic Order settled in Prussia in the thirteenth century.

The prince of the Wendish Obotrites, Niklot, anticipating the crusade, launched an attack first. A large German army led by Henry the Lion, duke of Saxony, Conrad duke of Zähringen, Albert the Bear, margrave of Brandenburg, and the archbishops of Bremen and Magdeburg marched out to meet his invasion. But the fighting ended without any clear victory. Indeed only the fact that the Wends went through a mock baptismal service prevented the real failure of the campaign becoming obvious.[50]

The crusade itself started at Regensburg in May 1147. The French set out from Metz a few weeks later. The German march through Hungary went off without incident. But once in the Byzantine Empire the excesses of the German troops so badly damaged relations with Manuel Comnenus, that when Conrad III reached Constantinople in September the two rulers did not even meet each other. Manuel was furious because the arrival of the crusading armies deprived him of all mobility. He had to remain in the capital while Roger II of Sicily seized the opportunity to ravage Corfu and to destroy the centres of the Byzantine silk industry at Thebes and Corinth. Two years passed before Manuel, with Venetian help, was able to drive Roger off imperial territory. For his part Conrad felt somewhat put out because Manuel, like his grandfather, had required an oath from him promising to respect Byzantine claims over Syria and Palestine. It was the approach of the French army more than the pressure applied by Manuel which persuaded Conrad to take his troops across the Bosporus into Asia Minor. Then, instead of keeping to the original plan and waiting for the French to join them, they decided to push on immediately in the direction of Edessa.

At Nicaea Conrad divided his army into two sections. One contingent, under the command of Bishop Otto of Freising, was instructed to take the longer coast road. Conrad had intended that this contingent should include all the non-combatants, but in fact some hangers-on remained behind to hamper the main army. This made its first contact with the enemy near Dorylaeum at the end of October. The Seldjuks won a convincing victory. The German retreat to the coast began in good order but control was soon completely lost and, in consequence, casualties were heavy. Most of the survivors who struggled back to Nicaea early in November left the army in order to return home. Otto of Freising's contingent meanwhile had marched south along the Aegean coast. It then struck inland only to suffer a severe reverse at the hands of the Turks at Laodicea. What was left of the army just about managed to reach the coast of Pamphylia but was then cut to pieces in February 1148. The bishop and a few other survivors finished the journey to Syria by ship.

Meanwhile the French army had reached Constantinople on 4 October 1147. On the surface relations with Manuel were good and the emperor himself went to some lengths to win over Louis VII. Within the French army, however, there was a strong anti-Byzantine party led by Bishop Godfrey of Langres. He was an unpleasant trouble-maker who claimed to enjoy the rights of a legate. In fact it seems that the pope had conferred them upon him but had later, at Byzantine insistence, subordinated him to Guido of Florence, cardinal priest of San Crisogono. But Guido failed to gain much influence in the army and Godfrey's party derived encouragement from the news of Roger II's success at Corfu and gained more support when it was learned that Manuel had made a truce with the Seldjuk sultan of Iconium. This shocked the Latins although it was precisely their approach which had helped persuade Manuel to come to terms. Thus even before they reached Constantinople the anti-Byzantine party was pressing for an attack on the city and for an alliance with King Roger in order to achieve this. They continued their agitation while the army was encamped outside the city but failed to convince the majority who pointed out that the pope had not authorized an expedition against Constantinople. Nevertheless here was the first sign that men were prepared to misuse the crusading ideal to the extent of turning it against fellow Christians. The capture of Constantinople by the crusaders of 1204 was foreshadowed.[51]

The French constantly postponed crossing the Bosporus until finally Manuel spread rumours about a German victory in Asia Minor. Fearing that they might come too late to quench their (typically medieval) thirst for booty—which made up an important part of a knight's income—the French hurried over into Asia Minor where they were reinforced by a contingent from Savoy. Manuel, however, refused to supply them with guides or provisions while the question of their relations with the Byzantine Empire was still unclear. Finally the French barons had to resign themselves to paying homage and Louis himself promised that he would not deprive the emperor of any town that rightfully belonged to him. Manuel now provided guides but in view of his treaty with the sultan he could give the crusade no more than half-hearted help. This gave further stimulus to the anti-Greek mood in the French army. At Nicaea they joined up with Conrad III and the remnants of the German army. From here they marched to Smyrna and then on to Ephesus where Conrad became so ill (Christmas 1147) that he had to return to Constantinople. Manuel took care of him personally in order to breathe new life into their old alliance. Meanwhile the French army had met the same fate as the German. Early in the new year they suffered a heavy defeat at Laodicea. The surviving contingents fought their way to the coast at Attalia but this Byzantine town was neither able nor particularly willing to accommodate so many crusaders. The Byzantines were asked to provide ships but so few arrived that only the king, the clergy, and the barons were able to sail. Those who were left behind tried to make their way overland to Syria, but soon after leaving Attalia they were routed by the Seldjuks; Louis and his followers reached Antioch in safety.

The position in Syria was not at all good. Joscelin II of Edessa had taken advantage of the death of Zengi in 1146 to try to recapture his capital, but Nur ed-Din stepped in and by massacring the Armenian and Jacobite population of Edessa ensured that it was lost beyond recovery. After this there were no important clashes; both Muslims and Christians were waiting for the arrival of the crusaders. Raymond of Antioch wanted Louis to lead an expedition against Aleppo to relieve the pressure on his northern border where he had to face the Seldjuks of Asia Minor as well as Nur ed-Din. It was a sensible plan. Only in this way was there any hope at all of reconstructing the county of Edessa, some fragments of which still remained on the west bank of the Euphrates. Nur ed-Din moreover was to become a most dangerous enemy of the crusader states, though this was perhaps not entirely clear in 1148. Even so, it must have been obvious that a victory over him could hinder the union of Aleppo and Damascus. But on his own Louis was too weak to be able to help Raymond in the north and in addition the rumours of an affair between his wife, Eleanor, and Raymond made him feel that he had been badly treated. What was left of the crusading armies was little enough already and a division of forces seemed stupid. So Louis marched south to join Otto of Freising and Conrad III who, after his convalescence, had reached the Holy Land in April 1148. After visiting the Holy Places the kings of France and Germany met at Acre. Louis's forces were reinforced by some newly arrived Provençal crusaders. Conrad who, during the crusade, began to add the imperial appellation of *Augustus* to his royal title, had been trying to raise a new army with Byzantine money. Since the paid troops enlisted by Conrad were mostly seasonal pilgrims wishing to return to Europe in the late summer, Edessa was simply too far away to remain the objective of the war. Moreover in negotiations with Baldwin III in Jerusalem, which were conducted in such secrecy that even Baldwin's mother Melisende seems to have been excluded, Conrad had already been won over to the idea of attacking Damascus instead.

At Palmarea near Acre on 24 June 1148 the High Court of Jerusalem met. The crusaders were admitted to the assembly as they were entitled to be according to a tradition of the court, though this is the first time that the historian can actually observe the tradition being followed. Besides Conrad III the Germans were represented by the bishops of Freising, Metz, and Toul, by the legate, the bishop of Porto, and by the duke of Swabia, Duke Welf VI and the margraves of Austria, Verona and Montferrat. For the French there were Louis VII, the bishops of Langres and Lisieux, Cardinal Guido of Florence, the counts of Perche, Troyes, Flanders, and Soissons. The kingdom of Jerusalem was represented by Baldwin III, Queen Melisende, the patriarch of Jerusalem, the arch-bishops of Caesarea and Nazareth, the bishops of Sidon, Acre, Beirut, Banyas, and Bethlehem, the Masters of the Temple and the Hospital, and the lords of Tiberias, Sidon, Caesarea, Oultrejourdain, Toron, and Beirut, as well as by the constable Manasses of Hierges and Philip of Nablus, an important royal vassal. North Syria was not represented. After some debate the assembly made the incredibly stupid decision to attack Damascus. Edessa had ceased to be a war objective and in view of the absence of the north Syrians the case for Aleppo rather went by default. But Damascus was the last place to attack. The existence of the kingdom depended on the continuation of the alliance made with Damascus against Aleppo in 1139. Its association with the apostle Paul made it a sacred city but the alliance with the atabeg of Damascus was a matter of life or death to Jerusalem and ought not to have been sacrified for reasons of this kind, no matter how idealistic. But Baldwin III had already made Conrad pledge his word in support of the campaign. Louis of France also seems to have been in favour of it; in any case he did not oppose it. The king of Jerusalem hoped that the conquest of Damascus would bring him the prestige which would at last free him from his mother's regency, which was still effective even though the king had attained his majority years ago. Melisende herself was probably sceptical about an enterprise which endangered both the kingdom's position and her own.

The plan was as ridiculous in execution as in conception. On 24 July they encamped among the orchards on the west side of the city. The approach of a relieving army under Nur ed-Din frightened the atabeg of Damascus just as much as it did the Palestinian barons. The latter, playing a dangerously devious game, persuaded the two kings that the orchards were adding to the difficulties of the siege and that it would be better to move the army to the south-east. But here the army was caught on a hot waterless plain; a prolonged stay was out of the question, so on the same day it was decided to raise the siege and withdraw. In his chronicle, William of Tyre, whose comments on the discussion at Acre had been very laconic, was later to try to put the blame on the count of Flanders or the influence of Raymond of Antioch. But contemporary public opinion in the West blamed, rightly, the barons of Palestine. The consequences of the campaign were bad. For one thing, public opinion in the West was shocked; for another, although the atabeg of Damascus still remained true to the alliance, the city population which had once accepted it also now distrusted the Franks and in 1154 opened the city gates to Nur ed-Din. The union of Aleppo and Damascus was helped rather than hindered by the campaign of 1148. On 8 September Conrad angrily left the Holy Land. Louis VII stayed on until Easter 1149 but achieved nothing of note. As William of Tyre observed: 'from this time on the position of the Latins in the East deteriorated visibly.'

Conrad III went to Thessalonica and there, probably in October 1148 before he returned to Germany, he made a treaty with Manuel Comnenus, renewing their old anti-Norman alliance from the days before the Second Crusade.[52] It was agreed that, with the support of Byzantine money and troops, Conrad would lead an expedition against Roger II next year. The European truce which Bernard of Clairvaux had brought about so that the crusade could go forward, was at an end. But Roger had made his preparations in good time. In 1148 he engineered a rebellion of the Welf family in Germany. This prevented Conrad III from entering Italy. In July 1149 when Louis VII visited the king of Sicily on his way back to France, Roger took the opportunity to strengthen their alliance. He advocated another crusade, again with the intention of turning it against the Greeks. He was helped by the fact that in France meanwhile Bernard of Clairvaux, Suger of St. Denis, and Peter the Venerable, abbot of Cluny, had also begun to preach a new crusade—a genuine one—which was intended to make amends for 1148. Bernard of Clairvaux might even have been chosen at Chartres to lead the expedition had not the plan collapsed because the French knights were unwilling to shoulder the burden of a new crusade so soon. The shock of the last failure was still too great; losses had been too heavy. But at least a great European war was narrowly averted when the pope refused to join the coalition against Conrad and Manuel because he was afraid of being politically dominated by the Normans.

The one success of the whole crusade took place in the wings. In 1147 a group of English, Flemish, and Frisian crusaders who were taking the sea route to Palestine, sailed up the River Tagus and, after a siege lasting several months, captured the city of Lisbon from the Moors.[53] The Englishman Gilbert of Hastings was chosen as the first bishop of the reconquered city while Henry of Bonn, a German knight killed during the siege, was buried in São Vicente da Fora in Lisbon, where his tomb may still be seen. He was soon counted among the Blessed and in the sixteenth century he was immortalized by Luis de Camões in the finest work of

Portuguese literature (*Os Lusiadas* VIII, 18). The Anglo-Flemish fleet sailed on in February 1148 and helped, as has recently been shown by Hiestand, with the conquest of Tortosa in Spain in December 1148. A good number of those crusaders can be shown to have settled permanently in Tortosa. Few can have reached the Holy Land and indeed there is very little evidence of their presence there. The conquest of Lisbon and Tortosa was a pitifully small return for a crusade which had begun in such an atmosphere of hope and enthusiasm and which had been organized on so large a scale. The disappointment was, of course, correspondingly deep. This is clear from the many attempts which were made to explain the failure. Some, above all the French chronicler Odo of Deuil, preferred rational explanations—the hostility of the Greeks and Turks, the difficulties of the journey. Others, like the Cistercians Otto of Freising and Bernard of Clairvaux, used metaphysical arguments—the sins of men, the inscrutable judgement of God. Between these extremes we find all manner of natural and supernatural explanations. Gerhoh of Reichersberg and the Würzburg Annalist, the two severest critics of the crusade, subsequently went so far as to regard it as the work of the Devil and Antichrist. The most important target for critics was naturally the abbot of Clairvaux who had done more than anyone else to set the crusade in motion, and had so closely identified himself with it. By his treatment of the crusade as a means by which a soul could find salvation he had aroused hopes which were brutally dashed by its failure. It would be a long time before the crusading ideal would recover from this. Bernard replied to his critics in the second book of his *De Consideratione*. There is no doubt that he took the criticism seriously and was hurt by it; he compared the judgement of God—and it was in these terms that he saw the criticism—to a hell in which he was now standing. It could not shake his faith but his writings show clearly that he found the subject a painful one. It is significant that he did not include his famous encyclical no. 363, his great call for the crusade, in his own carefully assembled collection of letters. In *De consideratione* he discussed the actions for which he had been—or might possibly be—reproached but he was not prepared to admit that he was in any way responsible for subsequent disappointments. It might, however, be argued that he had added to the difficulties of the crusade by widening its scope both internally and externally in a political situation which was not at all favourable to such a process of extension. Bernard's self-defence always ended with his taking cover behind the commission to preach the crusade which he had received from the pope. That he should try to evade responsibility for the crusade after it had failed reveals a side of his character which is not very attractive. To answer those critics who, rightly, would not accept this excuse, he constructed a second line of defence. He described himself as the shield of God, drawing upon himself the fire of the blasphemers, the critics, so that God would not be touched by their poisoned darts. For the critics, he argued, were really attacking God, not him.[54] The zeal with which the Cistercians, the monks of Bernard's own order, emphasized a metaphysical explanation of the fiasco, rather suggests that they wanted to cover up other reasons for the failure. But public opinion was not deceived. In future it was not going to be so easy to preach a crusade.

6

THE CRUSADER STATES, 1149–1187

THE division of Zengi's lands in 1146 whereby Saif ed-Din Ghazi obtained Mosul and Nur ed-Din (1146–74) Aleppo was unfortunate for the Franks. It meant that Nur ed-Din was freed from the responsibilities for the disorders in the east which had weighed so heavily upon his father. He could concentrate on the struggle against Damascus and the Franks.[55] His first success came when he beat off Joscelin II's vain attempt to recapture Edessa (see above p. 102). Then in 1147 and 1148 he attacked the principality of Antioch, occupying the best part of its territories east of the Orontes. But for the moment he made no decisive move. Indeed the Second Crusade forced him to go to the relief of Damascus. His own base Aleppo, however, remained out of danger since the crusaders proved incapable of making the decision to attack in north Syria. As soon as the crusade was over Nur ed-Din resumed his war against Antioch. In the summer of 1149 he appeared before the walls of Inab, a fortress belonging to Antioch. Raymond and his knights went to its relief but on 29 July they were routed and Raymond himself was killed. It was Nur ed-Din's finest victory against the Franks. His prestige throughout the Islamic world was enormously enhanced.

Sir Hamilton Gibb and Sivan have pointed out that the victory at Inab had other, more far-reaching consequences. From now on Nur ed-Din saw himself as the champion of Islam, as a man with a historic mission to fulfil. His task was to unite the Muslims against the Franks. *Jihad*, the Muslim holy war, which had in the early twelfth century been an idea of rather secondary importance, was turned into a driving force of Islamic politics under Nur ed-Din when it came to be seen as an expression of a general revival of Islamic orthodoxy. To understand Nur ed-Din it is essential to see that he was also a religious zealot; political unity presupposed unity of belief. Thus he took tough measures against the Shi'ites and promoted every cause which could help to reawaken and deepen Orthodox faith. Schools and mosques were founded. Poets and preachers were called upon to support his political and religious aims. Using propaganda slogans they worked to awaken the religious fervour of the people. Above all they condemned the 'scandalous' alliance between Damascus and the Franks which Nur ed-Din was determined to destroy. From 1150 onwards he steadily increased the pressure on Damascus; on several occasions he set up camp before its walls. After the death of Unur in 1149 the government of Damascus remained weak and unable to take advantage of his periodic campaigns in the region of Edessa where the capture of Joscelin II had permitted him to consolidate his conquests. The armed militias of the lower classes of Damascus withdrew their support not only from the city government but also from the upper bourgeoisie represented by the family clan of the Banu as-Sufi which had shamelessly enriched itself. In 1154, after a minimum of resistance, the people of Damascus opened the gates of their city to Nur ed-Din. His religious programme was at once extended to include the new state. Muslim Syria was now united and the gaining of Damascus brought Nur ed-Din a considerable addition to the strength of his army. Gibb has estimated the number of his Syrian troops at a maximum of 6,000 cavalry. Two thousand of these were his own household troops and the rest consisted of contingents under the command of men who were granted territorial fiefs (iqta) so that they could support the required number of soldiers. During this period there was a very noticeable influx of Kurdish soldiers into both the officer corps and the regular army where they counterbalanced the Turks. It was an army of foreigners.

Lack of leadership among the Franks made the rise of Nur ed-Din all the more menacing. Baldwin III, king of Jerusalem (1143–63) was still not grown up; Joscelin II of Edessa was a prisoner; the prince of Antioch had fallen in battle. After the battle at Inab and even before finally extinguishing the county of Edessa, Nur ed-Din dramatically demonstrated the extent of his power by taking a bath in the Mediterranean before the eyes of his soldiers. Antioch itself was saved by the efforts of the patriarch Aimery (1144–93). Unobtrusively controlled by him, the government of Antioch was formally in the hands of Raymond's widow, Constance, whose main concern was to preserve the principality for her children. The intervention of Baldwin III persuaded Nur ed-Din to withdraw from Antioch thus ensuring, for the moment, its continued existence. But Baldwin was not able to do the same for Edessa. Conditions in the kingdom of Jerusalem did not permit the ruler to stay away for long. The king was now nineteen and disliked sharing the government with his mother Melisende. When he came of age at fifteen, she had given no sign that she would terminate her regency, because the institution of joint rule gave her a share of her own in the kingdom. The majority of the barons disliked the arrangement just as much as the king. The quarrel between the young king and his mother was more serious than William of Tyre's account of it would suggest. Only an analysis of the royal charters of those years reveals just how deep the rift between them was. Melisende was by no means without allies. Above all she could rely on the support of the Church. She had pushed loyal men into great crown offices, notably into the most important office of constable to which she had appointed Manasses of Hierges, a nephew of Baldwin II, who had arrived in the Holy

Land in 1140. The viscount of Jerusalem, Rohard the Elder, held Judaea and the capital for her. In Samaria she had the support of the important Milly family represented by Philip of Nablus. She could also count on Prince Elinard of Galilee who brought into her camp his in-laws from the south-west, the Ibelins who had by then gained control of the lordship of Ramleh by marriage. Only very gradually was Baldwin III able to match this strength by building up a power base of his own in the crown estates in the north around Tyre and Acre.

From 1149 on the relationship between mother and son was more than chilly. The chancery of the kingdom was in complete disarray, dissolving in fact into two competing *scriptoria*, one the king's and the other his mother's. She built up her own household with her own officials separate from the royal household proper. These actions violated the principles of joint rule as established by Baldwin II, according to which the kingdom was one and indivisible, even though zones of influence might exist, and the share of the participants in joint rule remained territorially undefined. To create a separate household and, even more, to create a separate group of vassals came close to dividing the kingdom. The king's position was desperate when he had to go north in the summer of 1150 because Joscelin II of Edessa had been taken prisoner. A charter of this period shows Baldwin in control of Acre but otherwise deserted. His entourage consisted of just his chapel, plus a man who had been expelled as archbishop and dismissed as chancellor, an unknown Templar, a prince of Galilee fighting to keep his principality, and one undistinguished vassal. However, although this does not surface in the charter, he still had the support of the northern lordships of Beirut and Toron. In 1150 those vassals who acknowledged allegiance only to the queen mother, took the unprecedented step of openly ignoring the king's summons to follow him to the north, and this though he had resorted to the unusual means of summoning them individually by letter. Clearly they intended to weaken his position until it became impossible for him to exercise the traditional protectorate of the kings of Jerusalem over the principalities of Syria.

Their plan miscarried. In Antioch Baldwin proved himself a skilful diplomat, well able to hold his own in some delicate negotiations with Byzantium. But the discord made it impossible to solve the most urgent problem of the north, i.e. the remarriage of Princess Constance of Antioch. He had already—though without success—offered her three very respectable suitors and in 1150 he convoked the vassals of Antioch, Jerusalem, and Tripoli to meet in a special assembly at Tripoli in order to settle the matter. But here too Constance rejected all idea of marriage. William of Tyre said that she preferred a free and independent life and so chose to follow the advice of a patriarch of Antioch who was trying to preserve his own political power. This explanation is manifestly wrong because in 1153 neither of these factors prevented Constance from marrying someone so unknown (see below, p. 113) that she kept the project a secret from her own vassals until she had obtained the approval of the king of Jerusalem. The true explanation for Constance's refusal in 1150 must be that there does not seem to have been a suitable candidate on whom both the king and his mother, who was also present at the Tripoli assembly, would have been able to agree. In these circumstances any marriage would have cost Antioch the support of one half of Jerusalem.[56]

Melisende had, it is true, lost control of Galilee when Prince Elinard died *c.* 1148, but she offset this by creating her younger son Amalric count of Jaffa (1151). This gave her control of the central section of the coast. Yet it was at about this time that she made her decisive mistake. Probably in 1150, and certainly no later than 1151, she allowed her favourite Manasses of Hierges to marry Helvis of Ibelin, the widow of Barisan the Old. Almost all historians, relying on a passage in William of Tyre, have stated that it was this marriage which formed the basis of Manasses's power by assuring him of the support of the Ibelins. But in fact exactly the opposite is true. It drove them into the king's camp, a change of sides which can, indeed, be observed in the charters. Earlier, in about 1148, Helvis had inherited the important double lordship of Ramleh-Mirabel from her brother; it passed into the hands of her first husband, Barisan the Old of Ibelin. His three sons could justifiably look forward to a rich inheritance, but their hopes were dashed by their mother's second marriage, for it can be shown that at least Mirabel was now taken over by Manasses. The marriage of Barisan the Old had been the first really good marriage made by the Ibelins since their arrival in Outremer and what the sons would inherit from their father's side of the family, would neither provide properly for three men nor make them sufficiently eligible to attract the really wealthy heiresses. Thus unless the three brothers managed to bring down Manasses and the regime to which he belonged before he had sons of his own from his marriage with Helvis, they would have to face the ruin of all their hopes. The Ibelins, moreover, were one of the 'old families'—that group of baronial landowners which was becoming increasingly exclusive in outlook. Naturally they resented it when Manasses, a *homo novus* who had been kept on the sidelines, succeeded in entering the group only ten years after his arrival—and at their expense. Fortunately for them the Ibelins had influential kinsmen among the nobility. Only against this background can we understand the full significance of William of Tyre's explanation of the cause of the final break between Baldwin III and his mother: the dissatisfaction of the barons with the supposedly arrogant regime of Manasses. Undoubtedly the constable's marriage to Helvis added considerably to his power—and that, in fact, is all that William of Tyre tells us about it. He does not say, although these are the conclusions which modern historians have drawn, that the marriage formed the basis of his power or that it enabled him to count upon the support of the Ibelins.

Manasses had been constable since 1143 but cannot have married Helvis until 1150 at the earliest. In 1152 he was brought down. For this reason alone it is clear that the marriage to Helvis came too late to have been the basis of his power.

By early 1152 the opposition to Melisende and Manasses was sufficiently well organized for Baldwin III to make his move. He requested the patriarch to crown him for a second time at Easter without, at the same time, crowning his mother. To the assembled people this would have made it clear that Baldwin was now the sole ruler. Although urgently required in the interests of the state, such a ceremony would have undermined joint rule and thus Melisende's rights. Predictably the patriarch denied the request. On the surface it seemed as though Baldwin backed down but then he tricked the patriarch by appearing in public on Easter Monday in full regalia, wearing a crown, and without his mother. This amounted to a *casus belli*. When, immediately after this, the Haute Cour met, a compromise was worked out in the shape of a formal partition of the kingdom. That the king was already in the stronger position is clear from the fact that he had the right to choose his share first. He took Tyre and Acre, while Melisende received Jerusalem and Nablus. The real loser was the unpopular Manasses who had to yield his office as constable to Humphrey II of Toron.

But the partition was political nonsense and it lasted for only three weeks. Baldwin now switched to open war. He chased Manasses from Mirabel and forced him into exile. Next he dislodged his mother from the largely unfortified town of Nablus. Then he besieged the citadel of Jerusalem where, since shortly before 1150, the royal palace was situated (on property now occupied by the police station). Finally Melisende was forced to surrender the city and from then on was denied all right to take an active part in government. All that remained of her undeniable rights from joint rule was Nablus with the royal demesne in Samaria. Here she was able to live in a manner which befitted her station. The king solemnly promised to leave her undisturbed in these possessions, and he kept his promise until shortly before she died in 1161. From Nablus she still exercised a certain influence over appointments to Church offices. At any rate it was a kitchen cabinet of high ranking ladies, Melisende, her sister Hodierna of Tripoli, and a countess of Flanders living in Bethany as a nun, which, in 1157, secured the election of Amalric of Nesle, Melisende's chaplain from before 1143, to be patriarch of Jerusalem. From now on Baldwin III ruled alone but the civil war was hardly a good omen for the future and cannot have helped to enhance the authority of the royal family.

Baldwin III was a tall young man with fair hair and a thick beard. He had an unusually quick intelligence and a remarkable eloquence. He had been carefully educated and was much praised for his good manners, for the courtesy which he showed to all, for his military prowess, his legal knowledge, his preference for historical reading, and his pleasure in discussion. He was clearly of no more than average piety and even a favourably disposed observer like William of Tyre could not overlook his passion for dice and other games of chance as well as a certain sexual licence up until the time of his marriage.

As so often, Baldwin III's first task after his second 'coronation' was to march north where he and Melisende had to compose a marital discord between Raymond II of Tripoli and his wife Hodierna. But during the king's visit to Tripoli, Count Raymond was murdered by Assassins (1152). Baldwin persuaded the barons of Tripoli to do homage to the countess who would rule on behalf of her young son Raymond III (1152–87). In the following year Baldwin achieved a spectacular success in the south. By 1150 he had built a castle over the ruins of the ancient town of Gaza, thus blocking the route between the Fatimid south and Ascalon and so completing the encirlement of this town, the 'bride of Syria', which had been begun by Fulk. In January 1153 he concentrated all available forces on a siege. The garrison resisted obstinately but despite some reverses he never relaxed his pressure and on 19 August the fortress surrendered on condition that the garrison had three days in which to leave in safety. The plunder was enormous and the king rewarded his men magnificently with land and money fiefs. About 1154 he restored the county of Jaffa to his brother Amalric who had lost it in the wake of the civil war of 1152 because he had remained loyal to Melisende to the end. The king now added the city and district of Ascalon to Amalric's fief. From now on the double county Jaffa-Ascalon was the largest crown fief. Although it has been argued that the double county may have been regarded as two distinct and separable lordships, practically all the evidence points to it being considered an inseparable unit, even though, for purposes of administration, like other great crown fiefs, it was subdivided into two vicecomital districts, Jaffa and Ascalon. It was not just for the sake of family politics that Amalric was enfeoffed with the double county. As early as 1123, in anticipation of a conquest of Ascalon then under discussion, Hugh II of Jaffa had acted as though he expected to become lord of the city. In that year he had granted the great mosque of Ascalon, an important Shi'ite shrine, to the abbey of St. Mary Josaphat. It looks as though he may have withdrawn this claim in 1126 but in fact with the help of his constable Barisan the Old he was quietly laying the foundations for a feudal structure in this area. If Baldwin II and Hugh had come to an understanding that Ascalon and Jaffa would be united, then, regardless of Hugh's own downfall in 1134 (see above, p. 83f.), it had to be carried out once Ascalon was captured. The great mosque now became the cathedral of St. Paul and a canon of the Church of the Holy Sepulchre was elected bishop. But soon afterwards the bishop of Bethlehem protested about this to the pope; the new bishop had to stand down. Most likely

Bethlehem-Ascalon was, from now on, a double bishopric held by one bishop in personal union, but it is possible that Ascalon became just a parish in the see of Bethlehem. Although this would have reversed the ecclesiastical order of pre-crusade days, it would at least be in accord with a judgement made by a papal legate in 1108.

While the siege of Ascalon was still going on, Constance of Antioch suddenly decided to remarry. However, she chose not one of the politically suitable candidates but Reynald of Châtillon. He was handsome and recklessly brave, but he had no means, no followers, and no political common sense. To the end of his days he remained a dare-devil adventurer never able to measure and take account of the significance or the consequences of his actions.[57] Baldwin III was badly advised when he gave his approval to the match. Very soon after the wedding Reynald revealed the brutal side of his nature when he arrested the patriarch of Antioch and then had his face covered with honey before leaving him to the mercy of the Syrian sun and the flies. Vigorous representations by Baldwin III forced Reynald to restore the patriarch to his office but, not surprisingly, the latter decided that it was safer for him to live in Jerusalem.

The capture of Ascalon was undoubtedly a great achievement. The whole coast was now held by the Franks; the last Fatimid fortress in Palestine had fallen. It was easier now to forget about the difficulties in the north. But in a sense it was a Pyrrhic victory. Ever since Fulk's reign Ascalon had not represented a serious threat to Jerusalem. But once it had fallen the way seemed open for expansion to the south where Egypt, rich and with few fortified cities, was a tempting prospect for the would-be conqueror. The kings of Jerusalem yielded to this temptation. In doing so they not only drew valuable resources away from the defence of the north, they also provoked Nur ed-Din and, after him, Saladin to intervene in the affairs of Egypt. The end result was the fatal encirclement of Jerusalem by a united Islamic empire. Some of the other consequences very soon became clear. In equipping his army Baldwin III had incurred debts on a scale which diminished his freedom of political manoeuvre. Thus although both the treaty of 1139 and Frankish self-interest demanded that he should help Damascus against Nur ed-Din's final attack in 1154, he was in fact unable to do anything effective. He had to watch the creation of the menacing union between Damascus and Aleppo and was content when Nur ed-Din, in order to consolidate his gains, made a truce and ordered that the tribute formerly paid by Damascus should be continued. Even so, in the following years, there were frequent clashes between the Franks and Nur ed-Din, especially in the neighbourhood of Banyas below the castle of Subeibe. Town and castle controlled not only important roads in north Palestine but also the headwaters of the Jordan and, consequently, the water rights which were the life-blood of a rich agricultural region.

During this period Syrian affairs came to the forefront once again. Fortunately for both the Franks and the Byzantines Nur ed-Din fell dangerously ill in October 1157. He made arrangements for the succession but they were not sufficient to prevent a political crisis from developing, particularly in Aleppo where the Shi'ites rebelled against the Sunnite authorities. The revolt was quelled when the sick ruler intervened in person, but for a while there were signs that his army was breaking up. Nur ed-Din lived but his convalescence was a long one and afterwards he never again showed that warlike energy which had characterized the early part of his career. Reynald of Antioch took advantage of the situation and with support from Baldwin III and Count Thierry of Flanders who was on a visit to the Holy Land, he was able, in February 1158, to recapture the fortress of Harenc which protected Antiochene territory east of the Orontes.

Generally, however, it looked as though the prince of Antioch was doing everything he could to make himself disliked. In particular he had angered both the Byzantine emperor and King Baldwin by combining with the Armenian prince, Thoros, to attack the rich Byzantine island of Cyprus in 1156. For three weeks the troops of Antioch indulged in an orgy of destruction, murder, and rapine. This was the first occasion on which it became clear that, in Reynald's eyes, greed for plunder prevailed over every reasonable consideration. Reynald's behaviour persuaded the king of Jerusalem to seek an alliance with Byzantium. In 1157 he began the negotiations which ended, in September 1158, with the magnificent wedding between Baldwin and Manuel's young niece, Theodora, whose rich dowry gave the king temporary relief from his financial embarrassment. The terms of the alliance were that Baldwin would agree to the humbling of Reynald of Antioch in return for receiving Manuel's help against Nur ed-Din. In autumn 1158 the imperial army began its march. The Armenians of Cilicia were taken completely by surprise and Prince Thoros only just had time to flee to the mountains. Reynald did not wait for the arrival of the far superior Byzantine army. He went to meet Manuel at Mamistra in Lesser Armenia. Barefoot and bareheaded he threw himself at the emperor's feet, begging for mercy. He had to promise to instal a Greek patriarch and hand over the citadel of Antioch. Soon afterwards Manuel and Baldwin met for the first time and even the emperor was won over by the king's charm and diplomatic skill. He agreed to be reconciled with Thoros and to say nothing more about an Orthodox patriarch in Antioch. Then on 12 April 1159 Manuel made a triumphal entry into the city. A week later Manuel marched out again, but only to conclude a truce with Nur ed-Din and not, as the Franks had hoped, to make war against Aleppo. The terms of the truce, however, speak volumes for Byzantine statesmanship. There were advantages for all the parties to it—even for the Franks who believed that they had been betrayed. Nur ed-

Din was freed from the immediate threat of an attack by Manuel; Manuel won Nur ed-Din's support for a campaign against a far more dangerous enemy of the empire, the Seldjuks of Anatolia. Manuel moreover had achieved his aims in Cilicia and, although no Byzantine administration was set up in Antioch, he had established a preponderance in north Syria which was to last almost twenty years. But this discreet Byzantine influence would not have lasted long without Nur ed-Din's constant pressure on Antioch forcing the Franks to accept an imperial protectorate. Manuel had created a complicated balance of power system which would work just so long as Nur ed-Din did not destroy the crusader states. He had demonstrated that in an emergency he could intervene most effectively on the side of the Franks. The imperial campaign had been sufficient to convince Nur ed-Din of this fact and herein lay the advantage for the Franks. At very little cost in terms of human lives Manuel had brought about a new status quo in north Syria which was to last until 1176. The Franks understood the situation; when Nur ed-Din campaigned against the Seldjuks of Anatolia they kept their military operations on a small scale and made no serious attack on his Syrian bases so as not to disturb the Byzantine balance of power system. In one skirmish in 1160 Reynald of Antioch was captured. He remained a prisoner of the governor of Aleppo for the next sixteen years. No one exerted himself to raise the money for his ransom.

Once again arrangements had to be made for the government of Antioch and the barons turned, as they had become accustomed to do, to Jerusalem, not to their new overlord Manuel. Baldwin entrusted the government to the newly returned Patriarch Aimery, passing over the claims of Princess Constance. Obviously this settlement pleased neither Constance nor the Byzantine emperor. The latter was, at this time, negotiating a new marriage; his first wife, Bertha of Sulzbach, had died in 1159. Baldwin, not wishing to see a further increase in Byzantine influence in Antioch, proposed that the emperor should marry Melisende of Tripoli but, after hesitating for a year, Manuel decided in favour of Maria of Antioch, whose mother, Constance, had appealed to him against Baldwin's arrangement. Although, as a result, Baldwin III had to fear a strengthening of Byzantine claims on Antioch, he was in no position to oppose Manuel's choice; the alliance with Byzantium was now vital to Jerusalem as that with Damascus had once been. But not until 1163 was the governmental crisis in Antioch finally settled. In that year the barons drove Constance out of the city and installed her son, Bohemund III (1163–1201).

By this time Baldwin III was already dead. He was taken ill during a visit to Tripoli in 1162. When he realized that he was unlikely to recover he moved on to Beirut in order to end his days in his own kingdom. On 10 February 1163 he died. The funeral cortège took a week to reach

Jerusalem and even the non-Christian population is supposed to have mourned the dead king as his body passed slowly by. He was buried next to his forefathers in the Church of the Holy Sepulchre. For more than ten years he had steered his kingdom with great diplomatic skill between the Muslim enemy on the one side and the occasionally overbearing power of his Byzantine ally on the other. In September 1161 his mother Melisende had died after a long illness. She was buried at St. Mary Josaphat near the Tomb of the Virgin. But it is possible that this decision was made by the king and that she herself had wanted to be buried with the canons of the *Templum Domini* in the Dome of the Rock. Certainly she was lavish with her donations to the canons whereas the monks at Josaphat hardly got anything. If this was her intention, then she would have had a much more splendid mausoleum than the kings themselves had at the Holy Sepulchre, so Baldwin would have had good reason to thwart her hopes. But her named lived on in her religious foundations and in the magnificent Melisende Psalter in the British Library. Its fine miniatures are a striking testimony to the artistic heights attained in the scriptorium at Jerusalem.

Baldwin died childless and was therefore succeeded by his younger brother, Amalric, now twenty-seven years of age and formerly count of Jaffa and Ascalon. In spite of the fact that Baldwin, on his deathbed, had designated his brother as his successor, the succession was, in fact, hotly debated among the nobility. The reasons for this are not entirely clear nor is it known who the opposition proposed as an alternative. In the end hereditary right prevailed only because the Church strongly supported Amalric. But the price he had to pay was his separation from his wife Agnes of Courtenay, the daughter of Joscelin II of Edessa. He was related to her in the fourth degree. Later on she was to become the *femme fatale* of the Latin East and it may be that there were already objections to her lifestyle. The patriarch had vehemently opposed the marriage in 1157 so there could be no question of a dispensation at this stage. Amalric gave way when he was assured of the continuing legitimacy of his two children, Sibylla and Baldwin IV. Then, before the opposition to him could gather momentum he was 'suddenly'—as William of Tyre puts it—anointed and crowned. Against custom the ceremony took place on a Monday, and not on one of the major festivals of the Church.[58] In some ways there was a superficial resemblance between him and his elder brother. He had the same aquiline nose and blonde hair, though this was already beginning to recede. He too was extremely well-versed in law and enjoyed reading histories. Indeed he was the patron who persuaded William of Tyre to become court historian and to write his famous chronicle, and it was he who provided William with the works of Arab historians with the help of which the archbishop of Tyre wrote a chronicle—now unfortunately lost—of the Islamic states from the time of Muhammad. But otherwise the new king was very different from the old. He was of medium height and unusually fat—despite taking care not to eat or drink excessively. He was less well-educated than his brother, taciturn, introverted, unsociable, and troubled by a slight stammer. If he took little pleasure in gambling he made up for this by his taste for amorous adventures. William of Tyre accuses him of avarice and of oppressing the Church by his financial demands. Certainly he appreciated the need for a full treasury, but he was clearly not over-scrupulous in the methods he used to keep it well filled—as he once disarmingly remarked to William, the possessions of the subject were safe only when the ruler himself had enough. Money was vital if the strength of the kingdom was to be maintained; often enough already royal policies had been vitiated by its lack. Amalric had no intention of suffering in this way but occasionally—and unfortunately—he gave the acquisition of money an unreasonably high place in the priorities of his foreign policy. He was pious in a formal sense of the word—he seldom missed mass—but he deeply shocked his chronicler by expressing serious doubts about the resurrection of the body and by demanding to see some concrete proof of it.

In the realm of domestic policy Amalric was an outstanding legislator. That he was also a strong-minded judge is shown by the vigorous stand he took against the Military Orders. He played an active part in the great Hospitaller crisis of 1171–2 and it was from him that the Master sought permission to resign. Without hesitation and regardless of the order's claim, based on papal privileges, to be exempt from all secular jurisdiction, he had twelve Templars hanged in 1165 for surrendering a castle east of the Jordan. Towards the end of his reign he even seems to have been prepared for a showdown over this principle (see below, p. 123). His introduction of special courts to handle cases of commercial and maritime law worked well. In the 1160s he promulgated the famous *Assise sur la ligece* which, by means of an oath, brought the sub-tenants to recognize the king as their liege-lord, i.e. to recognize that the lord king's needs had priority over the needs of their own immediate lord. This assise was once thought to represent a vigorous attempt by the king to use the lesser vassals as a counterweight to the higher nobility, but today it is clear that it in fact marks the breakthrough of the higher nobility into fields formerly reserved to the authority of the crown (see below, p. 159).

Amalric's foreign policy was dominated by the assault on Egypt.[59] This was a policy which offered not only distraction from the reverses in the north but also the chance to furnish the cash resources which were urgently required by a royal demesne which was already becoming impoverished. After the capture of Ascalon such opportunities no longer existed within Palestine. Baldwin III had already prepared the way for this policy when, in 1156, he and the Pisans agreed to place an embargo on the import of timber, iron, and pitch (all ship-building materials) into Egypt. The result, of course, was that smuggling took the place of legitimate trade and neither the threat of the death penalty (in the thirteenth-century legislation of Jerusalem) nor the constantly repeated papal prohibitions were able to put a stop to it. Probably Baldwin's marriage to the Byzantine princess Theodora in 1157 should also be seen as an aspect of his policy towards Egypt. Certainly he discussed the conquest of Egypt in 1159 with Emperor Manuel I Comnenus. Prawer believes that Baldwin envisaged a 'Grand Alliance' of all the Christian powers of the Near East from Byzantium to Jerusalem, with the aim of eliminating Nur ed-Din and conquering Egypt. It was a sign of his serious intent that he promised to grant an Egyptian seignory of 100 knights to one of his ambassadors to Byzantium.

As count of Jaffa and Ascalon Amalric's attention had naturally been drawn to Egypt. The inexhaustible wealth of its natural resources exerted a tremendous attraction. There was the highly developed agriculture of the Nile Valley. There were fisheries, indigo deposits, and alum mines which facilitated the dyeing processes of an efficient textile industry (silk, linen, and cotton). Like much else these mines were a state monopoly. Soap, ointments, and ivory were also produced. Even greater profits were to be had from the trade in Sudanese slaves and from the control exercised over the transit of goods between India on the one side and Byzantium and the West on the other. By way of contrast the Egyptian political scene was in a state of disarray. The Fatimid dynasty had long since suffered the fate of all caliph dynasties; it had become a degenerate plaything in the hands of powerful viziers, two of whom Dirgham and Shawar, were at this moment engaged in a fierce power struggle. The bureaucracy was unusually well-developed, the system of financial administration being so complicated that right up until the nineteenth century it could only be understood by Coptic officials who were looked upon as bloodsuckers by the fellahin and as swindlers by the rulers of Egypt. It was clear that Nur ed-Din could easily become Amalric's rival in this part of the world. After 1158 when Syria was neutralized, Egypt was bound to become the decisive arena in the struggle between Franks and Muslims. Thus in 1163 Shawar, after having been driven out of the country by Dirgham, turned for help to Nur ed-Din. Nur ed-Din hesitated at first since he had problems enough in Syria, but finally decided to send an army under his Kurdish general Shirkuh into Egypt. Shawar was restored to power but immediately quarrelled with Shirkuh and had to seek a new ally, King Amalric of Jerusalem. Amalric had already made a brief entry into Egypt in 1163 and now, in 1164, he besieged Shirkuh in Bilbeis in Lower Egypt. Shirkuh's position began to look perilous so Nur ed-Din, feeling that the equilibrium in the Near East had been disturbed, launched a big offensive against the Syrian crusader states. In August 1164 at Artah he decisively defeated a joint army from Antioch and Tripoli, capturing both Bohemund III of Antioch and Raymond of Tripoli. Bohemund was soon released but Raymond stayed in prison for about ten years while Amalric governed Tripoli as regent. The fortress of Harenc again fell to the Muslims and the frontier of Antioch was pushed back to the line of the Orontes, this time for good. But in order not to provoke Byzantium Nur ed-Din did not seize the opportunity to attack the city itself. However in capturing Banyas and its fortress of Subeibe in 1164, he made a dangerous hole in the eastern frontier of the kingdom of Jerusalem. An unsuccessful attempt to recapture them after Nur ed-Din's death was to be King Amalric's last deed. But for the moment Nur ed-Din's offensive achieved its strategic as well as its tactical purpose when Amalric and Shirkuh came to terms and withdrew from Egypt.

In the following years Nur ed-Din forced the remaining semi-independent petty princes of Muslim Syria to recognize his authority. Then in 1167 he gave Shirkuh permission to lead another expedition into Egypt. If Amalric was to maintain the balance of power he also had to advance into Egypt. The Haute Cour met at Nablus. Amalric was unable to obtain a formal vote for a war beyond the kingdom's frontiers. This would have committed all vassals to military service. None the less he was able to persuade the Haute Cour to meet the costs of a campaign by levying a special 10 per cent tax on movable property belonging to the Church and to those vassals who chose not to follow the king into Egypt. The Frankish army then marched to the Nile and Shawar gladly agreed to an alliance with the aim of destroying Shirkuh. In return he promised to pay Amalric 400,000 gold dinars. Hugh of Caesarea who negotiated this treaty on behalf of the Franks insisted that it should be ratified by the caliph. So the Frankish envoys were taken to the palace in Cairo where they were amazed by the magnificent courtyards with their fishponds and aviaries. It is an eloquent testimony to the presumptuous self-confidence of the Franks at this time that Hugh demanded that he and the caliph should seal the treaty by shaking hands. This was bad enough in the eyes of the Muslim courtiers but their indignation knew no bounds when Hugh expressed dissatisfaction with the unwillingly proffered gloved hand and insisted on the caliph removing his glove.

After suffering some initial setbacks in Upper Egypt the allies succeeded in besieging Shirkuh in Alexandria and forcing him to make peace. Shirkuh and Amalric again agreed to leave Egypt thus restoring the *status quo ante*. But the Franks had gained a good deal. The alliance with Shawar was kept in being in return for an annual tribute of 100,000 dinars. The royal standard flew from the lighthouse at Alexandria and a Frankish garrison remained in Cairo. Egypt had become a kind of Frankish protectorate.

It ought to have been possible to maintain this state of affairs for some time since, as long as Egypt was not annexed, it involved no real loss of face for Nur ed-Din. But immediately after his return from Egypt Amalric strengthened the alliance with Byzantium by marrying the emperor's great niece, Maria Comnena. After long negotiations this marriage and Maria's coronation were performed with undue haste in Tyre rather than in the capital for, in the short space of time between his return from Egypt and the marriage, Amalric had admitted the Byzantine adventurer—later Emperor—Andronicus Comnenus into the Latin Kingdom and had enfeoffed him with Beirut. Andronicus had frequently given offence to the government in Constantinople and had embarrassed the Byzantine court with his many inopportune love affairs. Before fleeing from the wrath of the Emperor to Palestine he had embezzled the public funds of Cyprus and Byzantine Cilicia. This cannot have failed to attract the ever-greedy Amalric to him. On the other hand, he risked forfeiting his bride's very substantial dowry and, indeed, the whole marriage if news of his harbouring Andronicus leaked out before the wedding had taken place. Byzantium might at least have cut Maria's dowry by the sum of what Andronicus had embezzled elsewhere. That the whole arrangement was a delicate one is shown not only by the fact that the deal had been negotiated for two full years and was then concluded hastily in an inappropriate location, but also by the circumstance that, contrary to all custom, Maria was first crowned and then married to Amalric. It seems that the government in Constantinople insisted on this sequence of events to make sure that Maria would not remain uncrowned. Earlier, in 1165, Bohemund III of Antioch had married one of Manuel's nieces and had installed a Greek patriarch. The Latin patriarch was driven into exile and stayed there until the Greek was buried in the ruins of Antioch cathedral as the result of an earthquake in 1170. Amalric, his confidence bolstered by a formal treaty of alliance with Byzantium, believed that he could now conquer Egypt and so he embarked on a new adventure—no other description will fit the expedition of 1168. He did not bother to wait for the arrival of the Byzantine fleet which was essential if Egypt was to be blockaded from the sea. Instead he allowed himself to be persuaded by the militants among the members of the Haute Cour that the terms of 1167 had been too lenient to the Egyptians. Following their advice he launched a premature attack. William of Tyre returned from Constantinople, having successfully negotiated the treaty, only to find that the army had already left (October 1168). In their imaginations the Franks had already divided the spoils of Egypt. The Hospitallers, the leaders of the war-party, had promised themselves rich pickings, while the Templars had refused to take part—either out of loyalty to the treaty with Shawar or on account of their financial interests in Egypt. In desperation Shawar turned to Shirkuh for help and meanwhile employed a scorched earth policy to gain time. In November the Franks captured Bilbeis and then besieged Cairo. But they were unable to bring Shirkuh's relieving army to battle and so Amalric decided to call off his attack. He could not have annexed Egypt;

there were just not enough Latins for it to be possible to rule Egypt as thoroughly as the crusader states. And while no decisive success could ever be achieved in Egypt, the expansionist policy in this direction meant that Amalric had turned his back on what Prawer has rightly called the 'Golden Rule' of Jerusalem's foreign policy. This was the policy of ensuring that the northern crusader states were kept in existence so that they could stand as bulwarks in defence of Jerusalem. In accordance with this principle, the kings of Jerusalem had, up until *c.*1150, gone north time and again either at the head of an army or to supervise the arrangements for a regency. It is true that the neutralization of north Syria by Byzantium meant that significant alterations in the military and political structure of this region were now out of the question, none the less it should still have been possible for Jerusalem to provide the northern principalities with a certain amount of protection. But now, with so much effort being expended on the southern frontiers, the Golden Rule of yesterday was forgotten.

On 2 January 1169 Shirkuh marched into Cairo. At once he had his old enemy Shawar killed and took over the post of vizier himself. When he died two months later he was succeeded in that office by his nephew Saladin (Al-Malik al-Nasir Salah ed-Din Yusuf, 1169–93).[60] The fact that he was the fifth vizier of Egypt in only six years, is a revealing indication of the state of political confusion in which the Fatimid caliphate found itself. Saladin was to be the most terrible opponent that the Franks had to face. In the thirteenth century Sultan Baibars was as fierce an enemy but he never enjoyed the same universal respect within Islam. Saladin was born into a Kurdish officer family. He grew up in Baalbek where his father Ayub—the dynasty became known as the Ayubids—was governor. At first there seemed nothing to suggest a career out of the ordinary. The young officer was distinguished chiefly by his skill at polo. From 1152 he served in the household of Nur ed-Din and then assisted his uncle Shirkuh in the latter's Egyptian campaigns. Only after his appointment as vizier did he reveal what was in him. He at once consolidated his power by destroying the Egyptian-Sudanese army and building up his own military organization. He had an impressive citadel built in Cairo to defend the city against a possible Frankish assault. In 1169 he beat off an attack on Damietta even though this time the Franks were supported by a Byzantine fleet. This campaign, Amalric's fifth in Egypt, ended in disaster. Co-operation between the Christian allies was pathetic and finally, by secretly negotiating with Damietta, Amalric deliberately sabotaged the campaign himself. This was not, as Lilie suggests, because he was opposed in principle to a joint conquest of Egypt. He certainly wanted Byzantine aid, but in 1169 Byzantine naval support, consisting of an overwhelming 200 vessels, was simply too much of a good thing: a stifling embrace.[61] In his Egyptian campaigns Amalric showed himself to be a very skilful financier (see below, p. 170), but resources were now exhausted and this necessarily meant the end of expansion. There was, it is true, an attempt to mobilize the resources of the West in 1169. This involved an offer of the keys of Jerusalem being made in Paris, but although clearly meant as an invitation to the king of France to accept the status of suzerain over the Christian Near East, this and other similar attempts came to nothing as a result of the perennial tension between the Capetian and Angevin rulers.

In 1170 Saladin took his revenge for the attack on Damietta. He recaptured Gaza from the Latins and also Aila, their port on the Red Sea. He marched up the Nile and also into Arabia and the Yemen, thus securing Egypt's hegemony in the Red Sea area and over the trade routes to East Asia. After some initial hesitation he made an end of the Fatimid dynasty in September 1171 when he ordered that the Abbasid caliphs of Baghdad should be mentioned in the Friday prayers. Thus the unity of Sunnite orthodoxy was restored. The fact that there was no popular reaction to this order shows that Shi'ite doctrine had made little impression on the people of Egypt. Formally he still remained vizier, under the overlordship of Nur ed-Din, but in practice Saladin was sultan of Egypt. This inevitably led to tension with Nur ed-Din who, in 1171, added Mosul and Mesopotamia to the territories under his sway. Each of them looked upon his own area of influence as the real centre of Islam. Saladin refused to allow Nur ed-Din to treat Egypt merely as a source of money with which to finance his Syrian wars. The question was still unsettled when fate decided it in Saladin's favour. On 15 May 1174 Nur ed-Din died in Damascus. He had lived in a simple style and as he grew older he spent more time on pious exercises. His countenance was severe and he rarely laughed. After a century in which Syria had been ruled by the nomadic Seldjuks he had done much to strengthen the economy of the country. But his great achievement was his political and religious revival of Islam and his application of the *Jihad* idea to the war against the Franks. Even the Latin historian, William of Tyre, had to respect him.

On 11 July 1174, two months after Nur ed-Din's death, King Amalric died of dysentery. In 1171 he had enjoyed a splendid reception in Constantinople. It is far from clear but not altogether impossible that he recognized Manuel as some kind of feudal suzerain.[62] Seemingly the king had still been entertaining dreams of conquest in Egypt and only with Byzantine help could they be realized. This may have been why his visit had been so controversial in Jerusalem. The king had tricked his council, first securing a decision on the basic question of sending an embassy to Byzantium, and only then explaining to an astonished Haute Cour, that he was the only appropriate ambassador for so important a mission. Perhaps his council feared that at Constantinople he might be prepared to accept an unwelcome degree of political subservience. But however this may be it is clear that Manuel was unusually active in Palestinian affairs at this time. He had the Church of the Holy Sepulchre repaired and he ordered new mosaics for the Church of the Nativity at Bethlehem. In 1173 an Orthodox archbishop suddenly appeared at Gaza and a community of Orthodox priests at the Holy Sepulchre, to which the Orthodox faithful had been readmitted some ten years earlier. At about this time the ceremonial dress of the kings of Jerusalem was remodelled on the style of the court dress of the Byzantine emperor, so that Eustathius of Thessalonica criticized the king for improperly setting himself up as an emperor. (It is significant that this fashion was dropped after the fall of Constantinople in 1204.) Quite simply, Amalric was dependent upon Byzantium. As a ruler he had lacked any special gift of foresight but he had been an indefatigable fighter. In internal affairs he had ruled with as strong a hand as circumstances permitted. In his later years he was preoccupied by the problem of the Assassins. They had first made their presence felt in Syria at Aleppo under Ridwan but a Sunnite reaction after Ridwan's death in 1113 very largely—though not completely till 1124—brought their influence there to an end. In 1125 Toghtekin allowed them a foothold in Damascus but he went further in Upper Galilee, ceding them the fortress of Banyas. It was their standard practice to demand a castle and then use it as a base from which to launch their terrorist campaigns. When Toghtekin died the Assassins in Damascus found themselves the victims of a bloodbath just as they had in Aleppo. They were forced to surrender Banyas with its vital control over the headwaters of the Jordan to the Franks. In 1132 they purchased the castle of Qadmus. This marked their permanent establishment in the mountainous and impassable region east of Tortosa. Reaching out from Qadmus they acquired rather than built more fortresses, among them, in 1141, Masyaf, their principal Syrian stronghold, until they controlled the whole mountain range. William of Tyre numbered them at 60,000 and their fortresses at ten. Hitherto they had only murdered within Islam but in 1152 they assassinated' the count of Tripoli who had established the Hospitallers as a check on their southern flank in 1144. Perhaps because of their hostility to the Hospitallers, they came to look to the Templars for protection; they paid an annual tribute of 2,000 gold pieces to the new Templar fortress at Tortosa. After 1169 they were led by an energetic sheikh, Rashid ed-Din Sinan (d. 1193), better known as 'The Old Man of the Mountain', who was very satisfactorily described by Hodgson as a 'one-man-show'.[63] He attempted to form an alliance with Amalric of Jerusalem against the Sunnite Nur ed-Din[64] provided that the tribute be remitted. Negotiations promised well. Then in 1173 some Templars murdered the Assassins' envoys while they were on their way home. Amalric had no hesitation in using force to arrest the murderer and he then had him punished although this was a breach of the Order's privilege which made its members justiciable only by the pope. Amalric is even supposed to have considered dissolving the Order. Nevertheless, taken all in all, his superficially brilliant reign carried within it the seeds of internal decay.

Amalric's heir was a thirteen-year-old boy who was already seriously ill. It did not augur well for Jerusalem's future. The Syrian north was still suffering from the effects of the terrible earthquake of 1170 which had reduced Antioch and Tripoli to rubble. Then, to cap it all, Byzantium met with a catastrophic reversal. In 1176 Manuel Comnenus was completely routed by the Anatolian Seldjuks at Myriocephalum in Phrygia. In the aftermath of defeat it soon became clear that only an overstrained economy had made Manuel's brilliant foreign policy possible. Without exaggeration it can be said that the Battle of Myriocephalum—comparable in its results to the Battle of Manzikert in 1071—decided the fate of Outremer. Anatolia was finally lost to the Seldjuks, the Byzantine position in Cilicia and Syria was thus completely undermined, the ingenious balance of power system was finished, and the Franks had lost their protector. There were no other allies to be had, especially since a joint Sicilian–Frankish expedition to Alexandria in 1174 had failed owing to Saladin's energy and inadequate Frankish support. Unless help came from the West, the crusader states now stood entirely alone. And the more Saladin consolidated his position the greater the danger to the existence of the Frankish states.

After Nur ed-Din's death the Zengid empire rapidly broke up. A group of Nur ed-Din's officers became rivals, each struggling to be the guardian of his small son. In 1174 Saladin, who believed himself to be the true heir of Nur ed-Din's high-flying plans, occupied Damascus. Two years later he married Nur ed-Din's widow and was able to reach a settlement with the Zengids though this involved leaving Aleppo and Mosul in the hands of two members of that house. But the caliph now recognized Saladin as overlord of Egypt and Syria. The Frankish states were caught in a deadly encirclement and Saladin intended to take full advantage of his position to carry out the programme which Nur ed-Din had publicly proclaimed as early as 1169 when he commissioned a pulpit for the al-Aqsa mosque in Jerusalem. From then on Jerusalem's recapture was the overriding objective.

Saladin used the next few years to build up his strength. Campaigns against the Franks in 1177 and 1179 made it clear that he could not expect much help from the Zengids of Aleppo and Mosul. On the contrary they represented a permanent threat to his position. Saladin by no means gave up the fight against the Christians; none the less in the years 1179–85 he concentrated on his Muslim rivals. Until they had submitted there was no chance of a decisive war against the Franks. Against these rivals he used the same combination of diplomacy, propaganda, and armed demonstrations of his power that Nur ed-Din had used against Damascus. In 1180 he allied with the Anatolian Seldjuk sultan, Kilij Arslan II. This alliance was directed primarily against Mosul but was later to prove of great value in meeting the threat of the Third Crusade. In 1182 he prevented an imminent union of Aleppo and Mosul; in 1183 he brought Aleppo under his control. In 1185 he made a four years' truce with the Franks. This gave him the freedom of manoeuvre he needed to deal with Mosul. The opportunity was exploited at once. Mosul's firm adhesion to Saladin's system of alliances meant that the strength of his army was increased by about 6,000 men.

By 1187 he had an army of something like 12,000 cavalry. Until recently it was believed that the Turks in his army increasingly found themselves being supplanted by Kurds, but in fact Saladin was already using the system of Turkish Mameluks—and he was not the first one to do so—(see below, p. 264), though frequently with Kurdish officers in command. The quasi-feudal iqta system which was used to pay the troops created considerable problems for Saladin. Payment was made in kind as well as in cash and this meant that the payee had to remain on his estates to supervise the harvest. Thus it was very difficult to keep an army in the field for a long period of time. Overcoming this problem put a tremendous strain on Saladin's treasury and involved a highly complicated rota system between the Mesopotamian, Syrian, and Egyptian troops, as well as debasing the coinage. Since Saladin was not, in any event, a financial genius and was forced by his strict orthodoxy—his greatest political asset—to abolish all unorthodox taxes, he was almost permanently bankrupt, although his tax policies funnelled much money into private enterprise. What he had or acquired he distributed freely among his relatives and supporters, thus buying, in particular, the loyalty of his emirs. The Ayubid state which he founded was a semi-feudal family structure in which the sultan's chief vassals were the princes of the blood. Each of them had independent control over his own province, but was obliged to rule justly, to help finance the sultan's wars, and to provide troops. Each prince had his own vassals, all enjoying a limited amount of independence; below them were the iqta holders. What Saladin ruled was nothing like a unitary state; only the fact that a vizier was appointed to assist each prince enabled some uniformity of policy to be achieved. In Egypt the three main offices of the central government were the diwans for military, financial, and, most important of all, chancery affairs. Saladin, however, was a poor administrator and normally he left these matters to his brother al-Adil and to his secretary, the Qadi al-Fadil who was the head of the chancery and a kind of superminister for foreign and domestic affairs. As a general Saladin was a good tactician but a bad strategist. He was a politician through and through; his manoeuvres were successful because they were always carefully prepared and appropriate to the particular situation. He was borne up by the unshakeable conviction that he was destined to unite

Islam. In Gibb's view—a view unconvincingly attacked by Ehren-kreutz—his ultimate goal was not to drive the Christians out of the Holy Land but to re-establish the old empire of the caliphs as an expression of the rule of the revealed law. He wanted to see the end of the patent political demoralization of Islam which had already lasted far too long. He took over Nur ed-Din's political programme of a unification of all Islamic forces of the Near East under his leadership. In order to achieve this, they both relied on the idea of Jihad against the Franks and, inseparably linked with this, of the intra-Islamic struggle of Sunnites against heretical Shi'ites. Saladin enlarged even further Nur ed-Din's already powerful propaganda machine. He saw—correctly—that whether or not he succeeded would depend in large measure on the moral authority he possessed in the world of Islam. Owing to his magnanimity he became a favourite figure in the European romantic poetry of the late Middle Ages.

By 1185 the forces opposing the Franks were all in position. By skilful diplomacy Saladin had tried to isolate his intended victims from all potential allies. He built up the Egyptian fleet and at the same time tried to persuade the Italian maritime cities to transfer their trade to Egypt in order to deprive the Franks of support from this quarter. He also made diplomatic contact with Byzantium. After Manuel's death in 1180 his widow, Maria of Antioch, ruled as regent. Her policies were even more favourable to the Latins than Manuel's had been and in 1182 the tensions at Constantinople between Latins and Greeks flared up into a bloody massacre of western merchants. The Latin party was finished and a new emperor emerged, Andronicus Comnenus (1183–85), a vigorous man with an adventurous career behind him. After a short stay in Beirut (see above, p. 120) he had abducted Theodora, the widow of King Baldwin III, and with her had led a restless vagrant life at the Islamic courts of the Middle East until his submission to Manuel after Theodora had been taken prisoner by the Byzantines. As emperor, Andronicus was, of course, hostile to the Latins and so he expected the chief threat to his position to come from Europe; not so much from the Germans because the quarrel with them over 'the problem of the two emperors' belonged essentially to the realm of ideas; much more real was the threat from the Normans. In 1184 the latter drew closer to the western emperor as a result of the marriage between the Norman princess, Constance, and Barbarossa's son, Henry VI. In 1185 they sacked Thessalonica. In these circumstances Byzantium felt compelled to come to terms with Saladin (1185). This completed the isolation of the crusader states. It says much for Saladin's political skill that he was able to retain both the Byzantines and the Seldjuks of Anatolia as his allies.[65]

As Saladin's star rose so the Frankish one sank.[66] When Amalric of Jerusalem had his first marriage annulled he took care to ensure that the children of that marriage were declared legitimate. He had no more male children so he was succeeded by Baldwin IV (1174–85). William of Tyre, who was responsible for his education, gave him credit for no special qualities except perseverance, patience, and a talent for handling horses. In his childhood he became a victim of leprosy. This disease disfigured his appearance and led to an imperceptibly progressive paralysis of the limbs which eventually forced him to give up horses and take to a litter. Personally as well as politically his was to be a tragic fate. He was unable to prevent the disintegration of the kingdom into two quarrelling factions, yet he kept up a heroic struggle to maintain the authority of the crown. He must have seen all too clearly that his disease put a question mark against his suitability for royal office. Yet he did everything he could to frustrate all genuine or imagined attempts to replace him—and there were some genuine ones. The fear of being replaced became the *idée fixe* of his life and turned him into a suspicious person who tended to regard everyone as a potential anti-king. One wonders why the nobility ever accepted him as king in the first place. But William of Tyre's report on his accession has, perhaps, not been read closely enough. It would seem that one must interpret it as saying that although it was known during Amalric's lifetime that Baldwin IV was sick, the illness was not properly diagnosed until shortly before he came of age (mid-1176), i.e. after his accession. It is even possible that the few people with inside knowledge may have kept his illness secret. Thus in 1174, when Amalric's former favourite, Miles of Plancy, ruled *de facto* on the young king's behalf he was particularly criticized for hermetically isolating the king from the vassals, although doubtless there were also other reasons for this. The king was frequently compelled to appoint a regent (*bailli*), initially because he was under age, later on account of his illness. After Miles de Plancy's murder brought his unconstitutional regime to a sudden end, the first regent was the king's nearest male relative, Count Raymond III of Tripoli. As husband of Eschiva, widow of the last prince of Galilee, Raymond was also lord of Tiberias and thus, at the time, the most important vassal of the king of Jerusalem. He held office until Baldwin came of age. With iron self-restraint the thirty-four-year-old Raymond pursued a discreet, defensive policy, always looking for a settlement with the Muslims whom he had come to know well during his long captivity. He was the leader of the faction which can loosely be termed the party of the old families. Among its adherents were the constable, Humphrey II of Toron, the Ibelins, Reynald of Sidon—a man known for his fluency in Arabic—and, above all, William of Tyre. Raymond appointed him chancellor of the kingdom in 1174 and archbishop of Tyre in 1175. But after the end of Raymond's regency he was kept out of his office for some time. Not until the summer of 1177 did he return to the chancery. For a few years he was politic enough to maintain an independent position between the opposing parties. Up to 1180 he was the king's chief foreign policy adviser, representing the kingdom both at the Third Lateran Council (1179) and at the Imperial court at Constantinople. Just as he had under Amalric, he continued to advocate the policy of looking to Byzantium for support until the pogrom of 1182 made it quite impossible. The other faction was made up of more varied elements. It was dominated by the recent arrivals, men of the first generation in the Holy Land, who were anxious to find excitement and to obtain possessions. One of their leaders was Reynald of Châtillon. In 1176 he had finally been released but was unable to return to Antioch. Instead he made an advantageous marriage and acquired the important lordship of Oultrejourdain with its centre at the great fortress of Kerak. He also succeeded in detaching Hebron from the royal demesne, appearing in 1177 as the first lord of Hebron. This violated the unwritten rule that a lord of Oultrejourdain could not hold other seignories at the same time. Humphrey II of Toron must have been particularly offended since, by accepting the office of royal castellan of Hebron in 1148 and 1149, he had created the presumption that Hebron, if it ever did become a seignory, should belong to him. Reynald was joined by the brothers Aimery and Guy of Lusignan. They were restless and ambitious Poitevins who had been expelled from Poitou by Richard Coeur de Lion. Another member of the group was Joscelin III of Courtenay, titular count of Edessa (1159–1200), but a count without à county. Through sheer and unparalleled greed, he succeeded in building up the lordship known as the 'Seigneurie de Joscelin' in the region of Acre. There was also his sister, Agnes of Courtenay, who was the king's mother and the grandmother of Baldwin V. She was to exercise a particularly unfortunate influence over Baldwin IV. A chronicler said of her that she was greedy for money and loved power far too much. Until 1169 she was married to Hugh of Ibelin, her third husband, and this kept her away from politics. After Hugh's death and before 1171 she married Reynald of Sidon. This came as such a shock to the old families that Reynald's own father tried to have the marriage annulled although without success. After 1183 Reynald left his old friends and, at best, remained neutral. During Raymond III's regency Agnes's position was still a rather insignificant one, even though, as Hamilton observed, she must have returned to court as early as 1175 because in that year she obtained the election of her favourite Eraclius as archbishop of Caesarea; *les mauvaises langues* spoke of a love affair between them. After Raymond retired from office, she saw to it that her own influence and that of her camarilla, usually referred to by historians as the 'court party', was to grow quickly. In 1176, after having raised the money to secure her brother Joscelin III's release from captivity, she then obtained his appointment as seneschal of Jerusalem. In 1177 the marriage between Maria Comnena, the widow of King Amalric, and Barisan the Younger, the youngest of the Ibelin brothers, increased her standing at the court because this marriage meant that Maria was no longer queen dowager. The powerful constable, Humphrey II of Toron, though he remained in office, seems, like William of Tyre in 1176–7, to have been squeezed out. At all events, during the course of 1176 Humphrey, who had previously been omnipresent, vanishes from the witness lists of royal charters. Not until February 1179 did he surface again, when he participated in an important *finalis concordia* between the Templars and the Hospitallers. Only for part of this time can his absence be explained by a severe illness. In the meantime the command of the army was taken over by Reynald of Châtillon. But when in April 1179 there was heavy fighting near Banyas, Humphrey was present. There, with his customary loyalty, he saved the life of the leper king, receiving wounds which cost him his own. It was a heavy loss for the kingdom. Agnes saw to it that he was succeeded by Aimery of Lusignan, and once again gossip spoke of an affair. In a disputed election in 1180 Agnes secured the appointment of Eraclius of Caesarea (d. *c.* 1190) as patriarch of Jerusalem against the candidature of William of Tyre. For a long time Eraclius was condemned as a man lacking all moral principles but in recent years various writers have rehabilitated him. Like William of Tyre he studied law at Bologna. Doubt has been cast on the story that he kept the wife of a merchant of Nablus as his mistress. On the other hand he certainly offended European puritans when, as ambassador, he displayed great luxury in dress, jewels, and perfume, 'such as befuddles the brain' (wrote Ralf Niger). William of Tyre, however, was more and more pushed out of policy-making. In spite of all his diplomatic experience it was not he but Joscelin III who was sent as ambassador to Constantinople in 1180. In February 1183 he was appointed one of thirteen keepers of the special defence tax collected then but in March 1183 he officiated as chancellor for the last time. That Eraclius had him poisoned in Rome, is a demonstrably false slander. But it is possible that he excommunicated him in the summer of 1183 after the court party won a great victory in securing the appointment of Guy of Lusignan as regent. Such a step by the patriarch would have had the effect of ending, at least for a while, William's capacity to conduct the affairs of both the chancery and the archbishopric of Tyre. It would have forced him to appeal to the pope and thus would have taken him out of the country and out of politics. He died on 29 September 1186.

The election of 1180 completed the line-up of the parties. The greater part of the clergy now took the side of the patriarch and the Lusignans, undoubtedly in part because the king had clashed with the bishops on account of his miserliness towards the Church. The contrast with the generosity of his predecessors could hardly be more strikingly illustrated than by the fact that he, the leper king, did not even make a gift to St. Lazarus, the Jerusalem convent for lepers. After 1186 the Military Orders increasingly came over to the court party's side because the Master of the Templars, Gerard of Ridfort, had a bitter personal grudge against

Raymond III of Tripoli who had earlier—before Gerard's entry into the Order—refused to allow him to marry the rich heiress of one of his vassals. Since Baldwin IV was unable to marry, consideration of the succession question focused at first on his sister Sibylla. Raymond III as regent had arranged for her to marry William Longsword, marquis of Montferrat, and this gave William control of his wife's county of Jaffa-Ascalon. This (had he lived and remembered his debt of gratitude to Raymond), added to Raymond's own principality of Galilee, would have doubled the count of Tripoli's power base in the kingdom. But William died in 1177 leaving Sibylla pregnant. Their son was the future King Baldwin V. In 1177, before the child was born, the count of Flanders arrived in the Holy Land. In a series of confusing and erratic moves he brought to naught the renewed project of a joint Byzantine–Frankish conquest of Egypt. He also proposed Sibylla's re-marriage to a son of the advocate of Béthune but refused to reveal the identity of his candidate. Consequently it was easy for William of Tyre to defeat the project. Not only the lower social rank of the candidate, but also the unreasonable expectation that the heiress to the throne should be promised in marriage to an *inconnu*, demonstrates clearly how little Jerusalem now counted in international politics. There were also negotiations about the possibility of the count becoming regent and during these talks one can for the first time observe the king's fear that he might be relieved of his royal office. Three years later, in the spring of 1180, when the prince of Antioch and Raymond III of Tripoli advanced on the kingdom from the north, the king again feared that he might be deposed or, at least, that his sister might be married off against his wishes. To prevent this he hurriedly married her to Guy of Lusignan, a course of action he was to regret. It must have been clear to him that this marriage would offend the powerful Ibelins because in 1179 there had been endeavours to marry Sibylla to Baldwin of Ramleh, the head of the Ibelins. This project had had the support of the Byzantine emperor who provided the monumental ransom needed to buy Baldwin's freedom from Muslim captivity. Presumably the emperor saw him as the future king of Jerusalem. In 1186 Baldwin of Ramleh was to be one of the two barons who refused to do homage to Guy when he became king. In 1180 Guy stepped into Baldwin's shoes; a considerable coup for the court party. Guy became count of Jaffa-Ascalon. The only conceivable alternative to Sibylla was her half-sister Isabella, King Amalric's daughter by his second wife. She lived with the Ibelins in Nablus but, in 1180, the court party was able to counter this influence by arranging her betrothal to Humphrey IV of Toron. He was, of course, as grandson of the former constable, very much a member of one of the old families, but he was also, as heir to Oultrejourdain, where he lived, under the influence of his stepfather Reynald of Châtillon. Reynald is said to have been the principal match-maker but Agnes probably had a part in it too, because one of the terms of the marriage settlement was that Humphrey surrender his patrimony of Toron to the crown. And in 1184 Toron came into the possession of Agnes. Members of the court party now filled the most important crown offices; they had the support of the episcopate and, in addition to the royal demesne, they controlled Jaffa-Ascalon, Oultrejourdain, Hebron, and Toron. Only from Galilee under Raymond III and from the Ibelins in Ramleh and Nablus could there be any opposition to their power. In 1182 the king in another panic, urged on by his mother, peremptorily forbade the count of Tripoli to enter the kingdom, an unparalleled way to treat his own vassal!

In these circumstances it was not possible to put up an effective resistance to Saladin. It is true that Baldwin IV won a brilliant victory at Montgisard near Ramleh in 1177, but more important that he was unable to follow up his advantage. In 1179 he could do nothing to prevent Saladin from capturing the newly-built castle of Chastellet on the Jordan near Jacob's Ford. In 1180 a two years' truce was agreed. Saladin's successful advance against Aleppo in 1183 forced the Franks to take counter-measures. Again a special war-tax was imposed. Although the tax decree emphasized that everyone would be taxed equally, it contained important loopholes for the rich. The king's illness progressed steadily. He showed symptoms of paralysis and began to turn blind; by the time he was twenty-one he was a living corpse. According to an Arab traveller's report in 1184, his disease made him shun public appearances as much as he possibly could. In 1182 he offered to abdicate but only on the unrealistic condition that either the French or the English king would take over. A con-temporary letter collection even contains, though purely as an exercise in style, a letter of abdication written in his name. But by 1183, in spite of Baldwin's aversion to regents, it was plain that one had to be appointed. In the circumstances the only possible regent was Guy of Lusignan; he was regarded as the next king or, at the least, as the future regent for Baldwin V. The king distrusted Guy as much as anyone and made him swear that he would not aspire to the crown during his lifetime. It was characteristic of Baldwin that in addition to an annuity of 10,000 gold pieces, he decided to keep Jerusalem, the heart and core of the kingship, for himself. Everything else went to the regent. The court party seemed to have achieved all its objectives. But very soon afterwards the king changed his mind. The pretext for deposing Guy was that he had refused to let the army march away from a position which was well supplied with water. But in doing this Guy had avoided a very risky pitched battle, and this was entirely in accord with accepted military wisdom. Moreover, the king provoked a quarrel by suddenly wanting to exchange Jerusalem for Tyre and getting a predictable refusal from Guy. So, in the autumn of 1183, Baldwin IV once again took personal charge of the government, at any rate for the moment. The only alternative to Guy as regent was Raymond III and Hamilton has convincingly argued that it was to prevent him taking over that Agnes put forward a compromise solution on which, after considerable debate, both sides were just about able to agree. The king continued to rule without a regent. In practice this strengthened the court party's grip on government. But the problem of the succession was solved in a manner for which there was no precedent in the kingdom's history when, on 20 November 1183, Baldwin V was crowned king and received the homage of the vassals during the old king's lifetime. Immediately after this Baldwin IV marched to the relief of the fortress of Kerak in Oultrejourdain which had come under siege while the nuptials of Isabella and Humphrey IV of Toron were being celebrated. In order to keep the Ibelins out of Oultrejourdain Humphrey prohibited all contact between his wife and her mother at Nablus.

But in the king's eyes Guy had still not been sufficiently humbled. In the spring of 1184 he even attempted, although without success, to have Guy and Sibylla divorced. This pushed Guy into open disobedience. Although the king went in person to Ascalon to summon him to appear before the Haute Cour, he refused to do so. In consequence Jaffa was now confiscated and placed under royal administration. The agenda of a meeting at Acre which was meant to appoint a high-ranking embassy to Europe was disrupted when the patriarch broke in with an attempt to reconcile the king and Guy. When the king refused even to listen, the enraged patriarch walked out, and the king had to close the meeting because, after this denouement, he was politically too weak to be able to return to the agenda. The patriarch was one of the heads of the court party and a sizeable number of the nobles clearly did not wish to discuss the matter in his absence. At a later meeting the patriarch and the masters of the two Military Orders were appointed ambassadors to Europe. Simultaneously, however, Raymond III of Tripoli was appointed regent a second time. He imposed hard conditions. For himself he demanded Beirut as remuneration. He also took precautions against being deposed, insisting on a guarantee that he would remain regent for ten years. This covered the period of Baldwin V's minority and, if the figure was meant to be taken precisely, another two years after that. If Baldwin V should die prematurely then a committee consisting of the pope, the emperor, and the kings of France and England was to decide which of the two daughters of King Amalric, Sibylla or Isabella, had the better claim, either for herself or for her offspring, to succeed to the throne of Jerusalem. Raymond refused to be Baldwin V's guardian so as not to be suspected of the king's murder in the event of his premature death. Joscelin III of Courtenay, Baldwin V's great uncle, was appointed instead. Raymond's well-timed concession to Joscelin seems to have induced him to leave the ranks of the court party. Eight years' work by the court party had been in vain. Agnes probably did not live to see this defeat; at any rate she was dead by 1 February 1185. As

Guy of Lusignan seemed to be finished and Raymond's regency unacceptable, the patriarch in his European embassy openly pursued plans for a change of dynasty, even though at the moment Jerusalem had not just one king but two. Neither in France nor in England, however, could he find any support for such plans, and in 1185 he returned to the East with nothing to show for his efforts.

On 15 April 1185 the wretched leper-king finally succumbed to his disease. There was no real opposition either to Baldwin V's succession or to Raymond's regency, and this despite the fact that rumours that Raymond was aiming at the crown had been in circulation since 1184. They are reported in both Christian and Muslim sources but are difficult to assess. William of Tyre's chronicle was never finished. If, however, Hiestand's reconstruction of its original conception is correct, then book XXIII was to be the book of Raymond of Tripoli, just as the previous books had been devoted to individual kings. In that case William regarded Raymond at least as an equal of kings, and this strongly suggests that Raymond actually had some such plan. If Raymond's opponents hoped to make capital out of the guardianship of Baldwin V, these hopes were dashed when the child king died suddenly in the late summer of 1186. Joscelin III now showed his true face. He sent Raymond, who trusted him completely, to Tiberias, seized the royal demesne of Acre and Beirut and even kept Raymond away from the king's funeral. Baldwin V was the last king of Jerusalem to be buried in the Church of the Holy Sepulchre. There was no male heir and according to the terms of Baldwin IV's will it was now up to the committee of four to arbitrate between the claims of Sibylla and Isabella. But by a skilfully organized *coup d'état* Sibylla and her supporters outmanoeuvred Raymond of Tripoli shortly after Baldwin V's funeral. The men who pulled the strings seem to have been chiefly Reynald of Châtillon and Patriarch Eraclius. The final outcome of a series of dramatic events was that Sibylla was crowned queen of Jerusalem first and then she herself crowned her husband Guy of Lusignan. According to accounts recently rescued from oblivion by Kedar, Sibylla and Guy outwitted even some members of the court party who, although united in exploiting the kingdom in their own interests, were by no means unanimous as to who should be the next king. Indeed a majority of them seem to have been against Guy. Baldwin IV's plan had been revived and Sibylla required to get a divorce before being crowned. She refused at first but gave way when the needs of the kingdom were explained. She obtained guarantees, however, to secure Guy's livelihood and the legitimacy of their daughters. This seems to have lulled the opposition within her own party into a sense of false security and they agreed to the very considerable concession that after her coronation she should be entirely free to choose her new husband. To general consternation she then chose Guy from whom she had only just been divorced—but whom the patriarch now had to anoint. Raymond tried to persuade Isabella's husband to be an anti-king but he preferred to go over to King Guy (1186–90). The barons had to accept the *fait accompli*. Raymond withdrew in anger to Tiberias and it proved just possible to avert a civil war between him and Guy. But Guy and his supporters were unable to use wisely the power which they had seized so decisively.

Among Guy's supporters Joscelin III now came to the fore and was correspondingly well rewarded. He received the lordship of Toron and his elder daughter was to be married to a brother of Guy. Reynald of Châtillon seems to have been less satisfied. Early in 1187 he gave Saladin the *casus belli* he needed when, ignoring the truce, he ambushed a Muslim caravan travelling from Damascus to Egypt. Even before this he had angered Saladin by similar ill-considered actions—attacking, whether it was peacetime or not, pilgrims on the road to Mecca and, in a sensational raid, plundering the towns along the coast of the Red Sea. Saladin could not put up with these constant threats to the main route between Egypt and Syria and to Egypt's Red Sea link with India. After Reynald had refused to make any restitution, he declared war. The crown was too weak to force some sense into the head of the lord of Oultrejourdain. That Reynald should refuse the king's request was not entirely unheard of but it was totally unprecedented to reply—as he did—that in the Transjordan there was no truce with the Saracens and that there he was as much the lord of the land as the king in his territory. These defiant words amounted to a declaration of independence. Guy now succeeded in bringing about a reconciliation with the count of Tripoli who had earlier made an alliance with Saladin. Raymond now broke off relations with Saladin and sided firmly with his fellow Franks. Near Nazareth, in preparation for a decisive battle, there assembled the largest army ever mustered by the Franks. It numbered around 18,000 men, of whom, however, only 1,200 were heavily armoured knights and another 4,000 light cavalry. It was a mark of the special emergency that all able-bodied men had been summoned to arms, not just those who owed feudal service. Saladin, with his 12,000 cavalry outnumbered the Franks but the heavy Christian knights could still launch a charge with tremendous impact if only they were given the opportunity. Their strategy, however, was not to risk battle but, while avoiding contact with Saladin's army, to stop him turning the campaign into a war of rapid movement until the time when his army was affected by the usual seasonal withdrawals and he was forced to retreat. Saladin countered this by attacking Tiberias. This manoeuvre brought the Franks out of their safe defensive position where they had been well supplied with water. Raymond of Tripoli argued forcefully against the move even though it was his own wife who was besieged in Tiberias. His arguments were approved by the barons but during the night the Master of the Temple persuaded Guy to change his mind. Smail believes that Guy remembered how he had lost office in 1183 when, in a similar situation, he had remained encamped close to his water-supply, and that this memory produced the fatal decision of 1187. This may indeed have been in Guy's mind, but the part played by English money must also be taken into account. In penance for his involvement in Thomas Becket's murder, King Henry II of England had, ever since 1172, been transferring large sums of money to the East to be looked after, on his behalf, by the Templars and the Hospitallers. By the terms of his will, drawn up in 1182, Henry reserved the right to recall the whole amount if and when it pleased him. This effectively froze the money, a total of 30,000 marks of silver. It could only be spent with Henry's approval. But in 1187 the Master of the Templars seized that part of Henry's money which was in his care and used it to hire mercenaries—significantly they were to fight under the English king's banner. He and King Guy were now condemned to seek the kind of success which would justify this extraordinary step. Next morning, in the fierce summer heat, the march through the Galilean hill country to Tiberias began. The army did not get through. On 3 July 1187 the first brushes with the Muslims occurred at Hattin, west of the Sea of Galilee. The Franks were forced to halt for the night here, in a waterless region. Thirsty and with eyes smarting from the smoke of the bush fires which the Muslims had lit, they spent a terrifying night. When dawn broke they found they were completely surrounded. After a heroic fight they suffered a defeat far worse than anything yet seen in the history of the crusader states. Only Raymond of Tripoli and a few of his friends managed to break out. Many knights were killed in the battle. The rest were captured, among them the king, the Master of the Temple and Reynald of Châtillon. Reynald's head was struck off by Saladin himself. The Templars too were executed; only their Master was spared. The precious relic of the True Cross which had once fallen into the hands of the Sassanids but which the Emperor Heraclius, in the seventh century, had returned to Jerusalem, was lost again and this time for ever.

The immediate consequences of Hattin were catastrophic. The kingdom had lost practically all its fighting men. Only small garrisons in some towns and castles were left. In an unparalleled triumphal progress Saladin marched through Palestine and Syria. An Arab chronicler lists fifty-two towns and fortresses which he captured. Because the Franks knew that he would keep his word it was easier for them to agree on terms of surrender. On 10 July the important port of Acre fell; on 4 September Ascalon. Jerusalem was defended by Queen Sibylla, Patriarch Eraclius, and Barisan of Ibelin, but it capitulated on 2 October after a fortnight's siege. Even the most extraordinary rituals of penance had been to no avail. It was in vain that ladies had shaven the heads of their daughters and made them undress to take cold baths in public on the hill of Calvary. What the city lacked was fighting men and the few defenders had reason to be grateful that they were at the mercy of a merciful enemy. By the terms of a tariff which varied according to age and sex and which Saladin interpreted generously, those who had some money could buy a safe passage to the coast. The al-Aqsa mosque was again handed over to Islam in a ceremonial service and Nur ed-Din's pulpit was installed. Christian crosses on the roofs of churches were taken down, but four Syrian priests were allowed to continue to hold services in the Church of the Holy Sepulchre. The capture of Jerusalem, a holy place for the Muslims as well as Christians, was a triumph which resounded round the Islamic world. Practically nothing remained to the Christians. In his 1188 campaign in the north, Saladin had insufficient time to capture the strongly fortified castles of the Military Orders in Tripoli: Krak des Chevaliers, Chastel Blanc, Tortosa, and Margat. But in the kingdom of Jerusalem he made a clean sweep. High above the Jordan valley Safed and Belvoir were forced to capitulate at the end of 1188 and the beginning of 1189. About the same time the last strongholds of Moab and Edom, the supposedly impregnable castles of Kerak and Montreal, fell when the garrisons were starved into submission. At Kerak the Franks were driven to the desperate expedient of selling their women and children—whom they were unable to feed—in return for provisions. At Montreal a blockade of a year and a half led to a shortage of salt and to cases of loss of sight among the garrison. Yet thirty years later Master Thietmar met a French widow still living at Montreal who gave him food and showed him the way to Mount Sinai. The last fortress to surrender was Beaufort in the bend of the Litani River (April 1190). The Christians hung on grimly in three coastal towns which Saladin was unable to take: Tripoli and Antioch, which were saved by the opportune arrival of a Sicilian fleet, and Tyre which twice held out against Saladin's onslaught.[67] Tyre was commanded by Marquis Conrad of Montferrat who arrived there shortly after the disaster at Hattin. His stubborn and vigorous defence of the city made him famous far and wide in the West. As the man of the moment he saw that he was being offered the chance of a lifetime. Before the walls of Tyre he won a sea battle against the Egyptians. Saladin was then forced by his emirs to raise the siege on 1 January 1188. None the less it seemed impossible to save the Holy Land and Saladin is supposed to have announced his intention of sailing overseas and completely exterminating the infidels.

7

THE THIRD CRUSADE, 1187–1192

AFTER the Second Crusade Europe had had enough of crusades for a while.[68] But from the late 1160s the growing number of appeals for help coming from the Holy Land began to have some effect on public opinion. As always these appeals were sent primarily to Western Europe. Undoubtedly public opinion looked favourably upon the idea of a crusade, seeing it as a special duty of kings and as the highest fulfilment of royal dignity. But the political situation was anything but favourable. The emperor, Frederick I Barbarossa (1152–90), was fully occupied in Italy where he was trying to recover imperial rights in execution of the decrees of Roncaglia which he had issued in 1158. This had led to his entanglement in a fierce struggle with the Lombard towns which lasted until peace was made at Constance in 1183. Between 1159 and 1177 he was also fighting against Alexander III whom he was eventually forced to recognize as pope. At home in Germany his hands were tied by the Welf opposition headed by Henry the Lion, duke of Saxony and Bavaria. The powerful duke had himself been in the Holy Land in 1172 where he made a donation to the Holy Sepulchre. Not until 1184 when, at the Whitsun court held at Mainz, Barbarossa displayed the brilliance and power of the Hohenstaufen dynasty before the eyes of the world, was there any chance that he would be able to leave the empire. But then his awareness of the imperial dignity and his political common sense attracted him to the idea of a crusade. He saw that it would only diminish his reputation if the crusade were left entirely in the hands of the rulers of Western Europe. And, at the time of the crusade, he was indeed recognized in the West as the supreme lord of Christendom. A letter forged in England which purported to be sent from him to Saladin, described the emperor as ruler of the world. The leadership of the crusade was accorded, more or less spontaneously, to him. An English chronicler, William of Newburgh, even referred to him as 'our emperor'.

France was no longer the only kingdom in Western Europe to which men in Jerusalem looked for help. Above all they counted on Henry II of England (1154–89). The house of Plantagenet was related to the Angevin royal family of Jerusalem. Moreover since the king of England now ruled the greater part of France, the king of France would need the co-operation of England if he were ever to go on crusade. As vassals of the French king, Henry II and his sons ruled the duchies of Normandy, Brittany, and

Aquitaine and the counties of Maine, Anjou, La Marche, Poitou, and Auvergne. Plantagenet and Capetian regarded each other with ineradicable suspicion. Neither could afford to go on crusade alone. Each knew that the other was just lying in wait for such an opportunity to invade. Equally neither could permit the other to go alone because that would result in a loss of prestige for him and a gain in authority for his opponent. There was simply no way out of the situation. For the moment only financial help could be sent. Henry II was very active in this way, although he never allowed his money to be spent (see above, p. 135). The ever-increasing sum piling up in the East meant that for fifteen years Henry dominated European crusading politics. At the same time, it was his alibi for not going on crusade himself and even for preventing others, particularly his sons, from going. France seems to have done less though this impression may be no more than a consequence of the relative paucity of the sources for France. In 1166 Henry II levied a general tax on income and movables, to be paid by clergy as well as laity, the proceeds of which were to go to assist the Holy Land. This was the first clearly discernible crusading tax in the West. For the rest the years up to the late 1180s were taken up with an endless to and fro of diplomatic activity. In 1172 Henry II promised to take the cross but then had his promise commuted to the foundation of monastic houses instead. In the Treaty of Nonancourt of 1177 the two kings laid down rules which were to govern their behaviour towards each other in the event of one of them going on crusade or one of them dying. But the crusade remained just a project and the Treaty of Nonancourt reveals far more of the two kings' mutual distrust than of their enthusiasm for a good cause. When Philip II Augustus (1180–1223) succeeded to the throne of France he soon became involved in a wearisome quarrel with the count of Flanders; while it was as much as Henry II could do to cope with the rebellions of his wild and unruly sons.

In 1184–5 the special embassy mentioned above (p. 132f.) was sent from Outremer to Europe to emphasize the gravity of the situation to the rulers of the West, to try to make them see that something decisive must be done if there were to be any chance of saving Jerusalem. In November 1184 the ambassadors met the pope and the emperor at Verona. Barbarossa was inclined to promise a crusade for 1186. He was in the middle of revising his Italian policy and coming to terms with the Normans of the south. This was done by means of a betrothal between his son Henry VI and Constance, the daughter of Roger II and the aunt of the reigning Norman king William II (1166–89). He may have used the offer of a crusade in order to smooth the path of his negotiations with the curia but the project fell through when, in November 1185, Urban III was elected pope and at once raised new points of disagreement and incited some princely opposition to the emperor in Germany. When the envoys from Jerusalem reached Paris, the king of France took good care to push them on to

England as soon as possible. Henry II too merely assured them of his good will and, like Philip Augustus, immediately declined the rule of Jerusalem which was offered to him. Instead he once more promised money. But Jerusalem did not want yet more money which it was not allowed to spend, and it was one of the aims of the embassy, in the event as unfulfilled as its other requests, that permission should finally be given for the expenditure of the English money lying idle in the East. 'We want a prince who needs money, not money which needs a prince.' The patriarch's cry was in vain. Henry neither accepted the rulership of Jerusalem, nor sent one of his sons. He did not even open his purse in the Holy Land. Bitterly disappointed the envoys returned home. The embassy does, however, seem to have been the stimulus behind a new crusading tax imposed in England and France in 1185 (or 1184). There has been some debate as to whether or not the tax was actually levied since there is no record of any of the usual reactions to a tax. Nor is it known for certain whether the pope had agreed to the taxation of the clergy.[69]

A real change of heart came only after the catastrophic defeat at Hattin in the summer of 1187. Urban III died from the shock of the news. His successor, Gregory VIII, although he was pope for no more than two months, gave decisive momentum to the preaching of the crusade. His crusading encyclical, *Audita tremendi*, issued on 29 October 1187 is a moving document and a masterpiece of papal rhetoric though his proposal of a seven years' truce between the European powers was clearly unrealistic. The first ruler to respond was William II of Sicily. He sent a fleet of fifty galleys to the East and they played an important part in the relief of Tripoli. But any further help he might have given was brought to nothing by his death. The first to take the cross was Richard Coeur de Lion, count of Poitou, the most chivalrous of Henry II's sons, though in this—as in much else—he acted spontaneously and high-handedly, without his father's permission. But Richard was carried along on a tide of general sympathy and Henry II could do little about it. In all kinds of ways public opinion was stimulated and roused to a transport of enthusiasm. Poets composed crusading songs and elegies on the fall of Jerusalem both in Latin and the vernacular. According to the reports of Arab chroniclers, the mood of the populace was much stirred by rousing pictures. From Tyre there came a steady stream of progress reports and appeals for help.

The preaching of the crusade north of the Alps was entrusted to Archbishop Joscius of Tyre and Cardinal Legate Henry of Albano, a Cistercian of great diplomatic skill. They were even able to arrange a settlement between England and France. Amid popular rejoicing the two kings and many of their magnates took the cross at Gisors in Normandy on 21 January 1188. They planned to leave at Easter 1189 and to take the land-route. To finance the crusade a general tax of 10 per cent on all income and movable property (the Saladin Tithe) was imposed. The clergy objected to it most since the secular barons could not only avoid the tax by taking the cross but they could also keep for themselves the contributions paid by their tenants. In Wales the Cistercian archbishop of Canterbury, Baldwin, preached the crusade with the energy and style of Bernard of Clairvaux. In Germany the preaching was taken more calmly.[70] A crusading tax was not needed but each participant was required to take a two years' supply of money with him; this helped to limit the numbers of unwanted hangers-on. The first to take the cross did so at an imperial diet at Strasbourg in December 1187. The emperor delayed until March 1188 when, at the diet at Mainz known as the *curia Jesu Christi,* his old opponent, Archbishop Philip of Cologne, submitted to him. Now Barbarossa too was ready to take the cross; in April 1189, at Hagenau, he received the pilgrim's staff and scrip. In Mainz anti-Jewish pogroms had briefly flared up again but had been nipped in the bud by the emperor who threatened the imposition of draconian punishments. Owing to the shortage of ships he had no option but to take the land-route. A series of negotiations and treaties with Serbia, Hungary, Byzantium, and the Seldjuk sultan of Iconium prepared the way. It is not entirely clear whether Barbarossa sent an ultimatum to Saladin which the latter then rejected. Undoubtedly an exchange of letters to this effect between the two is a complete forgery, as Möhring has argued, and not just partly forged. But an imperial embassy is attested in western sources and it is going too far to deny its existence merely on the grounds that it is not mentioned in Arabic sources—a fate shared by other embassies sent by the emperor to the Ayubids. Barbarossa's negotiations with the Balkan states and his alliance with the Normans made the Byzantine emperor, Isaac II Angelus (1185–95) extremely suspicious and pushed him into diplomatic double-dealing between Barbarossa and Saladin. The German envoys in Constantinople were thrown into prison.

On 11 May 1189 Barbarossa's army moved off from Regensburg. If the crusade succeeded it would unquestionably make the emperor, now about sixty-seven years old, the dominating figure on the European political scene. With him there went his son, Duke Frederick of Swabia, the archbishop of Tarentaise, the bishops of Liège, Würzburg, Passau, Regensburg, Basle, Meissen, Osnabrück, and Toul, three margraves, and twenty-nine counts from all parts of Germany. An Austrian clerk known, wrongly, as Ansbert was the chief historian of this crusade. The men from Cologne, the Frisians, the archbishop of Bremen, Landgrave Ludwig III of Thuringia, and, later, Duke Leopold V of Austria chose the sea-route. The contemporary figure of an army of 100,000 men was a wild overestimate; none the less it was undoubtedly one of the largest crusading armies ever to leave Europe. The march through Hungary went smoothly but as soon as they set foot on Byzantine territory their troubles began. It became impossible to pass through in peace as had been planned.

Barbarossa occupied Philippopolis and threatened to take the capital and destroy the empire. He ordered his son Henry to rendezvous at Constantinople with an Italian fleet in March 1190 and to use the services of a leading Venetian financier Bernardus (Teutonicus), to transfer imperial crusading funds to Tyre. Meanwhile the emperor waited at winter quarters in Adrianople. In February 1190 the weak ruler of Byzantium gave in. At Easter the German army crossed over into Asia at Gallipoli thus keeping clear of the capital as had been agreed in the Treaty of Adrianople. The weakness of the Byzantine Empire now stood clearly revealed.

On 25 April 1190 the army moved into Seldjuk territory in Anatolia. It soon became obvious that the treaty with the sultan, Kilij Arslan II, was worthless. Despite the hostile accounts given in western sources this was not because of the sultan's attitude. He, in fact, was quite well-disposed to the crusaders, but it was now his eldest son Qutb ad-Din Malik Shah, who held the reins of power, and as Saladin's son-in-law he had no intention of allowing the German army to march, unopposed, to Syria. Putting up with unimaginable hardships, badly affected by hunger and thirst, the unwieldy formations dragged themselves through Anatolia, suffering severe losses on the way. On 18 May 1190, near Iconium, they encountered Qutb ad-Din's army which had been reinforced by the Turcoman hordes which had been plundering in Asia Minor since 1185. The Germans won a brilliant victory. In their service of thanksgiving they recalled Paul's tribulations in Iconium (2 Timothy 3:11). The old sultan re-assumed control of affairs and came to terms with the emperor. After resting a few days the army marched on in peace into Christian territory—Lesser Armenia. They crossed the Taurus Mountains and were approaching the sea at Seleucia when, on 10 June 1190, Frederick Barbarossa was drowned in the River Saleph which he had impatiently tried to swim across while the troops were being held up. He had been the last ruler to take the cross and the first to set out. He was the only one of them to meet his death while on crusade. 'At this point,' lamented a chronicler from Cologne, 'and at this sad news our pen is stilled and our account is ended.'

The German crusade broke up in confusion as a result of the emperor's death. His son Frederick lacked the personality needed to hold the despairing army together. Most of the crusaders made for Cilician or Syrian ports and then sailed home. The rest, led by Duke Frederick, marched to Antioch where, as a result of an epidemic, they suffered further losses. Here, in the cathedral of St. Peter, the emperor's body was buried after his bones had been removed in the hope that they might find a worthy resting place in Jerusalem. In fact they finished up in the church of St. Mary in Tyre. On 7 October the battered remnants of the once proud army reached Acre where they met those of their fellow countrymen who had chosen the sea route. But then the sudden departure of the landgrave of Thuringia again reduced the size of their contingent. The Germans played an insignificant part in the rest of the Third Crusade. Of great importance for the future, however, was the founding, outside Acre, of a German hospital community by some citizens of Lübeck and Bremen in 1190. By 1196 the hospital had developed into an order living under a rule and caring for the sick. In 1198 its range of duties was extended to include the fight against the pagans. In this way there came into being the Military Order of the House of St. Mary of the Germans in Jerusalem (Teutonic Order), an order organized on strictly national lines. This transformation was immediately approved by the pope. The knights lived according to the Templar rule until about 1245 when the Order received its own rule and took the white tunic and black cross as its uniform. In the most recent literature on the subject it has been claimed that the Acre camp hospital of 1190 was linked with an earlier German hospital in Jerusalem which, since 1143, had been administered by the Hospitallers as an independent and separate trust. But there seems to be more in favour of Favreau's theory of a new foundation. According to her, the hospital at Acre had nothing in common with the earlier one at Jerusalem and it was not until 1229 that the property of the Jerusalem hospital and, with it, the old corporation itself was taken over by the Teutonic knights.[71]

The Christians in the Holy Land were given fresh heart by Marquis Conrad of Montferrat's vigorous defence of Tyre (1187) and by the news that preparations for a crusade were under way. In June 1188 King Guy was freed on condition that he left the country. He at once secured his release from the oath that he had sworn. One after another his former battle companions were also freed. In Tripoli he collected a handful of knights together and marched to Tyre. But Conrad had no intention of handing over the city which he had defended; it was a crown possession but he no longer recognized Guy as king. The struggle for power which now broke out between Conrad and Guy and lasted until 1190 involved an unparalleled dissipation of the already much diminished royal demesne, from which the chief gainers were the Italian and French maritime towns. Guy had been encamped for several months before the walls of Tyre without making any progress when suddenly he showed that he had more in him than men had previously suspected. He allied with a newly arrived Pisan fleet and marched, to Saladin's great astonishment, straight to Acre. From a fortified camp on the hill of Toron he began to lay siege to the city on 28 August 1189. It seemed to be an act of incredible folly since Guy's forces were not even equal to the city garrison and there was the added danger that Saladin might come upon him from the rear and crush him between the relieving army and the city. But Guy needed a base from which to reconquer his kingdom and Acre had always been its strongest and richest city. With unyielding obstinacy he pursued the goal he had set himself. The possession of Acre became a question of prestige and it was a severe blow for Saladin when the city fell after a two years' siege. It was not Guy but Saladin who had committed the act of folly when he rejected his emirs' advice to raze the city to the ground after he had captured it in 1187. This decision reveals his inadequate grasp of strategy. Instead he improved the fortress and harbour and placed all his military equipment from Egypt and Syria in the city. Guy's attack on Acre—and indeed the whole Third Crusade—took Saladin by surprise and found him insufficiently prepared. He now had to deal with a problem never before faced by a Muslim ruler—how to keep a standing army together for three years (1190–2). According to al-Fadil he had 'used the revenues of Egypt to conquer Syria, the revenues of Syria to gain control of Mesopotamia, the revenues of Mesopotamia to win Palestine'. Now his financial reserves were running dry. The long struggle for Acre prevented him from pursuing his real aim, the propagation of Islamic Orthodoxy. Barbarossa's crusade had filled him with apprehension and he had collected information about it from every possible source. Before he knew that he had no more to fear from this quarter he was forced to take action against Guy.

From September 1189 onwards a steady stream of soldiers came by ship from Europe to reinforce the Franks besieging Acre. Frisians and Scandinavians brought the ships which were urgently needed to blockade Acre from the sea. Flemings, Frenchmen, Englishmen, and Italians came; a contingent of Germans under landgrave Ludwig III of Thuringia arrived. Even Conrad of Montferrat supported the venture in its early stages. On 4 October the Franks risked a battle against Saladin but were heavily defeated. Nevertheless the city had almost been starved into submission when, at Christmas, an Egyptian supply fleet managed to break through the blockade. The early months of 1190 were characterized by the changing fortunes of war. The Franks won a sea battle but an attempt to take the city by storm on 5 May failed. Their siege machines went up in flames when the wooden towers were bombarded by the dreaded Greek Fire, a mixture with a naphtha base which only vinegar could extinguish. From 19 to 26 May Saladin again tried to drive the Franks off but could win no decisive victory. On the other hand the Franks too suffered a setback when on 25 July the foot-soldiers, against the wishes of the commanders, tried a surprise attack on Saladin's camp. But it became increasingly clear that Saladin would not be able to defeat the Franks while they were entrenched behind a secure system of defence works. His troops were simply not equipped to deal with this kind of warfare. Reinforcements for the Franks continued to pour in. The most important new arrival was Henry of Champagne, count palatine of Troyes. As nephew of the king of England and the king of France he was well placed to reconcile the differences which the English and French troops had brought with them from Europe and which were visibly expressed by the fact that it had been necessary to set up a dual command in the crusader camp. On his arrival Henry of Champagne was given overall command. Then on 7 October the duke of Swabia with the remnants of the German army reached Acre; a few days later Baldwin, archbishop of Canterbury, arrived. On 12 November the Franks succeeded in driving Saladin out of his hill-top camp but he merely retired to a stronger position not far off.

Meanwhile Conrad of Montferrat had broken off his support for Guy. In the autumn Queen Sibylla and both her daughters died. Since Guy had ruled as Sibylla's consort, Conrad now sought the crown for himself. Guy and Sibylla had no surviving offspring so another claimant was Isabella, the younger daughter of King Amalric, and the wife of Humphrey IV of Torón. Conrad leaked the information that she had married before reaching the age of consent. With great skill he combined this legal, although most likely inapposite, argument with the political hostility of the barons to young Humphrey which had its roots in the latter's precipitate submission to Guy in 1186 (see above, p. 134). In a judicial farce the marriage between Humphrey and Isabella was annulled and she was then (24 November 1190) wedded to Conrad although he was, in fact, already married. The archbishop of Canterbury had opposed the match and died of grief when it went through. The papal curia hesitated but eventually reconciled itself to this bigamous arrangement. That winter (1190–1) the besiegers suffered terribly from a food shortage for which they blamed the marquis of Montferrat who had retired to Tyre. An egg cost a silver penny; a sack of corn cost a hundred gold pieces. In front of the ovens men fought among themselves for a morsel of bread. The situation did not ease until spring came. Then there arrived not only supply ships but also the soldiers who had long been looked for: on 20 April 1191 Philip II Augustus of France landed at Acre, followed seven weeks later by Richard Coeur de Lion.

The Anglo-French crusade had been delayed by a new war between the two kingdoms (1188–9). To make matters worse Richard Coeur de Lion again rebelled against his father. This state of affairs was openly criticized by poets as well as by the pope, but to no avail. The writer who was most active in promoting the crusade was Peter of Blois, author of a tract *On the Speeding-up of the Crusade*. At about the same time he wrote the *Passio Reginaldi* glorifying Reynald of Châtillon and pouring a stream of almost pathological abuse over Saladin's head. Against this kind of passion the cool approach of the Englishman Ralph Niger who, from exile in France, soberly pointed out all the problems in the way of the planned crusade, could make little headway. Indeed in his later chronicle Ralph dropped his criticism and spoke, like Peter, of Reynald of Châtillon as *beatus Reinaldus*.[72]

Peace was restored only with great difficulty. Shortly afterwards Henry II died in July 1189. His son Richard succeeded him both as king (1189–99) and crusader. He was thirty-two years old, fair-haired, tall and strongly built, a matchless warrior, a capable general; a superb knightly figure; but also a man who veered between a sensible generosity and an occasional show of cruelty and abject remorse. In contrast to him the twenty-five-year-old king of France was not a very compelling personality. He possessed a dry wit but he was also a hypochondriac who often suffered badly from a fear of death. He was as little interested in art or learning as Richard but he was a statesman who possessed patience as well as energy and who, step by step, cautiously but successfully built up the strength of the French crown. But he was poorer than Richard. Richard had inherited a well-filled treasury from his father and by selling crown offices on a large scale he raised even more money for the crusade. In his ten-year reign he saw England for ten months only; his kingdom was, in his eyes, just a bank from which he could draw the money needed to indulge his insatiable lust for war.

At last, on 4 July 1190, both kings left Vézelay, the appointed place of muster. They had, after all, decided to go by sea and at Lyons they separated. Philip marched to Genoa. According to the terms of his agreement with the Genoese there was transport for 650 knights and 1,300 squires with their horses, provisions and fodder for eight months, wine for four months. For all this the Genoese were to receive 5,850 silver marks. Richard marched down the Rhône to Marseilles where he awaited the English fleet of about a hundred supply ships and twenty men-of-war. In September the two fleets met at Messina and wintered there. Richard had a feud with the ruler of Sicily, Tancred of Lecce, over the hereditary claims of his sister Joanna, the widow of the previous king. However he found time for an interview with Joachim of Fiore, the Calabrian abbot of Corazzo who was well-known as a prophet and who foretold victory for Richard in the East. The arrogant behaviour of the English quickly fanned into virulent life the smouldering hatred of the Sicilians for foreigners. In turn Richard was forced to seize the city of Messina which he did in a lightning strike lasting just five hours. The Anglo-Norman poet Ambroise, whose *Estoire de la Guerre Sainte* is an imperishable memorial both to Richard's heroic deeds and to the sufferings of the poorer crusaders, wrote that Richard had taken the city into his hands in less time than it takes a priest to sing matins. Philip and Richard had arranged to divide the plunder between them and the first of their many quarrels arose out of this. On 30 March 1191 an angry King Philip sailed alone out of Messina. On 10 April Richard followed him. *En route*, in a boldly executed campaign, he captured the island of Cyprus from the 'emperor' Isaac Comnenus (May 1191). On Cyprus he met Guy, and being feudal lord of the Lusignan family in Poitou, he at once took Guy's part; Conrad of

Montferrat was supported by Philip Augustus and the duke of Austria, now the leader of the German crusaders. This split further intensified the Anglo-French hostility; and the Germans too found it difficult to get on with the Frenchmen and vice versa.

Despite these problems the siege of Acre was pressed more vigorously after Richard's arrival on 8 June; the big French siege machines were particularly helpful. Saladin's attacks on the crusaders' camp failed to achieve any result and on 12 July 1191—despite Saladin's objections—the dispirited garrison surrendered. Considering that Acre was a city without springs, it had held out for a surprisingly long time. In summer its cisterns could have provided only a very moderate amount of water, unless perhaps the occasional blockade-running ships had been able to bring in fresh supplies. Now the garrison was to go free on condition that Saladin restore the True Cross, release 1,500 named Christian prisoners and pay a ransom of 200,000 bezants. At last, after a siege of two years, the standards of France and England waved over the city. At Messina the two kings had made a deal on the division of the spoils and they now interpreted it to mean that all the booty went to them and their supporters and nothing to those who had been fighting outside Acre for up to two years before the kings' arrival. Leopold V of Austria tried to break into this syndicate by planting his banner in the city, but before this could develop into a general habit, Richard, with his own hands, tore down the Austrian flag. This was neither a *point d'honneur* nor an example of English high-handedness; it was simply a matter of business. The losses during the siege had been heavy. A semi-official list of the dead names Queen Sibylla, Patriarch Eraclius, five archbishops, six bishops, four abbots, a prior, an archdeacon, two dukes, a landgrave, ten counts, three viscounts, and thirty more great nobles. The losses among the lesser knights and the infantry were not counted. The list of the Saracen dead was considerably lengthened when, in a fit of anger, Richard had the 3,000 prisoners murdered because there had been difficulties with the payment of the first instalment of the ransom which was probably beyond Saladin's resources.

The problem of the kingship was settled by a compromise. Guy was confirmed as king; Conrad of Montferrat was made heir to the throne. But for the moment the real ruler of Outremer was Richard, especially after the end of July when King Philip went home. He had often been ill; he had the domestic question of the inheritance of the count of Flanders to worry about; and he would, if Richard remained away, have an opportunity to move against Normandy. From the French point of view his departure was well calculated, but the English chroniclers accused him of cowardice and oath-breaking. With him went Roger of Howden, a one-time royal clerk and one of Henry II's judges. Roger kept a crusade diary and after his return to Howden (in Yorkshire) he turned it into one of the best accounts of the Anglo-French crusade. Philip's army remained behind in the Holy

Land, now under the command of the duke of Burgundy but the latter was so short of money that he could pay the troops only by borrowing from the English.

For a whole year Richard campaigned against Saladin whose reputation had suffered a good deal as a result of the fall of Acre. His army showed ominous signs of breaking up; only the troops from Egypt and Mosul were at all reliable. Even his relatives, headed by his nephew Taqi ad-Din, plotted mutinies and engaged in quarrels which prevented him from devoting all his energy to the war. His main aim was to hold on to Jerusalem and so he concentrated on threatening the crusaders' supply lines in the interior of the country. This tactic did in fact stop Richard from making any serious attempts to take Jerusalem. But as a general Richard was Saladin's superior and was not to be tempted into a trap. On 22 August he marched south from Acre for if he wanted Jerusalem, he first had to be able to use Jaffa, the port nearest to Jerusalem, as a base. The march was a model of crusade tactics. The army's right flank was protected by the sea and the fleet, and the speed of its advance was dictated by the speed of the ships. The three squadrons of knights were in the centre, with their left flank protected by tightly packed infantry formations. To prevent too much strain being imposed on these footmen, they alternated with other infantry sections who otherwise marched right by the seashore. On 7 September at Arsuf, north of Jaffa, Saladin tried to break the Christian army in one decisive battle. But Richard stuck firmly to his order of battle and the much-feared English archers held the enemy at bay until they began to show signs of exhaustion. Only then did the massed English cavalry charge. The Muslims could offer no resistance. On both sides losses were small but the Latins had won a moral victory in the first big battle since Hattin. The legend of Saladin's superiority had been destroyed.

After taking Jaffa Richard allowed the army a rest. From now on he negotiated almost non-stop to end the war. Saladin was represented by his brother al-Adil, an exceptionally able diplomat who wore down the Franks by his delaying tactics. Moreover he split them into two camps by negotiating simultaneously with Richard and Conrad of Montferrat. The whole business was conducted in a most courteous fashion, revealing a political sense which was very far removed from the religious crusading spirit. At one stage even so recondite a project as a marriage between Richard's sister and Saladin's brother was said to have been discussed. The problem of keeping the crusader states in existence was, of course, a political problem which, despite the religious enthusiasm which was doubtless to be found in the ranks of the army, could only be solved by political means. Even a man as impulsive as Richard could not but realize this for, like revolutionary enthusiasm, the crusading spirit did not last for long. But there is no point in lamenting the decline of a noble idea when it is clear enough that what was urgently needed was pragmatic action.

An advance was made towards Jerusalem but in the New Year a halt had to be called at Bait Nuba about twelve miles short of the inadequately fortified city. Popular opinion in the army criticized this decision but in view of Saladin's tactics it was the right one. The French then returned to Acre while Richard kept the English busy rebuilding Ascalon.

In April news came that Richard's brother John Lackland had engaged in treasonable negotiations with the king of France. The situation was not immediately dangerous but Richard realized that he could not stay in Outremer for ever. The compromise settlement between Guy and Conrad had not worked for long. In response to pressure from the barons Richard dropped Guy and allowed the vigorous Conrad of Montferrat to be elected king; by the law of inheritance he now had the best claim. Richard compensated Guy for this loss by making him ruler over Cyprus though he had earlier sold the island to the Templars and Guy had to buy out their claim. But Conrad was never to wear the crown. According to the chronicler Ernoul, on the evening of 28 April 1192 Conrad went to dine with the bishop of Beauvais because dinner at home was late as a result of his wife Isabella staying too long in the bath. Unfortunately the bishop had already finished his meal so Conrad slowly walked back again to the palace at Tyre. As he turned a corner he was stabbed to death by two Assassins. It was the last deed of the 'Old Man of the Mountain' who died soon afterwards. Public opinion accused Richard of plotting Conrad's assassination and to clear their king English writers inserted into the chronicles a forged letter 'written' by the sheikh of the Assassins to Duke Leopold V of Austria who was now back in Germany. There is no way of telling who in fact was responsible.[73] After a few days Conrad's widow married Count Henry of Champagne who was then acclaimed king by the people of Tyre. Somewhat reluctantly Henry agreed, on Richard's advice, to take over the kingdom but he never claimed the royal title, probably because he was never crowned or because he did not want to give up Champagne. A daughter called Alice was born from this marriage (see the genealogy below, p. 250). She was illegitimate if Isabella's divorce from Humphrey IV of Toron in 1190 had been invalid. Because the inheritance to Champagne was involved, this question was later to keep all of northern France busy until eventually, in 1234, Louis IX was able to settle it, though only at considerable expense.

In the summer of 1192 the Christians again advanced on Jerusalem and again called a halt at Bait Nuba. While the army withdrew to Acre, Saladin captured Jaffa. As soon as Richard heard of this he gathered a handful of knights together, and sailed to Jaffa. There he carried out one of his most famous exploits, wading, still not in full armour, through the shallow water to the beach and rapidly clearing the town of Muslims. On 5 August he beat off an attack launched by Saladin. Then, on 2 September, the two adversaries made a three years' truce, recognizing that neither could inflict a decisive defeat upon the other. The Christians had to accept that they could not recapture Jerusalem. By the terms of the truce the coast from Tyre to Jaffa was to remain in Christian hands. Ascalon, which had been the chief bone of contention during the negotiations, was handed back to Saladin, but only after its fortifications, together with those at Gaza and Darum, had been razed to the ground. Jerusalem was kept by the Muslims but they agreed to allow pilgrims to visit the city. Richard himself did not trouble to take advantage of this concession. In October Tripoli and Antioch were included in the truce although they had remained neutral throughout the war.

On 9 October 1192 Richard left the Holy Land. He left behind an English hospital at Acre which English clerics had founded with his assistance and which was dedicated to Saint Thomas of Canterbury. In *c.*1230 it was reformed by the bishop of Winchester and became a Military Order with its seat in Montmusard, the suburb of Acre. Here it became the nucleus of the English quarter at Acre, but the English Order itself was never destined to be prominent. On his homeward voyage a shipwreck forced Richard to travel through Austria in disguise because the Austrian duke had not forgotten the flag incident at Acre. Richard was recognized in Vienna and the duke had him imprisoned in the castle of Dürnstein. Later he was handed over to the emperor, Henry VI, who finally released him in 1194 after an enormous ransom of 150,000 marks of silver had been paid and Richard had agreed to hold England as an imperial fief. In 1199 Richard died while still at loggerheads with Philip Augustus. Saladin had died earlier, in March 1193, aged fifty-five. With him there vanished one of the greatest personalities of medieval Islam, a man whose success was based almost entirely on the moral force of his ideas. As always in the Muslim world, his empire began to fall apart as soon as he was gone. This development effectively prolonged the truce and gave the crusader states half a century of peace before they had to face a decisive onslaught from the Ayubids. The greatest of the crusades was over. Its achievement was a modest one; most of Palestine was still in Muslim hands. The united forces of Outremer and the West had, it is true, ensured the existence of the crusader states for another hundred years, but the West was never again prepared to send help on this scale.

Even so a new crusade was soon planned. The new emperor, Henry VI (1190–7) had high-flying schemes and among them was a crusade—a crusade in which political considerations played a large part.[74] Owing to his marriage with Constance and to the fact that William II died without issue, he unexpectedly became heir to Sicily and south Italy though he had to conquer his inheritance before he could enter into it (1194). He was the heir not just to Norman lands but also to their policies, to their traditional plans for expansion into the eastern Mediterranean. In 1194 Leo II prince of Lesser Armenia under whose rule Cilician Armenia had its greatest days, successfully sought enfeoffment by the emperor. He and his Roupenian forefathers, while fighting a perpetual war against the Byzantines and their allies the Hethoumians (see above, p. 48), had built up a vigorous Christian state, economically founded on the Cilician plain and the cities of Tarsus and Seleucia and protected militarily and politically by the strong fortresses of the Roupenians high in the Cilician Mountains.

But Henry VI turned his attention chiefly to Byzantium. In 1194 his brother Philip was betrothed to Irene, daughter of the Byzantine emperor, Isaac Angelus. In 1197 the marriage took place; it was to have momentous consequences in the history of the crusades. In the meantime the alliance gave Henry a family interest in the Byzantine crown and when Isaac Angelus lost his throne to his still weaker brother Alexius III (1195–1203), it enabled him to clothe his political pressure on Byzantium in the guise of a right to an inheritance. Henry himself took the cross in 1195, partly in order to reach a settlement with the pope. He promised to supply and maintain at his own expense 1,500 knights and 1,500 squires quite apart from the normal crusading army. In the following years the crusade was preached in Germany, but for the moment nothing came of it. This was in part because the emperor's plan to make Germany and Sicily into a hereditary monarchy fell through as a result of opposition from the princes of north Germany and from the papal curia; in part because despite their religious differences, Rome came out decisively in support of Byzantium and pressed for a crusade to the Holy Land, not one against Byzantium. If the empire in the East had been unified with the empire in the West the papacy would have had to face the prospect of complete political impotence. In addition, the Greeks bought themselves a temporary respite by paying a heavy and unpopular tribute to the Roman Emperor—sixteen hundredweight of gold a year—known as the Alamanikon.

Henry had to give up his plan to lead the crusade himself. Instead he appointed the imperial marshal, Henry of Kalden, and the imperial chancellor, Conrad of Querfurt, bishop of Hildesheim, to be its leaders. From March 1197 onwards German troops embarked in south Italy. The main contingent left Messina at the beginning of September. They broke their journey to Acre in Cyprus where the chancellor crowned Aimery of Lusignan, Guy's brother and successor, as king—thus establishing a suzerainty of the empire over the island. In the Holy Land too, the Germans achieved a lasting success. Led by the duke of Brabant they were able to restore the land connection between the kingdom of Jerusalem and the county of Tripoli by capturing Sidon and Beirut (24 October 1197).

The sudden and unexpected death of Henry VI in Messina on 28 September 1197 plunged the medieval empire into one of its worst crises.

Henry had had no time to consolidate his great achievements. His power had rested entirely on his own personal authority as emperor and his only son was just a child. In these circumstances the German crusade soon broke up. Only Leo II of Lesser Armenia derived further profit from it when, in January 1198, he received the long-desired royal crown from the hands of the archbishop of Mainz. The union of the Armenian Church with Rome, part of the price to be paid for the title of king, was never to be anything more than a pure formality.

8

THE INTERNAL DEVELOPMENT OF THE CRUSADER STATES IN THE TWELFTH AND THIRTEENTH CENTURIES

WHEN the Muslim traveller, Ibn Jubayr, journeyed through the Holy Land in 1184 he was astonished to find it economically and socially flourishing despite the increasingly unhealthy political situation.[75] Here and there Franks and Muslims tilled the fields together and shared common pastures for their cattle. The great caravans were able to travel in safety to Acre where they were dealt with by a smoothly functioning customs system staffed by Arabic-speaking Christians. But this description should not lead one to suppose either that the Franks were tolerant or that a process of mutual assimilation between Christian and Muslim had taken place. If the yoke of Frankish rule did not press too heavily on the Muslims this was only because a shortage of manpower was at all times the greatest problem of the crusader states. At the conquest many Muslims were killed and others emigrated. Few of the crusaders remained behind in the Holy Land. In 1100 Jerusalem had only a couple of hundred inhabitants. Even in the towns, let alone in the countryside, living conditions were insecure. Those who did remain tended to settle in groups according to their place of origin. The men from Lorraine and north France stayed within the kingdom of Jerusalem; the Provençals went to Tripoli; the Normans to Antioch, though this principality was later to fall under French domination.

If Outremer were to survive then men who were prepared both to fight and to settle had to be attracted from Europe.[76] It soon became clear that the towns were more easily populated than the countryside. The view that the fiefs granted by Godfrey were almost always money fiefs from the municipal revenues is no longer taken for granted. None the less money fiefs played an important role in Godfrey's regime, and grants of land became relatively more important under Baldwin I. In addition there is also the question of arbitrary seizures of land during the conquest and, in consequence, property surviving for a long time as allod (i.e. where the rights of possession and control were entirely vested in the holder). Jean Richard demonstrated the existence of such estates in Cyprus and Tripoli; Joshua Prawer did the same for the kingdom of Jerusalem. This interpretation has recently been challenged by Riley-Smith, and it must be admitted that *fiés francs* were, in the final analysis, fiefs, not allods, even if no homage was paid, nor service rendered. But true allods did exist, both in real life and in the legal constructs of the thirteenth-century Jerusalem lawbooks. The debate is important because it touches on the other problem of whether feudalization occurred in a chaotic and muddled fashion during the disorder of the conquest (Prawer) or in an ordered fashion following a princely plan (Riley-Smith). In this debate the existence of allods is taken to indicate the former, their non-existence the latter. But if this rigid 'either-or' were avoided, then the conflicting views could be reconciled. There is nothing to prevent us assuming that Godfrey acted systematically so far as he was able to. But there is equally nothing to keep us from supposing that the way in which land was occupied by the conquerors frequently depended on accidental circumstances. For example the fief of Geoffrey of the Tower of David was created, *c*.1100, out of a number of Jacobite monastic estates because, as it happened, the monks had temporarily emigrated.[77] In any case the process of feudalization was a slow one. In the legislation of Outremer there were special provisions designed to persuade knights to come and settle. Here, in contrast to the customs of inheritance prevailing in Europe, a knight's fee could be inherited by daughters or, originally, also by collateral relatives. This meant that if the knight fell in battle his possessions were kept in the family even when he himself had no children; his kin in Europe could send another member of the family out to the East. Because new arrivals frequently found it difficult to find witnesses, the *Assise du coup apparent* was promulgated during Baldwin III's reign as a concession to lower-class immigrants. It exempted pilgrims and poor people from the requirement of the courts of law for proofs offered by witnesses.

Thanks to their economic situation it was fairly easy to find settlers who were prepared to live in the coastal towns. In Antioch too there were few difficulties; the city enjoyed the advantages of a pleasant climate and a fine situation between mountains and sea as well as the security guaranteed by the immense fortifications—four hundred towers—dating back to the period of Byzantine rule. Moreover, in a country where the city had always played a central role and which had known the advantages of the way of life common to both Byzantine and Oriental civilization, living in the city offered a standard of comfort unknown in Europe. The houses usually looked plain from the outside; but inside they were often magnificent. In Antioch there was an artificial sewage system and the citizens had running water in their houses; in these respects they were better off than a king from Western Europe. Ironically, although the whole point of the First Crusade had been to capture Jerusalem, it proved difficult to persuade men to live there. The entire native population of Jerusalem had been massacred in 1099 and indeed not until the capture of Sidon (1110) did the crusaders manage to find a different method of dealing with urban populations. Jerusalem was, it is true, the capital city, the seat of both secular and ecclesiastical administration, but apart from the pilgrim traffic and a goldsmiths' craft which served the gift-trade and seems to have stressed quantity rather than quality, Jerusalem had no economic stimulus, neither manufactures nor long-distance trade. The kings therefore had to take special measures to provide for its repopulation, notably the *Assise de l'an et jour* (see p. 59). In about 1115 Baldwin I established a colony of Christian Syrians from the Transjordan in what had been the Jewish quarter and gave them special privileges. In 1120, in response to a request from the patriarch, Baldwin II abolished all duties on imported foodstuffs, in particular on grain. This suited the financial interests of the Holy Sepulchre very well for it had a virtual monopoly of the Jerusalem bakeries.

Although Frankish society always remained essentially urban, it was clearly impossible to rule Outremer effectively without also bringing the countryside under the control of a system of colonization and administration. The extension of the area of cultivation often went hand in hand with the requirements of defence. Usually the king, but sometimes powerful household officials, began the process by building castles—purely for military reasons—whether in the south-west around Ascalon or in the Dead Sea region to the south-east. Naturally settlements and a church then clustered around these castles; a little further off villages grew up; the colonists farmed the soil more intensively and paid dues to the lords of the castles who guaranteed their safety and who held their castles as fiefs of the king. The extension of settlement and cultivation in the Gaza region can be closely observed. In 1149 a castle was built there within the ruins of the ancient town. After the fall of Ascalon in 1153 Gaza became less important militarily, but the settlement developed so rapidly that a new and bigger circuit of walls had to be built.

We are particularly well informed about the construction and function of Castle Safed. It controlled the road from Acre to Damascus and the most important crossing point on the Jordan, Jacob's Ford. In 1218 it was destroyed by the Saracens and then, in 1240, rebuilt at great expense by the Templars who made of it a strong and inaccessible fortress. In peacetime the castle held a garrison of 50 Templar knights, 30 serving brothers, 50 Turcopole cavalrymen, 300 archers, and another 820 men and 400 slaves. In wartime Safed could hold 2,200 people so it provided a safe retreat for the local Latin population. The arable farming, the cattle breeding, and fishing of the region were described in detail by a pilgrim. He mentions grain, figs, pomegranates, olives, grapes, and vegetables; he refers to the production of honey, to the excellent stone quarries which were being commercially exploited, and to the irrigation system which served the plantations. The castle's water supply was ensured by springs and cisterns within the walls. Grain delivered to the castle could be milled there by the castle's own mills, both wind and animal driven, and baked in the castle oven. It is probable indeed that the bread for the whole district had to be baked there. Mills, however, were also to be found outside the castle. Twelve water-mills are mentioned though there is nothing to indicate whether or not they belonged to the lord. The population of the region was estimated at 10,000, living in 260 villages. At the foot of the castle there was a settlement, rather larger than the rest, and a market. The writer described the castle's function as a centre of defence and settlement when observing that it prevented the Saracens from crossing the Jordan to raid in the direction of Acre and thus permitted agriculture and colonization (*terre colonia*) to be carried on in safety.

Also well documented is the Hospitallers' scheme for colonization at Beth Gibelin near Ascalon in 1168. This was settled exclusively by Franks, thirty-two families in all. Six of these had lived in Palestine for some time already; the others were new arrivals from Auvergne, Gascony, Lombardy, Poitou, Catalonia, Burgundy, Flanders, and Carcassonne. They each received 42 hectares (150 acres) of land in *tenure en bourgeoisie*;[78] they were personally free in the sense that they were free to move away if they wished; and they paid the *terraticum,* a payment in kind based on the harvest and assessed according to the customs of Ramleh-Lydda. (These customs seem to have been used as the customary model for agricultural organization which here, as usual in Outremer, was carried out on the European pattern.) They also had to hand over a proportion of the plunder they took from the Saracens, so presumably they must have had to go to war occasionally. As an additional attraction the Hospitallers' right of pre-emption was abolished and, in return for a moderate payment to them, the land could be freely alienated. By the end of the century the settlement had its own court (*Cour des bourgeois*) and thus enjoyed a certain amount of self-government. In the interior of the land the Church played a considerable part in the business of colonization. *Magna Mahumeria* near Jerusalem, for example, was a large settlement established by the canons of the Church of the Holy Sepulchre. Here the administration maintained a stricter control and occasionally a settler was forced out. The lord's agent, the *Dispensator,* kept a close watch on the quality of work. He could reprimand, impose fines, or confiscate land, though he had to act in co-operation with the local settlers' organization. The stringent terms of their contracts suggest that some of the settlers may have been pilgrims who ran out of money and could not afford to go home. But the picture drawn by Bernard of Clairvaux (*De laude novae militiae,* c. 5, § 10)—as also later by Burchard of Monte Sion—of the Holy Land as a kind of colony of criminals does the settlers an injustice. *Magna Mahumeria,* like Beth Gibelin, was settled exclusively by Franks, some 140 families in all, whereas in the south-east some of the colonies were composed of Muslims. There the unit of assessment of taxation was the hearth, as it still was in the great tax decree of 1183. After the coast, the region around Jerusalem was clearly the most densely settled part of the kingdom, for when the Hospitallers received 10,000 bezants in 1168 in order to buy land on behalf of the heir to the throne of Hungary, they had to report that they had been unable to acquire any in the neighbourhood of the capital. Thus a second class of free Franks developed beneath the aristocratic upper class. These were the *burgenses* or *Bourgeois* (see below, p. 176) whose numbers were kept up by a continual flow of immigrants. Presumably, except in those exceptional cases already mentioned, they came in order to better themselves socially, since a Frankish bourgeois was naturally the social superior of a Syrian landowner, no matter how rich the latter was. The crucial social dividing line was not, as elsewhere in the Middle Ages, between noble and non-noble but rather between Franks and non-Franks. The 'crusader states' were Frankish states in the sense that the Franks, i.e. the Latin Christians, monopolized all political rights. Officially, the king was the *rex Latinorum*. Even if the participation of the bourgeois in political life generally amounted to little more than a formality, it was none the less in some circumstances indispensable, e.g. in deciding the succession to the throne and after the coronation ceremony, when the bourgeois of Jerusalem had to serve the food at the coronation banquet. Most of the bourgeois lived in the towns—Jerusalem, Acre, Tyre, Tripoli, and Antioch—but the number who settled in the country should not be underestimated. The total Frankish population *c.* 1187, nobles, clergy, and bourgeois, has been estimated at 120,000, of whom 30,000 lived in Jerusalem, 40,000 in Acre, and 25,000–30,000 in Tyre.[79]

Fulcher of Chartres (above, p. 81) bears witness to the fact that from around 1120 the Frankish settlers had developed a sense of belonging to a community of their own. In the prologue to his chronicle (1184) William of Tyre gave eloquent expression to this same feeling. In their higher ranks the Franks were a fairly pure-blooded group and in the twelfth century they were all of them known as *poulains* (young animals, i.e. not actual crusaders but permanent settlers descended from them). Not until the thirteenth century was the sense of community seriously undermined by settlements of Italian merchants on the coast and the establishment of the Teutonic Order leading to the development of narrowly nationalistic foreign corporations which were prepared to put other interests above those of the Holy Land. The Italians put the commercial interests of their home town first; the Teutonic Order served the requirements of Hohenstaufen policy. For these reasons Jean Richard has referred to a process of 'de-nationalization'.

Below the Franks came a lower class made up of an exotic mixture of races. Politically, ethnically, and religiously it was kept apart from the ruling class.[80] At this time the religious barrier was the decisive one. If it could be overcome then ethnic difference would not prevent a man from rising in society (see below, p. 187). Fulcher of Chartres even talks of occasional marriages between Frankish settlers and baptized Muslim women. But sexual intercourse with an infidel was naturally prohibited and the man who kept a Muslim woman as a concubine was, according to the draconian measures laid down by the Council of Nablus (1120), to be castrated and have his nose cut off. The greater part of the native population consisted of Christian Syrians, themselves divided into several religious groups: going very roughly, from south to north they were Orthodox, Monothelete Maronites in Lebanon, and Monophysite Jacobites. Their language was very largely Arabic; Old Syriac died out in the thirteenth century. Even under the rule of Arabs and Turks the Syrian Christians had been a tolerated people, craftsmen and farmers, and their lot was little different under the Franks. Besides them there were considerable numbers of Armenians and Greeks living in the coastal towns, chiefly within the principality of Antioch but also in Palestine. Some were merchants; others, in Orthodox monasteries, served their Church. King Amalric tried to bring about 30,000 Armenian settlers into the kingdom of Jerusalem. Financially they were to enjoy the same lenient terms as the Muslims but they were also to do military service. The attempt failed, however, because the Church demanded a special tithe from which the Muslims—of course—and also the rest of the subject population were generally exempt (see below, p. 173). Where the numbers of Franks and Syrian Christians were insufficient to cultivate the land, men turned to Muslims, usually of Syrian origin, and only zealots like James of Vitry, bishop of Acre in the thirteenth century, would ever try to convert them. The number of Arabs and Turks tended to decrease but there were always the nomadic Bedouin tribesmen who, together with their flocks, were considered to belong to the royal fisc. In the coastal towns the Jews were of some importance. They had something like a monopoly of wool dyeing and glass manufacture. In Jerusalem itself, however, it was not until Saladin's reconquest in 1187 that the Jews were allowed to re-establish their religious community there. A few Jews still lived in the country, particularly in north Galilee. From the beginning of the thirteenth century there was a growing movement for the return of Jews, especially from France, to Palestine. A leading exponent of this movement was the Spanish rabbi Nachmanides who settled in the Holy Land in 1267 and, in his commentary on the Pentateuch, argued that the pious duty of a pilgrimage should be replaced by an obligation to live permanently in Palestine which he held to be especially reserved for the Jews. Finally there were some Georgians, Coptic Ethiopians, and a few Nestorian Christians from central Asia who lived in Jerusalem in order to fulfil religious functions.

At the head of the social structure stood the king or, in the north, the ruling prince. The king was elected but increasingly election did little more than confirm the hereditary right of the heir.[81] The view that the crusaders created an ideal feudal state with an all-powerful nobility and a feeble monarchy on the *tabula rasa* of a conquered land was based on the legal theory and practice of the thirteenth century and cannot simply be transferred to the twelfth—even though right up to the middle of the twentieth century some of the most distinguished legal historians did just this. In fact the process of feudalization was a slow one and, in the early days, the king quite clearly held the upper hand. Naturally he was not an absolute monarch. This was out of the question in a country where, in the twelfth century, war was normal and peace the exception. (For thirteenth-century conditions see below, p. 249.) In the course of time this state of affairs brought the king into a condition of increasing dependence on his vassals. But at first things were quite different. The king ruled directly through his viscounts on the royal domain with its centres at Jerusalem, Nablus, Tyre, and Acre. During the first three decades of the twelfth century an aristocratic class was gradually formed but the individual families remained unable to establish themselves in particular lordships. The king kept these firmly in his own hands transferring them often from one family to another. His legislation, which in accordance with medieval convention required the consent of those affected by it, applied uniformly throughout the whole land. Naturally the king also issued administrative ordinances on his own authority alone. Thus, in the thirteenth century, a royal ordinance on street cleaning in Jerusalem was held to be unconstitutional because it had been issued in the twelfth century without the consent of the inhabitants. The king alone had the right to make treaties with the Italian maritime towns or with Byzantium. He alone could mint coins and impose customs duties. In *c*.1150 there were cases where his courts enjoyed an overriding jurisdiction, e.g. cases involving thieves who were minors or rear-vassals caught in the act of stealing within the seignory of a lord who was not their own—though, in this case, they would probably have escaped more lightly than if they had been subjected to the draconian penalties of seignorial justice: whipping or branding where the stolen goods were of low value, mutilation or blinding where they were of high. In about 1170 the king still claimed the right to approve the resignation of the Master of the Hospital. Until the end of the century he continued to appoint the patriarch. This took place in an uncanonical procedure by which he chose one of the two candidates put forward by the canons of the Church of the Holy Sepulchre; but he was also entitled to reject both of them.[82] The *Establissement dou roi Bauduin*, a law probably issued by Baldwin II rather than by Baldwin III, seems to have allowed the king, in twelve precisely defined cases, to confiscate fiefs without due process of law. This right would contrast sharply with practice in Europe but, in harmony with Roman law, the cases include not only purely feudal offences but also crimes against the state as represented by the king (*crimina laesae majestatis*), especially those crimes which tended to deprive the king of revenue: counterfeiting or minting one's own coin, infringing his port and highway rights. The list also included such typical crimes against the state as high treason and apostasy. But Riley-Smith has recently adduced powerful arguments to throw doubt on this view, hitherto unanimously held. He believes that the law merely prescribed a penalty (confiscation of the fief in all twelve cases) and that this could be imposed only after a proper trial.

During a period of transition, approximately 1130–60, the nobility was able to strengthen its position relative to the king. Some families obtained a firm hold on certain lordships. If the king wished to remove them, he had to compensate them elsewhere. For the first time we hear of baronial rebellions. Within the knightly class a clear sense of caste developed. The nobility became more differentiated; a higher nobility of about a dozen families emerged, each of whom, in contrast to the earlier state of affairs, brought several fiefs together in one holding. The outstanding families were those which held the four great fiefs: the county of Jaffa-Ascalon, the principality of Galilee, the lordship of Sidon and Caesarea, and the lordship of Oultrejourdain with St. Abraham. According to thirteenth century legal theory these four were indivisible and their lords could be judged only by the other three. Jaffa-Ascalon was indeed impartible but the rest may be just a jurist's fiction. Only by marriage was it possible to enter the ranks of this self-assured élite. Beneath them came the great mass of lesser knights, most of them holding a fief from which the service of just one knight was owed. Usually these were money fiefs which just sufficed to maintain their standard of living and which kept them very dependent on their feudal lord. Amalric's *Assise sur la ligece* (above, p. 117) marked the decisive breach made by the higher nobility in the stronghold of royal power. Formerly it was believed that by making rear-vassals recognize the king as their liege lord, Amalric had raised them to the level of peers of the baronage and had thus created a useful counterweight to the higher nobility. But Prawer and Riley-Smith have shown that after 1198 appeals to the Assise were always made *against* the king, never in his interest. The rear-vassals became peers only in relation to the king; within the framework of the barony they remained subordinate to the baron. The witness lists of royal charters show clearly that the magnates continued to dominate the king's court and council. The lesser royal vassals and the rear-vassals would almost certainly have been too poor to have been able to exercise their right to sit and vote in the Haute Cour (theoretically a court of peers), especially since in this court the presence of three vassals was sufficient to establish a quorum. The Assise, in fact, was an instrument by which the nobles, in their own interests, could collectively renounce their obedience to the king just so long as they could find a legal justification for such a step. The earlier procedure for collective action, which can be observed during the revolt of Hugh of Jaffa (see above, p. 83), had required more effort and had entailed a higher risk. Then Hugh's vassals, in order to avoid rendering service, had been obliged to return their fiefs to him. Under the Assise, however, when the rights of one of their peers had been infringed, the vassals were entitled both to refuse service and retain their fiefs. The Haute Cour became increasingly important. In the twelfth century there had been a kind of royal privy council, but it vanished and by the thirteenth century the Haute Cour was not only the normal seignorial court for the royal domain but had developed into the highest—and indeed only—court of law for the ruling class. It acted as a legislative body; it elected king or regent, at any rate to the extent of deciding between competing hereditary claims; and, as an extension of the vassal's duty to give advice (*consilium*), it laid down the guidelines of policy. But not until the kingdom's last few years, if at all, were the acts of the Haute Cour recorded in its own register. Only in the most extraordinary situations did the Haute Cour and the Cour des Bourgeois deliberate together. An attempt has been made to project this practice back into the twelfth century. The cases cited, however, merely seem to show that certain decisions were thought to require the approval of the bourgeois, but not that this was necessarily obtained in joint meetings. The Haute Cour was composed not only of the nobility of the realm, but also, from 1120, of the bishops—in their role as councillors of the king—and, after 1148 (see above, p. 103), of high-ranking foreign crusaders. As the power of the Military Orders increased, so also their masters took an increasingly active part in the deliberations. After 1242–3 the presence of a middle-class element in the Haute Cour can be found. However, it was not the bourgeois as a class who were represented but the colonies of foreign merchants which were steadily increasing in power, and the confraternities which, in a time of collapsing public order, grew in number. Even so these non-noble participants were allowed only to talk, not to vote. Thus the nobility protected its plenitude of power and prevented the representation of the bourgeoisie as such. This made it impossible for the Haute Cour to develop into a parliament of estates. Equally inimicable to parliamentary development was the view of a leading feudal jurist that, in a dispute over pay for military services, the nobility had no right to lay a collective petition before the king. Instead he advised that everyone should put forward his own grievance individually and then, if necessary, should appeal to the *Assise sur la ligece*. To uphold the *Assise* seems to have been the overriding consideration in this lawyer's mind. Thus at all times the Haute Cour was dominated by the influence of the great barons. During the reign of Amalric, for example, they successfully defended the right of collateral relatives to succeed to their fiefs (*le cours des anciens fies est a toz heirs*), while at the same time the lesser vassals had this privilege taken from them. This only serves to confirm the fact that Amalric's reign witnessed not a weakening but a strengthening of the position of the higher nobility. They developed their own baronial courts and in the thirteenth century Jean d'Ibelin counted twenty-two fiefs possessing *court coin et justise*, i.e. having their own jurisdiction and the right to a lead seal. Such lead seals became, after *c.*1254, one of the main characteristics of the lordships (while the lords' wax seals were used to seal charters of only temporary validity). Towards the end of the twelfth century a few lordships (Beirut, Sidon, later on Tyre, and perhaps Jaffa) even usurped the royal prerogative of minting coins,—though possibly only in response to a demand for an increased volume of coin in circulation.[83] The greatest barons even had officials modelled on the pattern of the royal household.

Financial problems brought the kings into an even more difficult situation. By Baldwin III's time the king was already deep in debt. Amalric had to borrow money in order to pay his mercenaries. The royal domain shrank during Baldwin IV's reign and was then decimated by Saladin's conquests and by Guy of Lusignan's extravagant grants to those men who had supported his bid for the throne. In the thirteenth century King Aimery tried, without success, to reverse this process. The nobility became more and more powerful. In the second half of the thirteenth century the barons even made their own peace treaties with the Muslims, though at this date, of course, the king lived in Cyprus. In part this was the inevitable result of the fact that from 1225 onwards all the kings were outsiders who only occasionally came to the Holy Land and who generally ruled through *baillis* (regents).

Moreover during their struggle against Hohenstaufen centralization (see below, pp. 254) the nobles closed their ranks and energetically defended their rights. As a result they wanted to see them codified. According to thirteenth-century tradition the kingdom had always possessed a written code of law. Immediately after the conquest Godfrey de Bouillon is said to have had a collection of laws compiled and deposited in the Church of the Holy Sepulchre. It is then supposed to have been added to by a continuous process of legislation. This collection, known as the *Lettres de Sépulcre*, was believed to have been destroyed by Saladin in 1187. There may be a grain of truth in the story, but it is a very controversial question and certainly unlikely that there was ever a real code of law. King Aimery (1197–1205) wished to have the lost *Lettres de Sépulcre* (not Godfrey de Bouillon's 'code' but a collection of separate legislative acts) reconstructed by Ralph of Tiberias, a noble famous for his knowledge of the law, but Ralph excused himself from a task which was so incompatible with his own class interests. To some extent orally transmitted customary law helped to keep the tradition alive until it was written down in a partial codification, the *Livre au Roi* (drawn up at some date between 1196 and 1205), which still reflects something of the strong monarchy of the twelfth century and was, perhaps, an attempt inspired by King Aimery to achieve such a position of strength for himself.[84] Entirely different in character is the codification known as the *Assises de Jérusalem*[85] which is extant today only because it was also valid for Cyprus and was copied there. As part of the reaction to the Hohenstaufen policy of centralization, it summed up the rights of the vassals and is generally looked upon as the clearest and most comprehensive presentation of the structure of a highly feudalized state. But to be clear is not necessarily to be progressive. In fact the crass advocacy of class interests in this code of law together with its rigid formalism effectively nipped in the bud any possibility of vigorous development, even though it did produce fertile ground for the kind of legal trickery which left its mark on several treatises written by barons who were also learned lawyers, men like Philippe de Novare, Jean d'Ibelin, count of Jaffa, and Geoffrey Le Tort. The most important of these treatises was the *Livre de Jean d'Ibelin* (*c*.1265) a legal manual which left no room for unwritten customary law except in those cases where the code gave no answer. Naturally in this traditionalist age the formal character of the whole codification and, in particular, of the individual assises was one of an authentic interpretation of the 'good old custom' rather than the creation of new law. These collections described in detail an immensely complicated procedural law which, in various ways, ensured that the accused would have his rights, down to the right of all Franks to defend themselves in a judicial duel, but which also set such dangerous pitfalls in front of him that it became absolutely essential to have a lawyer in any case which was heard before the Haute Cour. Philippe de Novare in particular was an eminent authority on the art of procedural chicanery—those lawyer's tricks by which the hearing of a case could be accelerated or slowed down according to need. The most important means of coming to a judicial decision and one which, at the same time, could most easily be manipulated according to the shifting dictates of class interest was the *recort de court*, the court's collective memory of its judgements. In contrast to Philippe de Novare, Jean d'Ibelin's view of the law was clearly shaped by a guiding principle. For him the law of Jerusalem was based on a kind of treaty which had come into being, after the common enterprise of the conquest, as a result of the election of Godfrey de Bouillon. By this treaty loyalty to the feudal lord was the vassal's duty only so long as the lord observed the precisely defined rights of the vassal—rights which had been much extended since the twelfth century. In such a system the king and his *bailli* were playthings in the hands of various interests or, at best, merely first among equals.

So it was that as a class the nobility steadily improved its social and legal position. This did not mean that individual families were immune to the vicissitudes of fortune—on the contrary, as the example of the Mazoirs shows.* In the 1130s Reynald I Mazoir rose to be constable of Antioch. In the 1160s and 1170s we find his son Reynald II, as a vassal of Antioch and brother-in-law of the count of Tripoli, established in the huge, almost impregnable fortress of Marqab (Margat) not many miles distant from the sea. Reynald II had his own household, a castellan, six or seven vassals, a notary, a clerk with a master's degree, a few bourgeois, and a Syrian estate administrator. But his household expenses must have been burdensome, for from 1165 we can trace an accelerating process of sales and concessions to the Hospitallers. Here the Order of the Hospital created the nucleus of a new territorial domain which they rounded off in 1186, when Reynald's son Bertrand sold them the castle of Marqab, the town of Valania, three abbeys, and nineteen villages 'on account of the unbearable expenses and the all too close vicinity of the infidels', in return for an annual payment of 2,200 bezants. Bertrand then moved to Tripoli but by 1217 he was in Cyprus where he agreed to the payment being reduced to 2,000 bezants. His daughter married a wealthy Cypriot baron named Aimery Barlais who rose to be *bailli* but who later, being a supporter of Emperor Frederick II, suffered the forfeiture of his estates and had to go into exile. In 1226 his son Amalric cashed the annual payment for a lump sum of 14,400 bezants. Marqab, which had become the headquarters of the Syrian administration of the Hospitallers, capitulated to the Mameluks in 1285. Marqab had come into their possession relatively late. As early as 1144 they had already taken over Krak des Chevaliers with its extensive frontier march and in 1168 they took charge of Belvoir. In 1152 the Templars obtained Tortosa Castle from the local bishop on condition that they rebuilt it and in 1168 they received Safed as a royal gift. In all these castles the Military Orders embarked on a costly programme of building and extension.

The life span of the nobles was usually short. King Fulk was fifty-three when he died, Baldwin III thirty-three, Amalric thirty-eight, Baldwin IV twenty-four, and Baldwin V nine. Leprosy seems to have been common enough to call for legislation on the subject. The best known leper hospital in the kingdom was that of St. Lazarus outside the Damascus Gate of Jerusalem which developed into a Military Order. But two more are mentioned in the accounts of the executors of the count of Nevers (see below, p. 229), one at Bethlehem (then in exile at Acre), the other one, dedicated to St. Bartholomew, in Beirut. Within the ruling class wives were chosen almost exclusively from Frankish families, though two kings married Armenians and two others married Byzantine princesses. Concubinage with Christian women occurred at all levels of society— including the clergy. Child marriages were by no means rare and thus the men, worn down by war and the climate, often left young widows who

---

* The Mazoirs were, it is true, a family from the principality of Antioch, but conditions there were essentially the same as in the kingdom of Jerusalem.

were obliged by law to find a new husband soon in order to maintain the military value of a fief even when it was inherited by a woman. (They had to select one of the three candidates chosen by the king. Only if they could show that any of the king's choices was their social inferior did they have the right to refuse.) A classic example of this marriage pattern is provided by the career of Isabella, the younger daughter of King Amalric. In 1183 at the age of eleven she married Humphrey IV of Toron. At first sight this appears to constitute an exception to the convention (to which Prawer first drew attention) that royal princesses should marry either a prince of Antioch or a count of Tripoli—thus strengthening the influence of the court of Jerusalem over these principalities—or someone who was either an outsider or a new arrival (Fulk of Anjou, William Longsword of Montferrat, Guy of Lusignan, John of Brienne, Emperor Frederick II). The reluctance to make a marriage alliance with one of the old-established noble houses is probably to be explained in terms of doubts about the wisdom of adding to the hereditary claims of an already powerful family by a method which could only cause resentment among the other old families who were not so favoured. When King Amalric had his first marriage annulled (see above, p. 116), he ensured that the legitimacy of the children of this marriage was officially recognized, so that between Isabella and the throne there stood Baldwin IV, her elder half-sister Sibylla, and Sibylla's son Baldwin V. But in 1190 when Isabella's marriage to Humphrey was annulled for political reasons (see above, p. 144), she was the heiress to the throne, and her new husbands were chosen according to the old convention. From now on she brought both the crown and misfortune to successive husbands: Conrad of Montferrat (1190–2) was murdered by the Assassins; Henry of Champagne (1192–7) fell backwards out of a window; Aimery (1197–1205) died of a surfeit of fish. Both Conrad of Montferrat and Henry of Champagne were outsiders while Aimery belonged to the first generation of his family to live in the Holy Land even though he was the brother of King Guy of Jerusalem and was himself already king of Cyprus. Before Isabella married Aimery the question had been discussed in the Haute Cour and an alternative candidate had been proposed: Ralph of Tiberias. Ralph, who was famous for his knowledge of the law, belonged to the second generation of his family to live in the Holy Land although ancestors of his had been among the first crusaders. But if his candidature is said to have failed owing to his poverty and to German pressure in favour of the king of Cyprus, rather than to any other reason, this need not be taken as an argument against Prawer's thesis that candidates who belonged to the old families were at a disadvantage. In this case all these factors coincided. When Aimery died, Isabella at the age of thirty-three had been divorced once and widowed three times. She herself died shortly after Aimery.

In most respects the position of other women was very similar to what it was in the West.[86] James of Vitry, it is true, writes of them being shut away in harems, but to Orientals, with their very different ideas on the subject, it seemed as though they enjoyed far too much freedom. Women could hold fiefs—here there was a fundamental contrast with the position of noblewomen in Europe. So long as all their brothers, in order of birth, were already provided for, they could also inherit fiefs. Their position they owed simply to the particular environment of Outremer rather than to any special position midway between East and West.

By comparison with Europe the central administration was fairly rudimentary. The theory advanced by Riley-Smith that the kingdom's bureaucracy was relatively well developed because it took over pre-existing Fatimid institutions, is a rather implausible one.[87] It is undeniable that there was continuity in the methods of agriculture, perhaps also in some commercial practices. As the conquerors had to take over the old villages and left them untouched, there was inevitably a continuity in customs and in village life. It is also true that if the crusaders had not taken over Arab institutions, then they would have been very unlike other medieval conquerors. But the crusader conquest of Palestine destroyed the old units of land tenure much more thoroughly than in other conquered countries. Only the former Christian units remained more or less undisturbed. The vast latifundia of Muslim days, regardless of whether they had been state-owned or had been charities (*waqf*), were broken up with an arbitrariness which stopped short only of the basic unit of the village. This meant that the old archives, kept in Arabic anyway, were rendered useless. While it is true that the proportion of the harvest which the farmer had to pay to his lord was sometimes called *carragium* (from the Arabic *kharaj*), the fact is that it was more commonly called *terragium* and it was, in any case, something quite different from the old *kharaj*, which had been a public tax paid to the state.

The great crown offices developed out of the Lorrainer household offices of the first kings. The most important man was the constable who commanded the army, paid the mercenaries and exercised jurisdiction in military cases. His second-in-command was the marshal who was in charge of the mercenaries and was responsible for replacing horses which had been killed. The importance of these military offices was a consequence of the permanent danger of war. In contrast, the seneschal, so important in Europe, was less influential here. He was the king's deputy in the courts of justice, he administered the royal castles, and presided over the *Secrète*, a loosely organized financial office. Its name points much more to the Byzantine *sekreta* than to the Islamic *diwan* as the model for Jerusalem's fiscal administration. There are no indications that the *Secrète* of Jerusalem developed out of the chancery. We know next to nothing about the details of the *Secrète*'s procedures but one must agree with

Riley-Smith that it probably had, among other duties, cadastral functions. It is certain that it kept a register of money fiefs and it is likely, as Riley-Smith has surmised, that the crown retained overall supervision of the landed estates throughout the country. On the other hand, the sources lead us to believe that the *Grant Secrète* which we find in the thirteenth century, was not a central office for the whole of the royal demesne, but that the latter was administered by a number of regional *secrètes*. This seems to argue against a strict bureaucratization of the country. The chamberlain had certain honorary duties as well as having to supervise the royal household. For his remuneration there was a special 'fief of the chamber' assigned to him. The duties of the butler are unknown. The viscounts were royal officials, normally but not always of noble birth, who were responsible for local law and order. They presided over the *Cours des bourgeois* and administered the royal domain. Those barons who possessed their own courts also had their own viscounts at the head of local administration. The Jerusalem chancery remained a relatively undeveloped government department, sometimes consisting only of the chancellor, a vice-chancellor, a notary, and occasionally an additional scribe. They were all clerics, of course, but need not necessarily have begun their career in the royal chapel. The office of chancellor became a springboard for an epsicopal throne, though when chancellors were allowed to retain the office in addition to their episcopal dignity, they did in fact, here as elsewhere, give up the day-to-day routine of issuing charters. On the other hand they frequently made their influence felt in the field of foreign policy, none of them more so than William of Tyre. They were irremovable but, if necessary, they could be prevented from exercising their office. Chancery procedures were relatively rudimentary. We hear nothing of a register of outgoing charters and the charter business was mostly transacted in the form of the solemn diploma. This included the conclusion of bilateral treaties when the obligations of the other party were normally laid down by a separate oath. The simple administrative writ, one of the chief characteristics of highly centralized bureaucracies, was not altogether unknown, but extremely rare, at any rate up to the time of the absentee kings of the thirteenth century who used it at home.

On Cyprus, where there was a much longer period of constitutional development, the administration became more thoroughly organized. Here the chancery made use of the writ and seems to have kept registers. Moreover, there are registers for both the *Secrète* and the Haute Cour as well as documents recording the income and estates of individual landowners (*Remembrances de la Secrète, Remembrances de la Haute Cour, Prahtico*). On Cyprus the *Secrète,* presided over by a high royal official (*Bailli de la Secrète*), was more influential than in Jerusalem; the registrar of the Haute Cour was accountable to it. Because the *Secrète* dealt with fiscal business, the chamber, which in Europe was normally the central fiscal office, was restricted on Cyprus to its more classic role of maintaining the king's household (*hôtel du roi*). It purchased, for example, its own cloth and employed a special 'tailor of the chamber'. It also catered for the king's amusement, employing both falconers and keepers of the hounds. The king seems to have owned a menagerie; in 1468 it cost 365 bezants to feed a lioness for a year, an enormous sum given that on Cyprus a normal knight's fee was worth between 1,000 and 1,500 bezants a year. The nobility seems to have been passionately addicted to hunting. Ludolf of Sudheim tells of one Cypriot count who kept no less than 500 hunting dogs and 125 kennelmen. If this sounds exaggerated it is worth noting that another source reveals that after the fall of this particular count the king confiscated his hunting dogs and hunting leopards. In the fourteenth century a whole new set of royal officials appeared in Cyprus. The most important of these was the *Auditor* who had his own clerk and his own register. Originally he was probably an official of a court which supervised property transactions; later he became the attorney-general in the Haute Cour. The *Bailli de la Cour* was a steward of the household, while on the royal domain each of the ordinary *baillis* originally had a 'diocese', an administrative area in which he exercised jurisdiction in minor cases. In Nicosia the *bailli* was replaced by a royal viscount, the only official on the island to hold this title. In the fifteenth century the *baillis* dealt only with the economic exploitation of the royal domain. By then the five 'dioceses' had been replaced by twelve *contrées*. The *Maîtres des enquêtes* represented the interests of the fisc when dealing with the estates of the deceased (*Inquisitio post mortem*). Military organization on Cyprus produced further officers, the Grand Turcopolier (originally the commander of lightly armed auxiliaries) and the Admiral. In the fifteenth century there is evidence of a council of state, an institution imported from Europe which foreshadowed the cabinet of modern times.

On the surface the institutions of Antioch, which we can study in a rather fragmentary fashion in an Armenian translation of the assizes of Antioch, resembled those of Jerusalem. But, following Norman custom, it was an hereditary principality right from the beginning with the electoral rights of the Haute Cour limited to the choice of a *bailli*. Here the money fief was more fully developed and, in contrast to Jerusalem, the prince on each succession to a fief received one ninth of its annual yield. The native element in the administration was more significant than in Jerusalem. Indeed the whole administration was based on the Byzantine pattern as, for example, in the establishment of *duces* to supervise the administration of Antioch, Lattakieh, and Jabala. These *duces* were appointed and dismissed at the prince's pleasure.

The king had various sources of revenue. The viscounts rendered quarterly accounts of the income from the royal domain to the *Secrète* which kept a register of these accounts. The income was derived from feudal dues and taxes on both agricultural and urban production. Regalian rights like the right to mint coin also yielded profits. A special feature of the coinage were the rather poor imitations of Islamic gold dinars (*bisancii saracenati*) which were struck at the royal mints from 1124 on. During the twelfth century the percentage of bullion contained in them sank in successive stages.[88] When Pope Innocent IV (1243–54) protested about the minting of Islamic coins by Jerusalem, Christian inscriptions such as 'Minted at Acre in the year 1251. One Lord, one faith, one baptism' (cf. Ephesians 4:5) were added in Kufic script to these coins which were much used for trade with the Muslims. The numerous gold pieces which are extant only as fragments but most probably were never circular in shape are curious. On them they have the names of kings of Jerusalem in Latin. That they should have served to make up the weight of worn down coins is not very likely—since coins, when large sums were involved, were weighed rather than counted. It is more plausible, though far from certain, that they were sold to pilgrims to be given to churches. In his domain the king also had a financial interest in various industrial processes (soap production, dyeing, tanning and sugar production) which were farmed out for fixed sums to agents-general who ran the risks involved in actually collecting the duties. The Syro-Christian craftsmen were particularly burdened by taxation. The Muslims paid a moderate poll tax, the Bedouins paid tribute; the right of wreck belonged to the king; the general taxes on property imposed in an emergency have already been mentioned (see above, pp. 119 and 131). The most valuable sources of income were the customs and harbour dues of Acre and Tyre. The king very frequently made assignments on the harbour receipts of Acre though these were not always met. In the thirteenth century a customs duty varying from 4.16 to 11.2 per cent of the value had to be paid on imports from the East which were due for re-export. Higher duties, up to 25 per cent, were imposed on imports which were for domestic consumption. The preference rate given to the transit trade was designed to meet the competition from the Egyptian Nile Delta ports. In contrast to Fatimid Egypt a double system of graduated tariffs, taking into account the religion of the merchant as well as the kind of goods—with preferential treatment for co-religionists—did not exist in the Latin East. In fact Saladin decided to abolish this discriminatory system in order to compete with the Franks for the trade of Syria. In the *funda*, a cross between a bazaar and a warehouse, special market dues were levied by the market police. Foreign ships had to pay an anchorage fee of one mark of silver and the *terciaria*, i.e. one third of the sum paid by voyagers for their passage. This tax on pilgrims seems to have been important because it was expressly reserved to the king when other very extensive privileges were granted to the Venetians in 1123. The pilgrims themselves paid a duty on the property they brought with them until about 1130 when they were granted exemption by Baldwin II. But at all times the kings found this financial system inadequate and thus compared with their cousins in the west they were rarely in a position to indulge in policies which were deliberately designed to stimulate trade. Even so, we have already noted the important privilege which granted exemption from all internal customs to Jerusalem (see above, p. 154). The king of Cyprus was more fortunate in this respect and indeed in general he was able to maintain a preponderance of political power on the island. In 1367, according to Jean Richard, the royal domain in the diocese of Limassol was as large as the combined estates of the whole secular nobility. The king had a revenue of approximately 100,000 bezants, of which 86,500 derived from his lands; the rest came from various other rights. In addition he possessed valuable monopolies such as the dyehouses at Nicosia and the saltpans at Larnaca. Under James I the *mète du sel* was introduced and under this system all villagers were constrained to buy a certain quantity of salt. On Cyprus in the fourteenth century the revenues from the royal domain were usually farmed out, while in the fifteenth century direct exploitation prevailed. In addition the revenues of the king of Cyprus included the 'royal tithe' (see below, p. 246) and, under James II, the *rata*, a special three-year tax on all net income (i.e. income after ordinary taxation). To administer the *rata* the New Office (*nouvel ofice*) was set up.

The military system was based on the fief, above all on the money fief of 400–500 bezants a year for a knight.[89] Jean d'Ibelin preserved an (incomplete) list of knight's fees as they were *circa* 1180. This gives a total of 675 knights from the great and small crown fiefs to which, of course, we must add the knights belonging to the Military Orders. The Church and the urban bourgeoisie provided *sergeants* (foot-soldiers). The patriarch, the canons of the Church of the Holy Sepulchre, and the cities of Jerusalem and Acre each had to raise 500; the archbishops of Nazareth and Tyre, the bishop of Acre, and the abbot of Mount Sion 150 each; the bourgeoisie of Tyre 100, etc.; in total 5,025. In addition there was the light cavalry recruited from the native population. These troops were known as Turcopoles. They were frequently baptized Muslims, one of them in fact being named Geoffrey the Baptized. Among the highest officers of the Military Orders were the Turcopoliers who commanded these troops. Right from the beginning mercenaries were employed. In emergencies every able-bodied Frank could be called to arms; and every year there was the useful assistance of the crusaders who had come to the Holy Land for a season's fighting. In war the aim was almost always a localized conflict with a clearly defined geographical objective rather than the complete destruction of the enemy forces. As the Muslim armies grew stronger this concept of a limited war developed into a defensive war strategy, avoiding the risks involved in a pitched battle, intending only to contain the forces of the enemy until, as regularly happened, his army began to dissolve and he was forced to withdraw. Tactically the idea was to hold the troops together in tight battle formation in all circumstances; according to the Templar rule anyone who offended in this respect could expect to be punished severely. If this tight formation were lost then the speedier and more mobile Turkish cavalry soon gained the upper hand. The function of the infantry was to protect the heavily armoured knights both while on the march and in battle until the opportunity came for them to charge in a phalanx into the enemy. If properly delivered it was very seldom that the Muslims could stand up to the weight of such an attack.

The kings benefited from the fact that the vassals were obliged to do military service for much longer than in Europe where service normally seems to have been restricted to a period of forty days *per annum*. Indeed until recently scholars thought that in Outremer military service in return for a fief was unlimited—despite the fact that this would have spelt economic ruin for the king's vassals. But pioneering work by Riley-Smith has shown that this was not the case. Service always had to be rendered for the period for which the vassal had been summoned and no summons for more than a year was permissible. But this last clause was merely a long stop. In practice it was the first part of the regulation which was decisive because it forced the king to settle the length of a campaign before it began. When the announced campaigning period had expired, vassals were not allowed to go home but the king now had to pay them. As for service outside the kingdom, not only was this always paid service, but each and every expedition beyond the borders had to be preceded by negotiations between the king and his vassals. Out of the five invasions of Egypt undertaken by King Amalric, the one in 1164 was financed by one of the rival factions in Egypt, i.e. by Muslims, the one in 1167 by an extraordinary 10 per cent tax levied by way of a negotiated compromise on those who refused to take part. In 1168 both vassals and Military Orders were persuaded by the most grandiose promises of future possessions in Egypt; the expedition of 1169 was paid for by Byzantium. War was never simply a public responsibility, it was always an individual's way of earning a living as well. After 1168 (*Assise de Bilbeis*), however, the knights were permitted to refuse to do service on foot during sieges—a clear indication that a noble caste was in the process of formation. None the less the role of the footsoldier in medieval warfare in general, as well as in siege operations in particular, has recently been stressed by Gillingham and we should do well to be less exclusively concerned with the gallant exploits of the knight in shining armour. The castles were frequently sited so that it was possible to use lights to signal from one to another. The castle's offensive role as a *Gegenburg* has already been mentioned. But its chief function was, of course, an administrative and defensive one (see above, pp. 85 and 155), not because they could prevent enemy troops from penetrating into the interior but because they provided a place for refuge for the population and a base for counter-attack. The idea that Frankish castle-building techniques, using Byzantine and Arab models, were more advanced than those in Europe has been made to look a good deal less convincing by R. C. Smail's investigations; and the same fate, at the same hands, has befallen the idea that the Holy Land was divided into one outer and two inner rings of fortresses. In places the crusaders did take over Byzantine fortresses, and later the Ayubids and Mameluks made further additions to them, above all to the mighty Krak des Chevaliers. The contributions actually made by the crusaders to these castles seem to have been technically very similar to work being done in Europe. Their most striking features were the strength and solidity of the walls and their advantageous sites.

After the collapse of Patriarch Daimbert's attempt to create his own great ecclesiastical lordship, the Palestinian Church remained firmly within the community of Rome.[90] The authority of the pope was exercised through legates and judges-delegate. At the head of the ecclesiastical organization stood the patriarchs of Jerusalem and Antioch; the ecclesiastical boundaries followed the political ones, as was shown by the dispute over Tyre between the two patriarchs (see above, p. 76f.). The archbishoprics of Caesarea, Tyre, Nazareth, and Petra founded or promoted in this order to this rank belonged to the patriarchate of Jerusalem; so, therefore, did the bishoprics of Ramleh-Lydda, Bethlehem, Sebastea, Tiberias, Beirut, Acre, Sidon, Banyas, and St. Abraham (Hebron), where in 1119 the bones of the three patriarchs, Abraham, Isaac, and Jacob were found and which, from then on, became one of the most popular places of pilgrimage for Christians and Muslims alike. In Jerusalem the patriarch possessed a quarter of the city which had a special but ambiguous status. It was not a lordship of the kingdom because the patriarch did not render knight service for it, as was done by the archbishop of Nazareth (who owed six knights) and the bishop of Lydda (ten). They were the only two ecclesiastical tenants-in-chief in the kingdom enjoying both a seat and vote in the Haute Cour. On the other hand, the Patriarch exercised various rights of lordship in his section of the city. The patriarch's quarter may, perhaps, best be characterized as a liberty, i.e. a district from which royal officials were excluded. A special peculiarity of the church of Jerusalem was what I have called *Stiftsbistümer* (collegiate bishoprics). These were the bishoprics of Haifa, Jaffa, and Nablus which were bishoprics in theory only since they had no bishops of their own but were administered by the archbishop of Caesarea, and the priors of the canons regular at the *Templum Domini* and the Holy Sepulchre, respectively. The cathedral church of the patriarch was the Church of the Holy Sepulchre, the most important church in the land, possessing extensive estates in Europe (1128: sixty churches in eighteen European dioceses, mostly in Apulia) as well as in the Holy Land. A house of Austin canons under a prior functioned as the cathedral chapter of the

Holy Sepulchre. Until 1114 this was a community of secular canons but in that year, despite their opposition, Patriarch Arnulf regularized them. Other important religious institutions were the house of canons on the Mount of Olives, the abbey on Mount Sion, the Benedictine abbeys of St. Mary Latina and St. Mary Josaphat at Jerusalem, and the monastery of Tabor where the Cluniacs had settled. The Benedictine abbey of Palmarea near Tiberias, the family monastery of the lords of Beisan, became a Cluniac house in 1170. At St. Lazarus at Bethany there was the rare institution of a double monastery for nuns and monks under the rule of an abbess, a very wealthy foundation by the royal family, probably on the model of Fontevrault. The Premonstratensians had a small centre in St. Samuel on Montjoie near Jerusalem. The Cistercians had houses only in the county of Tripoli and the principality of Antioch. Kedar has shown that hermits played an important role in the Holy Land of the twelfth century. They preferred the seclusion of the Black Mountains of the north and the Judaean desert but they also populated the walls of Jerusalem in such numbers that their expulsion after 1187 was noticed and lamented. From early on the bishops strove to integrate eremitism into the church. Success came only in the thirteenth century when hermits living on Mount Carmel formed the nucleus of the Carmelite Order. The Mendicant Orders also set up houses in the Holy Land not long after they had been recognized by the pope. In the second half of the thirteenth century Dominicans were to fill many episcopal sees. As James of Vitry, the great promoter of the women's religious movement, was bishop of Acre for some years, it is not surprising that we find two beguines there in 1266.

The natural centre of religious life was in Jerusalem and its environs. Christmas was celebrated at Bethlehem; Candlemas with the canons of the Temple of the Lord—for this is what the Dome of the Rock, the superb octagonal Omar mosque which is the oldest surviving example of Islamic architecture, was believed to be. Other festivals were celebrated in the places hallowed by tradition: Ascension on the Mount of Olives, Whitsun on Mount Sion, the Feast of the Assumption of the Virgin at St. Mary Josaphat. Good Friday was observed on the Hill of Calvary. Every year on Easter Saturday in the Church of the Holy Sepulchre there occurred the 'miracle of the Sacred Fire'—a piece of pyrotechnic nonsense which was finally forbidden by Pope Gregory IX in 1238. The lamps in the Sepulchre Chapel were supposed to be lit by heavenly fire; it was probably spontaneous ignition brought about by a mixture of Mecca balsam and oil of Jasmine. When in 1101, the miracle for once failed to take place there was hopeless confusion in the crowd and some anxious hours for the clergy. Finally there was a special festival on 15 July to celebrate the capture of the city and the consecration of the Holy Sepulchre. For young clerks there were schools in the Holy Land, at the Holy Sepulchre for example, but those who showed real promise went to study in France and

Italy—William of Tyre stayed away for nearly twenty years. At Nicosia in March 1249 the papal legate Odo of Châteauroux promulgated statutes lamenting the fact that distance prevented the Cypriot clergy from obtaining the education available in the schools of Europe.[91] The clergy had their own courts, firstly to deal with cases in which they themselves were involved and, secondly, to deal generally with certain offences: heresy, witchcraft, testamentary and marital matters, and sexual offences. The Church was permanently involved in disputes with the Military Orders which remained outside and independent of diocesan organization and jurisdiction while, willy-nilly, the bishops were forced to consecrate priests belonging to these Orders. The Hospitallers infuriated the patriarch of Jerusalem by rebuilding their Hospital on a scale far surpassing the Church of the Holy Sepulchre. Then, in 1153, his fury knew no bounds when the noise of their bells drowned his attempts to preach a sermon in the chapel on the Hill of Calvary. One day they even entered the chapel armed and turned it into a kind of archery range; the arrows which were collected together at the end of the day were long left to hang in bundles in the church as a reminder of the outrage. Tithes, an important source of revenue for the Church, were a perennial bone of contention with both the Military Orders and the secular nobility. This was because, in contrast to the arrangement in Europe, in the Holy Land and Cyprus tithes were paid not by the subordinate tenant but by the lord of the land (including both the king and ecclesiastical corporations except where they were granted exemption by pope or bishop or possessed certain tithes as an episcopal gift—exceptions which prove the general rule). Moreover, these tithes did not go directly to the parish clergy but were paid into a central office at the cathedral and were then redistributed among the parishes. This arrangement ensured that the Latin Church received indirect financial support from the large group of non-Latin Christians and even from the Muslims since the income of the Frankish lords, on which the tithe assessments were made, included the dues paid to them by these groups whose wealth could not have been tapped by a tithe on the European model. This was expressly stated in 1113 when the pope granted the abbey of Josaphat, as part of its exemption from episcopal tithes, the right to retain full possession of dues paid by infidel peasants; without this the abbey would have had to hand over the tithe on this income to the diocesan, in this case the patriarch. From the pontificates of Anastasius IV and Alexander III and much to the indignation of the bishops, the Military Orders could claim exemption from tithes on those lands which they farmed themselves. Even so the survival of a tithes list of 1193 from the Antiochene see of Valania shows just how wealthy even an ordinary diocesan bishop could be, though of course much of this income was required to support his parish clergy. Obviously this was not a system which gave a bishop any incentive to create a dense network of parishes in his diocese. Normally there was only one parish church in each town—in the case of episcopal sees the cathedral itself. The Church of the Holy Sepulchre was the only parish church in Jerusalem, though there were at least twenty-seven churches in the city. Only in a very few towns, such as Acre with its thirty-eight churches, was more than one parish established. Of course in Acre, as well as in the other ports, the Italians in their quarters claimed parochial rights over their compatriots. These claims, and similar claims put forward by the Military Orders, were often fiercely contested by the diocesan, involving as they did such lucrative parochial rights as burial. Only in recent years has the rural parish been a subject for investigation, both by Hamilton and myself. It was even rarer than the urban parish but, contrary to earlier assumptions, it did exist. Its scarcity was essentially a consequence of the way the Latins settled the country. They were concentrated in the towns and not even the landed nobility lived on their estates. The few Franks who did live in the countryside, settled in villages which were exclusively Latin, containing neither Syro-Christians nor Muslims. Therefore it was only in these few places that rural parishes were needed. At *Magna Mahumeria* (al-Bira) and *Emmaus* (Qubeibeh), the Latin parish churches can still be seen. Where the monasteries engaged in internal colonization, they also built churches (e.g. *Legio* = Lajun, where there was a bitter dispute with the diocesan over parochial rights) or at least a chapel (*Sephoria* near Lydda). In order to prevent the balance of wealth in a small kingdom being upset by the continued alienation of land to the Church, the *Livre au Roi* forbade the sale of fiefs to the Church. This prohibition was also designed to prevent the king losing the military service due from the fiefs. But the practice of this prohibition was always less rigid than the theory and the church continued to acquire more and more land.

The kings themselves endowed the Church richly, not only because by doing this they conformed to the ideal standards expected of a medieval king, but also because they needed the Church's financial support. William of Tyre complained bitterly of the way in which his patron Amalric, for example, laid his hands on Church property in order to finance his policy. On the other hand it was largely the Church's financial contribution to Amalric's government that enabled it to exercise a significant influence over policy. No one embodied this better than William of Tyre himself. He championed the *libertas* of the Church against the king, but never for a moment considered that the clergy should abstain from politics. Episcopal elections required the king's confirmation; during vacancies the diocesan revenues seem to have been paid over to the king. Here, as in most matters of ecclesiastical organization, practice in Outremer was based on the custom in Europe. Inevitably then the question of the relationship between *sacerdotium* and *regnum* arose in the Latin East, but it was never disputed with the dogmatic bitterness that was characteristic of the West and particularly of the empire. In dealing with the crusader states the popes always held firmly to the basic demand for the *libertas ecclesiae*. On the other hand they recognized that only a strong secular arm would be able to protect these states against the infidel. But there were quarrels. The first king, Baldwin I, was a convinced adherent of pre-Gregorian ways of life who had abandoned his ecclesiastical career in Europe when church reform curtailed his income. It is true that after the shocking imprisonment of the pope by Emperor Henry V in 1111 he did not prevent a papal legate from being the first to excommunicate the emperor from the safe distance of the kingdom of Jerusalem.[92] None the less as early as 1101 he had clashed sharply with the patriarch of Jerusalem over the question of whether ecclesiastical revenues belonged to the Church or to the king. The patriarch accused him of infringing the liberty of the Church and in those days everyone knew the meaning of that slogan. Baldwin I kept a tight control over tithes, the Church's main source of income. Although this was now out of step with contemporary opinion, it was not abolished until 1120 when, in the Concordat of Nablus, Baldwin's successor solemnly relinquished his control. Returning tithes to the Church was probably the price he had to pay for his election (see above, p. 74). Having obtained this victory, the papacy then allowed the crown to intervene in episcopal elections, notably elections to the patriarchal see (see above, p. 158). Not until the pontificate of Celestine III (1191–8) was this royal prerogative reduced to the level of a mere right of confirmation. During the Alexandrine schism between Alexander III and a series of anti-popes (1159–77) the king at first tried to steer a cautiously neutral course; he wanted to allow Alexander's legate to enter the country only as an unofficial tourist. Finally, however, a majority of the episcopate forced him to align himself with the Alexandrine party. William of Tyre, who returned from his studies in France and Italy in 1165, seems to have been more inclined to support the imperial side, possibly under the influence of the Bolognese legists whose lectures he had attended. He complained of the financial burdens which Alexander's legate imposed upon the Palestinian Church. Relations with the other Christian Churches were tolerably good. Tension was greatest with the Greek Orthodox Church; only for a short while were they permitted to hold services in the Church of the Holy Sepulchre (see above, p. 123). But they retained most of their monasteries and in Byzantium a shadow patriarchate of Jerusalem was maintained; indeed its authority was acknowledged by the abbot-archbishop of the monastery on Mount Sinai (1166). Apart from isolated incidents like the plundering of the monastery of Barsauma by Joscelin II of Edessa in 1148, relations with the Jacobites were good. Queen Melisende gave them endowments—as she also did for the Armenian and Orthodox churches. In 1181 the Maronites entered into a permanent union with the Latins though within the Maronite Church there always remained a party opposed to this and prepared to use the weapons of homicide and murder. After 1187 as the kingdom became progressively smaller, the bishops and monasteries were forced to congregate more and more in Acre. After 1225 when the kings became outsiders who did not reside in their kingdom, they also lost the right to confirm the results of ecclesiastical elections. During the same period the prestige of the patriarch, the kingdom's *Seignor espirituel*, grew. From about 1220 he was, in real and not just in formal terms, the pope's plenipotentiary, for he was the *legatus natus* and cardinal legates *a latere* were now rarely sent to Outremer. From *c.*1262 onwards he also administered the bishopric of Acre. This permanent personal union of bishopric and patriarchate was a way of avoiding the unedifying clashes with the diocesan which had occurred ever since he had taken up residence there. During the last decades of the kingdom's existence the patriarch, willy-nilly, had to take over certain of the ruler's functions.

Below the nobility there developed a further class of freemen, the bourgeoisie, whose existence can be documented from *c.*1110. It should not be thought that they were anything like the bourgeoisie of today. Certainly there was, in the towns, a social class—a bourgeoisie in the modern sense—made up of Latin and Syrian Christians. But in the crusader states the term bourgeoisie meant something else: it meant the form of political organization common to the non-noble Franks. The fact that the indigenous population had long been organized into religious and ethnic groups stimulated the development of the Frankish bourgeoisie as also did the principle—so precious to the Middle Ages—that a man should be judged by his peers. The bourgeoisie was composed in part of the inhabitants of the small new settlements both in the interior and in the frontier regions (see p. 155) whose tenure of land was described expressly as *tenure en bourgeoisie*, and in part of the artisans and shopkeepers of Jerusalem and the coastal towns. It did not include the merchants from Italy and south France because they belonged to their own communities. The bourgeois were personally free but owed allegiance to the lord of the district or town. In Jerusalem their law is an obscure subject though it is clear that the economic solidarity of the family became less marked in the thirteenth century; the twelfth-century restrictions on the free alienation of family land have disappeared. In Antioch the marriage and property rights of the bourgeois remained firmly in the Norman mould. It is interesting to observe that in this respect the law of the first comers was preserved whereas the property law of the nobility, originally also Norman, kept in step with political developments in Antioch and became French.

The bourgeoisie in Jerusalem acquired their own code of law in about 1240 with the *Livre des Assises des Bourgeois*, based on the Provençal (and thus Roman Law) collection *Lo Codi*, and carefully amended to fit circumstances in Palestine.[93] But the legal organization of the bourgeoisie was much older than this. As early as the twelfth century we find the *Cours des Bourgeois*, their own courts and institutions of self-government, corresponding to the Haute Cour of the nobility. In the city of Jerusalem we can see this court developing from 1125 onwards; by 1149 it was a firmly established institution (and in Acre probably as early as 1135). In the thirteenth century there were four royal and thirty-three baronial courts of this kind, meeting three times a week under the presidency of the viscount who represented the local lord. Twelve jurors (*jurati*), exclusively Franks, declared the law in both civil and criminal cases involving the Frankish bourgeoisie. From these courts there was no possibility of an appeal. In the Haute Cour it was at least theoretically possible to escape the gallows by challenging the court to a duel and defeating all the judges within the space of one day. For non-noble Franks the judicial duel was permitted within the framework of the *Cour des Bourgeois*. But the bourgeois fought their duels against each other, not against the judges, and they used staves not swords. Syrians, Greeks, and Saracens were allowed to fight judicial duels before the *Cour des Bourgeois* only if they were accused of murder. In general the *Cour des Bourgeois* exercised blood justice over all non-Franks and acted as a register office for the records of property transactions; for this reason the court kept a register of its own from 1251. In addition it functioned as a court of appeal for the *Cour de la Fonde* and the *Cour de la Chaine*, the existence of both of which can be traced from the days of King Amalric.[94] The *Cour de la Fonde* dealt with commercial cases in the market towns and kept a register of business transactions not involving real estate. Since the parties in such disputes were often Christian non-Franks as well as Franks, the court was composed of two Franks and four Christian Syrians, but it also heard commercial cases involving Greeks, Muslims, Jews, and others. However, cases in which goods worth more than one mark of silver were in dispute automatically went before the *Cour des Bourgeois* which was composed exclusively of Franks. So too was the *Cour de la Chaine* (*Chaine* = the harbour chain) since it dealt only with questions of maritime and navigation law where disputes with the native population could hardly arise. Both courts also levied customs and trade duties and out of the proceeds made payments on the crown's behalf. In these special courts the judicial duel could not be used as a method of proof.

In the thirteenth century communes also developed, but in contrast to the situation in Europe they were few and far between.[95] Examples of this kind of political structure occur possibly in Tyre (briefly from 1187), and certainly in Antioch (from 1194), in Acre (from 1231), and in Tripoli (from 1288). They never had an important part to play in the history of Outremer precisely because a great part of the Frankish bourgeoisie already belonged to a legal community. Moreover there were alien bodies in the towns in the shape of the powerful Italian communities who would never recognize a commune as their overlord. Thus the Palestinian communes did not survive for long, especially when the Church opposed them, as it did at Acre at the request of Emperor Frederick II and at Antioch in a kind of reflex reaction to the egalitarian outlook of the commune there which had planned to tax all its members, clergy as well as laymen. But it was not only for these reasons that urban autonomy had no chance in the Latin East. It was also prevented by the unparalleled concentration of most Latin social strata in the towns. This included all the nobles and the idea of urban self-government was not for them. The kings, like some of their European colleagues, might have promoted urban autonomy and might thereby have won allies against the increasing power of the nobility, but since they themselves were the direct lords of the principal cities, this would have been against their own financial interest. Thus all the communes of Outremer came into being at times when the lord of the town had shown himself to be either unwilling or unable to defend the community. In Acre the commune was a product of anti-Hohenstaufen feeling. It was joined by the nobles, even of the highest rank, men like Jean d'Ibelin. In Antioch the numerous Greek inhabitants of the city joined the movement right from the start; in Acre, however, the commune was organized entirely by Franks. It originated in the religious fraternity of St. Andrew's church and then developed into a sworn community for urban government with the town itself as an abstract concept being looked upon as the town lord. The confraternity of St. Andrew's was particularly well-suited to serve as the nucleus of a commune because it possessed old royal privileges which permitted all Franks, regardless of origin and social status, to join it. This appeared to legitimize the creation of the commune since, in legal terms, all that happened was a massive influx of new members into a licensed confraternity. The commune was organized along European lines. At the head of the commune were the consuls or syndics under the chairmanship of a mayor; it had its own bells, its own budget and the right to tax its members, judicial authority, and doubtless also a militia. Whereas the commune at Antioch seems to have fallen into decay gradually, the one at Acre was formally dissolved in 1241.

Hardly any aspect of the history of the crusader states has given rise to such lively debate as the commune at Acre. La Monte regarded it as a normal Mediterranean commune aiming only at urban autonomy. Prawer, on the other hand, argued that the commune saw itself as the lawful government of the whole land when the Haute Cour was hamstrung by the refusal of Frederick II's lieutenant to convene it. Riley-Smith disagrees with both and interprets the commune in purely negative terms. In his view it served only to organize the opposition to the Hohenstaufen regime at a time when the chief political weapon of the Haute Cour, the *Assise sur la ligece* (see above, p. 117), had lost its sting because Frederick II's lieutenant commanded enough mercenary soldiers to render the withdrawal of service by the vassals under the *Assise* ineffective. But in that case it is difficult to see how the *Assise* could have been successfully employed as recently as 1229 against the emperor himself when he had nearly as many troops at his disposal (i.e. 600 knights) and why the commune was founded in 1231 when it was not until 1232 that the *Assise* was invoked and failed to work. Richard has directed attention back to the urban aspects of the question and, against Prawer, has pointed out that the leading barons of the commune were not willing to acknowledge its jurisdiction within their own lordships (e.g. Beirut and Caesarea). Since, as it seems to me, a first commune of Acre existed as early as 1198 and could only have been intended to achieve a greater degree of self-government, the purely urban aspects can clearly not be omitted. How else should we understand the terms proposed by the barons in 1241, when they deserted the bourgeois and offered to dissolve the commune, specifying that all communal offices should be abolished with the exception of those which were already in existence before 1225 (i.e. the offices of the first commune)? No better explanation of the barons' proposal which adheres strictly to the actual wording of the source has as yet been found. But perhaps a hitherto unused argument could be adduced in support of Prawer which might encourage acceptance both of the state-oriented *and* urban aims of the commune. This compromise solution lies in the report on the creation of the commune which states that there was 'in the land' (*en la terre*) a *Frarie de Saint-André*. And indeed, according to a charter of 1166 (Röhricht, *Regesta regni Hierosolymitani*, no. 422a) the church of St, Andrew's on the southern tip of Acre was situated outside the city walls (*extra muros*) and was, precisely because of this, a well-known landmark for navigators. A purely municipal commune would surely have chosen a church inside the city as its cradle. The fact that St. Andrew's lay just outside of Acre suggests that the aims and motives of the commune were more than merely urban ones.

When it became increasingly clear that the nobility looked upon the bourgeoisie only as a convenient and temporary ally, then the latter withdrew more and more into the numerous confraternities which, unlike the *Frarie de Saint-André*, were open only to members of one nationality. Here the bourgeois found mutual solidarity and a certain amount of social welfare such as assistance in case of illness or the provision of a proper funeral. In the thirteenth century these brotherhoods had a role to play both in politics and in urban defence (see above, p. 160). Riley-Smith has observed, however, that they could not replace the old organizational form of the *borgesie*, and given that their members also included knights, at any rate in the case of the Italian confraternity of the Holy Spirit in Acre, this is undoubtedly so. Moreover, their partial dependence on ecclesiastical corporations tended to make them ill-equipped to represent the political aspirations of their social class. At least this is true of the two non-Latin confraternities known to us in Acre. The Greek Orthodox confraternity of St. George was subject to the Hospitallers (as also was the Latin Spanish confraternity of St. James). The confraternity of the *Mosserins*, Chaldaean merchants from Mosul, was under the control of the Templars. With their common chests the confraternities also helped to overcome some of the supply problems of the crusades, presumably on the model of the *confraternitas* established to administer a common war chest during the First Crusade.

In the crusader towns there were no craftsmen's guilds. This means that one of the most vital ingredients in the struggle for urban autonomy in Europe was missing in the Latin East. Artisans of the same craft were concentrated in one street each, but only for surveillance and taxation. Only the physicians seem to have formed a college in order, under the bishop's chairmanship, to examine and license alien doctors. It is obvious why no guilds emerged. Frankish craftsmen would never have mixed in one guild with their Syro-Christian, Jewish, or Greek Orthodox fellow artisans, though such existed. This meant that a priori the essential function of a guild, regulating the supply side of the market, could never be achieved. And indeed in a country which was heavily dependent on immigration, it would have been impossible to deny newly arrived Frankish artisans admission into the guild.

The most striking feature of the towns was the presence of the Italian communities.[96] This went back to the early twelfth century when they were granted privileges on an unparalleled scale (see above, p. 76). When genuine grants had not been made, the cities did not hesitate to procure forgeries. When in 1248 the crusade of Louis IX of France was imminent, the Marseillais consul in Palestine contracted loans from merchants of Marseilles present in Acre against promissory notes. Twenty of them are still extant in the city archives of Marseilles. In the notes the consul explained that he needed the money to 'repurchase' charters issued by King Fulk and King Aimery of Jerusalem which had been fraudulently alienated from the commune of Marseilles. Actually he used the money to pay a flourishing forgery shop in Acre to produce them for him in the first place. When the merchants returned to Marseilles they handed in the notes to the city and were duly reimbursed. From 1155 onwards the Genoese even claimed that they had once had an inscription in golden letters in the church of the Holy Sepulchre extolling their part in the conquest of the Holy Land and listing their reward for this (a quarter in both Jaffa and Jerusalem and one third of Caesarea, Arsuf, and Acre). They now demanded that it be 'restored'. In the beginning they were unsuccessful but they kept pestering the papal Curia and the court of Jerusalem with the matter until in 1192 they finally obtained a privilege from the ruler authorizing its 'restoration'. In the thirteenth century a fictitious text of the inscription was then included in the Genoese *Liber iurium* and, eventually, as the story grew in the telling, the Bolognese even claimed to know that it had been one of them who had originally executed the inscription and how much had been paid for it.

The kingdom had no war fleet of its own and was therefore dependent on the maritime cities of Italy. They were needed to carry the kingdom's exports and imports; finally indeed it became necessary to try to stop them from sailing to Egyptian harbours. The great privilege of 1123 for the Venetians, however, has obscured the fact that the nature and extent of the Italian commitment varied considerably from one town to another. Holding one third of the city of Tyre and, more important, of the countryside around it, Venice had a complex of possessions which could have yielded considerable revenues and for which it rendered the king a token service of three knights, apparently on a voluntary basis. Yet in the twelfth century Venice's political commitment in the Levant remained a half-hearted one. Not until the thirteenth century and especially after the victory over Genoa in the War of St. Sabas (see below, p. 274) did it become the leading maritime power there. Attempts were then made to enlarge and fortify the increasingly important Venetian quarter in Acre. In 1286, for example, as D. Jacoby has shown, they imported seventy-two tons of stone from Venice, either because the stone from Istria is known for its particular hardness or—and more probably—because the Mameluks were already preventing the transport of building material into Acre. Another indication of the growing Acre trade of the *Serenissima* is the resolution of the Venetian *Maggior Consiglio* in 1288: between thirty and forty anchors were to be despatched from the Venetian arsenal and kept by the Venetian authorities at Acre to be leased to Venetian merchants in times of bad weather. But, as a forthcoming study by Favreau-Lilie will show, in the twelfth century it was Pisa, not Venice, which was the real driving force among the Italian powers in the Levant. Before and after the short annual trading season the Venetian quarters were often rather deserted. The Pisans, however, not only established their own independent quarters, but also actively pursued a policy of creating permanent settlements both inside and outside their quarters. Immediately before and during the Third Crusade they obtained a series of grants which effectively gave them control over the whole of the economically important part of Acre, from the southern tip to the arsenal in the north-east. At this time they also seem to have maintained a permanent naval presence in the Levant, though their ships frequently engaged in piracy—a perennial danger for all ships in Levantine waters. In any event for Henry of Champagne the Pisans were indispensable if awkward allies. Time and again determined kings tried to scale down the Italian privileges, as Henry did for Pisa. King Fulk, for example refused to pay the doge of Venice the

300 bezants from the port treasury of Acre to which he was entitled each
year according to the treaty of 1123. In 1164 the money was still owing.
But in the confusion before and during the Third Crusade (see above,
p. 142) everything was renewed and extended. Their settlements also
continued to grow and develop. At first the merchants had simply been
grouped as a community around their own national Church and had set up
a rudimentary kind of self-government. But soon the home towns took the
matter in hand. In 1157 we hear of the first Pisan administrative official
and soon each community had its own *bailli*, viscount, or consul who
directed the administration of the colony as the representative responsible
to the home republic. In addition Venice continued to make use of the
ecclesiastical organization. Then in the thirteenth century a higher
administrative structure was devised to which all the Syrian colonies of
each republic were subordinate; this made for more consistent policy-
making. The Venetians had their main settlement in Tyre where from
1200 to 1247 they quarrelled with the archbishop; both sides claimed
jurisdiction over the Venetian church of St. Mark. The Genoese and the
Pisans were based on Acre. Less important both politically and
economically were the colonies of Amalfi, Marseilles, and Montpellier.
But they all shared common characteristics: the merchants lived and
traded in their own quarter which was well situated by the harbour; they
had their own church, warehouse (*funda, fondaco*), bath, bakery, mill,
slaughterhouse, etc. They contrived to be economically self-supporting
and thus to escape the dues which they would have had to pay if they had
used the town lord's (i.e. the king's) monopoly services. Minor cases,
particularly commercial disputes, were dealt with by their own court if the
accused were an Italian, while blood justice remained the responsibility of
the viscount's *Cour des Bourgeois*. Where the crown, in a moment of
weakness, had renounced all jurisdiction over citizens of an Italian
maritime republic, it later on disputed this by means of an interpretation
unfavourable to the Italians or, if circumstances permitted, a modification
was introduced into a new grant. Throughout the land the Italians enjoyed
far-reaching trading liberties; they were exempt from every kind of due,
toll, anchorage fee, and from the obligation to use the royal weights and
measures. In their own quarters, especially in the market, they maintained
law and order themselves; elsewhere this was the viscount's job. In
exploiting their privileges all Italian cities adopted a policy of granting
non-citizens (although normally people from their native region in Italy)
temporary status as protected Pisans, Venetians, or Genoese in order to
secure for them the advantages conferred by these royal privileges. The
benefit of these must therefore have been great, both for the merchants
themselves and for the home town. To some extent, therefore, there must
have been a financial loss for the kingdom of Jerusalem. But the extent of
this loss is a matter of debate. Riley-Smith argues that it was relatively

small and emphasizes the stimulus which the Italian Levant trade gave to the economy. Favreau-Lilie is very sceptical but the argument depends on a detailed examination of the complexities of the customs system which goes beyond the limited scope of this book. The weaker the kingdom became, the stronger the Italian communes. They intervened, frequently with armed force, in the internal quarrels of the kingdom. If the different republics had not been so hopelessly at odds with one another the Holy Land would unquestionably have become an Italian protectorate in the second half of the thirteenth century. Despite this they were frequently despised. One Eastern chronicler reported that the French knights looked down on the Italians because 'most of them are usurers, corsairs, merchants, or sailors'—all professions equally alien to the author's outlook.

The volume of trade in twelfth-century Outremer was first over-estimated by historians and then underestimated.[97] Originally the markets of Syria and Palestine were not much visited by Europeans; before the crusades only merchants from Amalfi and occasionally from Genoa went there. Evidence from Genoa shows that the Levant trade, going mostly through Alexandria, was still in the hands of Jews, Greeks, and Syrians. The important Genoese notarial registers seem at first sight to show that this Egyptian predominance lasted far into the twelfth century. The Genoese notary Giovanni Scriba had fifty-eight clients from Alexandria during the period 1158–64 and only thirty-four from Syria. But the picture changes as soon as one turns from the number of commercial contracts to the amount of capital invested. The fifty-eight Egyptian clients represent 9,031 *livres genois;* the thirty-four Syrian ones add up to 10,075. The average investment in Alexandria was 156 *livres genois,* in Syria 300, although it must be remembered that Egypt's main imports (iron, timber, and pitch, i.e. shipbuilding materials) had been declared contraband by popes and councils and therefore could not be mentioned in the notarial registers. But a register compiled in 1248 in Marseilles confirms the impression that the average investment in the crusader states was higher than elsewhere.

The commercial framework was provided by two types of contract, both designed to spread the risk between the parties to the contract: the investor (*socius stans*) and the merchant himself (*socius tractans*). In what was known as the *societas* the merchant contributed one third of the capital and claimed one half of the profits while having to bear only one third of any loss. In allowing the merchant a higher percentage in profits than he would have to assume in losses, the investor provided the merchant with an additional incentive to aim for the maximum return on the capital of the investor, who had no control over how this money was employed while the merchant was overseas. The other type of contract, the *commenda*, became more common in the thirteenth century. Here the investor contributed the entire capital; the *tractator* would receive only 25 per cent of the profit but since he had risked no capital he could suffer no financial loss. In addition there was the sea-loan condemned by the Church because of the usury involved. Here the *tractator* raised capital at a fixed rate of interest of 35 per cent per annum—which presupposes a normal profit margin of at least 50 per cent if the business was to be at all worthwhile. A clear interplay of business and politics is revealed by an analysis of the investors whose names appear in the registers of Giovanni Scriba. Eighty per cent of the capital invested in the Syrian trade was put up by seven people; the remaining 20 per cent was shared between twenty other investors. During the same period about one hundred people had a share in the trade with Egypt. Of the seven leading investors in the Syrian trade one was a Jew, one a Christian Syrian; the five others all belonged to the political élite of Genoa, the group from which every year the consuls were chosen, indeed three of them were members of the Visconti family. This select and illustrious group monopolized the trade with Syria. In Syria itself their interests were supervised by trusted associates from the same class, families like the Embriaco who from 1109 held Jebail as a Genoese outpost and made of it an aristocratic lordship in the thirteenth century. Naturally the influential capitalists stayed home in Genoa; they acted only as *socii stantes*. It is, of course, true that Giovanni Scriba, as the official city notary, had close connections with the ruling class and quite a different picture emerges from an analysis of the 1191 register of William Cassinese. Here the number of middling investors is very much higher. 1191, however, was in every way an unusual year. The Third Crusade was under way and so trade with Egypt was completely prohibited. There was, none the less, a boom stimulated by two wars: the crusade and Henry VI's attempt to conquer Sicily. Thus both the sum total invested and the number of Sicilian and Syrian contracts were much higher than usual. In 1191, moreover, the Ghibelline party in Genoa asserted itself for the first time. It ended the regime of consuls chosen from the old families and entrusted the city government to an outside *podestà*. It is clear that this went hand in hand with the breakdown of the old Visconti monopoly of the Syrian trade. A later increase in the trade with Syria which was observable in other cities besides Genoa resulted from the destruction of Byzantium (1204) and from the long pause in the struggle against the Muslims in Syria (1229–44). At the same time trade with Egypt suffered considerably as a result of the crusades which were directed against Egypt in the first half of the thirteenth century. The wars waged after 1250 by the Mameluk sultans of Egypt were to some extent trade wars fought in support of the ports of the Nile delta and the Karimi merchants of Egypt. These were the men who were to monopolize the fourteenth-century spice trade in Egypt after the destruction of the crusader states, though in the Mediterranean itself the carrying trade still remained firmly in the hands of the Italians.

Throughout the twelfth and thirteenth centuries Egypt controlled the transit trade with India and Arabia, though some Indian spice did go through Acre and Tyre as did the trade of Persia, Syria, and Mesopotamia. The main exports to Europe were drugs and pharmaceutical goods including ginger, aloe, myrrh, camphor, senna leaves, bitter-wort, and the incense needed for liturgical purposes. There were spices like pepper, cinnamon, nutmeg, cloves, cardamom; fabrics and textiles like linen, silk, damask, muslin; dyes for use in European textile production, particularly indigo for blue colours, brazilwood, and alum for red. Until the alum mines of Phocaea in Asia Minor were opened up in 1275, alum was purchased mainly from an Egyptian state monopoly. Other commodities were fine wood (sandalwood), ivory, and steel manufactures from Damascus, perfumes, pearls from the Orient, jewels, and porcelain. In addition there were the products of Outremer itself: castor sugar (produced mainly in Tyre and Acre), Jewish glassware, and Galilean wines. Exports to Egypt included salted fish, fruit (dates, oranges, and citrus fruit), olive oil, and oil of sesame. Grain, salt, pottery, and poultry were imported from Egypt for domestic consumption in Outremer. European goods which went through the Holy Land on their way to Islamic countries included textiles from France, Flanders, and England; metals like copper, mercury, lead, and iron; wood, pitch, saddles, almonds, and nuts. This trade was mostly in the hands of Muslim merchants or people like the *Mosserins* (see above, p. 180). But in the thirteenth century we also find Venetians at Damascus and Sangimignanesi at Aleppo where they were offering a special luxury—saffron from Tuscany producing an expensive yellow dye. Salted pork for the Franks also had to be imported since this meat was not available in the Islamic world. To complete the picture there was the slave trade and the pilgrim traffic (see below, p. 229). Not until the thirteenth century did the Italians become active in the loan and banking business. Their importance in this field is indisputable but a collection of charters, the *Collection Courtois*, which used to be employed as the chief evidence for this, has been shown to be a nineteenth-century forgery. As early as the twelfth century the Procurators of San Marco in Venice accepted money deposits from crusaders for safekeeping and sent them on to them if needed, though at this date the transfers themselves were carried out by the Military Orders rather than by Italian merchants.

Agriculture was chiefly in the hands of the indigenous population, both Christian Syrians and Muslim Fellahin. Apart from the Muslim slaves, the lot of this class was not a bad one though of course they had no political rights. The Muslims now had to pay the poll tax which, in the old days, the Muslim rulers had imposed on the adherents of other religions. Otherwise the Frankish conquest made very little difference to the rural population, apart from the fact that the Syrian Christians and the Muslims were now placed into roughly the same legal category relative to the Frankish conquerors. If they lived in the country, Syrians and Muslims were both without rights. Only the Syrians who lived in towns, thanks to their personal freedom (*Stadtluft macht frei*), were legally better off than the rural *vilains*, as the peasants, both Syrian and Muslim, were called. In the country the village was a religious and an ethnic unit as well as being the smallest unit in the Latin Feudal system. As Prawer has made clear, the rural population was segregated into separate villages, each village being exclusively settled either by Syrians or by Muslims or by Franks. There was no village where the different races lived side by side. Outside the towns the Franks lived in enclosed and fortified Latin settlements. There were, in fact, far fewer Latin settlements than an over-hasty estimate had suggested. According to Prawer's calculations in the whole of the kingdom out of a total of 1,200 centres of population there were only fifty or sixty Latin settlements. The land was governed by Latins, but it was by no means settled by them. Not only was the Latin population sparse; it was also very unevenly distributed. It was concentrated in the coastal towns and in Jerusalem, and in rural settlements along the fertile plain and in the valleys; in the highlands, on the other hand, there were almost no Latin settlements and there were very few where, militarily speaking, they would have been most useful—along the threatened frontiers. To say that the change of rulers made little difference to the rural population does not imply that the countryside witnessed no changes at all. On this point Prawer's conclusions are important. Naturally the old landowning class was completely replaced by Franks. Moreover the old Islamic *latifundia* which, in the pre-crusade period, had been owned by the state or by individual magnates or religious and charitable institutions, were broken up. Since the Franks did not take over the land all at once but in a gradual process which kept pace with the piecemeal conquest of the country, there could be no question of the old units being preserved. Thus in two ways there was a completely new redistribution of the land. Firstly the landowners changed—for only the Churches and monasteries were allowed to keep their old possessions and they were, in any case, mostly Latinized. Secondly there was a change in the size of the landholdings. Nevertheless, these changes had only a minimal effect on the life of the rural population since recent research has shown that, on the eve of the crusades, Palestine was already caught up in a 'process of feudalization' (Prawer), i.e. the creation of big *latifundia* involving the depression of a once-free peasantry into a condition of servility or semi-servility. Even before the Frankish conquest the class of free peasants had almost disappeared. Perhaps this explains why Muslim rebellions were rare. Where conditions did become worse emigration seems to have been a more frequent course of action. When the Frankish lord of Mirabel imposed dues at a rate four times that sanctioned by custom and then stepped in to silence a Muslim preacher (ostensibly because the man, an expert in Islamic law, was urging the peasants not to work in the fields on Fridays, but probably because he was attacking this imposition) the population of eight Muslim villages emigrated *en masse* in 1156 and settled in a suburb of Damascus where they established a centre of counter-crusade propaganda which flourished right into the Mameluk period. It is not hard to trace their political commitment to the expulsion of the Franks from the Holy Land back to their position as refugees after 1156.[98] But in general the Franks could not afford to press the Muslims too hard. They were, it is true, tied to the land but they enjoyed freedom of worship (though they were, as a rule, allowed neither mosque nor qadi). Besides the normal dues they paid a moderate poll tax and, like the Syrians with the *Cour des Syriens*, they had a court of their own, the *Cour du Rais*. The opinion that the *Cour des Syriens* was gradually absorbed by the *Cour de la Fonde* seems to apply only to Acre. On Cyprus it certainly lasted into the second half of the fourteenth century. Muslim slaves could obtain their freedom by being baptized. From the lord's point of view this meant that he lost a slave but gained a dependent tenant. The lords do not seem to have favoured the conversion of their slaves, indeed sometimes they prevented it, even keeping Muslims willing to convert from attending Christian services. In 1237 and 1238 Pope Gregory IX intervened strongly on behalf of these would-be converts. But in return he had to promise that converted slaves could be forced to remain slaves—clean contrary to all previous customary law. Baldwin I had even allowed a Saracen to become his chamberlain after he had had him baptized and given him his own name. In the early twelfth century able Syrian Christians succeeded in becoming members of the Frankish knightly class, the family of Arrabit, for example, who from 1122 appear as vassals of the Ibelins. The Syrian *ra'is* were often wealthy landowners; we should not underestimate their position. The *ra'is* (latin: *regulus*) was a free man holding an office which was hereditary in his family. In the period of Turkish rule he had been a kind of chief of police; under the Franks he represented their authority over his own social class, presiding over the court named after him. He had jurisdiction in minor cases; serious offences were tried in the *Cour des Bourgeois*. But though we know little about the office, the distinction made by Riley-Smith between the urban and the rural *ra'is* is clearly fundamental. The former exercised judicial functions to a much greater extent than the latter, amongst whom there were very considerable differences. As a rule the rural *ra'is* had authority over a single village but there were cases both of *ra'is* who presided, like sheikhs, over several villages, and of villages which contained as many as three *ra'is*—in these cases they were probably just the heads of the leading family in the village. We are less well informed about a second native official, the *Mathessep*, successor to the Islamic *muhtasib* whose job it had once been to supervise public morals and local trade. There is very little evidence for the office in Jerusalem but in Cyprus the *Mathessep* was clearly a subordinate of the viscount exercising a certain authority over artisans.

Rural economic and social conditions in the lordship of Tyre have been studied in detail by Prawer.[99] An area of 450 square kilometres was densely settled. There were about 120 villages (*Casalia*); of these the king had originally held two thirds and the Venetians one third. By 1243 this distribution had changed. The king now held 36 per cent, the Venetians 31 per cent, the Church 13 per cent (not a great deal but acquired at the king's expense), individual lords 12 per cent, while 8 per cent was in other hands. The *casalia* differed enormously in size. The area of farm land in each varied from 190 to 1,120 hectares (470 to 2,770 acres) expressed in terms of *carrucae* each of about thirty-five hectares (86.5 acres). The *carruca* was originally supposed to represent the amount of land needed to support one family but it soon became a purely fiscal unit of measurement. All the farm land was divided into *carrucae* once and for all and this arrangement was entered into the registers of the *Secrète*. Included among the farm land were the sugar-cane fields, olive groves, vineyards, and also the pasture land (*gastina*, literally wasteland). The populations of the *casalia* varied from three to thirty-six families according to the size of each *casale*. Farming was carried on in a complicated two-year rhythm in a two-field economy with one field always divided. Within this system the growing of winter wheat alternated with vegetables, summer crops, and fallow. In this arid country water rights were regulated in great detail and jealously guarded; the distribution of water was fundamental to an often highly sophisticated irrigation system. A proportion of the harvest was paid to the lord as his due, but apart from that the farmer had to pay neither a formal rent to the landowner nor tithes to the Church. In contrast to Europe there was no demesne which the peasants were bound to work for the lord. This may be because the old pre-crusade system—which knew no such institution—was left unchanged, as in general there was a very high degree of continuity in the rural economy. Or it may be that peasant labour in the Holy Land was too valuable to be used in a way which was acknowledged to be uneconomic. The second hypothesis is supported by the fact that even the Military Orders held little demesne despite being exempted from having to pay Church tithes on it and on produce which was destined for their own consumption. A further reason for the absence of demesne land in Outremer is, of course, the fact that the landlords lived in towns, not on their estates. As Prawer has made clear, to them their villages were nothing more than revenue-producing units. For this reason not only was there no demesne land but also there was nothing of that patriarchal relationship which existed between the European landlord and the dependant peasantry who could look to their lord for protection. The landlord in Outremer felt no such responsibility. This emerges very clearly from those cases where a village was owned jointly by several lords. Prawer's analysis of charters which laid down the terms on which villages were divided up shows that it was rarely the village population which was shared out and even more infrequently was it the land. The lords divided the income between them; they had no interest in either the land or its inhabitants. The individual lord laid no claim to a share of the estates or to some of the *vilains*, but only to the income that could be derived from them. On Cyprus where the *casalia* were further divided into separate hamlets (*presteries*) about one seventh of the arable land of a *casale* was held in demesne. Here the peasants had to do labour services and thus each *casale* possessed a well-developed administration to supervise the apportionment of the various tasks.

Culturally Frankish society in the East remained basically provincial and thoroughly dependent on Europe.[100] The Islamic influence which was so fruitful in Spain and Sicily was rigidly excluded in Outremer. The Franks coexisted with the Muslims but there was no symbiosis. The number of those from the upper ranks of society who bothered to learn Arabic was tiny. Their everyday language—and in the thirteenth century also the written language of secular administration—was French. Tedaldo Visconti of Piacenza, the archdeacon of Liège who later rose to be Pope Gregory X, preached the same sermon in Acre twice, first in Latin, then in French (1271). Cyprus developed its own *lingua franca* out of French, Italian, and Greek. Only in superficial matters, dress, medicine, and domestic comforts was there any willingness to learn from Islam. It was not that the Franks achieved nothing of importance, but they hardly developed anything of their own. They were vigorous builders, as we can see not just from the great castles but also from the important additions to the Church of the Holy Sepulchre, from the impressive church of St. Anne in Jerusalem (later the burial place of the French consuls general in Jerusalem, those Great Moguls of nineteenth-century Palestine) with its massive and loftily simple Romanesque style; from the cathedral of Ramleh (today's mosque) so impressive in its dimensions as well as with its mighty piers of cylindrical columns; from the smaller but lovely Hospitaller church at Abu Ghosh near Jerusalem, built over a spring and thus clearly demonstrating the vital importance of water rights; from the beautiful church of St. Andrew at Acre—now to be seen only in a sketch done in 1681—and from the marvellous cathedral of Tortosa which still stands today. French and Venetian builders worked on the church of St. Mary at Tyre (formerly known as the cathedral). Measuring 75 metres in length, it was, so far as we can tell, the largest church building in the Latin East. Indeed in general it is probable that the artists who worked in the Holy Land were not born there but came from Europe or Byzantium. An exception to the otherwise purely western architecture was the palace of the Ibelins in Beirut. From the description written in 1213 by an astounded Willibrand of Oldenburg it is clear that it was strongly influenced by Byzantine styles. The front of the palace looked out over the sea; at the back there were orchards. The mosaic floor was ingeniously designed to look like the surface of water lightly rippled by the wind. In the middle of the palace there was a fountain, faced with marble and surmounted by a dragon; its high jet of crystal-clear water helped to keep the rooms cool and moist. It is possible that Frankish architects took over the pointed arch from their Muslim colleagues. The great cistern of Ramleh of 789 was already constructed with a full set of pointed arches and the crusaders must have seen it. Essentially however this question of the borrowing of an architectonic element depends upon the dating of the earliest examples of the pointed arch in the West—and it is not entirely clear whether these belong to the period before or after the First Crusade. A striking feature of crusader buildings is the superb tooling of the ashlar masonry. Executed at an angle of 45 degrees it creates a diagonal pattern of fine parallel grooves which is as characteristic of the work of these Frankish stone-masons as are their masons' marks (of which over 600 are known). These marks undoubtedly served as the mason's 'signature' but it is much less certain that they were also used for accounting purposes.

Some of the sculpture is outstanding. Five exquisitely carved capitals from Nazareth use scenes from the lives of the apostles to demonstrate the Church's victory over the forces of Satan. They are probably—though this has been disputed—the work of twelfth-century masons from Burgundy and Berry. The attempt to reconstruct from these and other sculptures in Nazareth the portal of the cathedral of St. Mary there remains highly conjectural, partly because there are no sculptural references to the Virgin as patron. There are also two fully sculptured capitals which, though different in measurement, depict the same biblical scene. It is argued that during the work the iconographical programme was altered and that this rendered one of the two capitals useless because its measurements would not fit the place where it was now to go. While this is not impossible, it is certainly a very bold hypothesis because it makes an inconvenient piece of evidence disappear on the assumption that in the twelfth century it was discarded as a piece of refuse. The study of the non-figural sculpture in the kingdom of Jerusalem has recently been reinvigorated by Buschhausen. In exemplary fashion he assembled the material in stylistic groups for the first time, but his wholesale ascription of it all to masons from Apulia (they supposedly came to the East in Frederick II's wake) has been forcefully—and probably correctly—disputed. An alternative theory postulates the existence of a 'Temple Area Workshop', in operation in Jerusalem between 1170 and 1187, and staffed by stone-masons chiefly from Provence but with some from Sicily and Campania. The works in question, however, are rather provincial, though there are a few exceptions such as the tomb of King Baldwin V—a precisely datable monument which has been convincingly reconstructed by Z. Jacoby. But imperialism seems to have crept into art history and now not only is the 'Temple Area Workshop' credited with most of the work done around Jerusalem and elsewhere in the kingdom, but Jacoby—neatly turning the tables on Buschhausen—has even argued that there were no Apulian masons who came to the East and that on the contrary, the 'Temple Area Workshop' emigrated to Apulia after its Eastern market collapsed in the catastrophe of 1187, decorating no less than eight churches there! Another group of stone-masons, this time from Fontevrault (Poitou) or from the Charente may possibly have worked in the Holy Land *c.*1130.

The Crusader coins were mostly crude products; the seals were better. Hardly any examples of applied art still survive. What little there is, was most probably imported from France. But in the Dome of the Rock the crusaders left behind eight wrought iron grilles (their remains can be seen in the Islamic Museum in the Jerusalem Temple Square) which are among the finest medieval examples of a smith's work. In recent years reliquaries in the shape of a Cross of Lorraine and containing pieces of the True Cross have been identified as the work of Jerusalem silversmiths from the first half of the twelfth century. Apparently they were designed for something approaching mass production since their decoration was punched onto them using identical dies. Probably they were intended as aids in the business of soliciting donations in Europe for the Church of the Holy Sepulchre. If high quality was required, it had to be obtained abroad—for example the 'very fine' (*delectabilia*) silver vessels which the renowned goldsmith Godefroid of Huy made for Bishop Amalric of Sidon in exchange for relics of John the Baptist.

The Franks made only a small contribution to literature. At the time of the conquest they destroyed the great Arab library at Tripoli and sold the Jewish library of Jerusalem. But later they did include Arab works in the fine cathedral library built up at Tyre (and certainly also at Jerusalem). In 1129 a charter was written by a priest Hugh who held the office of librarian of the church of Bethlehem. We also have a catalogue of the library of Nazareth cathedral of *c.* 1200. Apart from classical Roman authors, the names of St. Jerome, St. Augustine, and Gregory the Great stand out. Of recent authors only Anselm of Canterbury and Ivo of Chartres are there. In terms of the quality of its holdings it was a very average library. Nor, for an institutional library, was it at all large. Its little more than seventy works make a poor showing when compared with the thirty-six volumes which one dean of Chartres, admittedly a man of considerable learning, left to St.-Jean-en-Vallée in Chartres. Two Nazareth manuscripts of St. Augustine were on loan to the bishop of Sidon, perhaps so that he could have them copied, though they are not among the nine manuscripts still extant from the Sidon cathedral library.

From a library such as this Gerard of Nazareth, bishop of Lattakieh (1140–61), wrote a vigorous and learned defence of the identity of Mary Magdalen and Mary of Bethany against the Greeks. He also wrote several other works, among them a biography of abbot Elias of Palmarea, a former grammar teacher from the *Gallia Narbonnensis* who had a rather chequered ecclesiastical career in the East. But he poured all of his polemical energy into a treatise against a certain Sala who had succeeded in introducing a Greek bishop in Lattakieh: 'As necessity forces me to read the writings of this Sala, I feel barely able to swallow, as though I were chewing pitch or some other gluey substance with clogged-up teeth.'

In spite of William of Tyre's assertion to the contrary, Aimery of Limoges, patriarch of Antioch, was also a learned man and well-known as such in Europe. While still archdeacon of Antioch he had supplied the archbishop of Toledo with a fragmentary prose adaptation of parts of the Bible in Castilian to which was added an historical and geographical description of the Holy Land. It is by far the oldest translation of the Bible into any Romance language. When Aimery had risen to the patriarchate, Pope Eugenius III wrote to him, asking for a Latin translation of the commentary written by St. Chrysostom on the Gospel according to St. Matthew. Aimery, however, sent a Greek version to Rome, which the pope apparently did not find very helpful. Aimery himself asked for works by the Pisan theologian Hugh Etherianus. Hugh, who from the 1160s lived at Constantinople as adviser to the Emperor Manuel on problems of church union, sent him his bilingual treatise on the double procession of the Holy Ghost.[101]

William of Tyre was one of the finest historians of the twelfth century, an age peculiarly rich in excellent chroniclers. He was born in Palestine and for twenty years he studied the liberal arts at Chartres, theology at Paris, and law at Bologna. Upon his return to the Holy Land this education predestined him for a successful career (chancellor of the kingdom, archbishop of Tyre, tutor to a crown prince, court historian). Only the patriarch's throne eluded his grasp. William speaks highly of the kings' interest in reading history, though just what this means is not entirely clear. It could hardly have been solid but dry Latin chronicles such as Walter the Chancellor's 'Antioch Wars' or the History of Fulcher of Chartres (though Fulcher was one of the principal sources of William of Tyre's own History).

One would have thought that the kings had *chansons de geste* in the Old French vernacular read to them, were it not for the fact that there seems to have been an almost total absence of works of this genre in the East. Although crusading epics such as the *Chanson d'Antioche* and the *Chanson de Jérusalem* were tremendously popular in Europe, only one such work was actually written in Outremer itself, the *Chanson des Chétifs*, celebrating the events of the crusade of 1101 and a product of the court at

Antioch at some date before 1149. William of Tyre alluded to the epic cycle of the *Chevalier au Cygne* who was said to have been among the ancestors of Godfrey de Bouillon. Although he himself dismissed it as pure legend, he observed that it was widely believed. Given the long years of William's education in Europe there is no way of knowing whether he became acquainted with this cycle in Europe or in the East. In a penetrating study of the composition and diffusion of vernacular literature in the crusader states D. Jacoby has suggested that the romanticizing presentation of the crusades in the epics clashed to such an extent with reality that the nobility of Outremer did not care to read them. Certainly there seems to have been no lack of appreciation of epics on other themes, in particular the cycle of legends of King Arthur and the Round Table.

   The outstanding Old French author in the Levant was unquestionably Philippe de Novare, not a Frenchman, but an Italian immigrant into Cyprus from Novara. Philippe wrote not only history (see below, p. 254), but also satirical *sirventes* in the Provençal fashion, poetry occasioned by specific events, political satire couched in terms of scenes and characters from the famous *Roman de Renart*, as well as a moral treatise on *Les quatre âges de l'homme* in which he lamented the fact that in his youth he had written love poetry, but hastened to add that he had made up for this in his old age by composing pious songs on the Lord, the Virgin, and the saints. Not surprisingly he was known on Cyprus, as he himself tells us with characteristic *amour-propre*, as *le chanteor*. Compared to Philippe, the Frenchman Jean de Journy who in 1288 published on Cyprus a long allegorical poem called *La Dime de Pénitance*, cuts a poor figure.

   Apart from the codification of feudal customary law (see above p. 161f.), a field in which the crusader states produced work of the highest quality, thanks partly to native authors (Jean d'Ibelin) and partly to immigrants (Philippe de Novare), the Franks contributed little or nothing to the advancement of science and learning in the Middle Ages. In jurisprudence it is possible that John of Ancona wrote a *summa* of canon law in the East *c*.1265. But advanced medicine remained an Oriental domain, and of natural science we hear nothing at all. (The herbalist Rufinus is once referred to as 'abbot of Tyre', but this, whatever it may mean, was apparently an office held *in absentia*). The same is true of theology, for the treatise on the Christian faith which Benedict of Alignan, the bishop of Marseilles, wrote at Acre in 1261, can hardly be counted among the achievements of the Latin East. During the espiscopate of James of Vitry (letter IV) there was a lecturer in theology at Acre cathedral but we do not know for how long. The knowledge of Islam exhibited by the Dominican William of Tripoli in 1273 lagged behind that of contemporary Europe. The literary genre of Latin travel accounts was significantly added to by the Flemish Franciscan William of Rubroek when he temporarily lived in Acre (see below, p. 269).

The patient research of Weitzmann in the monastery on Mount Sinai succeeded in identifying a group of over 120 crusader icons. Most of them were painted in Byzantinesque style without remotely approaching the standard of the masterpieces of truly Byzantine icon painting. A few are from the twelfth century, the majority from the thirteenth and especially from its second half. The painters were mostly Italians and Frenchmen, with occasionally an Englishman or a German. Their products show certain similarities with the Acre school of book illumination but it is not entirely clear whether they were painted in Acre or by Acre artists staying in Sinai. And perhaps Cyprus too should be considered as a possible centre of production. The few remains of fresco painting in the crusader states (the stone of Bethphage, the fragment at Abu Ghosh, and the frescoes from Margat and from Krak des Chevaliers now in the museum of Tartus in Syria) have only very recently become the object of scholarly investigation. But, doubtless because Frankish rule in Outremer ended so much earlier, there seems not to have been anything on the scale we find in Frankish Greece in the fourteenth century. In the palace of the archbishop of Patras the hall, measuring twenty-five paces in length, was decorated all the way around with murals showing the destruction of Troy, whereas at Thebes the mansion of the St.-Omer family, distinguished crusaders from the beginning, had frescoes showing the Frankish conquest of Syria. In book illumination the scriptorium of the Church of the Holy Sepulchre reached an exceedingly high standard. The liturgical books used by the royal family were produced here—superb luxury editions based on older Byzantine models and influenced by English and Italian styles. In a country as cosmopolitan as Outremer the development of a style was very much a matter of chance and could be independent of the otherwise predominantly French way of life. Even in the Jerusalem of the thirteenth century manuscripts could be illuminated in a truly royal fashion with Byzantine and Latin elements fusing to form a genuinely original style. But after 1244 the only centre for book illumination was Acre; the Arsenal Bible produced there under St. Louis shows that they were still capable of first-class work. After this, however, the art of book illustration becomes even more provincial and second-rate, though the town nobility were still interested in French historical works and had them illuminated, such as the continuation of William of Tyre and the *Histoire universelle*.

A favourite form of entertainment at great feasts such as that in 1223 when two sons of the 'Old Lord of Beirut' were dubbed knights, or in 1286 after the coronation of King Henry (see below, p. 285), were dramatic performances. In both instances stories from the King Arthur cycle were enacted, *les aventures de Bretaigne* in 1223, *Lanselot et Tristan et Pilamedes*, i.e. Palamède, in 1286. There is no earlier reference to a dramatized version of the King Arthur theme than that of 1223. On both occasions scenes from the *Table Ronde* were also laid on, but D. Jacoby has pointed out that these were probably not subjects taken from King Arthur and the Round Table but, on the analogy of similar events in Europe, simply consisted of jousts accompanied by music and of dances which the participants entered under assumed names taken from the Arthurian cycle. In the festivities of 1286 there were still other and cruder plays in which knights dressed up as women jousted with each other as Amazons and later disguised themselves as monks and nuns and pretended to have sex. As has been seen, secular music had a part to play in these festivities and courtly lyrics were set to music in thirteenth-century Achaia (see below, p. 209), while the Turin National Library holds a collection of motets, virelays, and rondeaux, both text and music, from Cyprus (*c.*1400). From the same island, though from an entirely different category of writing, there survive two manuals devoted to the training and veterinary care of falcons—a subject dear to King Fulk in the twelfth century—he had even promulgated a special law to protect these birds.

9

THE FOURTH CRUSADE (1198–1204) AND FRANKISH GREECE (1204–1311)

THE collapse of the German crusade organized by Emperor Henry VI coincided with an important change on the papal throne. In 1198 Innocent III (d. 1216) was elected pope. He had been carefully educated in theology and canon law. He believed that the papacy should be set above the secular powers and that the pope should be a kind of priest-king. By a vigorous exploitation of the power vacuum created by the death of Henry VI he set out to turn theory into fact. In Innocent III's conception of the world there was no room for crusades directed exclusively by kings in which the pope's role was limited to his undisputed right of issuing the summons to the crusade. In his view the whole thing should be under the pope's control. But quite apart from this political objective, Innocent was deeply concerned to re-build the old Latin kingdom of Jerusalem which had been destroyed in 1187 and only very imperfectly restored in 1192. These two themes ran right through his pontificate, but in pursuing them, Innocent III overlooked the fact that it was no longer possible to finance and lead an army to the East except with the active co-operation of the rulers. The reality of the situation may have been veiled by the fact that the only successful crusade so far had been the First Crusade in which kings had had no share. None the less as a result of the advances made in state organization in the West since 1095 there was now a new reality which ought to have been taken into account. In Innocent III's strivings for a crusade there was this tragic element: that the ecclesiastical form of crusade organization which he established, particularly in the crusading decree of the Fourth Lateran Council, was not in fact an adequate substitute for the power of the state. So Innocent III's crusades either failed or achieved only an apparent success.

In August 1198, soon after he had ascended the papal throne, Innocent proclaimed a new crusade.[102] He concentrated his attention on France, writing to the higher ranks of the clergy and nobility, and on the Italian maritime cities whose fleets were indispensable. But he sent no letters to the kings. They were supposed to make peace with one another so that their quarrels would not disturb the preparations for the crusade, but they received no call to take part. Not that Innocent would have tried to prevent them from going on crusade if they had wished, but in fact they were much too absorbed in their own affairs. England and France had their old quarrel, while Germany was divided by the conflicting claims of two rivals for the crown, Philip of Swabia and Otto IV. But in any case the pope was not anxious to see kings taking part because in his proclamation he emphasized the failure of the nationally organized crusades.

In France the crusade was preached with great success up until 1203 by Cardinal-legate Peter Capuano and a parish priest, Fulk of Neuilly (d. 1202). Since 1195 and with ever-growing success Fulk had been active as a preacher. He was a fine figure of a man whose great rhetorical gifts were combined with a well-groomed appearance which made a favourable contrast with some of the unkempt popular preachers of earlier crusades. The content of his sermons was very different too. He was a product of the Paris schools and had begun his preaching career as an advocate of moral reform, fiercely denouncing usury, extravagance, and prostitution. The eschatological motif—with its hope that the end of time was at hand—which had played such a big part in the First Crusade, was pushed into the background and its place was taken by the preaching of a practical code of morals with the accent on a purifying act of penance here and now. Fulk was aided by the movement for apostolic poverty which had grown in strength during the course of the twelfth century and which Innocent III helped to bring within the framework of the Church. Earlier Peter of Blois had, in his disappointment over the delays to the Third Crusade, touched upon themes which were now to be heard more frequently. The rich, headed naturally by the kings, are unworthy of the true atonement and of the Holy Land, their crusades have failed; the true chosen ones are the poor. The idea that everyone is called to the crusade is rejected. Here we can see the effect of the christology of the poverty movement which had been taught by—among others—Peter Cantor, Fulk of Neuilly's old teacher. By the side of St. Paul's very spiritual Christ it set the humble, impoverished, and suffering Christ as the pattern of human behaviour; in place of the anointed Christ it emphasized the naked and defenceless Christ crucified. Like many other ideas for improving the world, the idea that the poor and the pure in spirit were called to free the Holy Land was ethically unobjectionable but completely out of touch with the real world. Less than ever was it now possible to renounce the help of princes. During the period of recruitment for the crusade it became clear that the machinery of the feudal system was needed if a sufficient number of knights were to follow the example of their lords and take the cross. The fact that this crusade was to be diverted from its original goal was in the last resort a consequence of that shortage of money which only the kings could have remedied. And in its noblest and purest form the idea of the poor crusaders led ultimately to the ill-fated children's crusade of 1212.

In 1199, after the first date set for the mustering of an army had come and gone with nothing achieved, the pope, while still continuing with his unremitting preaching of the crusade, tried to help the cause by decreeing a crusading tax of one fortieth on clerical incomes. Although on this occasion he promised that this would not be taken as a precedent for a regular papal taxation of clerical incomes, in 1215 he found that he had to resort to this measure again since he had no other means of financing the crusade at his disposal. The Cistercians—the great advocates of the Second Crusade—now refused to pay the tax of 1199. Indeed they accused the pope of persecuting their order and despite the severest pressure, Innocent could do no more than obtain a voluntary contribution from them in return for confirming the principle that they were exempt from such taxation. None the less success now attended his efforts. In November 1199 the first contingents gathered at a tournament in Champagne. Contrary to a widely held opinion there is no evidence for the presence of Fulk of Neuilly at the tournament. Count Theobald of Champagne and Louis of Blois took the cross as did also the marshal of Champagne, Geoffrey de Villehardouin (d. 1213) who became the semi-official historian of the crusade. Equally interesting is the account written by the Picard, Robert de Clari (d. after 1216). He consciously described himself as *pauvre chevalier*—poor knight—thus documenting his adherence to the ideal of poverty. Soon afterwards Count Baldwin of Flanders and Hainault took the crusader's vow. Many nobles of north France followed the example of their lords. The three counts then sent six envoys to Italy to negotiate a treaty about the transport of an army with one of the maritime cities. The negotiations became a milestone in the history of diplomacy. For the first time we hear of plenipotentiaries with complete freedom of action. The envoys had been provided with blank charters sealed in advance by their lords in readiness for the treaty. Even the decision to negotiate with Venice was made by the envoys. The treaty which they then concluded with Doge Enrico Dandolo (1192–1205) laid down that Venice would provide transport and victuals for a year for 4,500 knights, 9,000 squires and 20,000 footsoldiers; in addition the city was to take an active part in the crusade by supplying 50 warships. The price for this was fixed at 85,000 marks of silver payable in four instalments. The size of the army was based on estimates made by the envoys—estimates which later proved to be much too high. In a secret clause in the treaty it was decided that the expedition should be directed against Egypt, but both sides agreed that for the moment it would be wiser to allow the crusaders to think that they were going to the Holy Land; difficulties would certainly arise if the truth were known. Yet in fact Egypt was the only sensible target since effective help could not be given to Jerusalem until the centre of Ayubid power in Egypt had been decisively weakened.

   Hardly had the envoys returned home with their treaty when Count Theobald of Champagne, the crusade's unofficial leader, died. At a meeting at Soissons (June 1201), the barons chose Marquis Boniface of Montferrat as their new leader. The choice of an Italian seems a surprising one even though it was supported by the French king. But for generations the Montferrats had maintained contacts in the East, with both Byzantium and the Holy Land. Unquestionably the family had an 'Oriental tradition'. Whether or not Boniface at this stage voiced his claims to Thessalonica and already intended to fight on Greek soil is uncertain.

In April 1202 the date fixed for the army's departure passed by unheeded. The Burgundians and the men from Provence decided to sail from Marseilles because it was closer and by so doing they weakened the main army. Only the men from north France and a small German contingent led by a Cistercian abbot from Alsace, Martin of Pairis, made their way to Venice. Here they found themselves in an acutely embarrassing financial position. No more than about 11,000 men had assembled and the Venetians refused to lower their price even though it had been calculated on the basis of an army of 33,500. Despite all their efforts they remained 34,000 marks in debt. At this point the doge suggested a moratorium on their payments if they were prepared to recapture Zara, a city on the Dalmatian coast which the King of Hungary had taken from the Venetians in 1186. The leaders of the crusade had little choice but to comply with this suggestion for otherwise the Venetians would have pressed for immediate payment of the arrears. In the army there were some who protested at what they felt was an unparalleled sin, the attack of a crusading army on a Christian city. But this opposition was overruled and in October 1202 the fleet set sail from Venice. On 24 November Zara was captured, though not before opposition to this turn of events had broken out afresh, led by the Cistercians, under the abbot of Les-Vaux-de-Cernay, and a group of northern barons under Simon de Montfort. They obtained the pope's support but his intervention proved ineffective. As a result the entire army was excommunicated and only with some difficulty were the French and Germans able to persuade Innocent to lift the sentence on them at least. The Venetians remained excommunicated but the pope omitted to prohibit all human and political contact with them. He still hoped to save his crusade and so he sacrificed principles which ought not to have been given up. The attack on a city of Christian Hungary, whose king was himself preparing to go on crusade, was a most dangerous precedent. Now, as later, the pope's attitude to the Fourth Crusade remained ambiguous. Reluctantly Innocent was forced to reconcile himself to the twists and turns of a crusade which he looked upon as his own. He tried to make the best of every situation and by so doing he had only himself to blame when it became clear that he had laid himself open to the charge that his was the guiding hand behind the diversions of the crusade.

It was now too late in the year to do anything but spend the winter at Zara. The crisis of the crusade came at the turn of the year 1202–3. There arrived some unexpected envoys sent by the German king Philip of

Swabia (1198–1208) and by the pretender to the throne of Byzantium, Alexius IV Angelus. Alexius was the son of that Isaac II Angelus who had been blinded and driven off the throne by his own brother Alexius III. His sister, Irene, was the wife of Philip of Swabia. In 1201 the young Alexius IV managed to escape from a Byzantine prison but Pope Innocent III refused to aid his cause so he naturally turned to his brother-in-law. Philip could not give him any active support; he had just suffered a severe setback in his struggle to win the German crown in the shape of the pope's decision in favour of Otto IV (1198–1218). At this stage someone remembered the crusading army which Alexius had in fact already seen while it was mustering at Venice. So envoys were sent to Zara with the proposal that the army should restore the rightful ruler, Isaac Angelus, to the throne. In return Alexius, with the easy generosity of a pretender, promised the earth: reunion of the Orthodox Church with Rome, huge sums of money for the Venetians and the crusaders and support for the crusade in the shape of 10,000 Byzantine soldiers as soon as he was restored to power. The doge liked the idea and the most powerful leaders of the French signed the treaty—but only eleven barons in all. As an open supporter of the Hohenstaufen cause Boniface of Montferrat was also in favour of accepting the plan. But there was fierce opposition led once again by Simon de Montfort and the abbot of Les-Vaux-de-Cernay who in the course of this winter made the bitter decision to return home. Finally, however, even the bishops were persuaded to agree to the project. In their advocacy of the plan the leading barons made much of the legal argument in favour of a legitimate dynasty, an argument which made a considerable impression on the knights. In suppressing the opposition the ties of feudalism proved to be as effective as the fact that to leave in winter involved great risks. For the mass of the crusaders, as Frolow remarked, there was probably sufficient bait in the descriptions of the unbelievable quantity of relics which were to be found in Constantinople. This argument appealed not only to the medieval soldier's notorious greed for booty; it also fitted in with the hatred of the Greeks which had been steadily growing in intensity ever since the schism of 1054; the schismatic Byzantines, so it was asserted, were no longer worthy to be custodians of the richest treasure of relics in the world. The work in which Gunther of Pairis describes the journey of Abbot Martin provides ample evidence of this point of view. The opposition was all the more easily overborne because the pope, though he had known of Alexius IV's intentions as early as November 1202, did not protest to the crusaders about the change in their plans until June 1203. By then it was already too late. In April, soon after the arrival of the Byzantine pretender from Germany, the fleet had left Zara. On Corfu half of the army again rebelled against this most unchristian turn of events and Boniface and the Venetians had a great deal of difficulty in preventing the dispersal of the troops. In May 1203 in what

would have been a last-ditch attempt to buy support against the danger
approaching from Venice, Emperor Alexius III may have concluded
another treaty with Genoa in which he seems to have extended the
Genoese quarter in Constantinople to include even parts of the imperial
Blachernae palace. At any rate there are hints in the sources which permit
such an interpretation. But if there was such a treaty, it was never put into
effect. On 24 June 1203 the fleet dropped anchor at Chalcedon, opposite
Constantinople.

An enormous amount of ink has been expended by scholars discussing
the diversion of the Fourth Crusade. The question is basically an
unfruitful one and will probably never be settled, yet even today there is no
sign that the flood of literature on the subject will dry up.[103] The positions
taken up by the two sides in the controversy can roughly be characterized
as the 'chance theory' (i.e. that it was the result of a series of accidents) and
the 'intrigue theory' (i.e. that it was the result of a skilful plot, long
prepared). The chance theory is based essentially on Villehardouin's
account. Those who hold the intrigue theory—and in the nineteenth
century some of them were by no means free of national prejudice—are
sceptical of Villehardouin and look for a scapegoat. The debate was
opened by Louis de Mas-Latrie in 1861. He accused the Venetians of
treachery on the grounds that they had concluded a commercial treaty
with Egypt just before the army left Venice. One of the terms of the treaty
was supposed to be that they would ensure that the crusade was diverted
against Byzantium. This was what was reported by the Cypriot chronicler
Ernoul who was writing in the first quarter of the thirteenth century.
Ernoul reflected the opinion of the French in Cyprus who were anxious to
clear their fellow countrymen from any blame for such a scandalous
undertaking. And indeed it is true that the diversion of the crusade fitted in
well with the political schemes of the old doge, Enrico Dandolo, a
statesman of real stature whose cool assessment of *Realpolitik* meant that
he was indifferent to the emotion engendered by the crusading ideal. He
was determined to ensure the perpetual dominance of Venice in the
eastern Mediterranean. Although Venice had enjoyed an immensely
privileged position within the Byzantine Empire since 1082, her
merchants had suffered time and again from violent anti-Latin pogroms,
most recently in 1182. Moreover, the Byzantine government had tried to
free itself from Venetian pressure by granting commercial privileges to her
great rivals, Pisa and Genoa. But what cannot be proved is that in the camp
at Zara the doge plotted the complete destruction of the Byzantine
Empire. In 1867 the anti-Venetian theory gained impressively in weight
when no less an authority than Karl Hopf produced details of the
negotiations between Egypt and Venice, giving both the names of the
envoys and the content of the treaty of 13 May 1202. He did not supply any
evidence, however, and a painful shock was to come in 1877 when

Hanotaux and Streit, working independently, proved that Hopf's treaty had never existed and that, at best, Hopf had been looking at a treaty which had long been known but which was concluded in 1208, not 1202. This discovery seemed to acquit the Venetians at the right moment, for Count Riant, writing in 1875, had just introduced a new culprit. This time the conspirators were Philip of Swabia and his Ghibelline kinsman, Boniface of Montferrat. It had undoubtedly been Philip who had recommended his brother-in-law, Alexius IV, to the crusaders in the camp at Zara. Clearly then he had something to do with the change of direction but it is very unlikely that there was any skilful and long-prepared plot. Philip was, it is true, the political heir of the old Norman and Hohenstaufen schemes against Byzantium; his own marriage to Irene added to his interest in Byzantine affairs and the family alliance made it likely that he would support the pretender. But it must not be forgotten that at this time Philip was caught up in a life-and-death struggle with Otto IV and Innocent III and that he hardly had time to intervene actively and decisively in the Byzantine question. Indeed he may well have sent his brother-in-law to Zara simply because he could not help him and it was a convenient way of ridding himself of an additional problem—though this, of course, would not exclude the possibility that Philip hoped to gain something later should the expedition succeed.

So far as it is still held today the intrigue theory on the whole tends to hold Philip responsible. The theory, however, depends very much on the question of the date of Alexius IV's arrival—a question which is by no means easy to answer. The Byzantine historian Nicetas reports that Alexius escaped in 1201. Villehardouin appears to date his arrival in Europe to 1202 though recently Jaroslav Folda has observed that Villehardouin does not expressly say that Alexius escaped in 1202, but merely refers to Alexius's flight to Europe during his account of the year 1202 because it was then that the pretender opened negotiations with the crusaders. The other western sources are equally ambiguous. In November 1202 Innocent III wrote that Alexius IV visited him *olim* (i.e. once). H. Gregoire believed that this must have meant 1201, not 1202 at all events, but the argument is over-subtle and presses the source too hard. *Olim* can mean anything from the distant past to the distant future. If Alexius did not reach Italy until 1202 then there is no time for a carefully planned Hohenstaufen conspiracy; if he arrived in 1201, as is generally admitted today, then such a conspiracy is at least possible, though there still remains the need for a satisfactory explanation of Philip's intentions. Probably the most influential author in the whole debate was W. Norden, with what Queller called the 'modified chance theory' propounded as long ago as 1898: many, the Venetians and the Hohenstaufen among them, believed the conquest of Constantinople to be desirable, but no one deliberately conspired to bring it about. Inasmuch as any one view prevails it is probably the one first expressed by Norden.

Soon after their arrival the crusaders launched an attack on Constantinople. They seized the suburb of Galata and broke the chain which protected the entrance to the harbour of the Golden Horn. On 17 July they attacked Contantinople from both sea and land. The city was saved by the courage of the English and Danish Varangian Guard. But Alexius III lost his head and fled. So now Isaac II Angelus and his son Alexius IV came to the throne as co-emperors. In fact their government was entirely in the hands of the crusaders encamped outside the city. Although we can see from the text of a speech to the emperor, drafted—but never delivered—by a Byzantine court official, that there was a party at court advocating a peaceful agreement with the Latins, Alexius IV was hated by the anti-Latin population of Constantinople and his political position rapidly deteriorated. A revolt in January 1204 swept him and his father off their throne. They were both murdered. The new emperor was Alexius V Ducas Murzuphlus but the crusaders had no intention of putting up with his openly anti-Latin attitude. They decided to make an end of the venerable empire of East Rome in deliberate revenge for the Byzantine anti-Latin pogrom of 1182. In March 1204 they laid the foundation stone of the new state which was to replace the old empire by drawing up a treaty in which they made detailed provision for its constitution.

This time the city was stormed with more success. On 12 April 1204 the crusaders won control of the walls; on 13 April it was all over. For three indescribable days Constantinople was given over to killing and looting. Countless irreplaceable works of art were destroyed by a barbaric mob of soldiers. The most splendid article of plunder was the famous sixth century Quadriga which the Venetians took home with them and which today still adorns the facade of St. Mark's. For the relic hunter it was the chance of a lifetime. Gunther of Pairis, with naive openness, describes how Abbot Martin threatened to kill a Greek priest from the Church of the Pantocrator until he was shown a hoard of relics which impressed him more deeply than all the treasures of Greece. 'Quickly and greedily he plunged both hands in and, girding up his loins, he filled the folds of his gown with the holy booty of the Church which, laughing happily, he then carried back to the ship.' Gunther's list of these relics suggests that Abbot Martin must have been a very powerfully-built man for his loot included a trace of the blood of the Lord, a piece of the True Cross, quite a considerable part of St. John, an arm of St. James, a foot of St. Cosmas, a tooth of St. Laurence, relics of a further twenty-eight male and eight female saints, not to mention fragments, mostly of stone, from sixteen holy places. Many relics now to be found in France were also taken from Constantinople in 1204.[104] While Villehardouin boasted that never before was so rich a haul taken from a single city, another eyewitness, the Byzantine chronicler Nicetas, his own life saved by the kindness of a friend, a Venetian merchant, penned a moving lament to the fall of Constantinople, a document of helplessness and impotent rage, a rhetorical masterpiece richly studded with quotations from the Book of Job and the Lamentations of Jeremiah. In the conquest of Constantinople the Latin hatred of the Greeks which had been growing steadily ever since the First Crusade, celebrated its greatest and most disgraceful triumph.

In accordance with the terms of the treaty of March 1204 the Byzantine Empire was dismembered methodically and in cold blood; here the calculating hand of Venetian policy is evident.[105] The official booty was valued at about 900,000 marks of silver; 500,000 of this went to the Venetians in payment of their outstanding claims on the crusaders. Then, as was laid down, an electoral council of six Venetians and six Frenchmen met to choose a new emperor. The united Venetian front had no difficulty in blocking the candidature of Boniface of Montferrat and obtaining instead the election of the weaker Baldwin of Flanders (1204–5). On 16 May Baldwin was crowned in the Hagia Sofia as first emperor of Romania, the Latin Empire of Constantinople. The coronation service, though Byzantine in its magnificence, was celebrated according to the Latin rites. From now on, following Byzantine custom, the emperor signed his charters in red ink. He was to enjoy, however, only a shadow of the fullness of power once possessed by his Byzantine predecessors. Right at the outset the terms of the treaty of 1204 deprived him of any real power by excluding him from the distribution of the six hundred or so fiefs and thus preventing him from building up any dynastic wealth. The distribution was carried out by a commission composed equally of Venetians and Frenchmen. In accordance with the terms of the treaty the emperor received the palaces of Blachernae and Bucoleon in Constantinople as well as a quarter of the empire: Thrace and north-west Asia Minor, Lesbos, Chios, and Samos. Of the remaining three quarters one half each was allotted to the Venetians and the crusaders. Boniface of Montferrat had originally laid claim to Asia Minor but instead he went on to found, despite many difficulties, the kingdom of Thessalonica, consisting of Macedonia and Thessaly; here most of the new ruling class were Lombards. Boniface was never crowned king of Thessalonica but recently Pokorny reminded us of his letter to Innocent III in which he styled himself 'lord of the kingdom of Thessalonica and Crete'. Although the doge was to claim all of the Venetian share (three eighths) in his title, styling himself proudly 'lord of one fourth and one half [of a quarter, i.e. three eighths all told] of the empire of Romania', the Venetians were, in fact, realistic enough to take only what they could hold. Thus they renounced Epirus and Morea (the Peloponnese) but took the Adriatic coast, some ports on the west coast of the Peloponnese, the Ionian Isles, and bases on the Archipelago. Here in

1207 Marco Sanudo was to found a duchy of the Archipelago with Naxos and Andros as its centres and with suzerainty over the Cyclades. A Dandolo ruled Andros as his vassal and was succeeded by the Venetian Ghisi family. Euboea became a Venetian protectorate where the *baillis* of Negroponte exercised authority over the Veronese 'triple lords' (see below, p. 211) in the name of Venice. Venice bought out Boniface's claims to Crete which, as Candia, was to remain a Venetian outpost in the eastern Mediterranean until 1669. Nowhere did Venice colonize more actively than on Crete. By 1252 some 3,500 Venetians had been sent there, probably rather more than 5 per cent of the population of the Adriatic metropolis. But this was not sufficient to 'Venetianize' Crete and from 1219 onwards the rights of the old *archontes* (see below, p. 210) had to be recognized and a *modus vivendi* found. Compared with Frankish Morea, however, their integration into the Venetian system was limited. The most important harbours on the Hellespont and the Sea of Marmora also went to the Venetians; so did three-eighths of the city of Constantinople including St. Sophia in a new division of the empire drawn up in October 1204. The Venetians now had absolute control of the sea route between Venice and Byzantium. A Venetian colonial empire was springing up which was to last until it was overrun by the expanding might of the Ottomans in the sixteenth century. This empire was ruled by a Venetian *podestà* assisted by a council; after some early difficulties it remained firmly under the control of the republic of San Marco. In October 1205 a third treaty laid down the amount of military service which the Venetians owed to the empire and set up a kind of council of state composed of both Frenchmen and Venetians under the presidency of the emperor. The three treaties of March and October 1204 and October 1205 remained the backbone of the constitution; before he was crowned each new emperor had to swear to observe them. According to the *Assises de Romanie*, the law of Jerusalem was adopted by the Latin Empire but in fact this is only a later legend. It seems probable that unwritten customary law prevailed through the empire. The official language was Latin; only rarely and from the time of Baldwin II was it French, though from the beginning French was the language of the court. The imperial dignity retained its Flemish character inasmuch as the chancery was always headed by a clerk from Flanders. But the chanceries of the Latin patriarch and of the Venetians seem to have been more important than the imperial chancery. Whether the emperor's chancellor was also responsible for his treasury is not clear. In so far as one can speak of a constitution at all, the interests of its foremost parts, the emperor, the powerful feudal nobility, and Venice, were so much at variance that it only served to hasten the steady decline of the state.

The 'crusade' was at an end; no one spoke of sending help to the Holy Land. The conquerors settled down to life in their new land. The pope and the West were at first delighted by the news of the fall of Constantinople, the *civitas diu profana*. But when the pope heard of the atrocities of the sack he was deeply shocked. Even so, he was able to reconcile himself to the *fait accompli*. He was enough of an optimist to hope that a strong Frankish state in Greece would be of great assistance to the *terra sancta*. Moreover, he could look forward to the long-desired union of the Greek Orthodox Church with Rome. But it was entirely contrary to canon law when the cathedral chapter of St. Sophia was filled with Venetians—in accordance with the treaty of March 1204 which gave this privilege to Venice if the new emperor was chosen from among the Franks. Despite all papal efforts, the office of the Latin patriarch of Constantinople was from now on a benefice securely in the hands of the Venetians. In formal terms the union was achieved but it was always a hated union imposed by force. The Greeks remained intransigent in faith and ritual; they were merely made to accept a jurisdictional subordination. Most of the Greek prelates were replaced by Latins and the traditional hierarchy was drastically altered, generally for financial reasons, when bishoprics were changed, re-sited or newly founded. Later the Cistercians and the new Franciscan Order established houses in Greece. The most difficult question was the problem of the Church estates. The treaty of 1204 assigned the Church barely enough to exist; everything else was declared to be plunder. Outside Constantinople the Church had originally been granted one fifteenth of the land in the empire; finally in 1219 after various compromises it was fixed at one eleventh. Similar agreements had already been reached in north and central Greece (1210); in 1223 a settlement was reached in south Greece. The Latin inhabitants had to pay tithes; the Greeks were allowed to pay only one thirtieth in the hope of making the union more acceptable to them.

Thanks to the vigour and energy of the new king of Thessalonica (though this was a title which he never used officially), new Frankish principalities, loosely subordinate to the feudal authority of the emperor, rose in central and southern Greece. In Attica there was the duchy of Athens (the ducal title was in popular parlance from the start but did not become official until 1280) under the Burgundian Otto de la Roche. In France he was such an unknown that Alberic of Troisfontaines wrote that he had become duke of Athens and Thebes through a kind of miracle. On the peninsula of Morea there was the very French principality of Achaia under first William de Champlitte and then the house of Villehardouin. The surviving Byzantines grouped themselves in three centres where the traditions of the ruined empire were kept alive. Relatively insignificant was the empire of Trebizond on the Black Sea, ruled by Comneni until part of it became a Turkish vassal state while the remainder was absorbed by the empire of Nicaea. Nicaea, with its centre of power in Bithynia, was governed by the Lascarid dynasty. In north Greece there was the despotate of Epirus under the Angeloi. The Franks now had to face these three states as well as the Bulgars, the old enemies of Byzantium. Their first clash with the Bulgars ended in disaster at the Battle of Adrianople in 1205. The emperor was captured and never seen again. Soon afterwards Doge Enrico Dandolo died and was buried in St. Sophia. Baldwin's brother Henry became regent and then emperor (1206–16). He was the only effective ruler in the history of Romania. He saw rightly that his own power would be secure only if he was able to destroy the empire of Nicaea in Asia Minor. But at first he was himself almost completely driven out of Asia Minor and not until 1211 could he defeat the Lascarid emperor. Then, in the peace of 1214, he was at least able to restore the *status quo* of 1204 which left the north-western corner of Asia Minor in the hands of the Latins. Earlier he had been distracted by clashes with the Lombard barons of Thessalonica but by about 1210 he managed to settle things satisfactorily. His policy towards the Greeks was one of reconciliation.

Under his weak successors the Latin Empire went inexorably downhill. The vassal states became, to all intents and purposes, independent and the empire was thrown back on its own resources. Henry's successor, Peter of Courtenay, count of Auxerre (1216–19), did not even enter his dominions, being captured while he was still on his way to Constantinople. After a brief period of rule by his wife Yolande, the crown passed to his second son Robert, described by one chronicler as an ill-bred fool (*quasi rudis et idiota*). During Robert's reign the kingdom of Thessalonica was lost. Boniface of Montferrat had fallen in battle in 1207 and his young son Demetrius, crowned king in 1209, was unable to defend his realm against the violent assaults launched by the ruler of Epirus, Theodore Angelus Ducas Comnenus (1224–30) whose three imperial names were programmatic. In 1224, after the loss of his capital, Demetrius fled to Italy.

In Nicaea the fight against the Latins was taken up by Emperor John III Vatatzes (1222–54), a most able and economical ruler. In the peace of 1225 he forced the Latins to evacuate almost the whole of Asia Minor. His armies marched to Thrace and Adrianople. He was threatening to take Constantinople when his advance was halted by the ruler of Epirus who had ambitions of his own in Thrace and who drove back the Nicaean army to Adrianople. The Latin Empire was saved by John II Asen, King of the Bulgars, when he broke the power of Epirus once and for all in 1230. From then on the empire was at his mercy. Robert of Courtenay was succeeded by his eleven-year-old brother, Baldwin II (1228–61; after 1261 he was emperor in name only until his death in 1273). Baldwin II was the only Latin emperor to be born in Constantinople and for this reason he assumed the old Byzantine title *Porphyrogenitus* (born in the purple). In 1231, in an attempt to gain some relief from the pressure exerted by the Bulgars, the barons chose as co-emperor the titular king of Jerusalem, John of Brienne, who had earlier lost his kingdom in the Holy Land to the Emperor Frederick II. In 1236 John put up a stout defence against a menacing Bulgarian-Nicaean coalition but in the end it was only the disunity of the allies which saved the situation. When John died in 1237 the empire was completely surrounded by Nicaean territory and consisted of little more than Constantinople itself. A crusade organized by the pope for the support of the Latin empire proved ineffective. After the death of John Asen in 1241 the emperor of Nicaea was left as the only serious contender for mastery over the Byzantine Empire which John Vatatzes and his successors laboured to revive. Thus Nicaea also became the seat of the exiled Greek Church. The position of the Latin Empire became even more hopeless. No help from the West was forthcoming even though Gregory IX (1227–41) was prepared to accept participation in the struggle in Greece as a satisfactory fulfilment of crusading vows. The ruler of Constantinople lived in abject poverty. Probably there was no emperor or king who was ever so short of money. For years he travelled the world from England to the Nile in order to raise cash by selling both his European estates and precious relics from Constantinople. Even the Crown of Thorns was pawned to the Venetians to be redeemed in 1238 by Saint Louis of France and taken to the Sainte Chapelle in Paris. When all the relics had gone and the lead from the roof of the imperial palace had been sold, the emperor even pawned his son Philip for an advance of about 400,000 marks. This debt was redeemed by King Alfonso X of Castile. But Baldwin II was never able to organize the crusade he hoped for. Politically he remained utterly dependent on financial and moral support from France. Ethnically Romania was very much a French empire; as early as 1224 Pope Honorius III had called it *Nova Francia*. Baldwin received little or no help from the German Emperor whose quarrel with the pope led him to keep on good terms with the emperor of Nicaea. Even Pope Innocent IV (1243–54) was no longer prepared to back Constantinople; on the question of Church union he negotiated directly with Nicaea. It is one of the ironies of history that it took the fall of the Latin Empire to open the way to union. This was finally accomplished under Pope Gregory X in 1274 when Charles of Anjou was threatening to establish a new Latin Empire in Byzantium. It lasted only until 1282 however and was as ineffective in practice as the union of 1439 which was worked out at the Council of Ferrara-Florence in response to Turkish pressure.

The end of Latin rule in Constantinople came suddenly. One of the Nicaean commanders while marching past the city on his way to Thrace discovered that the Latins were relying on a truce and were in no state to defend themselves. Without hesitation on 25 July 1261 he took the city. On 15 August Michael VIII Palaeologus (1259–82), the first of a dynasty which was to rule Byzantium until 1453, made his entrance into Constantinople. Baldwin II fled to Europe. Earlier in 1261, on 13 March, Michael had concluded the Treaty of Nymphaeum with the Genoese, giving them privileges as valuable as those enjoyed by Venice. The

Venetian monopoly position in the eastern Mediterranean collapsed together with the Latin Empire. The Treaty of Nymphaeum proved to be the foundation stone of a Genoese colonial empire with its chief bases at Pera (on the Golden Horn) and at Caffa on the Black Sea and Asov on the Sea of Asov. For this reason the treaty led to a series of wars with Venice which lasted for more than a hundred years until, in 1381, Genoa conceded defeat at the Peace of Turin. Even so, by the middle of the fourteenth century the Ligurian republic had been able to extend its rule over the Byzantine islands of Chios, Lesbos, and Samos.

In the end it was the Peloponnese principality of Achaia which proved to be the most important Frankish state founded in Greece.[106] It was not until after the death of Prince Geoffrey I Villehardouin (1209–29?)—a nephew of the historian—that this became really clear as a result of the fall of the kingdom of Thessalonica in 1224. The rule of Geoffrey II (1229?–46) was marked by internal development and good government. His revenues enabled him to give forceful support to the Latin emperor during the wars of 1236 and 1238 against John III Vatatzes of Nicaea. The island county of Cephalonia, previously in the Venetian sphere of influence, now became a fief of Achaia. A knightly tour to Morea became fashionable for the young gentlemen of France who wished to learn the chivalric virtues for it was believed that nowhere could this be done better than at the prince's court of Andravida in western Elis. The Catalan chronicler Ramon Muntaner believed that the French spoken in Achaia was as good as in Acre or even in Paris (depending on which of his manuscripts one prefers). The highpoint of Achaian history came during the reign of Prince William II Villehardouin (1246–78). The richly illuminated *Manuscrit du Roi* (*Bibliothèque Nationale*, Franç. 844), although it probably never belonged to William II, none the less testifies to his cultivated taste, transmitting, as it does, two troubadour songs which the prince composed and had set to music. But he did more than just write poetry. He conquered the rest of the peninsula of Morea, built one of the strongest fortresses in the land at Mistra, near the ancient Sparta, and accompanied Louis IX of France on his first crusade to the Holy Land. From Louis he received licence to mint money on the pattern of the French royal coins. The duchy of the Archipelago, the duchy of Athens, and the lordship of Negroponte were brought to recognize the feudal suzerainty of Achaia.

Achaia was now the centre of Frankish Greece. As a result of its geographical isolation the interior of the state became steadily feudalized. It was ruled by customary law which was eventually (after a preliminary version completed *c*.1276) codified between 1333 and 1346 in the *Assises de Romanie*. In Morea this collection, though very influential, always remained private in character, and yet in the fifteenth century an Italian version of it became the official lawbook of the Venetian possessions in

Frankish Greece. This law did not, despite the assurances of the author of the *Assises*, come to Achaia from Jerusalem by way of the Latin Empire. Jerusalem lent no more than the lustre of its name and a few formulae. The importance of the principality can be judged from the fact that in its heyday Achaia and the states under its lordship contained about 1,000 knight's fees. In Achaia itself there were about 600 fees. Mostly they were created out of estates confiscated from the Byzantine fisc, from Greek landowners who fled or rebelled, and from the Orthodox Church. At the apex of the feudal pyramid stood the prince, bound to observe feudal custom and dependent on his vassals on matters of taxation and procedural law. But the moral authority and thus the real power of the dynasty was far greater than in Jerusalem. The bulk of the prince's estates lay in the west of Morea together with his capital and the economic centre of Glarentza. His household was controlled by the constable and the marshal (both hereditary offices), by the logothete (chancellor), the treasurer, and the protovestiarios (chamberlain) who farmed out the prince's revenues to tax collectors and kept the register of fiefs for which there is evidence from 1209 onwards. Despite the fact that some of the titles were Greek the structure of the state was thoroughly western. Four castellans administered the prince's family land and special officials (*enquêteurs*) supervised the administration of the barons (*bers de terre*). The dozen or so barons were ranked as peers and exercised blood justice. Their baronies varied in size between four and twenty-four knight's fees, of which about one third were subinfeudated while the rest formed the baronial demesne from which the baron met his own obligation to provide military service. Below the barons came the mass of liege vassals who only possessed jurisdiction over minor criminal offences. The service they owed was strenuous: four months service in the field and four months garrison duty; only for the remaining four months of the year could these knights stay at home on their own estates. Below them came the ordinary fief holders who enjoyed no more than civil jurisdiction over their own peasants. In arranging the marriages of their daughters they were subject to the consent of their lord and they were obliged to pay a special tax (*collecte*) in order to meet the cost of the prince's ransom or the dowry of his daughter. The amount of military service which they owed was in each case laid down in the charter of enfeoffment. Socially inferior to the ordinary fief holders, but in material terms more or less their equals were the *archontes*, the old Byzantine magnates who were especially numerous in the mountainous interior and who had resisted until they themselves were incorporated into the western feudal system. Whether the Byzantine institution of *pronoia*, which in some respects resembled a western fief, facilitated this integration or whether the western feudal order was imposed on a very different form of it is still a matter for debate—despite D. Jacoby's firm conviction that no *pronoia* existed in Morea before 1204. In any event the policy of integration pursued by the Morea Franks differed considerably from the initial Venetian attempt to supplant the *archontes* by introducing new settlers (see above p. 205). Finally there were the non-noble Frankish sergeants who held only half a knight's fee. The custom of primogeniture applied to all fiefs, with both female and collateral heirs enjoying the right to inherit, preference going to the nearest relative even if his claim was through the female line. In contrast to Jerusalem, widows here could choose their own husbands. Agriculture was chiefly in the hands of *vilains,* a term which conceals the fact that they were the descendants of the Byzantine *paroikos.* They were tied to the land, *stasis* as it was called, and they owed their lord fixed dues as well as labour services on his demesne. In return for this they could not be dispossessed of their *stasis.*

The period of peace which had been enjoyed by Achaia came to an end about 1255. William II broke with Venice over a dispute about the inheritance to a Euboean fief and the whole of Frankish Greece became involved in the war which followed. (It was known as the *Guerre des tierciers de l'Eubée* because the lords of Euboea called themselves *terzieri* in consequence of the island being divided into three large fiefs.) In the end William won this war. But then, in 1259, while fighting together with his allies Manfred of Sicily and Michael II of Epirus against Michael VIII Palaeologus, he was taken prisoner when the forces of Epirus changed sides during the decisive battle. He was not freed until 1262 after the restoration of the Byzantine Empire; in return he had to cede Monembasia and Mistra to Byzantium and acknowledge Greek overlordship. Not long after his return home he took up the fight again. This time he looked for help from Charles of Anjou who became lord of south Italy and Sicily as a result of his victory over Manfred at the Battle of Benevento in 1266. By the Treaty of Viterbo William granted Achaia and its dependencies to Charles while reserving the usufruct to himself for life. He was then to be succeeded by Charles's son Philip who married William's daughter Isabella. From now on Achaia was just an Angevin dependency, occasionally left to its own devices when the Angevins had more important matters to think about. It was largely thanks to the aid provided by Angevin money and troops, however, that Achaia held out against Michael VIII Palaeologus. The days of Frankish independence were gone. In this way Achaia was able to buy a period of peace for its most important northern and western parts, but it could not prevent the Byzantines driving a deep wedge in the south as far as Laconia and Arcadia. Since Philip of Anjou died in 1277, one year before William II, the next prince of Achaia was Charles of Anjou. But in 1282, his ambitious eastern plans were brought to nothing by the Sicilian Vespers, the revolt of the Italians against the hated French rule. Charles (d. 1285) managed to hold on to Naples but Sicily fell to Peter III of Aragon. Charles's son,

Charles II of Anjou, was kept fully occupied by the struggle against Aragon and he was, in any event, a weak ruler. In 1289 he granted Achaia as an Angevin fief to William's daughter, Isabella. She married Florence of Hainault (1289–97). Nominally Achaia was independent again but the frequent interventions of Charles II show that Angevin predominance was still very much a reality. Thanks to his sensible policy towards Byzantium Florence enjoyed a peaceful reign in which some of the chivalrous splendour of earlier years was revived. Isabella's next husband, however, Philip of Savoy (1301–6), was an overbearing man who earned the dislike of both the native aristocracy and Charles II of Anjou. In 1306 Charles deposed him for a felony (breach of faith) and granted Achaia to his own son Philip of Taranto, the 'Despot of Romania'. The disaster which befell Athens in 1311 (see below) also had an effect on Achaia. The French ruling class was almost completely replaced by Italians; Italian became the language of the country. The principality went down amidst the growing complexity of the tangled Balkan policies of Venice, Byzantium, and the Ottomans. It became smaller and smaller in size until in 1432 it succumbed to the Greek despot of Morea; soon afterwards it was taken over by the Turks.

In Athens the last duke from the Burgundian house of de la Roche died in 1308. He was succeeded by Walter of Brienne, count of Lecce, who then lost his duchy to one of the most adventurous bands of brigands ever to plague Europe. A former Templar named Roger Flor (d. 1305) had founded the Catalan Company, a kind of itinerant republic, out of Catalan, Aragonese, and Navarrese mercenaries. For many years the company fought in south Italy in the service of Aragon against the Angevins of Naples.[107] When it became redundant as a result of the Peace of Caltabellotta (1302), Roger and his 6,500 men took up an offer of employment made by the Byzantine emperor, Andronicus II Palaeologus (1282–1328) who could see no other way of defending himself against the Turks in Asia Minor who, in their turn, were retreating before the western advance of the Mongols. But the Catalans themselves soon proved to be a menace to an empire which was badly shaken by both internal and external pressures. In 1305 they began to make war on Byzantium from their base at Gallipoli. First they plundered Thrace. Then in 1309 they turned their attention to Thessaly. In 1311, when this province too had been reduced to poverty, they overran the duchy of Athens. Catalan took the place of French as the vernacular; the *Assises de Romanie* gave way to the customary law of Barcelona. From their base at Thebes a band of Catalan brigands now ruled a considerable part of southern Greece. The allegiance which they owed to the kings of Aragon and Sicily who appointed a non-resident duke from 1312 onwards, was purely nominal. Even after Thebes itself fell to a Navarrese Company in 1379, they still remained in control of Athens with its mighty fortress on the Acropolis where the Propylaeum served as a palace and the Parthenon as the Church of St. Mary. In 1388 the Florentine banking house of the Acciajuoli came to power in Athens and ruled as dukes, sometimes subject to the Turks, sometimes to Byzantium, until 1456 when the Ottomans took over for good.

Most of the islands held out longer against the Turks. Negroponte finally became Venetian between 1366 and 1369 and remained so until 1470. The Sanudo and then the Crispo families ruled Naxos until 1539 and Andros until 1566. In 1304 a Genoese dynasty established itself on Chios and in 1346 the island became a Genoese dependency, remaining so until 1566. For all practical purposes it was in the hands of the *Mahona*, an institution rather like a joint stock company. It originally consisted of those Genoese shipowners who had conquered Chios for Genoa and who recouped their investments by obtaining the right to administer and exploit the island, in particular its valuable mastic production. In 1364 nearly all the shareholders adopted the name of Giustinani—despite the fact that none of them belonged to this family—and in this curious, though characteristically Genoese fashion, Chios was turned into a family business—of a sort. Lesbos was a Genoese duchy from 1355 to 1462; Rhodes was held by the Hospitallers from 1309 to 1522. The last of the islands to fall to the Ottomans was Crete in 1669.

IO

THE CHILDREN'S CRUSADE OF 1212 AND
THE CRUSADE AGAINST DAMIETTA
(1217–1221)

ALTHOUGH the outcome of the Fourth Crusade might have been
expected to produce a cooling-off in enthusiasm for the crusade in Europe
during the period of the establishment of the Frankish states in Greece, no
such development in fact occurred. On the contrary the precedent of
a crusade against Christians was followed by a period of considerable
crusading activity within Europe itself. In 1212 the kings of Castile,
Aragon, and Navarre defeated the Muslim Almohads in the Battle of Las
Navas de Tolosa. It was the greatest victory so far in the *Reconquista* and
was won with the assistance of an officially approved crusade. More
important were the Albigensian Crusades 1209–29.[108] During the course
of the twelfth century the Albigensians, heretics who had taken up the
dualist doctrine of the Cathars, had made an increasing number of
converts in Western Languedoc. Innocent III hesitated at first but then
ordered the preaching of a crusade against their protector, Raymond VI of
Toulouse. Owing to the fanaticism of the papal legate and the military
commander, Simon de Montfort, the crusade degenerated into a
humiliating scandal, all the more disgraceful in that it was precisely the
Second Crusade which had encouraged the spread of this heresy outside
the Balkans. The Albigensian Crusade became a power struggle for
control of a Pyrenean kingdom consisting of Catalonia and south France.
In the Peace of Paris (1229) the Capetian monarchy emerged as the real
victor and began at once with the work of assimilating Languedoc into the
French kingdom. The Albigensian heresy, though not entirely eradicated,
was reduced to insignificance and the Church of Rome's hold on south
France was assured. It is very difficult to escape the fact that the original
crusading ideal had been perverted by being used to justify war against
Christians even if they were heretics. The canonical justification for this
extension of the crusade which was later worked out by the canonist
Hostiensis did not alter the situation. The same applies to the whole series
of political crusades launched by the thirteenth-century papacy against its
Hohenstaufen enemies in south Italy. Here it was not even heretics who
were preached against but orthodox Christians. What was right for the
head of the Church was just for its members. Thus the archbishop of
Bremen had the Stedinger peasants branded as heretics in order to be able

to launch a crusade which quite clearly served no purpose except the political aims of Bremen and which finally sealed the fate of peasant freedom in the Weser marshland as a result of the defeat of the Stedinger in the battle of Altenesch in 1234. The secular arm also played a part in these events since it was the recently tightened up heresy legislation of Frederick II which provided the legal basis for the dispossession of the Stedinger which was then carried through on a massive scale. But lack of space means that none of these expeditions can be examined at all closely; this applies equally to the 'crusades' against the Slavs mounted by the Teutonic Order in Prussia after 1226 in a style similar to that already used for the conquest of Livonia after 1184 by the north-German crusaders known as the Brethren of the Sword.

The children's crusade of 1212, however, cannot be passed over.[109] Probably it began in the Rhineland and Lower Lorraine. In the spring of that year large crowds of adolescents gathered together with a sprinkling of adults and a few clerics. Their leader was a boy from Cologne called Nicholas whom they venerated and whose promises they believed. Asked where they were marching to they replied 'To God'. Their goal was clear. They intended to capture the Holy Sepulchre and thus accomplish the task which had proved too much for the mighty of the world. Only to the rationalist is it inconceivable that they should fall victim to the erroneous notion that they could achieve this unarmed and deficient in both money and organization. The participants themselves all of whom seem to have come from the poorer strata of society, were absolutely confident. The year 1212 was a time when religious enthusiasm was at a height, whipped up everywhere by the encouragement to fanaticism which was contained in the preaching against the Albigensians. In addition there were more profound psychological causes. Children's 'crusades' were not entirely unprecedented. In earlier years there had been penitential movements which had seen the path to salvation in the work of helping to build a great cathedral like Chartres. Among these movements there had been groups made up entirely of adolescents under the leadership of youthful miracle-workers. In north France and elsewhere at this date there was a deeply felt reverence for the Innocents, the children of Bethlehem murdered on Herod's orders, who were represented on this earth by the youngest members of the Church, the children. On Innocents' Day (28 December) the children were accustomed to choose and consecrate their own child-bishop. In the idea that the innocent children were specially chosen we can see one of the roots of the naive belief that they, the poorest and the purest, would be able—though unarmed—to recapture Jerusalem. The children's crusade marked both the triumph and the failure of the ideal of poverty.

Neither the ecclesiastical nor the secular authorities took sufficient trouble to disperse the children. Only the French king seems to have persuaded a large French group to go home. They were led by Stephen, a boy from the Vendômois, to whom Christ was said to have appeared in a vision in the guise of a poor pilgrim bearing one of those highly popular letters from heaven. Fired with enthusiasm the children marched to St. Denis; whether or not they intended to go on to Jerusalem is uncertain. On the whole it is true that the comments of the ecclesiastical chroniclers on the children's crusade were acid; the majority of educated adults can have been under no illusions about its chance of success. But no effective steps were taken to prevent the departure of the unfortunate children. Where the clergy did oppose it they were held back by an over-enthusiastic laity. None the less the enterprise never enjoyed the official blessing of the Church so it was not, technically, a crusade.

Early in July the main body of children set out and, led by Nicholas, marched up the Rhine and then over the Alps to Italy. On 25 August they reached Genoa. Despite their losses *en route* they were still said to number 7,000. But at Genoa there were disappointments. The expected miracle failed to materialize; God did not allow them to walk across the sea. The Lombards, who had followed the march with much greater scepticism than the Germans, refused to supply them with ships. What happened next is unknown. According to one report, some of the children sailed in two ships from Pisa and were never heard of again. Others are supposed to have gone to Rome to seek the pope's release from the vows in which— even though this was not an official crusade—they were caught. But even the pope could only free those who, in any case, were not yet old enough to swear valid oaths. A few are said to have got as far as Brindisi, but the rest marched back over the Alps in November and, exhausted and disappointed, made their way home, now mocked by the very same people who had greeted them with such joy on the way out. Alberic of Troisfontaines mentions another group who left the main body and made their way down the Rhône valley to Marseilles, but confuses them with the group led by Stephen. His account is full of legends and is based entirely on a story allegedly told by a man who returned home after eighteen years as a slave in the East. But it contains some facts which can be confirmed from other sources and thus at least a grain of truth. According to Alberic two Marseilles merchants provided seven ships for the children. Two of the ships were wrecked off Sardinia, while the passengers on the other five were sold in the slave markets of North Africa and Egypt. After the miserable failure of an enterprise begun with so much fervour the chroniclers had little trouble in pointing to the absence of any help from God in order to brand the whole crusade as the work of the Devil. Behind this explanation there are clear signs of an uneasy conscience.

But the papacy too was preparing for a new crusade. Innocent III must have been hit hard by the way in which the Fourth Crusade had so completely slipped from out of his control for since the time of Urban II there had been no pope who had fought more keenly to make the crusade an ecclesiastical and specifically a papal enterprise. Besides he was genuinely determined to help the Holy Land and had hoped that the elimination of the Byzantine Empire would bring about this result as well as a union of the Churches. Instead, knightly families emigrated from Palestine and Syria and settled in the newly founded Frankish states in Greece—states which were at a safe distance from the forces of Islam. Inevitably Innocent became convinced that when secular powers like Venice or the Hohenstaufen exercised considerable influence over the course of a crusade there was little chance that it would be of any help to the Holy Land, to the crusading ideal, or to the political objectives of the papacy. From this point of view alone more vigorous papal leadership of future crusades was clearly called for. Moreover, the children's crusade had shown that there was still an untapped reservoir of popular support for a war for the faith which, if it were possible, under papal leadership, to guide into the right channels, might well be used to the advantage of the Holy Land and the Church. Nor should it be overlooked that to Innocent a crusade was an essential means of realizing his hierarchical ideas. Like Frederick II after him he saw that high reputation and the support of public opinion—and thus political leadership—would belong to the man who could both make himself champion of the crusading ideal and bring such an enterprise to a triumphant conclusion.

After the bitter lessons of the early period of his pontificate, in his later years Innocent pursued his goal unwaveringly. In 1213, with the bull *Quia maior*, he opened a vigorous campaign for a new crusade.[110] The incident which gave him his opportunity, the fortification of Mount Tabor in Galilee by the Ayubids, was not in itself important; it carried no special threat to the crusader states. But the European political situation was favourable to the pope's aims. The kings of England and France were caught up in a murderous war, on the outcome of which depended the existence of the French monarchy and the Angevin continental possessions. This was decided at the Battle of Bouvines in 1214. Closely tied up with the Anglo-French conflict was the equally momentous struggle for the German crown between Frederick II and the Welf, Otto IV. Thus there could be no question of the kings taking part in the projected crusade. This was just as Innocent wanted it; his summons was sent to all the peoples of Christendom. *Quia maior* calls for the participation of all Christians irrespective of rank or ability; in Alphandéry's phrase, the bull authorized a kind of *levée en masse*. Spiritual as well as material weapons were to be used. The pope ordered that processions should be held monthly in order to intercede for deliverance of the Holy Land. In this way even the poorest and weakest was given a part to play in the war against Islam. Innocent can have had few doubts about the successful outcome of his plan; he was filled with the quiet certainty that, as was promised in the Book of Revelation, the days of Islam were numbered. (Revelation 13:18: the number of the Beast is 666, i.e. Islam would last at most 666 years and, reckoning from its inception in AD 622, that meant that its end would come in 1288 at the latest.)[111]

In order to make provision for the organization of the crusade, the pope called a council for 1215. But the preachers were at work as early as 1213. In France the outstanding preacher was the legate, Robert of Courçon. He and the pope had been fellow-students. His actions made crystal clear the intention behind *Quia maior*. He distributed the cross to all—to children, to old men and women, to the blind and the leprous. Despite the success of his preaching there was some opposition from the clergy, whom he wished to reform, and from the feudal nobility, whose jurisdiction he wished to limit in the interest of the Church. Even the pope had to disavow some of his actions. Nor could the king afford to keep silent. In evident rejection of the one-sided claims to leadership made by the Church, a royal decree of March 1215 regulated the legal standing of crusaders. In north-west Germany, Flanders, and Holland the preaching of Oliver, the master of the cathedral school of Cologne, met with a great response. But together with the success went an increasing amount of criticism. This is suggested by the fact that it was found advisable to supervise the preaching more strictly. A kind of propaganda office was envisaged for each diocese; from here the preachers were provided with collections of papal and other letters which gave them the arguments they needed to make their work effective; the collection known as the Rommersdorf Letterbook was one of these.[112] Soon overall control of crusade propaganda was made the responsibility of a newly established department of the curia, the penitentiary, which had already been assigned the job of dealing with the steadily growing volume of business concerning dispensations. The connection between the crusades and the penitential system could hardly be made clearer.

The pope saw that a new organization was needed if the kings— together with their financial resources—were to be excluded from the crusading movement. It was to meet this need that he called the Fourth Lateran Council. In November 1215 1,300 prelates assembled at Rome; as a muster of the *ecclesia militans* it was most impressive. They debated the problem of heresy, settled the fate of the county of Toulouse which had been conquered during the Albigensian Crusade, formulated the doctrine of transubstantiation, and set limits to the translation of the Bible into the vernacular. But Innocent's chief concern was the crusade. A special decree was issued in which every aspect of the crusade was dealt with. The development of the papal doctrine of the crusade had now reached its climax. Later (*c.*1250) this doctrine was fully interpreted and given a thorough legal underpinning by the famous canonist Hostiensis, first of all in his *Summa aurea* and then in his main work, the *Lectura*.[113] It was intended that the crusaders would muster in June 1217 in the south Italian ports of Brindisi and Messina, where the pope himself wished to bless the fleets. Clerks who accompanied the crusade were to be released from their residential obligations, i.e. they could continue to enjoy their revenues even while they were away on crusade. All prelates were to see that crusading vows were properly kept; if necessary they were to enforce them by using the weapons of excommunication or even interdict. A man who did not go himself was at least to equip others for three years. Because the sea-route was now regarded as the only possible way to transport large armies to the East, shipbuilders were given special privileges. The curia promised to contribute 30,000 pounds of silver to the crusade itself and it imposed a three-year tax of one twentieth of their income on the whole clergy with the cardinals having to pay as much as one tenth. Those who sold strategic material to the Saracens were threatened with excommunication; confiscation of their property and enslavement was laid down for those who entered the service of Islam as freebooters. For the next four years the entire Levant trade was prohibited in order to ensure that there would be enough transport ships available when needed. All crusaders were exempted from taxes and tolls and were placed under the protection of the Apostolic See until their return or until the arrival of reliable news of their death. There was to be a moratorium on their debts. Christendom was bidden to remain at peace for the next four years.

Particularly momentous was the decree, now approved for the first time by a council, though it had been proclaimed by the pope as early as 1198, that a man who equipped another man should receive the same plenary indulgence as a genuine crusader. In the interests of sound finance this decree was probably as unavoidable as the taxation of the clergy; nevertheless it was a distortion of the original crusading ideal. From here it was but a short step to the commutation of crusading vows in return for a straight money payment. Taken together with a development which was, in itself, admirable—the organization of the Apostolic Chamber and the collectorates into a model of bureaucratic efficiency—this meant that the door was wide open for all kinds of abuses in the financial administration of the curia and the Church—the abuses which were to culminate in the intolerable pre-Reformation traffic in indulgences. Indeed as early as the thirteenth century the popes, often with the thinnest of arguments, were to elevate their Italian wars against the Hohenstaufen to the status of crusades in order to be able to use crusading taxes to meet the costs of their campaigns. But secular rulers also took advantage of the system. By taking the cross, but without ever actually fulfilling their vow, they could time and again have the income from crusading taxes assigned to them. Haakon V of Norway did this three times. Finally Boniface VIII was forced to recognize the right of kings to tax the clergy of their lands for their own secular political ends. Innocent III could not have foreseen consequences as far-reaching as this but even during his lifetime his policy was subjected to biting criticism from poets like Walther von der Vogelweide. The extension of the indulgence to cover those who made no more than a financial contribution to the crusade, however, was not just an economic necessity. It was also the only way to involve the entire population in the papal enterprise. He who wished to lead a crusade had to finance it and Innocent saw himself as sole leader of the movement. For this reason he was most unpleasantly surprised when the young Hohenstaufen, Frederick II (1215–50), suddenly took the cross in 1215. In part Frederick was undoubtedly fired by genuine zeal—he was under the influence of some Augustinian canons who were crusade enthusiasts—but in part he was persuaded by political considerations, and to this extent Innocent was justified in fearing that Frederick wanted to follow in the footsteps of Henry VI and challenge the papal position. The danger of this happening had been increased by Innocent himself. The extension of the crusading indulgence to cover paying non-combatants had its positive side; it meant that this instrument of salvation now became something more than just one of the class privileges of the knightly order and was restored to the common people who had played such a large part in the First Crusade. But the greater the number of those who could enjoy this privilege, the more likely it was that the leadership of the crusades would become a political bone of contention between Church and state, between pope and emperor or king, as is amply demonstrated by the later history of Frederick II.

In the midst of his preparations for the crusade Innocent III died at Perugia on 16 July 1216. His successor, Honorius III (1216–27) was as dedicated to the cause of the crusade as Innocent had been but he was a lesser man, lacking the political strength and energy of his great predecessor. It now became clear that not many crusaders could be looked for from France where the Albigensian wars still kept men busy. But there was great enthusiasm in Austria and Hungary; the king of Hungary had taken the cross as long ago as 1196. In return for the final cession of Zara the Venetians agreed to transport the Hungarian army. In August 1217 the Austrians and Hungarians assembled at Spalato. Leopold VI of Austria sailed at once and Andrew of Hungary left soon afterwards. Apart from a few French troops who embarked at Brindisi the ports originally designated by Innocent III were hardly used. At Acre the crusaders were joined by the prince of Antioch and King Hugh of Cyprus. But neither a single high command nor a clear-cut war aim emerged from the discussion which they held with the king of Jerusalem, John of Brienne, the Masters of the Military Orders, and with the Frankish barons. Finally, with only lukewarm support from the king of Hungary, they undertook three expeditions against the Saracens during the late autumn and early winter of 1217. But since the Saracens were not prepared to give battle nothing decisive was achieved. In vexation King Andrew left to march home through Anatolia in January 1218. With him went Hugh of Cyprus, who died on the way, and Bohemund IV of Antioch. The remaining crusaders were too few to undertake military operations and so they spent the time helping to rebuild Caesarea and enlarging the Templar 'Castle of the Pilgrims' (Athlit) until it was an almost impregnable fortress overlooking the sea and guarding the pass on the road from Carmel to the south. Not until April and May 1218 when the crusaders from Frisia and the Lower Rhine under the command of Oliver of Cologne arrived at Acre after an adventurous journey lasting a year and including some fighting in Portugal, was it at last possible to think again of taking the war to the enemy. A council of war decided to attack the town of Damietta in the Nile delta, thus reviving the old plan of destroying the Muslim centre of power in Egypt as a prelude to the reconquest of Jerusalem. The bishop of Acre, James of Vitry, undertook the task of informing the pope of the decision and his letters constitute an important source for the history of the crusade.

At his death Saladin had divided the Ayubid empire between his sons and his brother and spiritual heir, al-Adil. The latter was able to out-manoeuvre his nephews and from 1200 to 1218 he was generally recognized as the overlord of the whole Ayubid state. He had no fixed residence and governed from wherever his presence was most needed. With the exception of Egypt, the Ayubid empire was in no sense a centralized state; within it there existed a whole range of centrifugal forces which it required great diplomatic skill to hold in check. It was largely owing to these difficulties that the Franks on the Palestinian coast enjoyed a period of peace during the days of al-Adil. Unlike Saladin, moreover, al-Adil was unable to count on the alliances either with the Seldjuks or, after 1204, with the Byzantines. Al-Adil's sons ruled the separate parts of the empire under their father's suzerainty. Al-Kamil, who was designated to succeed al-Adil, held Egypt, the heartland of the empire; al-Mu'azzam ruled Syria and Palestine; al-Ashraf governed al-Gazira, Upper Mesopotamia. In Syria and Mesopotamia there were a number of subordinate city states ruled by collateral branches of the Ayubid family or by dynasties of the second rank (Ortoqid, Zengid).

As has been shown by Gottschalk the Franks had given diplomatic backing to their Damietta project by accepting the offer of an alliance made by the Seldjuk sultan of Rum (Anatolia), Kaikhaus (1210–19). Kaikhaus had ambitions of his own in the direction of Aleppo and Mesopotamia; so he supported the Frankish plan of a crusade against Egypt in the hope that this would tie the main Ayubid forces down in Egypt, leaving him with a fairly free hand in the north. The pincer attack began simultaneously on both fronts. At the end of May the crusaders arrived before Damietta, a strong fortress and the second most important port in Egypt; they pitched camp on the west bank of the Nile opposite the town. In June Kaikhaus attacked Aleppo but by August his campaign had already broken down in the face of al-Ashraf's determined resistance. It ended too quickly to give the Franks the flank support they had hoped for.

The key to the defences of Damietta was the Tower of Chains built on an island in the Nile. (The tower took its name from a chain which stretched across the river from the tower to the east bank on which the town lay.) The channel to the west of the tower was apparently unnavigable so in effect it controlled the entire breadth of the river. The crusaders made this tower their main objective. Al-Kamil, who had been taken completely by surprise by the Frankish attack, hurriedly set up camp some distance south of the town on the east bank. His tactical aim was to prevent the Franks from crossing the river and completely encircling Damietta from the land. Using ships and fire-ships the crusaders launched several attacks on the tower but although they were supported by a ceaseless barrage from eight stone-throwing 'engines' they were beaten off each time. At this point the cathedral schoolmaster, Oliver, whose *Historia Damiatina* provided a valuable account of the crusade, took a hand in events. He had a special kind of siege-engine constructed and paid for with German money. Two cogs were lashed together and four masts erected; at mast-top a wooden fort was built, and lower down draw-bridges controlled by a pulley system were constructed. On 24 August 1218, despite the fierce resistance put up by the defenders who almost managed to destroy the 'engine' with Greek fire, the Franks succeeded in lowering the bridges on to the battlements and in occupying the upper floors of the tower. The next day the garrison surrendered. The crusaders cut the chain, destroyed the bridge of boats which connected the island to the town and built instead their own bridge to their camp on the west bank. This success made a great impression on the Muslims. Sultan al-Adil died of grief. From now on it was always possible that the latent tensions in the Ayubid empire would come to the surface for neither al-Mu'azzam nor al-Ashraf had any intention of remaining permanently subordinate to their brother al-Kamil (1218–38). For the moment, however, they were united in their opposition to the Franks.

From September 1218 onwards the crusaders received a steady flow of reinforcements from Europe: Italians, Frenchmen, Englishmen, and Spaniards. Unfortunately from early 1219 onwards the arrival of new soldiers was offset by a thin but continuous stream of men returning home—despite the promise made by the leading churchmen with the army that, if they would stay, their families too would be covered by their plenary indulgence. Despite the capture of the Tower of Chains they were still unable to gain a foothold on the east bank of the Nile. They suffered from the usual camp diseases. A great part of the army succumbed to dysentery and only a religious fanatic like James of Vitry could believe that the victims of the epidemic had greated their illness joyfully as 'an invitation to a heavenly banquet' and had died almost painlessly. There has never been a time in history when the interested parties have not found some means or other of glorifying death in war.

Among the new arrivals of autumn 1218 were two cardinal legates sent by the pope. One of them, Robert of Courçon, soon died; to the other, the Portugese cardinal, Pelagius of Albano, fell the task of putting into practice Innocent III's conception of a crusade run by the Church. This was a task requiring great diplomatic skill, for although John of Brienne was supposed to be military commander there was in fact no unity of opinion in the army. Pelagius had been granted the plenipotentiary authority to enable him to carry out this task but he lacked the necessary personal qualities. He was a man of driving energy but hopelessly shortsighted, autocratic, self-satisfied, and uncommonly pigheaded. Robert of Courçon's death had deprived him of the influence of a colleague who might have been able to hold him in check. Once already a legate in the Latin Empire of Constantinople he had distinguished himself by his intransigence. Now he looked for support from the new arrivals, the Military Orders and the Italian merchants of Palestine; relying on them he could outmanoeuvre King John, the Frankish barons of the crusader states, and the Frisians and Rhinelanders led by Oliver. Before long the army was split into two hostile camps. Untroubled by the prohibitions of canon law, Pelagius intervened actively in military matters. None the less events went well for the crusaders. An attack on their camp launched by al-Kamil on 9 October was beaten back thanks to the watchfulness of John of Brienne. During the winter the crusaders made some rather hesitant attacks and in February the energetic Pelagius took command. Now and later he demonstrated that once he had decided on a tactical plan he was not to be put off by early lack of success. This time he was assisted by the collapse of al-Kamil's position. The sultan's demands for troops together with the heavy taxes unremittingly imposed by him on the Coptic Christians and on the urban population led to a conspiracy among the Egyptian emirs. Al-Kamil fled followed by the rest of his panic-stricken army. So, on 5 February 1219, the crusaders were able to occupy al-Kamil's camp on the east bank, making a rich haul of booty. All supplies to Damietta were now cut off; the blockade was complete. Al-Kamil was thinking of fleeing to Yemen when his brother al-Mu'azzam arrived from Syria and took vigorous action. The leading plotters were transported to Syria and the conspiracy collapsed. This restored al-Kamil's confidence. But the threat to Damietta had now become serious enough for him to proclaim a holy war in March 1219. Previously he had tried, unsuccessfully, to come to terms with the crusaders. In return for the evacuation of Egypt by the crusaders he had offered a long-term truce and the restoration of the whole former kingdom of Jerusalem with the exception of the Transjordan for which he was prepared to offer 30,000 bezants compensation. The legate would not allow this offer of peace to be accepted. Once again the sultan resumed the struggle but his attack on the Christian camp was thwarted by its good defence works and the two pontoon bridges (one of them consisting of as many as thirty-eight boats) which the crusaders had built. Al-Kamil also tried to barricade the Damietta branch of the Nile and to divert the full flow of the river through the Rosetta branch but the attempt failed when the dams burst. In May 1219 the gallant Leopold VI of Austria returned home despite Pelagius's efforts to persuade him to stay. In July and August the legate organized a series of attempts to take the town by storm. They did not succeed but at least they kept the Muslims in a state of uncertainty. Not until 29 August was al-Kamil able to win any real success in battle. He then took advantage of his improved position to make another peace offer. This time he was even prepared to return the True Cross and to rebuild, at his own expense, the castles and walls of Jerusalem which he had carefully had dismantled in the previous March. Al-Kamil's overriding concern was to protect the Ayubid heartland, Egypt. Despite his military success at the end of August his overall position had deteriorated owing to the fact that the Nile floods had not come and the land was threatened by a harvest failure. In Damietta itself conditions were almost impossible. The population was starving. A hen cost 30 dinars, a cow 800; grains of sugar were as rare as precious stones. Even so the capture of Damietta was by no means the same thing as the conquest of Egypt and al-Kamil's offer was extremely generous. John of Brienne spoke in favour of accepting these terms; over and above the immediate campaign in Egypt it was, after all, Jerusalem that they were fighting for. But again Pelagius turned it down. The Masters of the Military Orders believed that without the Transjordan it was impossible to defend Jerusalem and, as for the True Cross, Saladin had not been able to find it after the fall of Acre. The Italians were most anxious to set up a trading colony in Damietta. Thus it was that the chance to bring the crusade to a successful conclusion was allowed to slip by.

Staying in the crusaders' camp at about this time was St. Francis of Assisi who was to help bring about the triumph of the movement of apostolic poverty by his foundation of the Franciscan Order and through the example of his own purity. He hoped to succeed by preaching where the sword had failed. After some hesitation the legate allowed him to visit al-Kamil. The latter listened to him with the attention that was appropriate to a period of negotiations but never for a moment considered being converted. The political significance of this attempt was ephemeral but it did mark the beginning of a lasting Franciscan interest in the Holy Land and in the Christian mission to the heathens of Asia which the Franciscans initiated and to which they devoted themselves with great zeal if with relatively little success. Their zeal was all the greater since their founder, in his rule, had made missionary activity one of the Order's special tasks. From 1333 to 1524 the Franciscan *Custodia Terrae Sanctae* was based on Mount Sion just outside Jerusalem's Old City (today it is in the Franciscan convent in the Old City). It was charged by the papacy with the task of looking after the Christian Holy Places in the Middle East. From the thirteenth century onwards the curia showed a special preference for Franciscans when choosing embassies to the Near, Middle, and Far East, though the new Dominican Order of Preachers was also active in this field.[114]

By the autumn of 1219 it had become impossible to hold Damietta. On 5 November the crusaders found several sections of the wall undefended and there was practically no resistance when they occupied the town. Damietta fell so easily not because of treachery within the walls but simply because the townspeople were worn out by hunger and disease. The children were rescued by James of Vitry who had them baptized; all the other survivors were either dispersed or enslaved. The fall of Damietta made a devastating impression on the Islamic world. Al-Kamil did what he could. He withdrew up the Nile to Mansourah (i.e. the victorious) and there built a camp which blocked the road to Cairo and was to have a famous place in the history of the crusades. He sent al-Mu'azzam back to Palestine in order to keep the Franks there fully occupied. Otherwise his main aim was to gain time, for only with the united forces of all the Ayubids was a counter-attack possible and throughout the years 1218–20 his brother al-Ashraf had his hands full, initially with the Seldjuk invasion and then with a disputed succession in Mosul where a pretender was threatening to take the city state out of the Ayubid empire.

The crusaders settled down in Damietta but internal dissensions meant that the whole of 1220 was lost and not until the summer of 1221 was decisive action again a possibility. John of Brienne claimed the town for himself and had coins minted which proclaimed his right to rule Damietta.[115] Against him Pelagius declared that the town belonged to the community of all crusaders whom only the Church could properly represent. Early in 1220 John sailed back to Acre angry because the legate had made his provisional acceptance of John's lordship dependent on the decision of the pope and there could be little doubt what the outcome of this would be. Moreover the king had run out of money and in Palestine al-Mu'azzam had been operating very successfully; not much more than Acre and the half-deserted Tyre were left in the hands of the Franks. John's departure left Pelagius as the only possible commander but he was no more than partially successful in controlling the jealousies of the different national groups which sometimes resulted in armed clashes. The best that could be done was to assign them separate quarters of the town. Only the Italians continued to support the legate and then only after he had ordered a redistribution of the booty in their favour.

In order to spur the crusaders into action Pelagius had some Arabic prophecies translated into French and preached to the troops; he also had copies despatched for circulation in the West.[116] The most important of these prophecies, the *Prophetie de Hannan, fils d'Isaac*, was supposed to have been written by a ninth-century Persian doctor and translator who was a Nestorian Christian. In fact it was put together by the Nestorians during the winter of 1219–20 and so, not altogether surprisingly, it accurately 'prophesied' the history of the crusade up to the fall of Damietta. In the figure of the tall and emaciated leader of the Christians Pelagius had no trouble in recognizing himself. The next stage would be the coming of two kings and since one of them was believed to be Emperor Frederick II, all the crusaders now pinned their hopes on him. Pelagius himself was firmly convinced of the truth of these prophecies. For him they were very much more than mere instruments of propaganda and his apparently irrational refusal to have anything to do with al-Kamil's offer of peace only becomes comprehensible on the assumption that he was completely under the spell of these writings. Victory therefore was inevitable. A King David, whose historical identity cannot be established, stood no more than ten days march from Baghdad—or so Pelagius had reported to the pope.

Things did not turn out quite as Pelagius had expected. To begin with, Frederick II did not come although at his imperial coronation in 1220 he had once again taken the crusader's vow. He did, however, send about 500 knights under Duke Louis of Bavaria who, in defiance of the emperor's express command, supported the legate's demands for a war of conquest in Egypt. It was in vain that John of Brienne who had arrived back in Damietta on 7 July 1221 in response to the pope's reproaches, opposed so rash an enterprise. Al-Kamil offered peace once again but talks broke down when the Franks demanded Transjordan as well. This region served as a bridge between Syria and Egypt and from the Ayubid point of view it was indispensable. On 17 July the crusaders marched out to conquer Egypt, moving up the east bank of the Nile until 24 July when they took up a defensive position before Mansourah. Their camp lay in the angle formed by the Nile and one of its tributaries and only ignorance of the hydrography of Egypt could have made the crusaders believe that this was a good defensive position.

Meanwhile the situation in the Ayubid empire had altered. In early 1221 al-Ashraf had concluded the third Mosul war and had prevented the secession of a part of Mesopotamia. He was now able to comply with al-Kamil's ever more urgent appeals for help, although this meant that he had to refuse to go to the assistance of the Georgians against the Mongols. Like almost all the princes of Islam he underestimated the Mongol danger. By early August the troops of the three Ayubid brothers were united in Egypt. Manoeuvring skilfully they circled round the Frankish army and on 10 August cut its land and river communications with Damietta. Neither provisions nor a relieving army could reach the crusaders because al-Kamil had opened the sluice-gates and, it being high water on the Nile at this time of year, this meant that the surrounding countryside was completely flooded. On 26 August the crusaders tried desperately to cut their way through on the one road to Damietta that was still open, though well guarded by al-Kamil. But the sultan now gave instructions for this road to be flooded as well so after advancing a few miles they became bogged down in the morass. Pelagius was forced to sue for peace and on the following day an eight years' truce was made. The Christians were free to leave but they had to leave Egypt altogether. The crusade which might have witnessed the recovery of Jerusalem instead ended dismally owing to the legate's pigheadedness. On 8 September 1221 al-Kamil entered Damietta in triumph. Shortly afterwards in victory celebrations at Mansourah the unity of the Ayubid empire was once again demonstrated. Women sang: 'Most unjustly did the pharaoh of Acre come to Egypt to plague the land, but Moses came to help us with a rod in his hand and he drowned them, one by one, in the sea.' It was not in fact the pharaoh of Acre (John of Brienne) who was responsible. Honorius III tried to blame Frederick II but public opinion, accurately reflected in the songs of the troubadours, came to a different conclusion. The Norman Guillaume le Clerc wrote in his satire *Le Besant de Dieu* (*c*.1227): 'We lost this town owing to our stupidity and our sins, on account of the legate who led the Christians . . . for it is surely against the law [i.e. canon law] for clerks to command knights; the churchman should recite his Bible and the Psalms and leave the battlefield to the knight.' Still more indignant were the poets of Provence, already embittered by the Albigensian Crusade. Fiercest of them all was Guillem Figueira with his terrible sirventes against Rome. But the Damietta expedition proved to be the Church's final attempt to turn the crusade into an enterprise directed and led by her alone.[117]

I I

THE CRUSADE OF FREDERICK II, 1228–1229

ALREADY the reader will have noticed that in the thirteenth century crusades followed each other in more rapid succession than in the twelfth century and that they have been described here without reference to events in Palestine (for which see below, pp. 246ff.). The crusades of the thirteenth century were not in fact brought about by the alarm caused in Christendom by particular events as had been the case with the Second Crusade (the fall of Edessa) and the Third Crusade (the fall of Jerusalem). Instead, leaving purely political motives aside for the moment, they were the result of the permanent state of weakness from which the Holy Land never recovered after the catastrophe of 1187, even though during the Ayubid period it was never exposed to any menace serious enough to jeopardize its very existence. Without some special spark, however, it would hardly have been possible to rouse the great masses that went on crusade in the twelfth century. Instead of the large but quite distinct surges of the twelfth century, there was now a steady stream of crusaders, sometimes no more than a trickle but never quite drying up. A similar stream had existed in the twelfth century; it was from this source that the steadily increasing number of permanent European settlers in the Holy Land had been drawn. In the thirteenth century the immigration of settlers seems to have stopped. Conditions were now too insecure and the competition from the Frankish states in Greece was too strong. There was instead an influx of knights who, every year, came at certain well-defined times in increasing numbers—'seasonal crusaders' they could be called, for their military services were placed at the disposal of the Holy Land for short periods only. The importance of these seasonal crusaders should on no account be underestimated. Apart from the Military Orders who, however, often pursued their own policies indifferent to the interests of the state, they constituted the only reasonably large force whose availability could definitely be counted on. Nor was their enterprise any less dangerous than that of their ancestors on one of the big crusades. In May 1227, for example, William of Queivillers (a hamlet in the French *département* Somme) was at Acre negotiating with the Hospitallers about an annuity which he had previously assigned to the prior of the Hospital in France on condition that the Order assisted him in obtaining the release of his father, Peter of Queivillers, captured while on crusade and imprisoned in the former crusader castle of Sahyun (above, p. 89). Discussions were still going on when William received the news that his father had died in Sahyun. But generously assuming that had his father lived, the Hospitallers would have been able to secure his release, William decided to confirm the gift. It is at this time, too, that a change in the contemporary notion of a crusade becomes apparent. The tumultuous *commotio* (mass movement) of the First Crusade gave way to the orderly *passagium*. This term, drawn from the vocabulary of economic life, is an indication of the way in which the twelfth-century crusades developed into a definite seasonal rhythm in the thirteenth century. Typical of this concept of an established rhythm is the statement made by the annalist of St. Médard at Soissons (*c.* 1250). He reported that even before the Children's Crusade animals of the most diverse kinds had set off for the Holy Land at regular ten-year intervals; the departure of the animals had always been looked upon as a portent of the approach of the Last Days.

The Italian maritime cities staged two *passagia* a year, the March or Easter voyage and the Autumn voyage. Originally these terms meant no more than the convoys of merchant ships; but these, of course, also offered the best chance of making the pilgrimage. The Easter voyage appears to have been the more popular and the conditions of payment attached to it were more favourable. Whether the Easter date, *ver sacrum*, always had religious associations, as Alphandéry believed, is very much open to doubt, but it is incontestable that pilgrim traffic flourished greatly in the thirteenth century. The financial interest of the cities in this traffic was such that in 1234 Marseilles imposed limits on the monopoly of the Military Orders; from then on the Orders were not allowed to transport more than 6,000 pilgrims a year from Marseilles. In 1233 Venice fixed 8 May as the deadline for the return journey of the Easter voyage and 8 October for the Autumn voyage. The 'season' therefore was very short unless a pilgrim decided to stay for half a year or a full year.[118] One of those who did was the immensely rich count Eudes of Nevers. He landed at Acre on 20 October 1265 and died there in the odour of sanctity on 7 August 1266. Rutebeuf lamented his death in his *Complainte du comte Eudes de Nevers* portraying him as a model crusader. The count's testament even attracted the attention of a contemporary chronicler and the executors' accounts vividly illustrate the style of an aristocratic pilgrimage—the luxuries in his luggage, fine manuscripts and jewellery, altar plate and rich hangings, as well as the quantities of supplies, arms, and money. The majority of pilgrims being poor, made the voyage to Outremer under appalling conditions on the lower deck. James of Vitry on the other hand, as a bishop, travelled 'first class'. He rented five cabins for himself, his household and his horses and laid in a three months' supply of wine, meat, and ship's biscuit. But in stormy weather, when the ship lurched in all directions, even the bishop had an uncomfortable time. Nobody dared light a fire, so there was nothing hot to eat, and most of the passengers did not feel like eating anyway. When James disembarked at Acre the voyage from Genoa had lasted about a month.

This change in the nature of the crusades was associated with an altered attitude to heathens. The poets, in particular Wolfram von Eschenbach in his *Willehalm* (*c*.1220), created the image of the 'noble heathen' as represented by a man like Saladin. In terms of his human qualities and virtues this 'noble heathen' is unquestionably the equal of the Christian knight and it is precisely on account of this that a tragic conflict arises when, in the struggle between Christian and heathen, the knight must take up the sword against an honourable adversary, a man who, like him, has been created by God. It would be too much to speak of tolerance in this context but there was certainly a genuine humanity springing from a courtly culture. A change of this kind in the attitude to heathens presupposed, of course, a more accurate view of Islam as the most important heathen religion. The theory that the Muslims were idol worshippers had been losing currency since the middle of the twelfth century. It was now recognized that, on the contrary, the Muslims were rigorous monotheists and hostile to image worship. From the Christian point of view their error lay not so much in their concept of God as in their attitude to Christ. In 1143 Peter the Venerable, abbot-general of Cluny, had the Koran translated into Latin by the Englishman Robert of Ketton. As a result Muslim doctrine was, for the first time, made available to the Christian world. Peter was also one of the first to prefer peaceful persuasion to the force of arms. He wrote: 'I attack you not with arms, as many of us often do, but with words, not with force but with reason, not with hate but with love. . . . I love you; out of love I write to you and with the help of the Scriptures I show you the way to salvation.' Peter still believed that the Muslims, who in terms of numbers represented by far the greater part of the known heathens, made up as much as a third to a half of the total population of the world. But the appearance of the Mongols from 1220 onwards revealed that this estimate was completely false and that beyond the Muslims there were enormous numbers of other heathen peoples. This meant that the proportion of Christians to heathens was altered very much to the disadvantage of the former; and Roger Bacon, in particular, recognized this in his famous *Opus Maius* (*c*.1266).[119] Differing conclusions could be drawn from this changed situation: either there would have to be a tremendous increase in the military commitment—a vigorously debated possibility, though a purely theoretical one—or, instead, an unarmed crusade might be tried—an illusion to which only the children of 1212 yielded. One thing, however, was absolutely clear; 'conversion or destruction', the choice offered by Bernard of Clairvaux (letter 457) when writing about the 'crusade' against the Wends (see p. 99), was no longer a choice which made any sense in the East. Thus besides military aid which was intended to preserve the crusader states there also had to be a greater emphasis on missionary activities. This change in men's knowledge and attitudes created the basis for the intensified missionary activity of the mendicant orders which was to reach deep into Asia and which, in contrast to Cistercian efforts in Europe, never envisaged the possibility of forced conversion. The most impressive testimony to these tiny Christian communities in the Far East is the tombstone of Catherine Vilioni who died in 1342 in Yangchow north of Nanking. The local Franciscans composed the Latin funerary inscription but the artist who depicted the martyrdom of Saint Catherine (giving both her and her torturers Chinese features) was obviously Chinese, though presumably baptized.

The new appraisal of the situation also made possible an approach that would have been unthinkable in the twelfth century and would have met with bitter resistance from public opinion. Even in the thirteenth century it aroused opposition enough but it could, none the less, be undertaken by a man who was ahead of his time, without, however, being able to detach himself from it completely: Emperor Frederick II (1220–50), the first person to try to bring a crusade to a successful conclusion by using political rather than military means.[120]

At the Fourth Lateran Council Innocent III had completely ignored the crusading vow sworn by Frederick II in 1215; the king's participation would not have fitted in with his conception of a papal crusade. Likewise at first Honorius III also made no attempt to persuade Frederick to fulfil his vow; in any event until 1218 the latter was far too busy with the fight against his rival Otto IV to be able to give any thought to a crusade. Only when this danger had been overcome did Honorius, under some pressure from public opinion, call upon the king to lend active support. This was at about the time of the departure of the first contingent—the Hungarians—on the Damietta Crusade. Without the secular power there could be no crusade and so, because the pope needed the king, he was prepared to make concessions. In 1220 he crowned him emperor and, still more important, resigned himself to allowing Frederick to rule his native kingdom of Sicily as well as the empire. The union of south Italy and the empire under one ruler threatened the very existence of the papacy and Innocent III had tried to prevent it by forcing Frederick to promise to hand over the reins of government in Sicily to his son Henry. But immediately after Innocent's death Frederick had frustrated this plan by having Henry elected as king of Germany, thus ensuring that both realms would be united in the hand of his son. In these circumstances it made little sense for Honorius to hold Frederick to the promise which he had made to Innocent III. At his imperial coronation Frederick renewed his vow to go on crusade. He had already successfully requested the pope to threaten to excommunicate all those who had not fulfilled their vow by the summer of 1219. This was a mistake on Frederick's part for it meant that he had deprived himself of the possibility of choosing a date for his own crusade to suit himself. For this reason his vow became increasingly burdensome to him in the following years. Since the imperial coronation had opened the way to Sicily he now gave first priority to the task of putting an end to the conditions of near anarchy in south Italy. In these years and particularly after his return from crusade he turned the kingdom of Sicily into an efficiently governed, centralized state. Here he built the power base from which he subsequently engaged in his great struggle with the curia. This time it was to be a struggle for political dominance in Italy and not, as in the eleventh century, a contest of primacy between emperor and pope.

At first, however, relations between the new emperor and the curia remained harmonious. Time and again he was granted licence to delay his crusade. H. M. Schaller has shown that his chancery was dominated by a group of churchmen headed by Richard, a Templar who had formerly been papal chamberlain and who now served the emperor in the same capacity. Also influential was Hermann of Salza, Master of the Teutonic Order, and since 1216 a close friend and adviser of the emperor. Both of them tried to act as peace-makers between emperor and pope and they found a sympathetic helper in the curia in the person of Cardinal Thomas of Capua, the Grand Penitentiary. But the efforts of these men could do no more than postpone the threatening conflict.

The failure of the Damietta Crusade in 1221, dealing a severe blow to the pope's prestige, meant that the curia now pressed unremittingly for a new crusade. In July 1225 the final arrangments were made in the Treaty of San Germano. The emperor agreed to pay 1,000 knights for two years and to provide transport for another 2,000. He himself was to go on crusade in August 1227; if he failed to carry out his promise he was to lose an enormous deposit of 100,000 ounces of gold and he would incur the sentence of excommunication to which he had, in advance, expressly given his consent. If the emperor died, his successor in Sicily was to assume his obligations. But in contrast to similar treaties with other rulers in the Treaty of San Germano, no allowance was made for the possibility that the emperor might fall ill. Only by accepting these harsh terms could Frederick obtain another two years' delay. It was not, however, a complete victory for the Church. It was to Frederick's advantage that the emperor was once again entrusted with the sole direction of the crusade. The treaty contained no reference to papal financial assistance in the shape of a crusading tax imposed on clerics and laymen. As late as 1223 Frederick had been asking for such a tax, but in fact if the curia made no financial contribution to the crusade it was also unable to exert much influence over the course of events. It ought to be more widely recognized that there were elements of compromise in the Treaty of San Germano.

In November 1225 the emperor acquired a dynastic claim to Jerusalem; he married Isabella, daughter of John of Brienne, king of Jerusalem. At the pope's wish Hermann of Salza had been negotiating this marriage since 1223 but at first Frederick himself had remained very cool on the subject. Now, however, the alliance fitted into his political schemes. John had hoped to be able to rule for the rest of his life but, in the event, he had to resign himself to seeing Frederick assume the royal title immediately after his marriage. Formally Frederick was in the right. John had ruled only as husband of Maria of Montferrat, daughter of Conrad of Montferrat, and then, after her death in 1211, as guardian of their daughter Isabella. His rights were now transferred to Frederick as Isabella's husband. The Frankish barons of Outremer raised no objection; they had higher expectations of the emperor than of John and as yet they knew nothing of Hohenstaufen centralization.

In March 1227 Honorius III died. His successor, Gregory IX (1227–41) was made of sterner stuff; he belonged to the same family as Innocent III. He soon saw that the curia could not tolerate the menacing power of the Hohenstaufen in Italy. But both in Germany and Italy preparations for the crusade were going so well that it was impossible for the pope to intervene. Hermann of Salza had succeeded in persuading Ludwig IV, landgrave of Thuringia, to take the cross together with a large following. In August 1227 an unexpectedly large army mustered at Brindisi and, despite the outbreak of an epidemic, it set sail for Palestine. The emperor and the landgrave followed but they had only been at sea for three days when Ludwig died and Frederick too became seriously ill. To turn back might have the most serious consequences since this eventuality had not been provided for in the treaty of 1225. But even Hermann of Salza advised Frederick to return, so the emperor retired to the spa of Pozzuoli near Naples. Immediately afterwards, on 29 September, Gregory IX denounced him in the most extravagant language and placed him under a sentence of excommunication. Frederick replied with a manifesto which was all the more effective for being a restrained and sober account of the facts. It is clear that, according to the terms of the Treaty of San Germano, Gregory was in the right, but it is equally clear that for him the interruption of the crusade was just a welcome excuse to put the overmighty emperor in his place. The first great power struggle between Frederick II and the curia had begun. From now on both sides waged an incessant propaganda war, attacking each other in fiery manifestos which utilized to the full all the techniques of that art of retoric which reached the climax of its development in the thirteenth century. In Palestine meanwhile peace still prevailed. The truce of Damietta (1221) was supposed to last until 1229 and could only be broken by the arrival of a crowned king; in these circumstances the army which had sailed on ahead of Frederick to Palestine did not dare to begin a war. Instead, in the region between Acre and Tyre, the crusaders built Montfort, the castle which was to be the chief stronghold of the Teutonic Order in the Holy Land.

By his sentence of excommunication Gregory IX had, according to canon law, prevented the emperor from using the crusade as an instrument of politics; for all forms of contact, both in material and in spiritual matters, with an excommunicate were prohibited. When Frederick sought a reconciliation, the pope, who was obliged to pardon the penitent sinner, laid down unacceptable conditions—for example, papal supervision of the government of Sicily. If the emperor had given way and had remained in Italy the pope's actions would have seemed to be justified and Frederick would have lost the game almost before it had begun. So he ignored the pope's express command that he should not go on crusade until he had received absolution and announced that he would leave in the summer of 1228. Gregory, however, clearly continued to rely upon the effectiveness of his sentence, for he was utterly astonished when, on 28 June 1228, the emperor embarked at Brindisi and sailed to join his army. It was a move of unparalleled boldness in a game played for high stakes. Frederick left without having succeeded in reaching a peaceful settlement in Lombardy. Still worse was the possibility that the pope might now regard Sicily as an escheated fief of the papacy and might depose him as emperor. But in fact Frederick had very little choice. Only success in the East could secure and enhance his lordship in the West. In all ages, to rule the East had been looked upon as the ultimate achievement of the world-ruler; with this crusade the emperor proudly confronted the Church with the fact that his policies were universal in their range. He was carried high on the waves of those eschatological hopes and promises which were so powerful at that time. It was foretold that the Last Emperor, in a messiah-like role, would win Jerusalem, unite East and West under his universal rule and, as a sign of the advent of perpetual peace, would hang his shield from the branches of the withered tree which would, at that moment, begin to put forth green shoots. Most manuscripts of the *Prophetie de Hannan* of 1219–20 (see above, p. 226) had allotted the greatest task, the destruction of Islam, to the Ethiopian negus, but in some texts the negus was replaced by the king of Calabria, i.e. Frederick II. We can safely assume that Frederick, imbued like no other either before or after him with a sense of the dignity of his imperial position, was swayed by ideas like this as well as by all the calculations of *Realpolitik*. By the same token his crusade exposed the papacy to an unprecedented danger. Never before had anyone disputed the exclusive right of the pope to call a crusade. Bernard of Clairvaux had guarded this right jealously (see above, p. 94). It meant that in the last resort the pope always possessed the possibility of controlling the crusading movement. But even this right was now threatened by the emperor, an excommunicated man, going on crusade in flagrant disregard of the express prohibition of the pope. It is understandable that Gregory should have done everything in his power to prevent the crusade from succeeding.

After a brief halt at Cyprus while Frederick renewed the feudal overlordship of the empire over the island kingdom and installed imperial garrisons in the castles, he landed at Acre on 7 September 1228, ten years after men had first begun to look for his arrival. None the less he was greeted by an outburst of popular enthusiasm as the man 'by whose hand deliverance was given unto Israel' (I Maccabees 5:62). But the army had shrunk considerably; moreover, it was split into two parties. Frederick could rely on the support of Hermann of Salza and the Teutonic Knights, on the Germans and Sicilians, and finally on the Pisans and Genoese. But ranged against him was the might of the Templars and Hospitallers together with most of the clergy led by Gerold of Valence, the patriarch of Jerusalem (1225–39) and the moving spirit in the opposition of the emperor. But the poet Freidank reflected the popular mood. He lamented the excommunication of Frederick and its effects:

> The cross was given for sin
> To save the most holy sepulchre.
> Now they want to forbid that with the ban
> How then shall a man's soul be nourished?

He also expressed his conviction that he who took the cross in good faith

> Could be sure of the remission of sins
> That is my firm belief.

Frederick was not so rash as to go on crusade without first preparing the way diplomatically. The situation was a favourable one for him because the Ayubid brothers, who had united to drive the Franks out of Egypt, had quarrelled more and more since 1221. A power struggle had developed between al-Kamil and al-Mu'azzam. In 1227 al-Kamil, faced by this difficulty and wishing to secure his rear, repeated the offer of 1219 whereby Saladin's conquests would be restored to the emperor. Al-Mu'azzam, of course, would have nothing to do with this offer. His death on 12 November 1227 freed al-Kamil from the danger of a war on two fronts, but by then it was too late to stop the crusade. Immediately after his landing Frederick began negotiations with the sultan, negotiations which the latter prolonged in order to exploit the emperor's difficulties with the ecclesiastical opposition. Frederick's military operations were on a small scale, intended only to exert some occasional pressure in support of the negotiations. The emperor's engaging gaiety—a quality inherited from his Hohenstaufen ancestors—was praised in the Christian sources, but the Muslims were not much impressed by his appearance. They described him as bald and short-sighted; one of them observed dryly that in the slave market he would not have been worth twenty dirhems. They were impressed, however, by his lively interest in Arab scholarship.

The sultan kept the emperor waiting and forced him to lower his demands considerably and to admit that his imperial prestige would be finished if he had to return home without having achieved some success. Meanwhile rapid negotiations had led to a new partition of the Ayubid empire in the Treaty of Tel-Ajul which was agreed towards the end of 1228. Syria with Damascus was assigned to al-Ashraf, while Palestine fell to al-Kamil. Thus the treaty strengthened the position of Egypt at the expense of the other parts of the Ayubid empire and maintained the overlordship of al-Kamil. As yet, however, the partition existed only on paper and al-Mu'azzam's son, an-Nasir, would have to be defeated by force of arms if it were to be put into effect. In order to equip himself for the struggle which followed immediately after the conclusion of the treaty, al-Kamil came to terms with Frederick in a peace treaty signed at Jaffa on 18 February 1229. The peace was to last ten years, five months, and forty days;[121] Jerusalem—its fortifications had been dismantled by al-Mu'azzam in 1219—was restored to the Franks together with a few places between Jerusalem and the coast including (certainly) Lydda and Bethlehem and (perhaps, but only according to Christian sources) Nazareth, the lordship of Toron and Sidon. So the Franks gained not only their capital city but also considerable territory in the north. For the rest, the *status quo* was to be upheld, in particular in the case of the castles of the Orders. In Jerusalem itself the Temple area, with the two Islamic shrines of the Dome of the Rock and the mosque of al-Aqsa, was to remain in Muslim hands; they were to have their own administration headed by a qadi. It is not clear whether or not the treaty permitted the rebuilding of the walls of Jerusalem, but there are indications that al-Kamil regarded the cession of Jerusalem as purely temporary and he is therefore unlikely to have allowed it. The emperor's attitude on this question is unknown. In fact Jerusalem remained unfortified until it was lost again to the Muslims in 1244.

The treaty meant that with a stroke of the pen Frederick II had achieved the objective sought for so long: Christian lordship over the Sepulchre of Christ, which all the military efforts of the years since 1187 had failed to attain. More than this it meant that al-Kamil could now concentrate on the ordering of his empire while, for his part, Frederick had immensely enhanced both his reputation in the eyes of the world and his own self-confidence. The efforts made by the curia in the fight against him had been brought to nothing. Both the Christian Church and the orthodox Muslims were angered by the treaty; it was condemned by pope and patriarch. The latter, a fanatical Saracen-hater, was particularly dismayed by the Muslim enclave in the holy city and by the fact that the treaty contained nothing at all about the rights of his church. The area around Jerusalem, where most of the estates of the Church of the Holy Sepulchre had lain, remained Muslim territory. Frederick tried in vain to obtain Gerold's approval of the treaty. On his side the patriarch made a last-minute attempt to prevent the emperor from entering Jerusalem. He sent the archbishop of Caesarea to Jerusalem in order to lay an interdict over the city. This meant the prohibition of all divine services and was the most severe ecclesiastical punishment. The archbishop reached Jerusalem on 19 March, but Frederick had already entered the city on 17 March and had even viewed the Muslim quarter. It is an indication of his excessive self-confidence that, though under sentence of excommunication, he now formed the reckless plan of having mass said in his presence in the Church of the Holy Sepulchre. Hermann of Salza was just able to make him see reason and drop the idea. Since the patriarch was absent and had, in any event, refused—with good legal reasons—to crown Frederick as king of Jerusalem, the emperor placed the crown on his own head in a crown-wearing ceremony at the Church of the Holy Sepulchre on 18 March 1229. The archbishop had arrived one day too late. It was undoubtedly a bold and challenging act but it was in no sense—as has been suggested—a kind of Napoleonic self-coronation. In contrast to the Corsican, Frederick would have welcomed an ecclesiastical coronation. As things were this was impossible, but equally Frederick could not afford to leave Jerusalem without the sacred dignity of the crown, and bad news from Italy made it necessary for him to leave soon. Moreover, his dynastic claim to the throne of Jerusalem had been badly in need of strengthening since his wife Isabella had died in childbirth on 8 May 1228—even before Frederick left Italy. Thus although he might choose to call himself king, according to the law of Jerusalem he now ruled only by virtue of being guardian of their son, Conrad IV.

On the coronation day an important imperial manifesto was addressed to all the peoples of the earth, the first to be written in that overpoweringly emotional style that was to be characteristic of the late Hohenstaufen chancery. In it the emperor had himself raised up to a more than earthly position. He stood between God and mankind; in his nearness to God he was like the angels. What he had done, God had done through him. Then he was placed in the context of the tradition of the kingdom of David. In medieval thought David was both king and prophet, a prefiguration of Christ to whom he was occasionally likened. 'Thus,' wrote the emperor, 'all those who honour the true faith shall from henceforth know and shall publish it far and wide to the ends of the earth that he who is blessed for all time has visited us, has brought deliverance to his people, and has raised up an horn of salvation for us in the house of his servant David.'

Meanwhile the situation in south Italy had become critical. John of Brienne, still embittered by the loss of his kingdom, had allowed himself to be talked by the pope into invading Sicily at the head of a papal army. There was a distinctly unpleasant flavour about Gregory's actions at this point, for it was still regarded as particularly despicable to infringe the possessions of an absent crusader and this point of view had always been supported by the Church. Frederick's presence in Italy was now urgently required. So he made sure of the succession of his son Conrad to the Kingdom of Jerusalem—though, in theory, this would depend upon the year-old boy coming to Acre within the next twelve months to claim his inheritance—and then he embarked at Acre on 1 May 1229. The people who once had welcomed him so warmly now treated him with unexampled insolence as he rode down to the harbour; the butchers are said to have pelted him with entrails. Quite clearly the patriarch's propaganda had had its effect. But the most powerful lord in Christendom gave no sign that he had noticed anything amiss. On 10 June he landed at Brindisi. Not until a month later did the pope even know that he had left Acre, and by autumn the papal army had been routed. Gregory IX had lost the first round. He could do little against a ruler who was victorious in war, who had returned from Jerusalem surrounded by the aureole of the Last Emperor who had restored the Holy City to Christendom—a ruler who moved around the countryside accompanied by an exotically magnificent court and later by a rare menagerie of wild beasts. In May 1230 peace was made at San Germano. Superficially it looked as though the emperor had humbled himself. But although there was some compensation for the Church, in reality he was unquestionably the victor. His rule of Sicily could no longer be disputed and in the next year he issued the constitutions of Melfi, re-organizing the kingdom's centralized administration. The sentence of excommunication was lifted and the emperor who, not long ago, had been called the 'disciple of Muhammad' was once more the 'beloved son of the Church'. The success of his crusade was now recognized by the Church. Even before the conclusion of this peace the emperor had had a pulpit constructed in the cathedral of Bitonto, a town which had just been forced to submit to him. The relief on this pulpit has been the subject of a penetrating analysis by H. M. Schaller who has shown that it represents the Hohenstaufen Last Emperors from Frederick I to Conrad IV and thus illustrates a sermon delivered by Nicholas of Bari in which the emperor was glorified as divine majesty and elevated to a godlike position. Schaller has rightly emphasized that the Hohenstaufen conception of the Last Emperor begins with the coronation manifesto of 18 March 1229 together with Nicholas of Bari's sermon and the Bitonto pulpit. From now on his supporters saw the emperor as the long-awaited Messiah and even his most extreme opponents succumbed to this eschatological point of view when, from 1239 onwards, they described him as the forerunner of Antichrist. No one doubted that he marked the end of an era.[122]

12

THE HISTORY OF CYPRUS (1192–1489) AND THE CRUSADER STATES (1192–1244)

As a result of the emperor's determination to incorporate the kingdom of Jerusalem and the island of Cyprus firmly within the Hohenstaufen empire, Frederick II's crusade had momentous consequences for the Holy Land. The Frankish barons were far too conscious of the privileges of their class to allow such a project to go unresisted. Thus the most important episode in the history of the crusader states from 1192 to 1244 is the anti-Ghibelline party's struggle against Hohenstaufen centralization. In the end Frederick was defeated partly because he had underestimated the obstinacy of the barons and partly because he was unable to devote sufficient energy to his Mediterranean plans, particularly after his second excommunication in 1239 when the opening of the last round of his contest with the Roman curia forced him to concentrate his resources in Italy.

The question of Cyprus played an important part in the conflict between the emperor and the Palestinian barons. This then is an appropriate point at which to give a brief survey of the history of the island kingdom until its loss of independence in 1489, before going on to recount the history of the mainland states up until 1244.[123] From the time of its conquest by Richard Coeur de Lion in 1191, Cyprus was of great significance to the crusader states. Once Byzantium had resigned itself to the loss of the island, the possession of Cyprus gave the Franks an unassailable base; not until the days of the Ottoman Empire was Muslim seapower sufficient to make a complete or a lasting conquest of Cyprus possible. The island lies so close to the mainland that from the heights of the pilgrimage centre at Stavrovouni the mountains of Lebanon can be seen across the sea. It served as a supply base, as a port of call for traders and pilgrims, as a springboard for future crusades and as a place of refuge for those who had to flee from the Holy Land. Naturally its secure situation attracted just as many knightly families away from the Christian lordships of the mainland as did Frankish Greece; on the other hand because it was so near the Frankish barons who kept or recovered their estates as a result of the treaties of 1192 and 1229 treated Cyprus only as a place to retreat to in case of emergency. On the whole they retained their fiefs on the mainland and were available for military operations there. Thus it was that in the following years, through a process of intermarriage and property settlements, the great Palestinian families became firmly established on both sides of the sea.

This process was warmly encouraged by Guy of Lusignan who received the lordship of Cyprus in 1192 in compensation for the loss of his kingdom of Jerusalem (see above, p. 148). In his two years' reign he laid the foundations of a new feudal state on the western pattern which was to remain in the hands of his descendants for nearly 300 years. If he was to maintain himself against the native Greek-Cypriot population he had to have vassals. So he freely distributed state property to the knights whom Saladin had driven out of Palestine. Altogether he granted out some 300 knight's fees to the value of 400 bezants a year each and an additional 200 Turcopole fees worth 300 bezants each to non-knightly soldiers who possessed two horses and a coat of mail. By this policy Guy almost completely emptied the state treasury. His brother and successor, Aimery of Cyprus (1194–1205; king from 1197) believed therefore that his primary duty was to refill the royal coffers. Using a mixture of persuasion and force he made his vassals return a part of their incomes. When he died he had an annual revenue of at least 200,000 bezants. In 1367 the king was to receive 100,000 bezants as the yield from landrents and fiscal rights in the diocese of Limassol alone. The total income of the entire lay nobility in this diocese only equalled the king's and it was this economic preponderance—so different from the situation on the mainland—that established the king's political supremacy. When, in 1197, Aimery took over the throne of Jerusalem[124] he made an important decision. Instead of uniting Jerusalem and Cyprus under one crown, as the pope would have liked, he created a purely personal union and thus, by keeping the administrations separate, he prevented Cyprus from being financially milked to the unilateral advantage of Jerusalem. This arrangement was confirmed when the Lusignans recovered the throne of Jerusalem after the Hohenstaufen interlude. But this did not mean that the rulers and knights of Cyprus contributed nothing to the needs of the Holy Land. They took part in the crusades of Henry VI (1197), of the king of Hungary (1217), of John of Brienne at Damietta (1219), and of Louis IX of France (1249). Within the limits of reasonable political action Cyprus played its part in the defence of the mainland states.

During Aimery's reign the Latin Church in Cyprus was organized (1196). The capital, Nicosia, was made an archbishopric with suffragan sees at Limassol, Famagusta, and Paphos. An unusual feature of the Cypriot Church was that it consisted almost entirely of the upper ranks of the hierarchy. Apart from the cathedral churches there were hardly any parishes; in his analysis of the state of the diocese of Limassol in 1367 Jean Richard found only three, one of which, as well as the cathedral, was in Limassol itself. The parishes, as dependent priories, came directly under the authority of the cathedral church. To celebrate the important religious festivals the Latin population, which was mainly concentrated in Nicosia, Famagusta, Limassol, Paphos, and Kyrenia—leaving the countryside to the Greeks—travelled to the cathedrals in the episcopal cities unless there was a house belonging to one of the Mendicant Orders near where they lived or unless, like many of the nobility, they had a chapel of their own. The most important religious houses were the Dominican convent in Nicosia where the kings had their family vault, and the Premonstratensian house, Bellapais. The fourteenth-century ruins of Bellapais still survive as does the thirteenth-century cathedral of Sainte Sophie in Nicosia: two of the finest examples of Latin Gothic architecture in Cyprus. As in the Frankish states in Greece the crucial problem of Church politics was the question of the relationship between the Latin and the Greek Orthodox Churches. The chief points of tension were the subordination of the Greek hierarchy to the Latin and the azyme question, i.e. the debate as to whether the host should be made of leavened or, according to the Latin custom, unleavened bread. The differences of ritual led to attempts at conversion, but also to persecution, the burning of heretics, expulsion, emigration, and other equally unfortunate developments. In practice the azyme question was never solved; the Greeks remained true to their own rite. As for the first problem, this was settled in theory by Alexander IV's *Constitutio Cypria* of 1260. The Greek bishops kept their episcopal rank but were regarded in canon law as being vicars of the Latin archbishop of Nicosia. They had to swear an oath of fealty to him and were subject to his jurisdiction in matters of faith and discipline. Fierce quarrels had preceded this settlement but it was by no means always observed strictly, nor did it lead to a lasting peace, for besides the tensions between Latins and Greeks there were also bitter internal disputes between the Greek conformists who were prepared to compromise with the Latin Church and the strict Orthodox who were not. As early as 1222 the fourteen Greek bishoprics had been reduced to four and the bishops themselves were not allowed to reside in the diocesan capital. Thus the Greek bishop of Limassol lived in Lefkara and the bishop of Nicosia in Soli. The possessions of the Greek Church had been badly mauled by the Frankish nobles at the time of the conquest. Even so the bishop of Nicosia had an income of 1,500 florins (9,000 bezants) in 1329. This, of course, was a modest sum compared with the 18,400 bezants which the Latin bishop of Limassol obtained from his much smaller diocese in 1367.

Like Jerusalem, Cyprus suffered from its kings dying early and leaving heirs who were under-age. Aimery's son Hugh I (1205–18) was only ten years old when he came to the throne; his own son and heir Henry I (1218–53) was only eight months old; and Hugh II (1253–67) no more than two months old. Henry I's mother, Alice, daughter of Henry of Champagne, acted as guardian and regent, but the barons appointed relatives from the famous Palestinian family of the Ibelins to serve as administrative *baillis*, first Alice's uncle Philip (1218–27) and then Jean d'Ibelin, the 'Old Lord of Beirut' (1227–8). When Frederick II stayed on the island in 1228 he forced Jean to hand over the young king and the four strong royal castles in the north (Kyrenia, Kantara, Buffavento, and St. Hilarion, called Dieudamour by the Franks). Frederick claimed the *bailliage* for himself and in 1229 farmed it out to his supporters on Cyprus. By doing this without obtaining the consent of the Haute Cour—which was just as important in Nicosia as on the mainland—he offended against the feudal ideas of the time. There are some faint indications that the Cypriot barons had begun by promulgating their own assises, but the law of Jerusalem was soon recognized to be more favourable to them and by 1230 it can be shown to be valid for Cyprus as well. The famous *Assise sur la ligece* by King Amalric of Jerusalem offered the best way of proceeding against Frederick II because it obliged all the liege-vassals to band together against a feudal lord who confiscated a fief—in this case the *bailliage*—without a judgment of their peers. It should be noted, however, that although the law of Cyprus was in many ways based on the customs of Jerusalem it was not until 1369 that it was completely and officially replaced by the latter. Hardly had Frederick left the island when a revolt broke out against the rule of his *baillis* and Cyprus became caught up in the long drawn out War of the Lombards. However, since this war was fought out chiefly on the mainland it will be described later (see below, p. 254) as part of the history of the Holy Land. In Cyprus the war ended in 1233, ten years earlier than in Palestine, with the capitulation of the imperial fortress of Kyrenia. This marked the end of the Hohenstaufen attempt to seize Cyprus and in 1247 Pope Innocent IV took the island into the protection of the Apostolic See, absolving King Henry I from any oath of allegiance which he may have sworn to the emperor.

The collapse of the Hohenstaufen empire in the eastern Mediterranean put an end to the Oriental plans made by the Master of the Teutonic Order, Hermann of Salza. In 1220 he had bought Count Otto of Henneberg's Palestinian inheritance and thus obtained the important *Seigneurie de Joscelin* (see above, p. 128) for the Order. As the emperor's chief support during his crusade the Order received great privileges from Frederick II, and if the War of the Lombards had not been lost the Teutonic Knights might have achieved a position similar to that of the other Military Orders, with Cyprus, as an imperial fief, playing an important part in their history. In 1230, when it became clear that this was not going to happen, Hermann of Salza obtained from the pope a privilege for the Kulmerland and then devoted his energies to the realization of the Prussian programme for which the foundation had already been laid in the emperor's Golden Bull of Rimini of 1226.[125]

In 1246 Henry I of Cyprus succeeded his mother Alice as regent of the kingdom of Jerusalem, taking the title *Seigneur du Royaume de Jérusalem.*

Thus, in the absence of the lawful king, responsibility for the government of the mainland kingdom rested once again in the hands of the king of Cyprus. Henry's son and successor, Hugh II (1253–67), the prince for whom St. Thomas Aquinas began to write his important treatise on statecraft, *De regimine principum* (completed by Tolomeo of Lucca), died before he reached adult years. With him the house of Lusignan died out in the direct male line. The next king was his cousin Hugh of Antioch-Lusignan. His mother was a Lusignan and he used her name exclusively in order to emphasize dynastic continuity. As Hugh III of Cyprus (1267–84) he was, like his predecessor, *Seigneur de Jérusalem*. Indeed after the death of the last Hohenstaufen king of Jerusalem, Conradin, in 1268, he became King Hugh I of Jerusalem. His primary concern was for the mainland kingdom which was under severe pressure from the attacks of the Mameluks. In 1271 in order to give it additional support he tried to impose military service which was unlimited both in time and place on those Cypriot barons whose only fiefs were on the island. Since they were to receive no payment for this service, the king's demand was turned down by James of Ibelin. He declared proudly that such service had always been purely voluntary, that, when rendered, it had been paid for and that if there was anyone who had the right to demand it, it was the Ibelins, not the king, for they had led the Cypriot army to the mainland more often than he had. In 1273, as a compromise, it was agreed that four months' mainland service might be done. As a result of this limitation which preserved the principle—crucial in the eyes of the vassals—that the obligation to do military service abroad was more restricted than service within the kingdom, Hugh's attempt to defend the kingdom of Jerusalem, was doomed to failure (see below, p. 284). Only after Charles of Anjou's death did the kings of Cyprus recover the throne of Jerusalem. In Cyprus itself Hugh III was succeeded by his two sons, John I (1284–5) and the epileptic Henry II (1285–1324). During the latter's reign the last part of the mainland kingdom was lost (1291) and henceforth the Lusignans ruled Cyprus only, though they continued to be crowned as kings of Jerusalem at a ceremony in Famagusta. As a result of the fall of the Holy Land Henry II suffered much personal misfortune. In 1306 his brother Amalric, the dispossessed lord of Tyre, used his epilepsy as a pretext for seizing power and ruling for four years as a despot with the title *Gouverneur*. Henry was shipped off to Lesser Armenia; not until after Amalric's murder in 1310 was he able to return.

Apart from this palace revolution the internal history of Cyprus had been peaceful since 1233. Of course there had been differences of opinion between king and barons; as in Jerusalem the king theoretically was only *primus inter pares* and was subject to the Haute Cour in Nicosia. But for various reasons he was much more powerful than the king of Jerusalem. He was richer than the mainland king for a start. The Cypriot crown fiefs never attained the size of the four great mainland baronies; in 1367 the revenues of his tenants-in-chief varied between 100 and 21,000 bezants but 'ordinary' fiefs of 1,000 to 1,500 bezants were fairly common. Thus at this level the holders of fiefs were two or three times as well-endowed as on the mainland. In addition the important legal principle of collateral succession to the great fiefs in Jerusalem did not apply in Cyprus. Thus if the direct male line died out the fief escheated to the crown and there was no *Leihezwang*, i.e. the king was not obliged by law to regrant the fief immediately. So he was in a position to build up his landed wealth. The right to mint coin and to exercise jurisdiction over the bourgeoisie remained exclusively royal prerogatives. Thus the barons were clearly subordinate to the king even though the nobility as a corporation seems to have kept an archive of its own as early as 1311; it is significant, for example, that the notary of the Haute Cour had to render account to the royal *Secrète.* Above all, as a result of the absence of any external threat, the barons held no castles. Only the king and the Military Orders disposed of such fortresses. Thus, as Jean Richard has pointed out, it was impossible for individual barons to rebel. In Cyprus resistance could only take the form of a palace revolution or a rising of the entire nobility. Otherwise state and society in Frankish Cyprus were basically similar to the situation in Jerusalem and for that reason the reader is referred to the description of the kingdom of Jerusalem in chapter eight where attention is drawn to those features which were peculiar to Cyprus, usually as a result of Byzantine influence. The impoverished native Greek population still lived as they had done during the days of Byzantine rule. They were divided into three classes: the *paroikoi* who were tied to the land and had to pay a poll tax and one third of their produce as well as do labour services on two days a week; the *perperiarii* who, though personally free, had to pay an annual tax of fifteen hyperpers (bezants) and one third of their produce; and the *eleutheroi* or *francomati* who held free land and only had to pay one fifth of their produce to the former lord of the land. After the fall of Acre (1291) the economic importance of Cyprus grew as Famagusta took over Acre's role in the Levant trade. The population of Famagusta grew so much that the old cathedral became too small and had to be replaced by the beautiful Gothic building still to be seen today. For a long time the city enjoyed the special status of being regarded as the kingdom of Jerusalem in exile. From 1232 onwards the Genoese held a privileged position in Cyprus and their great economic power meant that the king was constantly either at odds or at war with them. They kept a consul or *rector* at Famagusta, but until 1301 their senior administrator in Cyprus, the *podestà* or *rector*, preferred to reside close to the royal court at Nicosia. The Venetians were still based at Limassol in the mid-thirteenth century, but soon after 1291 their consul was to be found at Famagusta. The Pisans seem to have stuck to Limassol longer, but there was undoubtedly an

Italian shift to Famagusta which Jacoby has explained as the result of an influx of refugees from the mainland, initially from the northern mainland states of Antioch and Tripoli in the 1280s and then in still greater numbers after 1291. In Cyprus the system of 'protected' citizens (see above, p. 182) was extended to include native Greeks and Syrian Christian immigrants. They were known as 'white Venetians' or 'white Genoese'. Who the 'black Genoese' were remains a mystery, but in any event there were very few of them. Sugar, salt (obtained by a process of evaporation), and the famous Cyprus wines and fabrics were the island's most valuable exports. In addition Famagusta was of some importance as a shipbuilding centre.

The later history of Cyprus can only be briefly touched upon. Hugh IV (1324–59) distinguished himself in the war against the Turks. Under his successor, Peter I (1359–69) the Lusignan dynasty reached its high point. Peter undertook successful campaigns of conquest in Cilicia and in 1368 he was elected king of Lesser Armenia though he did not live long enough to take over the reins of government. In fact Lesser Armenia's days were numbered. It was hard pressed by the Mameluks and finally collapsed in 1375. After the death of its last Christian king Leo VI (1393), Lesser Armenia was joined in permanent union with the crown of Cyprus, but the union existed in name only—the country itself was controlled by the Egyptians until 1516 when it became part of the Ottoman Empire. When this broke up after the First World War, the Armenian attempts to revive their old Cilician independence were crushed by the new Turkey in a series of indescribable massacres. Besides his Armenian adventures Peter I also organized a serious crusade to reconquer the Holy Land; in this he had the vigorous support of his chancellor, Philip of Mezières, a figure of some importance in the world of literature. For years Peter travelled Europe preparing his crusade. The enterprise began well with the capture of Alexandria in 1365 but then immediately came to a halt because the booty was so immense that the army had no thoughts of further war, only of getting their plunder safely away. In 1369 Peter became the victim of a general revolt of the nobility—the result not, as was thought until recently, of court intrigue and marriage policy, but of the determined resistance put up by the barons to his somewhat absolutist tendencies. He had appointed non-noble bourgeois to crown offices and employed foreign mercenaries who threatened to undermine the baronial privilege of carrying arms. Taxes which had been granted for a fixed period he continued to levy after the expiry of that period. The last straw came when he imprisoned vassals without a judgment by their peers in the Haute Cour. As a consequence of the revolution of 1369 it was officially decided to make the law of Jerusalem apply to Cyprus and a baronial committee was commissioned to search out the best (i.e. the most favourable to the vassals) manuscript of the *Livre de Jean d'Ibelin*. In theory this destroyed the predominance of the crown. And indeed from now on the Haute Cour had a voice in the administration of crown lands; from 1369 all royal charters which concerned the extent or the administration of the crown estates were 'guaranteed' (i.e. countersigned) by two members of the Haute Cour. In practice, however, borrowing the law of Jerusalem made little significant difference. The kingdom changed by evolution not by revolution. From 1369 onwards growing numbers of Greeks and Syrians (i.e. Eastern Christians of all kinds) entered the administration and the landed aristocracy. Internal decline set in under Peter's successor, Peter II (1369–82). In the course of a war with Genoa he lost control of the port of Famagusta (1373). This soon became a dependency of the Genoese bank of San Giorgio. Since Famagusta was the economic centre of the island its recapture now became the most important objective of royal policy. In the Great Schism Cyprus remained neutral until 1382, then opted for the pope at Rome. In 1396 the king changed sides, giving his allegiance to the pope at Avignon in the vain hope that French pressure on the Genoese would then force them to relinquish Famagusta. Under James I (1382–98) and Janus (1398–1432) the kingdom became steadily weaker. The lower classes profited from this development. Even Peter I's policies had been partially financed by the fees paid by villeins to obtain their freedom. The nobles too were forced to resort to the same expedient in order to be able to pay the 'royal tithe' (as distinct from the ecclesiastical one) introduced during the war with Genoa. By the beginning of the sixteenth century there were only 47,185 *paroikoi* left in contrast to 77,066 *francomati*.

In 1426 the Mameluk sultans took revenge for the attack on Alexandria by overrunning and laying waste the island which was then reduced to the status of a tributary vassal state of the Mameluks. Under John II (1432–58), Charlotte of Lusignan and her consort Louis of Savoy (1458–60), and James II the Bastard (1460–73) who came to power through a revolution, the internal dissensions of Cyprus became increasingly savage. Famagusta was recaptured in 1464 but James II obtained little advantage from it because by marrying Katharina Cornaro, the daughter of a Venetian patrician, he had acknowledged that Cyprus lay within the Venetian sphere of influence. After the death of James III (1473–4) Katharina Cornaro ruled the island until 1489. When she abdicated on 26 February 1489 the Lusignan period came to an end. The standard of St. Mark was hoisted over Famagusta. Until 1571, when it fell to the Turks, Cyprus was a Venetian colony.

We are less well-informed about the internal development of the crusader states on the mainland in the period after 1192 than in the years before that date. Too much archive material has been lost and there was not another chronicler of the stature of William of Tyre. It is true that his chronicle was continued in Old French versions, some of which go up as far as 1277, but these continuations are not in the same historiographical class as their

Latin model—and some of them were even written in Europe, not in Outremer. Equally inadequate as histories are the chronicles assembled in the collection known as the *Gestes des Chiprois*. Despite the title some of these chronicles were written on the mainland or, at any rate, by mainlanders. Above all, we lack the finely drawn portraits of the kings which were such an outstanding feature of William's chronicle.[126]

Saladin's truce with Richard Coeur de Lion in 1192 (see above, p. 149) had restored the kingdom of 'Jerusalem' but the old capital itself was not returned and its place was taken by Acre. Essentially, the Franks held little more than the littoral, the coastal region from north of Tyre to south of Jaffa. This did not include either Nazareth or Beaufort on the Litani; thus the natural frontier to the east, the Jordan, was lost. Lydda and Ramleh were partitioned between Muslims and Franks. A land connection between Tripoli and the kingdom of Jerusalem no longer existed. Further north Muslim territory around Lattakieh separated Tripoli from Antioch which had managed to hold firm on the line of the Upper Orontes. Internally the thirteenth century witnessed some shifts within a nobility which had been decimated by the events of 1187 and by emigration to Greece. Some 'old' families managed to maintain themselves despite these developments only to die out in the male line (Arsuf before 1198; Haifa *c.*1244; Scandelion *c.*1260). Their places in the higher nobility were taken by other families, not all of whom came from France—e.g. Walter the German in Mergecolon, the Flemish family of Termonde in Adelon, the Spaniard Alvarez *c.*1250 in Haifa. The Ibelin family—which was probably of Italian extraction—succeeded in making itself the undisputed head of the baronage.[127] It controlled Beirut (from before 1205; carefully planned development of the port from 1220 onwards), Arsuf (after 1206), Ramleh and the county of Jaffa-Ascalon (from 1246–7; Ascalon itself was in Hospitaller custody from 1243 until it fell to the Muslims in 1247); it owned extensive estates in Cyprus and was related by marriage to all the leading families of Palestine.

After the murder of Conrad of Montferrat, his widow, Isabella, married Henry of Champagne, count palatine of Troyes. The count, as the candidate supported by Richard I of England, then took over the government of the Holy Land. The former king, Guy of Lusignan, had already been granted Cyprus by way of compensation. For reasons which are not entirely clear Henry of Champagne never assumed the title of king, being content to call himself 'lord of the kingdom of Jerusalem'. A man of considerable diplomatic skill he saw that his main task, apart from the material reconstruction of the kingdom, would be to put an end to the terrible feuds which had originated in the days of Baldwin IV and which had contributed so much to the fall of Jerusalem. The heirs to these feuds were the families of Montferrat and Lusignan. Henry relied much more on the supporters of the murdered Montferrat, including the Genoese, than

Richard of England may have foreseen. Although initially he sought the support of the Pisans, who had always been closely associated with the Lusignans, when their piracy in Levantine waters could no longer be restrained he drove them from the kingdom. This caused a breach with the constable of the kingdom, Aimery of Lusignan. He too was forced into exile and went to Cyprus where, in 1194, he succeeded his brother Guy. Henry now thought it advisable to come to terms with Aimery. He went to Cyprus and arranged marriages between his daughters and Aimery's sons. In return Aimery finally paid off the arrears owing from Guy's purchase of Cyprus, and the Pisans were allowed to return to the mainland. Henry's plan was a sensible one and, if carried out, it would have established a strong new dynasty, but in fact only one of the projected marriages actually took place and this proved insufficient to ward off the claims of other candidates. Henry also tried to uphold the rights of the crown in ecclesiastical matters. In 1194 this led to conflict over the king's right to confirm the election of a patriarch. After beginning by acting in an altogether too heavy-handed way—he had the canons of the Church of the Holy Sepulchre imprisoned—Henry was forced to climb down. On 10 September 1197, shortly after Henry VI's troops, the heralds of a new crusade, had arrived in Palestine, Henry died as a result of a fall from a window. The plans for a new crusade came to a miserable end (see above, p. 150); indeed even before Henry of Champagne died Jaffa had fallen.

As his successor the barons elected Aimery of Lusignan who had recently become king of Cyprus. The election was in no sense a free one, untrammelled by the claims of hereditary right, for essentially what the barons were doing was choosing a new husband for Henry's widow, Isabella, who continued to wear the crown. Under pressure from the Germans they opted for the rich Aimery of Lusignan in preference to the native baron, Ralph of Tiberias, who was learned in the law but also poor. Thus a personal union of Jerusalem and Cyprus was established. Aimery's election initiated a period of Hohenstaufen influence in the Levant though Jerusalem, of course, unlike Cyprus, was not an imperial fief. King Aimery (1197–1205) concentrated his attention entirely on the Holy Land. After his coronation, a ceremony which meant that Isabella had been crowned at last, he seems never to have returned to Cyprus. With the help of the German crusaders he was able to recapture Beirut and restore the land connection with Tripoli. The most distinctive feature of his reign was his attempt to restore the old customary law. The task was first assigned to Ralph of Tiberias but he preferred to evade it. Some time later Aimery issued the first code of law for Jerusalem, the *Livre au roi* (see above, p. 161f.), in which a faint glimmer of the strong monarchy of the twelfth century still shines through, revealing Aimery's intention of re-establishing that authority. But already the opposition of the barons was too strong, and when Aimery, perhaps with the additional idea of confiscating Ralph's fief, tried to exile him without first obtaining a judgment from the Haute Cour, he was met by open and prolonged resistance. Only with great difficulty was it possible to find a compromise which enabled both sides to save face. For the first time the vassals, acting in response to a petition from Ralph and collectively threatening to withhold their service, had applied the *Assise sur la ligece* against the king. But no action was taken because Ralph voluntarily went into exile. The king's treatment of Ralph was probably not the only reason for his vassals to grumble. The troubles and the loss of territory in the years since 1187 meant that there was no longer sufficient royal revenue to pay the traditional money fiefs in full. Aimery therefore asked the vassals to elect two from among them to help supervise the collection and expenditure of royal revenue. But this was not intended as a constitutional reform giving the vassals an equal share in matters pertaining to the royal fisc. On the contrary since it was stated that all vassals were due to receive from the commissioners their money fiefs 'if this were possible' (*s'il pooit estre*), it is clear that they were being asked to accept, at least temporarily, a reduction in income. In other words their right to elect two commissioners was merely a tactical device by which the king hoped to avoid taking the sole responsibility for this unhappy state of affairs. Since Aimery refused to use his Cypriot resources to alleviate the problem, doubtless despite the fond hopes of his vassals at the time of his accession, it would hardly be surprising if they felt somewhat disenchanted. Moreover, the next crusade, the fourth, came to a halt at Constantinople and brought no help to the Holy Land. Time and again, however, it proved possible to renew the truce with the Ayubids. In 1204 Jaffa was recaptured. Until almost the middle of the thirteenth century the kingdom was by and large spared the danger of a decisive Muslim attack thanks, in the early years, to the conciliatory attitude of the sultan, al-Adil, and later, to the civil wars between the Ayubid brothers. The crusader states would never have held out for nearly a century had it not been for these constantly renewed truces (1192–7, 1198–1204, 1204–10, 1211–17, 1221–39, 1241–4, 1255–63, 1272–90). The later Ayubids had little intention of attempting what Saladin had failed to achieve. They resigned themselves to the existence of the crusader states.

On 1 April 1205 Aimery died of a surfeit of fish. Isabella then ruled alone until her death shortly afterwards. Their two sons had not survived their father. Because his other son, Hugh, was the child of a former marriage, with an Ibelin, he could inherit only the crown of Cyprus, not that of Jerusalem. On the mainland the throne returned to a representative of the Montferrat line. From now on the descendants of Isabella from her last three marriages followed one another in the succession to the throne or to the regency. Until 1291 they were kings of Jerusalem. The following family tree illustrates these relationships. It is much simplified, but within this compass it is quite impossible to clarify all its ramifications.

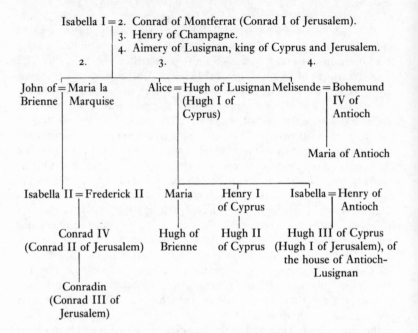

Isabella I = 2. Conrad of Montferrat (Conrad I of Jerusalem).
     3. Henry of Champagne.
     4. Aimery of Lusignan, king of Cyprus and Jerusalem.

Isabella's successor was her child from her second marriage, Maria la Marquise so called because her father was Conrad, the marquis of Montferrat. Jean d'Ibelin, the 'Old Lord of Beirut' was appointed *bailli* (regent). He was a half-brother of Isabella but had no claim to the succession. With him there begins the long series of thirteenth-century *baillis*, not all of whom can be mentioned here. Riley-Smith's seminal work on the *bailliage* showed that, following the precedent of the regency for young Baldwin V, relatives had the first claim to be considered for the position of *bailli*. A surviving parent had the best claim; thus John of Brienne became regent for Isabella II, Frederick II for Conrad IV. If both parents were dead, then it was the turn of the closest male or female relative from that branch of the family through which the crown descended who was present in the East (Alice of Cyprus for Conrad IV, 1243; the system applied as early as 1118, see above, p. 73). Claimants for the office of *bailli* had to appear in person before the Haute Cour. This does not mean that the Haute Cour elected the regent. It only ruled on the question of whether the degree of relationship claimed was correct and so entitled the claimant to the regency or on the question of which of two claimants had the better claim. Such a judgment was necessary every time a regent had to be appointed. So the *bailliage* was not yet a strictly hereditary office, at least not before 1268 (see below, p. 283). Only if there were no relatives who could be considered did the Haute Cour have the right of freely electing a regent from amongst the barons of the kingdom. The separate office of the guardian of a minor ruler seems to have gone to the closest relative from that branch of the family through which the crown did not descend. The rationale behind this rule seems to have been to ensure that a guardian could not murder his ward and then inherit his right to the throne. Therefore this rule was not applied in those cases where the father was appointed *bailli*. He was allowed to retain the charge of the minor king's person, not necessarily because it was assumed that a father would never murder his own son but rather because the succession of the throne was restricted to descendants, i.e. lineal relatives in the ascending line—such as a father—could never succeed. The *bailli* exercised all the functions of the king and therefore had the crown's revenues at his disposal. But he had to render account to the king when the latter came of age. The barons were at all times on their guard against the possibility of a usurpation and so did not permit the *bailli* to control the royal castles. These were granted to individual noblemen chosen by the Haute Cour. Because the crown vassals were not obliged to swear to the *bailli* the oath of allegiance which they owed the king, the *bailli* was allowed to resume their fiefs for the period of the regency since otherwise he might have been deprived of the service due from them. The law of the *bailliage* became increasingly complicated as a result of two developments. Originally regencies had been intended to cope only with the case of minor rulers but later on regents also had to be appointed to act for the absentee Hohenstaufen rulers. Then there were the regents, especially Frederick II and the Cypriot Lusignans, who were themselves frequently absent abroad. They appointed administrative *baillis* of their own—lieutenants in Riley-Smith's helpful terminology. Frederick II's were particularly important. A minor regent for a minor ruler was inherently possible in a system of legal thinking based on blood relationships, but at first no such manifestly useless appointment was made. Thus Jean d'Ibelin became regent for Maria la Marquise in 1205, taking precedence over her two minor half-sisters Alice and Melisende, even though, following the precedent of the succession to the throne in 1163, they were entitled to succeed Maria should she have no children of her own. As late as 1253 there was still an obvious reluctance to claim the regency for Hugh II of Cyprus; he was, after all, only a few months old. But in 1258 his claim was entered and in the logic of the situation this meant that a minor regent now needed a guardian as well as a deputy to act on his behalf (see below, p. 274). By the time Hugh II died in 1267, still a minor, he had needed four deputies with five tenures of office and they, in their turn, had appointed three lieutenants with four tenures. The law of the *bailliage* was undoubtedly an ass.

The regency of Jean d'Ibelin lasted until 1210. Then Maria la Marquise was married to John of Brienne. He was brave and energetic, but by no means a statesman or diplomat of the first rank. His career was remarkable for his continual attempts to obtain one crown after another. His wife died in 1212 leaving him as regent for their daughter Isabella II. Two years later he married Stephanie, daughter of King Leo II of Lesser Armenia. During the Fifth Crusade, the climax of his career, involving war in Syria as well as in Egypt, he tried in vain to wrest control over the crusading army out of the hands of Cardinal-legate Pelagius and to keep Damietta for himself. Outmanoeuvred by Pelagius he then laid claim to succeed to the throne in Cilicia (1220) on the basis of his marriage to Stephanie, but once again in vain. In 1225 he married his daughter Isabella to Frederick II. Again he was outmanoeuvred, this time by the experienced imperial diplomats, with the result that immediately after the marriage he found, much to his astonishment, that he had lost the throne of Jerusalem. He saw no reason to give up, however, and in 1231, six years before his death, he actually succeeded in getting himself crowned as Latin emperor of Constantinople (see above, p. 207).

During the whole of this period it was in the north that the most important events took place. Count Raymond III of Tripoli had died soon after the battle of Hattin (1187) and with him the Toulousan dynasty in Tripoli came to an end. As his successor he had designated his godson Raymond of Antioch, the eldest son of the ruling prince of Antioch, Bohemund III (1163–1201). Instead Bohemund installed his younger son, Bohemund (IV), in Tripoli. But in the following years Bohemund began to feel himself increasingly threatened by the 'great power' policy initiated by one of his own vassals, the Roupenian prince of Lesser Armenia, Leo II. The threat was all the more serious since after 1187 Antioch could no longer rely upon support from the kings of Jerusalem. In 1194 Bohemund III was tricked by Leo and taken prisoner, but Leo's attempt to seize Antioch failed in the face of resistance put up by the city commune which was organized to meet this crisis. Then at the request of the Antiochenes Henry of Champagne intervened. He travelled to Lesser Armenia and persuaded Leo to release Bohemund (1194). In return Bohemund renounced Antioch's feudal overlordship over Lesser Armenia. This opened the way for Leo to obtain a royal crown. In 1198 he received it from the hands of the German chancellor and recognized the emperor as his lord. As a symbol of the reconciliation between Antioch and Lesser Armenia Bohemund's son Raymond married Leo's niece Alice; unfortunately he died soon, shortly after a son, Raymond Roupen, had been born to him. His early death left the question of the succession in Antioch wide open with the result that Bohemund III's death in 1201 was followed by a fierce war of succession between Tripoli and Lesser Armenia lasting for fifteen years. Leo II championed the cause of his great-nephew Raymond Roupen who, according to the accepted rules of primogeniture in Antioch was, in fact, the rightful heir. Leo was supported by the higher nobility and by the pope who treated him indulgently on account of the union of the Armenian Church with Rome which had accompanied the coronation of 1198. But Innocent had to observe with disappointment the way in which (on several occasions) Leo first dissolved and then renewed the union according to the requirements of his policy towards Antioch. On the other side stood Bohemund of Tripoli, claiming to be the nearest relative of the last ruling prince and thus stating a principle which was to become increasingly more important in the history of the crusader states. The city commune, in which the anti-Armenian Greeks played a great role, supported Bohemund. At first the count of Tripoli could also rely on the support of the Latin clergy of Antioch but he forfeited this in 1207 when he installed a Greek patriarch who was to remain in office until 1213. Bohemund's intention was to ensure himself of lasting Greek support and now that Constantinople had fallen into Latin hands there was no danger that the installation of a Greek Orthodox patriarch might lead to a revival of Byzantine claims over Antioch. In these circumstances the Latin clergy withdrew their support from Bohemund and then, on a question of taxation, they broke with the commune as well. They were now clearly in the Armenian camp. Bohemund was still able to count on energetic help from Aleppo; like his predecessors he had no qualms about making alliances with Muslims. On several occasions az-Zahir of Aleppo drove Leo out of Antioch, the citadel of which always remained firmly in Bohemund's hands. Only in 1213 did Leo's position begin to improve, when rumours of a new crusade—the preaching of which began with the bull *Quia maior* in 1213—persuaded az-Zahir to associate himself more closely with Sultan al-Adil who favoured Leo's cause. The marriage between Stephanie and John of Brienne ensured that Leo would have the help of Jerusalem. Thus in 1216 he was at last able to take Antioch and instal Raymond Roupen. But the new prince was soon on thoroughly bad terms with the citizens. In 1219 he was ousted by a revolt and Bohemund of Tripoli returned to take over the government of Antioch for good, as Prince Bohemund IV (1219–33).

Leo's frequent interventions in North Syria were paid for in West Cilicia where he suffered losses at the hands of the Seldjuks of Rum. Even so, he was an outstanding ruler. At home he was able to outmanoeuvre the Hethoumians who, as vassals of Byzantium, had for many years fought a fierce struggle against the Roupenians. He did much to promote trade. He reconstructed his kingdom along Frankish lines, to such an extent indeed that under his successor the Assises of Antioch, translated into Armenian by the constable, Sempad, were introduced as the new code of law for the kingdom. When he died in 1219 a struggle for the succession ensued. In the interests of his daughter Isabella, the old king had disinherited Raymond Roupen and though both pressed their claims neither Raymond nor John of Brienne, who championed the right of his wife, Leo's elder daughter Stephanie, were able to make much headway. But in this situation an alliance with Antioch seemed vital so in 1222 the regent, Constantine of Lampron—a member of the Hethoumian dynasty— arranged for Isabella to marry Philip of Antioch, a son of Bohemund IV. But two years later Constantine dropped this plan and then, in 1226, he married Isabella to his own son Hethoum. As Hethoum I (1226–69), this king was able to bury the old feud between the two princely families of Armenia.[128]

One year earlier a new era in the history of the Holy Land had been ushered in by the marriage of Frederick II to John of Brienne's daughter Isabella. Until the death of his wife (1228) Frederick was king of Jerusalem; after that date he was no more than regent for their son Conrad IV (Conrad II of Jerusalem) who had been born on 25 April 1228. The barons refused to recognize him as king so the coronation of 1229 had no validity in constitutional law except perhaps as a retrospective legitimization of Frederick's kingship of 1225–8. Frederick's crusade and the subsequent attempt to incorporate the Holy Land firmly within his empire unleashed a fierce war of resistance. The barons believed that the rights of their order were threatened and they were never prepared to sacrifice their group interests. Clearly they were fighting against an opponent who was equally self-interested, but the account given by the historian Philippe de Novare presents only one side of the coin in surrounding the baronial reaction with the aura of a struggle for liberty. Over and above the dynastic interests of the Hohenstaufen it is clear that what the emperor had achieved in the treaty of 1229 held out some promise for positive development—for if the Holy Land needed anything it was strong government. Instead from 1228 to 1243 the War of the Lombards raged in Palestine and reduced the kingdom to a state of 'legalized anarchy' (Runciman). The war was named after Frederick's German and Italian mercenaries—not because they came from Lombardy but because many of them came from south Italy, i.e. from the old Byzantine *theme* (province) of Langobardia. Unfortunately we possess only the one-sided accounts written by the anti-imperial party, in particular the memoirs of the famous jurist Philip of Novare which he deliberately entitled *History of the War between Emperor Frederick and Messire Jean d'Ibelin*, in this way elevating the leader of the anti-Ghibellines to an imperial level. The trouble began in Cyprus when the *bailli* on the island, Jean d'Ibelin, handed over the young king to his feudal lord Frederick, but refused to resign either the *bailliage* or the mainland fortress of Beirut to the emperor. Both of Frederick's demands were illegal in that they had not been discussed and approved in the courts of Nicosia and Acre—the course of action recommended by the 'Old Lord of Beirut'. The immediate solution was a compromise which left Cyprus in the hands of the emperor while the fate of Beirut was to be decided in the Haute Cour of Acre. But Frederick did not keep his promise to consult the court and this turned the Ibelins into obstinate and bitter opponents. Nevertheless the emperor began well with the success of the treaty with al-Kamil to his credit. In two places, Jerusalem and Nazareth in Galilee, the kingdom's territory was extended eastwards. Before returning to Europe, the emperor farmed the *bailliage* of Cyprus to a consortium of five loyal barons. Understandably enough these men were determined to recover their costs and so their administration soon ran into trouble. By June 1230, with the help of reinforcements from the mainland, Jean d'Ibelin had driven them from the island.

Hardly had Frederick II made his peace with the pope in 1230 when he intervened in the East. In 1231 he sent a squadron of galleys to Palestine. It was commanded by the imperial marshal, Richard Filangieri, who was accompanied by his brothers Lothar and Henry. They did not venture to land on Cyprus but sailed straight on to Palestine where they took up their headquarters in Tyre. Leaving Lothar in command here, Richard moved on to besiege Beirut; his instructions from Frederick were to dispossess the Ibelins. This had the effect of uniting almost the entire baronage behind the Ibelins and so once again the kingdom was split into two warring camps. On one side there were the imperial troops together with the Teutonic Knights, the Pisans, and the exiled Cypriot consortium of five. On the other side were the forty-three most important barons in the Holy Land supported by the Genoese and the king of Cyprus. The chief centres of Ibelin power were Beirut and Acre. At Acre a commune made up of the urban patriciate and city nobility was formed. Determined to resist to the end, the commune elected Jean d'Ibelin as its mayor in 1232. As the man most directly threatened he was the moving spirit behind the rebellion. He was an upright, brave, and cultivated man. In these circumstances he can hardly be blamed for preferring to defend the privileges of his class rather than submit to a centralized Hohenstaufen state which though it might well have led to a strengthening of the Holy Land, would not necessarily have done so. While Gregory IX attempted to mediate in the interests of the emperor, the Church in Palestine remained neutral; so did the north under Bohemund IV and Bohemund V (1233–52) of Antioch-Tripoli. In any case, Antioch, cut off from the other crusader states by the Muslim enclave at Lattakieh, went downhill economically and so declined steadily in influence after the death of Bohemund IV in 1233. For almost thirty years north Syria practically disappears from history. Meanwhile the barons of Jerusalem recognized Richard Filangieri as the lawful representative of the regent but still continued to oppose him vigorously. On 3 May 1232 at Casel Imbert

between Tyre and Acre the imperial marshal defeated the Ibelins in battle
and then, encouraged by this victory, carried the war to Cyprus. But here
he was himself beaten by Jean d'Ibelin on 15 June at Agridi near the castle
of Dieudamour. When Kyrenia surrendered in April 1233 the second, and
final, liberation of Cyprus by the Ibelins was completed. On the mainland
the imperial bureaucracy continued to function but in reality the Holy
Land was ruled by the clan of the Ibelins whose far-flung family
connections included many of the higher nobility of Europe. During the
years 1234–6 Hermann of Salza and the pope tried to arrange a
compromise which would have ensured the continuity of the imperial
administration. But since they disputed the right of the barons to choose
the regent and demanded the dissolution of the commune of Acre—the
key to Jean's strong position—their efforts were bound to remain fruitless.
In 1236 Jean d'Ibelin died but his brilliant family at once found a new
leader in the person of his son Barisan. Then in 1239 Barisan was in his
turn succeeded by his cousin, Philip de Montfort, a relative of Simon de
Montfort, the powerful earl of Leicester.

Three years after Jean's death Frederick's treaty with al-Kamil expired.
The Muslims at once seized the opportunity to occupy the undefended
city of Jerusalem but were persuaded by the imperial garrison to retire.
Very early in 1240 another Muslim force captured the city once more and
it was at this time that the only section of the fortifications still standing,
the citadel of the Tower of David, was destroyed. Shortly before this had
happened, an imposing group of crusaders led by Theobald IV, count of
Champagne and (since 1234) king of Navarre, had arrived in the Holy
Land. The pope had been planning this crusade ever since 1234. At one
time, though without achieving any noteworthy success, he had even tried
to send it to Constantinople to help John of Brienne (see above, p. 208) in
his war against Byzantines and Bulgars. In 1240 the position of the Franks
in Palestine was not at all bad. Since 1229 al-Kamil had been occupied
with the reconstruction of the Ayubid empire consequent upon the treaty
of Tel-Ajul. In addition he had to cope with the Khwarismians. At the end
of the twelfth century the Shah of Khwarism had created a powerful state
out of the ruins of the Seldjuk empire of Iran. With the help of his only
superficially Islamicized Kipchak Turks he was, for a short while,
overlord of the whole of the Islamic East from his power base in west
Turkestan (Khwarism, Transoxania and Khorassan). Then in 1220 his
empire was overthrown by the Mongols and the Khwarismians withdrew
westwards. By 1230 they were ruling parts of Armenia and Azerbaijan,
serving both as a buffer state against the Mongols and as a threat to the
eastern frontiers of the Ayubids and the Seldjuks of Rum. In 1230 a
coalition of these two powers defeated the army of Khwarism. They did
not foresee that this setback would weaken the shah to such an extent that
within a year the rest of his kingdom had been totally destroyed by the

Mongols. The gates by which the Mongols would enter the Near East were now open. Soon al-Kamil was at war with the Seldjuks, his former allies. He was defeated and, as a result, had to face a rebellion led by his brother al-Ashraf. Not until al-Ashraf died in 1237 did the civil war come to an end. But al-Kamil himself died a year later and the Ayubid empire collapsed into the turmoil of a civil war between his sons as-Salih Ayub (Damascus) and al-Adil II (Egypt). In 1240 as-Salih took over Egypt. Taking advantage of these convulsions Theobald's crusaders had struck southwards in 1239 and recaptured Ascalon but their vanguard had been heavily routed by the Egyptians further south near Gaza. From now on military action was seriously restricted by the threat which this might present to the lives of the Frankish prisoners held in Egypt. Because as-Salih, based in Egypt, now found himself in the position of having to try to reconquer his former territories in Syria, Damascus found it advisable to come to terms with Theobald in the summer of 1240. This allowed him a certain amount of campaigning and the reoccupation of Jerusalem, as well as substantial territorial concessions in the north and in Eastern Galilee. In addition Damascus recognized Jerusalem's right to all territories held west of the Jordan in 1187. Although the alliance with Damascus quickly collapsed and this contributed to Theobald's precipitate departure for Europe in September 1240, it seems unlikely that he would also have made a truce with Egypt, as has been thought. For this would have undone the truce with Damascus as well as the one he had concluded with the Muslim prince of Kerak and southern Palestine and which effectively implemented the treaty with the ruler of Damascus in as much as the latter's territorial concessions had not really been his to give. That Theobald's crusade has not had a better press from scholars until very recently, seems to be due to Richard, earl of Cornwall. He and his army arrived in the Holy Land in October and sided with the pro-Egyptian party in the Latin Kingdom. Before returning to England in May 1241 he concluded a treaty with as-Salih of Egypt which confirmed the concessions made by al-Kamil in 1229 as well as most of those previously granted by Damascus and Kerak: the hinterland of Sidon, Tiberias, Eastern Galilee, and the area around Jaffa and Ascalon where Richard rebuilt the citadel in the northern part of the area encompassed by the great semi-circular land wall. Only Samaria and Hebron remained in Muslim hands; in Galilee the Jordan frontier had been restored and, at least in theory, the Holy Land had a greater extent than at any time since 1187—Theobald's truces excepted. In a letter to England Richard described his own achievements in grandiloquent terms and deliberately belittled those of Theobald. But the concessions won by him had in part already been granted by Theobald. Some of them, moreover, were not in as-Salih's gift but had been held by the prince of Kerak who by shifting back and forth between Egypt and Damascus, kept forcing the Franks to change sides in turn if they were to recover in full their old territories west of the Jordan.[129]

Soon after Richard of Cornwall had gone the War of the Lombards began again. On 25 April 1243 Conrad IV became fifteen years of age and no longer a minor. The barons, their minds attuned to such legal formalities, had waited until then or almost until then before renewing the war against the imperial administration. Probably in June 1243—June 1242 is a possible date but is, as Riley-Smith has shown, at variance with the constitutional legalities—the barons at a meeting in Acre made Alice of Cyprus, the daughter of Henry of Champagne, regent of Jerusalem, though back in 1229 they had rejected her claims to the throne itself. They declared that the regency of Frederick II had automatically lapsed with his son's coming of age. This was arguable but so too was the view (*Livre au roi*, chapter 6) that the regency should continue until the king was crowned. The barons had indeed taken this line in the summer of 1241 when they had offered to accept the earl of Leicester or some other candidate of Frederick II's choice as the imperial lieutenant if only he would dismiss Richard Filangieri, even saying that they would be willing to accept this new *bailli* until Conrad was of age and, beyond that, until he had come in person to claim his throne. Whether this offer was meant seriously or not, we do not know. If it was a trick, then the emperor certainly walked into the trap. He recalled Richard Filangieri; but the attempt to appoint a successor, this time in Conrad's name, failed disastrously. The barons reversed direction and not only declared Frederick's regency at an end but also refused to receive Conrad's appointee. Instead they recognized Alice when it was pointed out—though it had long been obvious—that not only was she, after Conrad, the next heir to the throne but she was also the nearest one actually residing in the East (*plus dreit heir aparant*). This was beyond dispute, but despite what the baronial lawyer, Philippe de Novare, said, it was in point of fact, not customary for the *plus dreit heir aparant* (Alice) to hold the royal inheritance until the arrival of the most rightful heir (Conrad). No sooner had Alice been installed than she asked the barons to pay no further attention to anything that Conrad might command by letter or by messenger. She next revoked, in an illegal and only partially successful move, all those grants which Frederick had made as regent for Conrad. The barons then settled down to besiege Tyre. The unfortunate Richard Filangieri, having been shipwrecked and driven back to Tyre, was captured and Lothar had to surrender the city in order to save his brother's life. The Hohenstaufen take-over bid had finally failed and the more or less complete predominance of the barons in the Holy Land was now assured. It was a clear sign of the weakness of the monarchy that Tyre, the brightest jewel in the crown's estates, was not restored to the king but gradually slipped into the possession of Philip of Montfort. The commune of Acre was no longer needed and had already—probably in 1241—been dissolved, though the religious fraternities of the city, the seeds out of which the commune had grown, continued to play some part in politics. After the death of Alice of Cyprus in 1246, her indolent son, Henry I of Cyprus, succeeded to the *bailliage*, but he called himself *Seigneur de Jérusalem*—not king certainly but clearly claiming to be more than just a *bailli*. In reality, however, he was merely a plaything in the hands of the Ibelins.

The growing tension between as-Salih and his Syrian opponents led to a rapprochement between Damascus and the Franks. The old alliance of 1139 was renewed and in 1243 the Muslims even evacuated their quarter in Jerusalem. But such was the power of thirteenth-century Egypt that the alliance with Damascus no longer possessed its former value. In 1244 the Ayubid rulers declared war on each other. In preparation for this as-Salih had made an alliance with the Khwarismian troops who had been soldiering in Mesopotamia ever since their defeat by the Mongols and who were ready to serve any lord who could pay them. Moving down from the north they swept through the Holy Land and occupied Jerusalem without meeting any resistance worth mentioning. This time Jerusalem had been lost for good. As a memorial of the brief second period of Christian rule over the Holy City there still exists on the *parvis* of the church of the Holy Sepulchre—unfortunately covered up and hardly ever to be seen—the fine tombstone of Philip d'Aubigny, governor of the Channel Islands for John and Henry III and mentioned in the preamble to *Magna Carta*. Matthew Paris, the chronicler of Saint Albans, tells us that Philip fought several campaigns in the Holy Land. It was on one of these that he died in 1236 and was buried, as he had wished, among the Holy Places. After the conquest of Jerusalem the Khwarismians then joined forces with the Egyptian army and together they inflicted a crushing defeat on the Frankish-Damascene army at Gaza on 17 October 1244. It was the greatest setback since Hattin. Among its results were the re-unification of the Ayubid Empire (1245) and the loss of east Galilee and Ascalon (1247). By 1250 the south had gone; and in the north the Jordan frontier had been lost; from now on the kingdom's eastern border ran through Beaufort and Safed.

13

SAINT LOUIS'S FIRST CRUSADE
(1248–1254) AND THE MONGOL INVASIONS

THE Khwarismian conquest of Jerusalem, despite the brutal way in which it was carried out, did not make much impression on Europe. In 1245 Innocent IV held a council at Lyons where he had taken refuge from the power of Frederick II. Here he began to preach a new crusade—but with little success. He himself was just as involved as the emperor in the great struggle between the two universal powers. The war of Guelf against Ghibelline was raging in Italy. The disciples of Joachim of Fiore mocked at all attempts to organize a crusade; they relied upon a pseudo-Joachite commentary on Jeremiah according to which Christ himself was opposed to the recapture of Jerusalem. Here they differed from Joachim who had only expressed the hope that the crusades would become unnecessary through divine miracles and who had in any case believed that they could only be successful after a spiritual purification of Christianity.[130] Henry III of England (1216–72) was kept far too busy by his unruly barons to be able to think of going on crusade. France was the only European power that, at that moment, was capable of mounting a crusade and in fact King Louis IX, Saint Louis (1226–70), had anticipated the pope by taking the cross in December 1244. Owing to the silence of the sources it is not clear whether he had been influenced by the news from Jerusalem. The immediate occasion of his decision had been his recovery from a serious illness. Once again, in the person of St. Louis, a great leader of the crusading movement had arisen, a man capable of inspiring enthusiasm, a man who was himself devoted to the pure and unadulterated crusading ideal. From 1245 until his death in 1270 French policy was based on the crusade.[131]

Louis IX was most likely born in 1214 and succeeded to the throne while still a boy. He had the good fortune to have his kingdom ruled by a most vigorous and intelligent regent, his mother, Blanche of Castile. When he came of age in 1234 she married him to Margaret of Provence and continued to exercise a dominating influence over his government. It was only by taking the cross, an action which at first met with determined opposition from Blanche (and not only from her) that Louis cast off his mother's influence. The royal vassals who had scented an opportunity during the regency, rebelled again and were again put down by Blanche. In 1242 England too was made forcibly aware of the revival of French

power. Under St. Louis the southward expansion of France continued
unabated. In 1247 the Capetians acquired Provence; in 1249 Toulouse.
The stronger north had triumphed over the more civilized south. At home
Louis proved to be an able, uncompromising, and a just ruler. He
reformed the administration of justice and prohibited the judicial duel.
Under him the French economy flourished. The Church could always
count on his support—but not at the expense of the rights of the crown
which he upheld emphatically. He remained neutral in the great struggle
between empire and papacy; both sides put pressure on him in the hope of
gaining his support, but in vain. He allowed the pope's excommunication
of the emperor to be published in France, but prevented the crusade
against the Hohenstaufen from being preached there. In his eyes
Frederick II was still the emperor and he tried to persuade the pope to be
more moderate. Louis's greatest strength was his character—so highly
praised both by his contemporaries and by posterity. But he was by no
means always the peaceful saint that he was made out to be by some
contemporary hagiographers. Though essentially gentle and always ready
to listen to justified criticism, he was still capable of fierce outbursts of
anger. Despite his delicate health he lived frugally and ascetically;
sometimes his indisputably profound religious feeling brought him to the
brink of ecstasy. The bonds between him and his mother were unusually
close, certainly much closer than those with his wife, but when it was a
question of his faith or his crusade then even his mother could be
overruled. He was a man who in his daily dealings with his fellow men
proved that power had not corrupted him and that he was as much a man
as a king. In this respect Louis appears very much to advantage when
compared with Frederick II who surrounded himself with a mystical veil
so that he might be raised up to a godlike dignity. Louis's strength and
influence lay in the decisiveness with which he pursued a moral ideal; only
Saladin was his equal here. The impression he made on men is best
illustrated not by the fact that he was canonized just twenty-seven years
after his death but by the fact that even Voltaire considered the
canonization to be fully justified.

Louis prepared his crusade with great care. The Church had to bear the
chief financial burden. A general crusading twentieth voted at the council
of Lyons brought Louis nothing from outside France or, at least, so little
that he persuaded the French Church to pay a tenth for five years. This
brought in 190,000 *livres tournois* annually, 950,000 all together. The
towns too were heavily taxed. Paris contributed 10,000 *livres parisis*, and
even the tiny Rigny-le-Ferron near Sens raised three *livres parisis*. By the
somewhat hazardous process of extrapolation the total contribution of the
towns has been estimated at 274,000 *livres tournois*. In the fourteenth
century the royal treasury estimated the total cost of the crusade at 1.3
million *livres tournois*, itemized as follows: on court expenses 200,000, on

the king's ransom 210,000, military expenses 750,000, on ship-building 40,000, on the construction of fortifications in the Holy Land 120,000, on the ransom of Christian prisoners 1,300. The significance of this treasury estimate becomes clearer in the light of an annual royal income of 1256-9 of about 250,000 *livres*, i.e. the crusade cost about five times the annual budget. In principle Jean de Joinville was correct when he wrote that the king did not spend his own money but only the Church's, though this is an assessment which fails to take account of the time and effort spent in collecting such levies. It is evident, however, that the Church and the towns had to bear an enormous burden. The arrangements for the transport of the troops were made in treaties concluded with Marseilles— a port which, in formal terms, still belonged to the empire and which Louis hoped to replace by the newly founded port of Aigues-Mortes. The complicated financial arrangements were made by the bankers of Genoa. Louis took the precaution of having large stocks of wine and grain built up in Cyprus over a period of two years. In August 1248 he sailed from Aigues-Mortes while, to the singing of the old crusader hymn *Veni creator spiritus*, the main army embarked in the Old Harbour at Marseilles. Here it was that the expedition was joined by the twenty-five-year-old knight Jean de Joinville. He had been brought up at the civilized court of Count Theobald IV of Champagne and his *Histoire de Saint Louis* is the most vivid as well as the most important account of the crusade, though it should be borne in mind that he did not write it until he was an old man (*c.* 1309) and that historical objectivity is often sacrificed for hagiographical glorification. Particularly one-sided is Joinville's attempt to make the king's brother, Robert of Artois, alone responsible for the failure of the crusade. This, of course, in no way detracts from the work's literary value.

Louis decided to winter in Cyprus while awaiting further reinforcements though the prospects for an immediate attack on Egypt—which was now the only possible target—looked to be good since as-Salih was involved in a war with Aleppo. The army of between 15,000 and 25,000 men which assembled in Cyprus was well organized and included 2,500 knights and 5,000 crossbowmen. It was made up almost entirely of Frenchmen, with a very few participants from other nations (Germans, Norwegians, English, and Scots). It also seems to have been a predominantly feudal army.[132] The fleet left Cyprus at the end of May and anchored off Damietta on 5 June 1249. The sultan had naturally been kept informed of their approach so the coast was held in force by the Egyptian army. But by using flat-bottomed landing craft the Christians sailed in almost to the beach and then the knights waded the rest of the way. The defenders soon gave way before the onslaught of the dripping wet knights. Although they had as yet lost little the Egyptians decided to withdraw not to Damietta but, for some strange reason, further up the Nile. This led to a panic in Damietta and on 6 June the town was evacuated without there being any resistance offered. In the face of this unexpected success for the crusaders it was as much as the mortally sick sultan could do to restore order in his own army. This then took up position at Mansourah.

Louis decided to spend the summer in Damietta. He wanted to wait for the reinforcements promised by his brother, Alfonso of Poitiers. Perhaps he remembered the catastrophe of 1221, when the crusaders had become bogged down in the summer mud of the Nile. In the meantime the war was carried to Syria where Sidon had been lost to the Muslims. In November Louis established an archbishopric at Damietta. Its foundation charter— the only one of its kind to survive from the Latin East—has been subjected to a searching analysis by Jean Richard.[133] He has shown that although the Capetian tradition of an expansionist territorial policy had had nothing to do with Louis's decision to take the cross, once out in the East he began to think in these terms. Just as Philip Augustus in his treaty with the Genoese (see above, p. 145) had granted them territorial concessions in the Holy Land—which, though he might help to reconquer it, in no way belonged to him—so now even Louis looked upon Damietta as his by right of conquest, though as late as 1218 it had been assigned to the king of Jerusalem. Egypt, as yet unconquered, he regarded in the same light and used its territory to assign revenues to both the archbishop and the chapter. In addition he granted ten fiefs to the archbishop. Louis may have thought of his brother Robert of Artois as the future ruler of Egypt. The charter is a good illustration of the way in which Louis was able to combine ideals with practical politics.

On 20 November 1249 the French army began to march south along the east bank of the Nile towards Cairo, following in the footsteps of the crusaders of 1221, although there had been many who had advised an attack on Alexandria which might have offered better hope of success. The Ayubid empire was in a difficult position because as-Salih died on 22 November. But, with the help of his bodyguard, his favourite wife saved the situation by acting in an unusually vigorous fashion until the heir to the throne, Turanshah, arrived from Mesopotamia. Meanwhile Louis's army advanced very laboriously and not until the middle of December did it arrive near Mansourah where, once again, the crusaders found themselves caught in the angle created by the Nile and one of its tributaries. Louis now planned to cross the tributary, then circle around Mansourah and attack from the rear. The river was bridged on 8 February 1250. Then the French advance guard under Robert of Artois made a premature attack on an Egyptian camp, captured it and killed the Egyptian commander-in-chief in his bath. Tempted by this partial success they pressed on to Mansourah and were slaughtered in the narrow streets of the town. When Louis IX with the main army crossed the river he was attacked by the Egyptian forces which had been rapidly reorganized by the new commander, Rukn ad-Din Baibars Bundukdari. The king who, with his golden helmet and German sword, was recognizable from afar, struck fiercely about him. His energy and coolness saved the battle, but the campaign was lost. The losses had been considerable and Louis did not retreat soon enough to Damietta. Not until the end of March did he make up his mind to withdraw and by then it was too late. The troops were weakened by disease and hunger; the Muslims had prevented supplies from getting through to them. The king himself was enfeebled by dysentery and by 6 April when only half-way to Damietta, he saw no other course open to him but to capitulate. He refused to save himself by ship, preferring to be taken prisoner together with his army. The entourage of the king of France was reduced to just two people, his chaplain William of Chartres and his cook Isambard. Damietta, however, was saved thanks to the intervention of the French queen who, though she had just given birth to a son there, managed, by dint of great efforts, to persuade the Italian merchants to stay; their going would undoubtedly have caused a panic in the town. This meant that the crusaders still held something with which they could bargain with the Egyptians. On 6 May a treaty was concluded; Damietta was exchanged for the person of the king. In addition Louis paid at once the first half of a total ransom of 800,000 bezants = 400,000 *livres tournois* for his imprisoned army. Of this first instalment 'only' 177,000 *livres* were found in the royal coffers which were evidently still well stocked; the remainder of 23,000 *livres* was taken from the Templars, notwithstanding their formal protests, using moneys they held as deposits by third parties. On 8 May Louis sailed from Damietta for Acre. His brother Charles of Anjou assumed the crusade was finished and at once went back to gambling which had been forbidden for the duration. For Louis, however, the crusade was not over yet. He tore the dice from Charles and threw them overboard. But his army was dissolving. He now had hardly more than 1,400 men left but, ignoring the urgent pleas of his mother who was acting as regent in France and overruling the objections of his own council, Louis decided to stay in the Holy Land. His help was much needed there and, in addition, his army was still in captivity.

Four days before the king's release there had occurred a palace revolution in Cairo which was to have the most far-reaching of consequences. The *coup d'état* had been organized by the Mameluk bodyguard.[134] The Mameluks had always been important as élite troops. They were white Turkish slaves, mostly from the Kipchak steppes, bought when young and then converted to Islam and brought up to be soldiers. Generally they were freed when they were of an age to bear arms. They had no family ties—their patronym is invariably the same, i.e. purely fictitious: Ibn Abdallah—and no patriotic feeling, only a sense of personal loyalty to their lord. This made them well-suited to being bodyguards but their position as a kind of Pretorian Guard turned them into an arrogant warrior caste. Many of them could not even master the

Arabic language yet they were well aware that they were indispensable to their master. He ruled only for as long as he made them his power base. Conversely, they only stayed in power as long as he ruled. The career and the fortunes of a Mameluk, like that of a black eunuch in the administration, lasted only for a single generation. Unlike the eunuchs they could, of course, have children but because their children were born into Islam they could not, in Islamic law, be enslaved. Yet only former slaves could become members of this warrior élite so, paradoxically, the sons of these aristocrats could never inherit their father's rank. The Mameluks, moreover, were always threatened, as the eunuchs were not, by the tendency of new rulers to get rid of the old ruler's Mameluks and acquire Mameluks of their own. The Mameluk system was thus an immensely costly one, but it undeniably achieved striking military successes against both the Franks and the Mongols. So long as the bulk of the Ayubid army was composed of Kurds, or at least was commanded by them, the Mameluks posed no threat to the state, but as-Salih, thinking in terms of centralization, had brought the Mameluk system to perfection; with the help of this Turkish military machine he had hoped to re-establish the unity of the disintegrating Ayubid empire. The most important troops were the Bahriya Mameluks, named after the island in the Nile where they had their barracks. They made up a fearless cavalry regiment which, though only one thousand in number, controlled the capital city. When as-Salih's successor, Turanshah, seemed to be on the point of saturating the administration with men who had come with him from Mesopotamia, the Bahriya Mameluks saw in this a threat to their own position and so they had him murdered on 2 May 1250. This brought a period of Ayubid rule in Egypt to an end. Aibek then became the first Mameluk sultan. The hereditary Kurdish system was replaced by a Turkish military oligarchy in which the sultans were elected because it was almost impossible for a Mameluk sultan to install his son as his successor. An-Nasir of Aleppo now became the leader of the Ayubid legitimists in Syria which, in contrast with the economically strong Egypt, was the centre of Islamic culture in the Arabic-speaking world. War between Mameluks and Ayubids followed and it was not until April 1253 that some agreement was reached. The Ayubids kept Syria and north Palestine while the Mameluks held Egypt and south Palestine. The next development was the outbreak of fierce fighting within the Bahriya regiment itself. This lasted until 1254 and was only half settled by the emigration of a part of the regiment; up until 1260 these Mameluks in exile in Syria formed a militant group which threatened the security of Egypt.

Saint Louis profited from these quarrels. Both Ayubids and Mameluks bid for his support. He saw clearly enough that the future lay with Egypt and in 1252 made a treaty with the Mameluks as a result of which his army was liberated and he was released from payment of the second instalment of his ransom. But, from a military point of view, the Franco–Egyptian alliance came to nothing. The Ayubids were not so easily defeated. For the four years that he was in Palestine, from 1250 to 1254, Saint Louis ruled the Holy Land. There was no one, neither baron nor Master, who could challenge his authority. With great prudence Louis rebuilt the fortifications of Jaffa, Acre, Caesarea, and Sidon. He tried to settle the family feuds in Antioch and had no hesitation in exiling the marshal of the Templars who, without his knowledge, had come to terms with the Ayubids. Nevertheless the regency (*bailliage*) of the king of Cyprus on the mainland was more than merely nominal. Whenever he could he tried to assert his own position at the side of the French king. In 1251 his lieutenant, John of Arsuf of the Ibelin family, tried his hand at a revolutionary administrative reform. He proposed to introduce a system of written registers in both the Haute Cour and the Cour des Bourgeois. The barons accepted the latter. They held many *tenures en bourgeoisie* and could see the advantage of the extra security of a written record. But they would not have a register in the Haute Cour because it would have threatened to displace an institution dear to their hearts, the *recort de cort* (see above, p. 162).[135] Louis also became the patron of the school of painting at Acre and once more a masterpiece was produced there—the superb Paris Arsenal Bible for which Byzantine manuscripts, possibly purchased by Louis himself from the permanently bankrupt Emperor Baldwin II of Constantinople, served as models. During the winter of 1250–1 Joinville was inspired by the king's sermon-like conversation to write his *Credo*, in which the most important articles of the Christian faith were elucidated. This work, decorated with miniatures, was designed to be read and shown to the dying, as a comfort to them and to protect them from the temptations of the devil.

In the spring of 1254 the king came to realize that he could stay no longer in the Holy Land. His mother had died towards the end of 1252 and his brothers, though they took her place as regent, were but poor substitutes. The consequences rapidly became visible in the East. In 1253 Louis's money ran out and he had to live on credit; he borrowed 100,000 *livres* from the Italians. Now that his purse was empty the barons of Jerusalem, without mincing words, advised him to depart. On 24 April 1254 Saint Louis, the last crusader-king, left the Holy Land. He had sought to win glory for God but he had also won it for himself. Such was the moral prestige which still accrued to a king who went on crusade that Louis became the arbiter of Europe and the 'uncrowned emperor'— especially since Frederick II had died in 1250 and the empire was now in a state of disintegration.

Before leaving the Holy Land, Louis IX entered into discussions with the Mongols in the hope that in them the Franks might find a powerful ally against the Muslims.[136] And in fact the Mongols were the only people in the second half of the thirteenth century who were capable of destroying Islam, though in this event the Christians would have had to face the very real danger that they would be their allies' next victims. A vital consideration in the plans which were eagerly discussed at the curia and in Europe generally until about 1300, was the fact that the Mongols, though the vast majority of them were neither Christians nor Muslims, had been influenced by Nestorians. These were Christians who, in the fifth century, had been declared to be heretics for emphasizing the human rather than the divine aspect of Christ's nature. They had then withdrawn to Central Asia and their descendants had now won some influence over the Mongol Great Khans and their wives. Some Mongol tribes indeed were solidly Nestorian. For this reason it was hoped that the Mongols were more likely to be converted to Christianity than to Islam; in that event it was believed that it would not be too difficult to deal with the Nestorian heresy. As early as 1245–7 Innocent IV had sent a Franciscan friar, John of Piano del Carpine, to the East in order to convert the Great Khan of the Mongols. The latter had replied by demanding the submission of the pope. Equally unsuccessful were two other attempts at conversion, the mission of the Dominican Ascelinus (1245–8) described in detail in the *Histoire des Tartares* written by his companion Simon of St. Quentin and the mission (1249–52) of Andrew of Longjumeau, a Dominican despatched from Cyprus by Louis IX. What the Christians had failed to grasp was that the Great Khans were indifferent in religious matters and treated the unorthodox Muslims and Buddhists hardly less well than they treated the Nestorians. These attempts do, however, reveal just how much the Mongols had become the decisive factor in the politics of the Near East. The attitude of the individual powers to the Mongol problem increasingly became the measure by which they themselves were judged by other powers.

Neither before nor since has there been anything in history to compare with the empire of the Mongols.[137] It was astounding both for its immense size and for the explosive speed with which it grew. It was precisely this extremely rapid expansion which led the Muslims into the initial mistake of underestimating the Mongol peril, particularly during the period when the Khwarismian empire still lay between them and the Mongols. The Mongols were a nomadic people divided into several tribes. Like the Turks they originated from the infertile steppe regions between Lake Baikal and the Altai Mountains. They first appeared in the light of history in the tenth century when they pushed southwards, driving before them the Khitai who went on to establish the empire of the Liao in North China. This empire was destroyed *c*.1125, whereupon the Liao withdrew westwards and built up the empire of the Kara Khitai east of the Jaxartes. After this first contact with the culture of China the Mongols sank back again into the chaos of tribal warfare. Their meteoric rise began shortly after 1200. Within a decade one of their leaders, Temujin, had made himself lord over all the Mongol tribes. In 1206 a tribal assembly acclaimed him as Great Khan of the Mongols with the (linguistically unexplained) title of Genghis Khan. From now on the great hordes of the Mongols were prepared to act as one political unit; they believed that it was their divine mission to unite the world under Mongol lordship—'one sun in the sky, one lord on earth'. Within a few years Genghis Khan had organized his empire. He had the customs of the Mongols collected and written down in a law-book, the Yasa, in which regulations of draconian severity protected private property. The army was organized in groups of ten and multiples of ten; a group of 10,000 formed a unit which could operate independently. Its strength lay partly in the audacious, death-defying courage of the Mongols, but chiefly in the army's extraordinary mobility which enabled the Mongol horsemen to attack their enemy before he had time to organize his defences properly. The 'whistling arrows' of the Mongols—in flight their pierced arrowheads produced a howling sound—struck fear into the hearts of man and beast. The Mongol army was held together by iron discipline. During the years of conquest it was increasingly reinforced by Turkish units. The Mongols made war in the most brutal fashion. They ruthlessly harnessed their subjects to the transportation of immense quantities of siege materials. Unless they had surrendered in advance, the citizens of a captured town were nearly all massacred. The best that men capable of bearing arms could hope for was to be used by the Mongols at later sieges, driven on in front of the army to act as 'arrow-fodder'. The women and children were enslaved; only craftsmen and engineers, who could be of use to the conquerors, could count on being spared. Thus the nomadic Mongols destroyed the economic and cultural life of Central Asia which was based on an old urban civilization, and drove a permanent wedge between Persian Iran and the Arab world. But in the Far East, attracted by the superior Chinese civilization, they completely accepted Chinese customs.

When Genghis Khan had completed his work of reform he set about satisfying the land hunger of his nomadic steppe tribesmen. In 1211–12 he attacked north China; its subjugation was completed when Peking fell in 1215. Then in 1219–20 he destroyed the eastern part of the Khwarismian empire in Transoxania and Khorassan. The rapid collapse of these two empires which had previously been thought of as unconquerable, established the reputation of the Mongols and created a state of panic in the minds of their prospective victims. They drove the once-powerful Shah of Khwarism helplessly before them until in desperation he sought protection south of the Indus, though only shortly before this he had himself threatened to extinguish the Abbasid caliphate. The unfortunate neighbours of the Mongols were left only 'the choice between voluntary submission—which generally meant annihilation—and a resistance which they believed was hopeless' (Cahen). From 1220 to 1223 the conquerors devastated Azerbaijan, south Russia, and the territories around the middle Volga; then they withdrew for a while. Genghis Khan died in 1227 but his sons, under the Great Khan Ogodai, continued the expansion. In 1230-3 Iran and the rest of the Khwarismian empire fell; this opened the way to the Middle East. In 1231-4 Korea was captured. South Russia followed in 1237-9; here the Mongols founded the Tatar lordship of the 'Golden Horde' which was to endure for centuries. In 1240 they swept westwards through the Ukraine and Poland and destroyed a German army at Liegnitz in 1241. Only Ogodai's death in 1241 saved Europe from their onslaught; they turned back for home, moving eastwards through the Balkans. In 1243 they made Anatolia into a Mongol protectorate. During the rest of this decade internal dissensions temporarily prevented further conquests, but with the accession of Mongka Khan (1251-9) the expansion, both to the east and to the west, was renewed and accelerated. In the east, with the help of his brother Kubilai Khan (himself Great Khan 1260-94), Mongka Khan conquered south China; here his brother, the founder of the Yuan dynasty, developed the brilliant, purely Chinese court culture which was to be described by the Venetian Marco Polo who lived there for twenty years. By about 1280 the whole of China had submitted to the Mongols; Cambodia and Tonkin were reduced to the status of dependent protectorates. In the west, Iran and Mesopotamia were thoroughly subjugated during this period. It was now possible to travel from Kiev or Baghdad to Peking without once crossing a frontier. But the Great Khan became increasingly involved in Chinese politics. As a result the western parts of the empire, Iran, Transoxania, and Russia, were left more and more to their own devices.

From the Holy Land, and with the knowledge and support of Louis IX, another Franciscan missionary had set out for Mongolia: the Fleming William of Rubroek. He had only had missionary work in mind but had then been relayed by stages all the way to Mongka Khan's court at Karakorum because a simple letter of recommendation written by Louis IX had been mistranslated and, as a result, was thought, much to William's dismay, to contain the offer of an alliance. In Karakorum William met an enslaved goldsmith Guillaume Boucher from Paris who made him a gift of a silver cross 'in French fashion', i.e. showing Christ crucified. The Nestorians immediately tore the figure from the cross because for them the cross signified not Christ's passion but his second coming. And there were other 'abuses' which shocked William. The Nestorians mangled their Syriac liturgy 'in the manner of those monks of ours who know no grammar'; like Muslims they washed their feet before entering a church; occasionally they practised polygamy; and they overcame the perennial danger of a shortage of priests by the simple method of getting the bishop, on his rare visits, to ordain all male children. William returned from his long voyage (1253–5) convinced that the Latins were theologically superior to all other Christian denominations and that the East was probably not too difficult to convert. But Mongka Khan would agree to an alliance only if Louis became his vassal and on these terms agreement was impossible. When William returned in 1255 he wished to report to Louis IX in person but true Bible experts were as rare in the Latin East as anywhere else. His provincial kept him in the Holy Land, installed him in the Franciscan convent at Acre as lecturer on the Bible and it was here that he wrote the story of his journey, one of the most fascinating of all reports on conditions in the Far East. Eventually Louis was able to secure his release from a post he disliked and in 1257 he was in Paris where Roger Bacon made his acquaintance. By the time William returned from Karakorum, Mongka's brother Hulagu had already begun the conquest of the Islamic lands in the west. In 1255, with about 120,000 men, he had entered the Middle East. In 1256 he annihilated the Persian Assassins at Alamut. On 10 February 1258 the Mongols took Baghdad by storm and smothered the last Abbasid caliph al-Mustasim in a carpet. Dismissed as puerile by the contemporary chronicler Bar Hebraeus, he had been a degenerate creature who wasted his time playing with birds. In this way the orthodox Sunnites lost their spiritual head and the Shi'ites could breathe again. Between 1258 and 1260 Hulagu subjugated Upper Mesopotamia. The Christians in the Holy Land, though they saw in him the enemy of the Mameluks, awaited his coming with mixed feelings. In 1259 and 1260 he captured Damascus and Aleppo and then sent a section of his army under Kitbuqa south towards Egypt. But in September 1260, at Ain Jalud in Galilee, Kitbuqa was met by the Mameluk army under Sultan Qutuz and his general Baibars. After a fierce fight the Mongols were defeated. It was one of the decisive moments in history; the legend of the invincibility of the Mongols was destroyed, their expansion to the west towards North Africa was halted for good, the continued existence of Islam was ensured and the Mameluk suzerainty over Syria and Palestine established. Refugees from Mesopotamia and Syria ensured that from now on Cairo would be the cultural centre of the Arabic-speaking Islamic world. At Ain Jalud the first cracks in the structure of the great Mongol empire had been revealed; fighting on the Mameluk side there were some Mongol troops sent from the Golden Horde which had for some time been at loggerheads with Hulagu's Mongols. Hulagu (d. 1265) contented himself with Iran where he founded the empire of the Il-Khans (princes of the land) and beat off the attacks of the Mameluks. In religious matters he and his immediate successors tended towards Buddhism and they continued to co-operate closely with the Great Khan. But after Kubilai Khan's death in 1294 the system broke down. Quite simply the empire had grown too big—it took six months for a man travelling from the empire's western frontier to reach its capital at Karakorum. The eastern part of the empire became thoroughly Buddhist while in 1295 the Il-Khans were converted to Islam—the final blow to all the hopes which, since 1245, the Christians had placed in the Mongols.

14

THE CRUSADER STATES, 1254–1291

THE departure of Saint Louis in 1254 left a power vacuum unparalleled in the annals of the Latin Kingdom of Jerusalem. The regent, Henry I of Cyprus, had died in January 1253; his son and potential successor as regent, Hugh II, had only just been born. In May 1254 Conrad IV, the Hohenstaufen king of Jerusalem, died in Italy. His son Conradin was also a child, only two years old and clearly no more likely to travel to the East and to rule the kingdom of Jerusalem in person than his father had been. Despite this—or perhaps because of this— the barons, assembled at Acre, recognized him as the rightful king of Jerusalem (Conrad III 1254–68). A king residing abroad was probably what the barons liked best of all. Clearly there was no special loyalty to the Hohenstaufen dynasty in this adherence to Conradin although a certain respect for the law may possibly have played a part. But like the state the Church too was totally without leadership. The patriarch of Jerusalem died in 1254. His successor James Pantaleon, Bishop of Verdun and future Pope Urban IV, was not elected until April 1255 and did not come to the East until June 1256. The archbishop of Tyre, second in command in the absence of a patriarch, had died in 1253 and in the autumn of 1254 his successor had not yet been consecrated and was therefore still only archbishop-elect. The most important bishopric, Acre, had also been vacant since 1253 and here the new bishop likewise did not arrive in the East until June 1256. Odo of Châteauroux, papal legate for Saint Louis's crusade, left in September 1254. The royal chancery had ceased to exist under Frederick II and the barons did not revive it after the collapse of the Hohenstaufen administration. In 1252 no one seemed to be bothered by the fact that the regent's seal was out of the country, in Cyprus. In 1245, after pronouncing the deposition of Frederick II, Pope Innocent IV had actually taken it upon himself to grant commercial privileges in the kingdom of Jerusalem to the city of Ancona. Significantly it was in 1253–4 that the barons adopted a new sealing formula on their charters (*bulle de plomp empreint en mes dreis coing de ma seignorie*) so that from now on their lead seals became true symbols of lordship. For the last half century the writers of law-books had advocated this formula but up to the mid-thirteenth century only the regents had used it and the increasingly important class of notaries public would have nothing to do with it, so its employment by the barons seems to have been unauthorized. Between 1253 and 1258 government—in so far as one can use the word at all—was in the hands of the vassals, after that we return to regents with a dynastic claim, but their rule was generally purely nominal, and in practice the reins of government were held by their appointed lieutenants, in other words by members of the nobility once again. Between 1253 and 1258 the house of Ibelin dominated the regency, though in the persons of two very different men, the centralist John of Arsuf (regent 1253–4, 1256–8) and Count John of Jaffa (1254–6), the champion of aristocratic class interest (see above, pp. 162, 266). They were not above exploiting the regency for their own ends, e.g. when John of Jaffa in the spring of 1256 attempted to reconquer Ascalon, a part of his county, with the aid of the feudal host. The enterprise miscarried and involved John in a very awkward series of negotiations with the Hospitallers who, ever since the loss of Ascalon in 1247, had been demanding compensation for their loss as had been promised them by Frederick II. In addition to the regents and their lieutenants other powers to be reckoned with were the Masters of the three Military Orders, the *baillis* and consuls of the Italians in the Levant, the principals of the urban confraternities and, increasingly after 1265, the patriarch of Jerusalem (see above, p. 176).

Initially the kingdom's foreign policy was directed towards maintaining intact the old system of constantly renewed truces which were familiar from the Ayubid period.[138] Before his departure Louis IX had arranged such a truce for two and a half years with Damascus, though he himself was inclined to prefer Egypt. A year later (1255) the Franks in fact concluded a ten years' truce with the Egyptians. Internally the little kingdom was plagued by fierce quarrels. In 1256 the first big colonial war in the Levant broke out between Venice and Genoa.[139] A dispute over the ownership of some houses of the monastery of St. Sabas in Acre had been smouldering in the courts ever since 1251. In the summer of 1256 new Levantine officials from the two republics began their period in office and both brought with them contradictory papal letters concerning the dispute. The result was open fighting. One day, while the lawyers were still arguing, the Genoese occupied the hill of Montjoie in Acre where the disputed property was situated—and which separated the quarters of the two republics. Then they took the whole Venetian quarter. Only with difficulty were the Venetians able to drive them out again. Philip de Montfort seized the chance to expel the Venetians from his new lordship of Tyre where they had held a third of the town ever since the treaty of 1123 (see above, p. 76). Although the Venetians already had their hands full with the trouble at Acre they could not possibly reconcile themselves to the loss of Tyre, their most important settlement in the Holy Land. In 1257 what had once been a local conflict broadened out into the War of St. Sabas involving also the feudal nobility. The whole land was up in arms. On one side were the Venetians, supported by the Pisans, the Provençals, the majority of the Ibelins (especially by John of Jaffa), the Templars, and the Teutonic Knights; on the other were the Genoese, John of Arsuf—who had just succeeded in ousting John of Jaffa from the regency—Philip de Montfort, the Hospitallers, and the Catalan merchants. Most of the fighting was done by the Italians and by the fleets which were sent out by their home ports. There were fierce battles in Acre and many houses were destroyed by stone projectiles. The sources give the number of dead as 20,000, though this is clearly an exaggeration. In February 1258 John of Jaffa staged a *coup de théâtre* intended to overthrow John of Arsuf. He had the boy-king Hugh II of Cyprus brought to Acre and made his mother, Queen Plaisance of Cyprus, claim the regency on her child's behalf—exactly the step which had been carefully avoided ever since 1253 precisely because Hugh's claim was unassailable in law. Now a ruling guardian had to be appointed for the minor regent and John of Jaffa's real trick was to manoeuvre Plaisance into this position. As guardian she became *de facto* regent. The land now had a minor king, Conradin, with a minor regent, Hugh II, whose office was exercised by his mother. Since Plaisance had been at loggerheads with John of Arsuf, it was natural to expect that he would, in addition to losing the regency, be excluded from all participation in government. But in a surprise move Plaisance came to terms with him and appointed him as lieutenant to the regent, thus allowing him to rule in her place. John of Jaffa's only success was in persuading Plaisance and her brother Bohemund VI of Antioch-Tripoli to unite the Jerusalem vassals in a common front against the Genoese. When Bohemund's vassals from Tripoli were required to take up arms, one of them, Bertrand of Gibelet, from the Genoese Embriaco family, not surprisingly refused. When none the less he was forced to attack, he did so unarmed and loudly shouting his name. This was just one of the incidents which, in 1258, drove the vassals of Tripoli into open revolt. Bohemund VI had also made himself unpopular by filling the Haute Cour of Tripoli with 'Romans', i.e. foreigners who had come as followers of his mother Lucie of Segni (from a family which produced three thirteenth-century popes), thus weakening the capacity of his vassals to resist arbitrary action by their lord. Because the Haute Cour was no longer capable of containing these quarrels, in 1260 a committee of thirteen with six from each side and an impartial chairman had to be appointed to settle the dispute. In 1258 the Genoese fleet suffered a severe defeat in a battle off Acre while Philip de Montfort's simultaneous attempt to seize the city itself was beaten back. This meant that in practice the Venetians had won the war. Acre had become a sort of Venetian dependency. As symbols of their triumph the Venetians were supposed to have taken two pillars from St. Sabas and erected them in the Piazzetta of San Marco in Venice. This, at any rate, was the official Venetian version of how these *Pilastri d'Acre*, still standing today, came to be there. But in fact they are identical down to the last detail and even to the stonemason's mark with pillars which archeologists from Dumbarton Oaks excavated in Constantinople; they are part of the Venetian booty of 1204.

After 1258 the scale of military operations diminished somewhat though with each *passagium* the conflict automatically flared up again, i.e. twice a year when the Italian fleets came to Outremer. In 1261 a temporary peace was patched up. The Genoese kept an establishment in Tyre but were barred from Acre which was to remain the resort of the Venetians and Pisans. The Genoese took their revenge by signing the Treaty of Nymphaeum (1261) with the Greeks, thus threatening the Venetian monopoly of trade within Byzantium (see above, p. 208). The Byzantine Empire now became the main theatre of war but sea battles continued to be fought off the Syrian coast until 1270 when at last St. Louis was able to bring about a genuine peace. The Genoese were allowed to return to their quarter in Acre though it was now lying in ruins; in 1277 the Venetians went back to Tyre. But Pisa would have no part in the peace and so the war between the Tuscan and Ligurian republics raged on until 1288. In Palestine the continuing civil war further revealed the weakness of the central administration. When John of Arsuf died he was succeeded by Geoffrey of Sergines (May 1259). John of Jaffa (d. 1266) countered this by taking Queen Plaisance (d. 1261) as his mistress, much to Pope Urban IV's anger.

One reason for the diminishing scale of military activity in the War of Saint Sabas after 1260 was the growing urgency of the Mongol problem. The North took an emphatically pro-Mongol line—indeed it had very little choice. As early as 1243 the Mongols had established a protectorate over the Anatolian state of the Rum Seldjuks and from that time the Armenians of Cilicia had also looked for support from the new lords. In 1247 King Hethoum I despatched his constable Sempad, an important chronicler, to offer submission to the Great Khan. From Samarkand in 1248 Sempad wrote a letter to Cyprus reporting on the devastation wrought by the Mongols which he had seen along the way. In 1254 Hethoum thought it wise to go to Karakorum himself to make a firm alliance with Mongka Khan. Hethoum was one of the few who understood the full extent of the Mongol danger and was determined to co-operate with them. Mongka granted concessions to the Armenian Church in the Mongol Empire and appointed Hethoum as a kind of consultant for Christian affairs. In return Hethoum promised to take part in Hulagu's Middle Eastern campaign. From Hethoum's point of view this alliance was obviously sensible. To resist the Mongols was impossible and anyway it was in fact the Mongols who had released the Lesser Armenians from the pressure of their arch-enemies, the Seldjuks of Anatolia. In addition there was always the hope that the Nestorian influence would in the end convert the Mongols to Christianity, especially since Mongka's principal wife was a Nestorian. A late thirteenth-century Armenian historian greeted Hulagu and his wife (another Nestorian) with the old imperial acclamation as a new Constantine and a new Helena, as instruments of God's vengeance on the enemies of Christ; and it was as Constantine and Helena that they were depicted in 1260 in a west Syriac book illumination (Cod. syr. 559 in the Vatican). For his part, Hethoum always remained true to the alliance, first with the Mongols and then with the Il-Khan. In 1254, the year that Hethoum went to Karakorum, the ancient quarrel between Lesser Armenia and Antioch was finally ended. Ever since 1224 when the Hethoumian regent of Armenia had ousted the country's legitimate ruler, a member of the princely house of Antioch (see above, p. 254), relations between the two states had been difficult. But now Bohemund VI of Antioch-Tripoli (1252–75) married Sibylla, Hethoum's daughter, and whether or not this was the occasion for Bohemund to become Hethoum's vassal for Antioch, there can be no doubt that Antioch was swept completely into the orbit of Armenian politics. From now on Antioch was in practice ruled by the king of Lesser Armenia while the prince of Antioch resided exclusively in Tripoli. There is further evidence for the rapid way in which the two states were merging in the fact that during this period Lesser Armenia took over the law code of Antioch. Thus Antioch too was incorporated into the Armenian–Mongol alliance, an alliance which was at first clearly advantageous to both sides. The Armenians helped the Mongols at the siege of Aleppo and the Antiochenes may have joined their army before Damascus, though this, like the report that after the conquest of Damascus Bohemund had the Great Mosque turned into a Christian church, has recently been doubted. As a reward for his help Hethoum was allowed to extend his territory in the direction of Anatolia at the expense of the Seldjuks and in the south-east at the expense of Aleppo. The protective shadow of the Mongols enabled Bohemund to recapture the Muslim coastal enclave at Lattakieh and thus to re-establish the land connection between Tripoli and Antioch that had been broken since 1187. In return Bohemund had to install a Greek patriarch in Antioch, since the Mongols were well aware of the importance of the Greek element in the population of the city. As a result, Bohemund was excommunicated by the pope.

The Franks in the south were unsure how to react to the Mongol advance; here Egypt seemed both nearer and more menacing than the Mongols. Both John of Jaffa and Julian of Sidon obtained separations from—or were separated from—wives belonging to the royal family of Lesser Armenia, the principal Mongol ally. None the less the Franks were far too afraid of the Mongols to risk provoking them. In 1260 they painted a sombre picture of the Mongol danger in an urgent though ineffective appeal which they sent to Charles of Anjou. Meanwhile the Mameluk sultan, Qutuz, had already made up his mind to counter-attack. He sought an alliance with the Franks and, under his pressure, they were at first inclined to agree to this suggestion, but finally they took the advice of the Master of the Teutonic Order and opted for neutrality. They allowed Qutuz free passage through Palestine but would not give him any military support.

The Master of the Teutonic Order may have taken the line he did out of consideration for the policies of Lesser Armenia. Relations between the different Military Orders were just as bad as were all relations between evenly matched powers in the Holy Land. The Hospitallers and the Templars had long pursued opposing policies. This had first become apparent in 1168 when the Hospitallers had supported King Amalric's expansionist schemes in Egypt while the Templars had held back. Later the Hospitallers supported Conrad of Montferrat's party so the Templars went over to the Lusignan camp. In their opposition to Frederick II the two Orders were, for once, united, but even here the Hospitallers were noticeably less enthusiastic than the Templars. Then during the last stages of the War of the Lombards the Hospitallers moved towards the imperial side with the result that the old rivalry reasserted itself—amost to the point of open war. In 1243 the Templars and the barons made an alliance with Damascus while the Hospitallers had been inclined to look towards Egypt. On the other hand since the collapse of Hohenstaufen power in the Holy Land the Teutonic Order had concentrated its interests in Cilician Lesser Armenia rather than in Palestine. The kings of Lesser Armenia, as vassals of the emperor had endowed them richly. Hethoum I and his whole kingdom seem to have entered into a vaguely defined affiliation with the Order (*in veram fraternitatem et sororitatem*). It may have been concern for their possessions in Lesser Armenia that persuaded the Master to advise against military action against the Mongols although, as Jackson has pointed out, the Order had recently acquired very considerable interests around Sidon, a city that had just been exposed to a savage Mongol attack (see below, p. 278). After 1243 the kingdom of Jerusalem became smaller and weaker, but the Templars and the Hospitallers grew more and more powerful. While the Italians controlled the towns, the Military Orders dominated as much of the countryside as was still in Christian hands. They held the great castles, particularly north of Tripoli, where the power of the Hospitallers was concentrated at Marqab and Krak des Chevaliers, and where the Templars held Chastel Blanc and Tortosa. But the situation was no different in the south. Here the Templars held Safed and Athlit (Château Pèlerin) and the Hospitallers Belvoir. Only the Military Orders were able to recruit European knights who were prepared to fight for long periods in the Holy Land. Thus they controlled the only effective fighting force. In addition, thanks to the innumerable gifts of land which they had received in Western Europe, they were immensely rich and their far-flung network of establishments enabled them to carry out important financial transactions; naturally they found themselves cast in the role of bankers. But between themselves relations were no better after 1243 than they had been before. A never-ending series of clashes sometimes flared up into open war—as in the War of Saint Sabas (1259)—with a regrettable loss of human life as the result. The pope was unable to find any satisfactory solution to their differences; in the West he relied upon the goodwill of both Orders and could not afford to alienate either of them.

As the nobles of the Holy Land became increasingly impoverished they were forced to relinquish their castles and lordships to the Orders.[140] The fate of the lord of Marqab in the twelfth century (see above, p. 163) was shared by the lord of Sidon in the thirteenth. Between 1253 and 1261 he sold a considerable part of his lordship to the Orders, in particular his estates in the Shuf mountains to the Teutonic Knights; finally after the Mongols had devastated Sidon in 1260, he lost the whole of his remaining fief, including the castle of Beaufort in the bend of the Litani River, to the Templars. Bit by bit the lord of Arsuf, a member of the once so powerful Ibelin family, had to sell his lordship to the Hospitallers until by 1261 it had completely gone, just four years before the Mameluks moved in and occupied it. The history of the small fief of Casel Imbert north of Acre, assigned in 1252 to John II of Ibelin-Beirut, is particularly instructive. In 1256 John leased it for ten years to the Teutonic Order in return for an annuity of 13,000 bezants. When he was taken prisoner in 1261 and had to buy his freedom for 20,000 bezants, the time for complicated and shady deals had come. Without the required government approval John, in a preliminary contract dated December 1261, sold both his fief of Casel Imbert to the Teutonic Knights for an annuity of 11,000 bezants, i.e. less than the former rent, and the fort of Toron Aghmid in the mountains of Beirut for a one-off payment of 5,000. The preliminary contract expressly stipulated that the 5,000 were not to be mentioned in the final version of the contract as indeed they were not. In return for allowing the Order to terminate the original lease early John received an additional 4,000 bezants. Altogether this would give him by the end of the year precisely the 20,000 he needed. But in order to raise the amount at once he had to borrow 16,000 from his cousin Julian of Sidon. As Julian did not have so much ready cash he in turn had to borrow 10,000 from the Hospitallers. The final contracts are still extant. Although it had been agreed in December 1261 that they were to be drawn up by the following Whitsun, when they were finally issued, they were backdated to November 1261. This gave a veneer of legality to the unauthorized sale since at that date there happened to be no deputy for the regent (still a minor). The documents, moreover, represented the sale of Casel Imbert as an exchange, and the sale of Toron Aghmid as a gift in free alms—which is why all mention of the 5,000 gold pieces had to be suppressed, even though, in a separate document, John issued a receipt for them. By

September 1263 John had repaid 6,000 of what he owed Julian. He repaid the balance of 10,000 directly to the Hospitallers, transferring to them the annuity which the Teutonic Knights owed him for Casel Imbert.

Another interesting case is that of the Amigdalas, lords of Scandelion north of Acre. After half of the lordship had fallen into Mameluk hands in 1272 the Teutonic Order, which held the *Seigneurie de Joscelin* just south of Scandelion, began systematically to steer the Amigdalas towards bankruptcy. They advanced them money and stood surety for them. Then, in 1280, when they owed the Order no less than 17,000 bezants and no longer had credit elsewhere, the Order called for all the loans to be repaid within the year. Since this was evidently impossible, it must be assumed that the Order took over that half of the lordship which was still in Christian hands. Out of the three brothers Amigdala, one, the principal heir, emigrated to Apulia while the other two entered the Teutonic Order—even though their family origins lay in Calabria.

The breakdown of public order since the departure of Saint Louis was all too obvious. Yet, ironically enough it was precisely at this time, in 1265 on the eve of the great Mameluk offensive, that Jean d'Ibelin, count of Jaffa, undertook his codification of the law—a codification which gives no hint of the disintegration but instead builds up a picture of an aristocracy which, if greedy for power, was also powerful. And this at a time when the count of Jaffa was himself deep in debt! In reality the kingdom had fallen apart into a number of warring groups of which only two, the Italian communes and the Military Orders, were relatively (i.e. in comparison with the barons) powerful. Thus the chief characteristic of this period in the history of the crusader states was the absence of any consistent and purposeful policy.

A few years after the battle of Ain Jalud, probably in 1264, a new deputy to the regent, Hugh II of Cyprus, still a minor, had to be appointed. Two candidates presented themselves to the Haute Cour: Hugh of Antioch-Lusignan and Hugh of Brienne. According to the hitherto prevailing custom of primogeniture, Hugh of Brienne ought to have been successful (see the genealogy on p. 250). The decisive factor should have been their degree of relationship to their common grandmother, Queen Alice of Cyprus. After days of debate, however, the Antioch-Lusignan claim was upheld by the Haute Cour on the grounds that he was the older man. The reality behind the decision was probably the fact that Hugh of Antioch-Lusignan was already *bailli* of Cyprus and might succeed to the throne there, that he was, in other words, a man who counted for more than Hugh of Brienne. Indeed the new *bailli* turned out to be a vigorous leader who took his office seriously and who divided his time fairly between Cyprus and Acre—even after 1267, the year in which he became king of Cyprus. For a while it looked as though Hugh might succeed in restoring the authority of the crown. He managed to obtain the support of the Military

Orders; he won over Philip of Tyre by renewing the grant of that city to his family. (Though it really belonged to the royal domain, it had earlier been given to Philip by the regent Henry I of Cyprus). By marrying one of the Ibelins he was at least able to neutralize them. But in the end Hugh's work was brought to nothing by the grandiose, expansionist schemes which Charles of Anjou pursued from Italy.

The mainland kingdom desperately needed a strong regent, indeed to save the country he would have to have been much stronger than Hugh. For in the meantime there had been more changes in the political situation in the Mameluk Empire. Sultan Qutuz had been murdered shortly after the Battle of Ain Jalud and one of the conspirators, Rukn ad-Din Baibars Bunduqdari (1260–77) had taken his place.[141] Baibars was the greatest statesman ever to emerge from the Bahriya regiment. The only man in any way comparable with him is Saladin. It is true that the blood of two murders—that of Turanshah in 1250 and that of Qutuz in 1260—stained his path to power, but that does not alter the fact that he was an extraordinarily gifted and able ruler. If, in contrast to Saladin, there was no moral ideal which he was seeking to achieve and which might have carried him still higher, he compensated for this by possessing a fine sense of strategy. He was the only Mameluk to try to build an Egyptian navy, though even he could not entirely free himself from the ways of thought engrained in a people who fought on horseback—he never saw that it was only the Italian domination of the Eastern Mediterranean that enabled the Franks to resist the Mameluks for as long as they did. He was unable to comprehend the kind of strength that was possessed by all sea-powers in contrast to purely continental powers. After his whole fleet had been lost in an attempt to make a landing on Cyprus in 1271, he wrote a letter to the king of Cyprus in which all the pride of the nomadic mounted warrior was reflected: 'Your horses are ships, but our ships are horses.' As for his sailors he contemptuously dismissed them as 'peasants and scum'. He could never forgive the Franks for the alliance which North Syria had made with the Mongols—though he was, as it happens, a great admirer and imitator of Mongol legislation. He was determined to ensure that even the Franks of the south who had remained neutral would pay for that alliance. His declared intention was to drive the Franks into the sea once and for all. This would have the additional advantage of diverting the trade of Syria into Egyptian ports. His great advance was prepared thoroughly. First he brought the Syrian hinterland, especially Aleppo and the Transjordan, firmly under his control. Everywhere he ensured that the castles were carefully repaired and put into a state of readiness. He took particular trouble to see that he obtained news quickly—for this enabled him to react with unexpected speed. He made use of pigeon post on an hitherto unprecedented scale and he insisted on being informed of every piece of news as soon as it was received, even if he was undressed at the time.

While still engaged in subduing the last Ayubids, Baibars began to threaten Antioch. In 1263 he sacked Nazareth and destroyed its famous church of the Virgin. He appeared unexpectedly before the walls of Acre, supposedly acting as Genoa's ally in the War of Saint Sabas. Then in January 1265 he launched the big offensive which was to be pressed forward until 1271. First he captured Caesarea and thus cut off Jaffa from the rest of the kingdom. Then, further to the north, he occupied Haifa, Toron, and Arsuf. Acre itself was saved only by the prompt intervention of the *bailli*, Hugh. In this campaign Baibars used the scorched earth policy which his successors were to continue. The ports were completely destroyed in order to prevent them being used by the Franks as assembly points or beach-heads. In 1266 he attacked on all fronts simultaneously. His first concern was to wreak vengeance on the Armenians now that their Mongol overlord Hulagu (d. 1265) was dead. He sacked the Armenian capital. Soon afterwards King Hethoum I abdicated in favour of his son Leo III (1269–89) and retired to a monastery. By making a new alliance with the Mongols Leo was able to win a breathing space for a few years. In 1270 Baibars turned against the Syrian Assassins, always the foci of a special kind of unrest, and destroyed them. In the south, Baibars's 1266 campaign had been aimed principally at Safed and when it fell the whole of Galilee was effectively his. Further south the cathedral of Ramleh was taken over and used as a mosque—it still survives today—while in the neighbouring Lydda the church over the tomb of Saint George was pulled down and its stones probably used for the small bridge north of Lydda (built 1273) which, until the recent construction of the motorway, carried all the coastal traffic from the north to Ascalon and Jerusalem. In 1268 Jaffa capitulated after a siege of just one day; a few weeks later the new line of defence running through the Litani river and the castle of Beaufort, the line built up by the Franks after the fall of Safed, was breached. Shortly afterwards the sultan suddenly appeared before Antioch. The city soon surrendered and its inhabitants had to pay dearly for the Frankish alliance with the Mongols; Antioch was turned into a bloodbath. The rest of North Syria yielded without a fight. Antioch had been the first Syrian city to fall into Christian hands (in 1098) and they had held it without interruption for 170 years. Its fall was a portent of approaching disaster.

Baibars's victorious campaign made an impression in Europe. That tireless crusader, Saint Louis, took the cross again in 1267, possibly under the influence of Dominican missionaries. Joinville, the king's old brother in arms, this time flatly refused to follow him to Egypt. But as Richard has shown, there is no warrant for the widely held belief that the nobility of France was in general so unenthusiastic. Similarly Lefèvre, using the evidence of the Angevin chancery registers, has demonstrated that it was not the king's brother, Charles of Anjou, who had received Sicily as a papal fief in 1265, who caused Louis to change the direction of the campaign to Tunis (supposedly in support of his brother's Mediterranean ambitions). In fact as late as July 1269 Charles believed that Louis was going to take his fleet to Egypt via Syracuse and at that point Charles did not contemplate joining the crusade. Only from mid-June 1270 does he seem to have known of Louis's secret plan to convert the sultan of Tunis en route. Not until 13 July when his fleet was at Cagliari did Louis announce his intentions to his astounded troops and it was only on 27 July that Charles publicly announced that he was going to accede to his brother's request for armed support. All supplies were then re-routed to Trapani as the Sicilian port most convenient for an assault on Tunis. But the enterprise came to nothing. His strength gone, Louis died in the camp outside Tunis on 25 August 1270, only a few days after the death of his son Jean-Tristan who had been born in Damietta in 1250. On 1 November Charles of Anjou brought the campaign to an end.[142] Only one latecomer, Prince Edward of England, having arrived too late in Tunis, sailed on to Acre where he landed in 1271, just in time to learn that Baibars had broken through Tripoli's line of defence by capturing the last great castles of the Military Orders there, Chastel Blanc from the Templars, Krak des Chevaliers from the Hospitallers, and Montfort from the Teutonic Knights. Edward remained in the Holy Land until September 1272. His only successes were in mediating between the king of Cyprus and his knights (see above, p. 243) and in arranging an eleven years' truce with Baibars.

With Prince Edward in the Holy Land was the archdeacon of Liège who, in 1271, was elected pope as Gregory X (d. 1276). He made tremendous efforts to organize a crusade but met with nothing except disappointments. From 1272 to 1274 he called for reports and plans for a new crusade and four of these are still extant. In them we have clear evidence for contemporary criticism of the crusading movement, criticism which was directed chiefly at the trade in indulgences and at the misuse of crusading taxes. The critics regretted the decline of the belief in the crusade's spiritual merit. Their plans for reform included ideas like giving more weight to the crusade in eastern Europe against the Slavs or setting up a kind of standing army of crusaders. But recommendations such as these could do little to combat the general lack of enthusiasm. The council which Gregory X held at Lyons in 1274 could do nothing to help the crusading cause and almost its only achievement was to bring about a short-lived union of the churches which was made a practical possibility by the fact that the Greeks were worried by Charles of Anjou's plans for expansion. A meeting which the pope held with the representatives of the leading powers and the Military Orders turned out to be brutally revealing. All those present either remained silent or asked that others should speak, not they, and the ambassador of the French king, according to an

Aragonese report, even compared the planned crusade to a tiny pup barking at a big dog (*una semblanca del xen petit quan lladre al gran Ca*).[143]

Meanwhile the shadow of Charles of Anjou had reached out over the kingdom of Jerusalem. When King Hugh II of Cyprus, regent of Jerusalem, died in 1267, he was succeeded on the island by his cousin Hugh of Antioch-Lusignan. He became Hugh III of Cyprus and also claimed the regency of Jerusalem after having already been deputy to Hugh II for some years. But a dispute over this with Maria of Antioch in the Haute Cour of Acre resulted in a remarkable constitutional development. Maria rested her claim on the undeniable fact that she was the nearest relation of the then titular king Conradin as well as of his grandmother Isabella II who had been the last person in seizin of the throne (see the genealogy on p. 250). Against this Hugh argued that he was the nearest relation of the last regent Hugh II. This was a point of law which may have been discussed in 1246 when Henry I of Cyprus was appointed regent of Jerusalem, assuming that his aunt Melisende contested Henry's claim at Acre as well as before the Curia. If the Haute Cour had followed the precedent it had set *c.* 1264 (see above p. 279), the case should have been decided in favour of Maria, for although she belonged to a junior branch of the royal family not only was she older than Hugh but she was also a whole generation closer to their last common ancestor, Isabella I of Jerusalem. Moreover the Haute Cour of 1268 upheld the point of law which had been established in 1264, i.e. that the issue of primogeniture was irrelevant to the case so that it was not necessarily an advantage to belong to the senior branch of the royal family. This also favoured Maria. Despite this Hugh III was made regent of Jerusalem on the slender legal argument that he was the nearest relative, not of King Conradin, but of the last regent.[144] In other words the regency had been turned into a hereditary institution even though the Haute Cour may have made no formal pronouncement to this effect, probably because it looks as though Maria's claim was turned down on procedural grounds. In these circumstances it is hardly surprising that there should be further strange twists in the case. When Conradin tried to reconquer Sicily for the Hohenstaufen, he was captured by Charles of Anjou and then executed at Naples on 29 October 1268. This marked the formal end of Hohenstaufen rule in Palestine. Acre celebrated with a firework display and illuminations. The contest between Hugh and Maria for the regency now became a contest for the crown itself. Hugh became king of Jerusalem. But Maria did not resign her claim. In 1269, on the occasion of Hugh's coronation, she issued a formal protest through a notary public who, having transacted his dangerous business, at once ran out of the church. In time the crown of Jerusalem became a piece of merchandise for, in 1277, in a hitherto unimaginable act, Maria sold her right to Charles of Anjou. He at once sent a detachment of troops to Acre together with Roger of San Severino to act as his *bailli*. As though Baibars had not created problems enough, the Franks managed to make things infinitely worse for themselves by indulging in the luxury of two kings. Acre, Sidon, and the Templars opted for Charles of Anjou while Tyre and Beirut continued to recognize Hugh I. Hugh had made himself somewhat unpopular with his few remaining vassals, particularly by demanding—unsuccessfully—to be made guardian of the young Bohemund VII of Tripoli (1275–87) after the death of Bohemund VI in 1275. He tried to reverse the sales of the lordships of Sidon and Arsuf (above, p. 278) to the Military Orders. He did not succeed in wresting Tyre, one of the crown jewels of the royal domain, from the grasp of the Montforts but he did marry his sister into the family and arrange that Tyre would escheat to the crown should she remain childless. In this event, however, he was to pay the Montforts an indemnity of 150,000 bezants. When the opportunity came in 1283, Hugh lacked the money. Indeed he had effectively given up his attempt to restore the power of the crown as early as 1276 and, significantly enough, had done so because the Templars had purchased a village without his consent and their great power meant that he was unable to take them to task. Grumbling about the unruly men of Acre, he retired to Cyprus.

In 1277, the year that Charles of Anjou became king, Baibars died in Damascus. The state of truce with the Franks in his last years had permitted him to concentrate on fighting the Mongols, the Armenians (in 1275), the Nubians, and the Seldjuks of Anatolia. During the seventeen years of his reign he undertook thirty-eight campaigns, travelled about 25,000 miles and personally fought in fifteen battles. He banished the double threat to the Islamic Middle East which was posed by the Franks and the Mongols. He fought nine times against the Mongols, five times against the Armenians, three times against the Assassins of Syria. Most of all, he had defeated the Franks twenty-one times. They had lost all the strong points which they had held in the interior of the country. All that was now left to them was the coastline from Athlit (Castle of the Pilgrims), south of Haifa, to Lattakieh in the north. Baibars's death vouchsafed them another short breathing space since it took his successor, Qalawun (d. 1290) some three years to establish himself in power. The government of Roger of San Severino lasted until 1282; it might have achieved some success if the country had been united but, as it was, Roger had no choice but to make a ten years' truce with Qalawun. His example was followed by Bohemund VII of Tripoli who from 1277 to 1282 was at war with the Templars and with rebel vassals in Jebail whom he finally punished by having them immured in the moat of Nephin, leaving them to starve.

In March 1282 the Sicilian Vespers brought down the government of Charles of Anjou and Charles himself was driven out of Sicily. Acre and Sidon, however, continued to recognize him as king until his death in 1285. Then Henry II of Cyprus, the son of Hugh I (d. 1284) was able, as

Henry I Jerusalem, to reassert his family's claim to the mainland kingdom. But it was no longer possible to talk of an ordered royal administration. Each man had to look after himself. Already some vassals had been forced to make separate treaties with Baibars, without obtaining the king's permission, for example at Beirut in 1269. This development continued under Sultan Qalawun. A treaty he concluded in 1283 with the representatives of Charles of Anjou and the Military Orders expressly applied only to Acre, Sidon, and Château Pèlerin. This meant that the Sultan no longer recognized Tyre and Beirut as territories belonging to the kingdom, a bitter pill for the government at Acre to swallow. The Lady of Tyre had to make very great concessions in order to obtain a ten years' truce in 1285. She had to promise to stay neutral if war broke out between Franks and Mameluks, to build no new fortifications and to share the whole lordship with the sultan: administration and justice outside the city of Tyre were to be their common responsibility and they were each to take half the profits, a frequent clause in the treaties regulating such condominia.[145] In the same year Marqab, the chief fortress of the Hospitallers, was captured although it had always been regarded as impregnable. Qalawun no longer took any notice of truces. A year later, in 1286, Henry I was crowned king of Jerusalem in Tyre and for the last time the royal court at Acre was the scene of splendid festivities. For two weeks the coronation was celebrated in the Great Hall of the Master of the Hospitallers. Scenes from the story of King Arthur and the Round Table, Lancelot and Tristan, and many other knightly romances were enacted. But there was nothing that could stop the Mameluks now. In 1287 Lattakieh fell; in 1289 Tripoli. In Tripoli after the death of Bohemund VII in 1287 the ruling dynasty had been ousted and a commune under the Genoese Bartolomeo Embriaco, lord of Jebail, had been formed when the dowager countess appointed a regent whom the vassals found unacceptable. The commune then sought Genoese support against Lucia, Bohemund's sister, who came out from Europe to claim the county. But when Genoa proposed that a Genoese *podestà* be installed in Tripoli, thus *de facto* incorporating Tripoli into the Genoese republic, then even an Embriaco was willing to recognize Lucia. In a complete volte-face, however, Lucia went over to the Genoese and they set her up in Tripoli. This was to be the end of Tripoli, both commune and city. The enemies of the Genoese in the Levant, perhaps the Venetians or the Pisans, are said to have been so disturbed by this strengthening of Genoa's position, that in 1289 they urged Qalawun to attack Tripoli. The last attempt to build up an alliance against the Mameluks was made by the Mongol Il-Khan Arghun (1284–91). Reading the situation correctly he did not bother to look for support from the Palestinian Franks but went directly to the West. From 1285 to 1289 his envoys toured Europe; the Il-Khan's letters were read in Rome, Paris, and London. But all the European powers were busy with their own affairs and the envoys met with nothing except empty promises and polite excuses.[146]

In 1290 Qalawun moved against Acre. Then his sudden death looked as though it might save the Franks but next spring his son, al-Ashraf Khalil, returned to Acre with an enormous army and 100 siege engines. With its forty churches, its many towers, and its double line of walls, Acre was an imposing monument to Frankish rule in the Holy Land. The Franks mustered all available troops in the city. The Military Orders summoned knights from Europe and there was a company of English soldiers under a Swiss commander, Otto of Grandson. At last the true extent of the danger had been realized and differences were forgotten in the will to resist—but it was too late. On 6 April the siege began with a non-stop barrage from the mangonels and catapults and with an incessant rain of arrows. On 4 May King Henry arrived from Cyprus bringing reinforcements, but on 15 May the outer wall was breached. Three days later the Muslims began a general assault along the entire length of the wall. They took a tower known as the Accursed Tower by storm and then forced their way into the city. Everybody now tried to escape by ship and there were, of course, far too few available. At the quayside there were terrifying scenes of panic. Among the more prominent defenders to escape were King Henry, his brother Amalric, and Otto of Grandson; the patriarch, Nicholas of Hanape, was drowned while trying to get away. By evening it was all over. The population was decimated. The Dominicans, with the old hymn *Veni Creator Spiritus* on their lips, were cut down in their own church. Only the Templars, in their city castle, held out for any length of time, but on 28 May their fortress was undermined and came crashing down.

The rest of Palestine yielded without a struggle. Tyre capitulated on 19 May; Sidon at the end of June although the Castle of the Sea there held out until 14 July. Beirut followed on 31 July and the two Templar fortresses, Tortosa and the Castle of the Pilgrims, were evacuated on 3 and 14 August. Deliberately and carefully the Mameluks devastated the whole coast in order to ensure that the Franks could never return. The political victory of the Mameluks was won at the cost of the destruction of the ancient Syro-Palestinian city civilization. In 1335 Jacob of Verona wandered sadly through the deserted ruins of the coastal cities. Only the ruins of palaces survived to tell of former splendour. The city walls had collapsed and within their perimeters there was no one except a few Saracens living in the most primitive conditions. The fine Gothic doorway of the church of Saint Andrew in Acre, once the headquarters of the commune, had been transported to Cairo where it has stood from 1295 until the present day as part of the sepulchre of a son of Qalawun.

The days of Frankish lordship in the Holy Land were past. As Edward Gibbon put it: 'A mournful and solitary silence prevailed along the coast which had so long resounded with the World's Debate.' Only Peter

Embriaco, lord of Jebail, though under Mameluk surveillance, held on to his domain until 1298, possibly because he could count on the traditional support of the Maronites of the Lebanese mountains, whose resistance the Mameluks were unable to break until after 1300. In 1303 the Templars evacuated their last base, the waterless island of Ruad off the coast near Tortosa. But if the Holy Land was lost, it was not forgotten. In 1295 Charles II of Naples provided grain to be distributed in Cyprus to the impoverished nobles who had fled there from Acre. And when an Italian, Martoni, visited Cyprus in 1394 he noticed that when the noble ladies went out of doors they wore long black garments which revealed only their eyes. When he asked for an explanation of this custom, he was told that it was a token of mourning for the lost city of Acre in 1291.

In contrast to the situation in 1187–8 there were no more Christian beach-heads on the Syro-Palestinian mainland. Yet in Europe men continued to hope that the Holy Land might be recovered and the crusader states re-established. During the first Jubilee in Rome in 1300 rumours that the Mongol Il-Khan who had defeated the Mameluks was going to restore Latin rule in the Levant caused mass hysteria for a while. The flood of memoranda advocating a new crusade did not only offer military advice. They also provided blueprints for the new constitution of a re-established crusader state. Discussion of ways of financing the enterprise drew men's attention to the immense properties belonging to the Military Orders. Between 1307 and 1312 on a trumped-up charge of heresy the French king got the pope at Avignon to dissolve the Order of the Knights Templars. He then confiscated all the Templar properties he could lay his hands on. But in reality talking about the crusade had now taken the place of action. In so far as subsequent generations did act, it was less in terms of a crusade and more in terms of defence against the Ottoman Turks, though the persistence of the old ideology made the change an almost imperceptible one. Resistance to the Turks gave the Hospitallers at Rhodes (1310–1522) and at Malta (from 1530 on) a new *raison d'être* and a task which should have been treated as a common European responsibility but often enough was not. From the days of Francis I onwards France was time and again to ally with the Great Turk against Austria-Hungary and the Holy Roman Empire. On another level the crusading indulgence continued to be used as a recruiting device in quarrels within Christendom. In 1412, for instance, Pope Gregory XII had no qualms about offering a crusading indulgence to those who would take up arms against his rival, the conciliar pope, John XXIII. Further west the crusading idea lived on as a means of driving the Moors out of Spain. After the conquest of Granada in 1492 the Church continued to sell crusading indulgences in order to raise money for liturgical purposes. The popes periodically issued the *bula de la cruzada* to the kings of Spain for a specific number of years until the last such bull expired in 1940 and there was no longer a Spanish king to receive another.[147] By this stage at any rate it is obviously impossible to speak of a crusade. Similarly when the French army in 1914 established its first camp in the Levant where the Templars had left their last base in 1303, i.e. on the island of Ruad off Tortosa, it did so not as a distant reminder of the crusades but simply as a matter of military tactics.

BIBLIOGRAPHY

THE notes are primarily intended to refer the reader to the literature on the subject; only occasionally are they concerned with matters of controversy. The titles listed there represent only a selection from the literature which was used in the preparation of this book; they do not represent a critical survey of all the authorities. They were chosen with an eye to referring the reader to the most important recent literature where he can easily find for himself both a discussion of problems of detail and a guide to the rest of the literature. Thus the bibliography here is limited to the most important general works which, in consequence, are normally omitted from the notes.

COLLECTIONS OF SOURCES: *Recueil des Historiens des Croisades* (1841–1906; abbreviated as *RHC*) divided into the following classes: *Historiens Occidentaux (Hoc.),* 5 vols.; *Historiens Orientaux (Hor.),* 5 vols.; *Historiens Grecs,* 2 vols.; *Documents Arméniens (Arm.),* 2 vols.; *Lois,* 2 vols. *Documents rélatifs à l'histoire des croisades,* so far 15 vols. (1946–84). *Archives de l'Orient latin,* 2 vols. (1881–4). Supplementing this is the *Revue de l'Orient latin,* 12 vols. (1893–1911). *Corpus scriptorum historiae Byzantinae,* 50 vols. (1828–97). As a guide to this there is **G. Moravcsik,** *Byzantinoturcica,* vol. 1 (2nd edn. 1958). **J. P. Migne,** *Patrologiae cursus completus, Series Latina,* 217 vols. (1844–64). In addition there are the great national collections: 'Monumenta Germaniae Historica' (abbreviated as MGH), 'Recueil des Historiens des Gaules et de la France', 'Rerum Britannicarum scriptores medii aevi,' 'Rerum Italicarum scriptores', which are cited in every historical bibliography.

SOURCES: To make space for a more complete coverage of the modern secondary literature, which will in any case lead the reader to the sources, individual chronicles or other primary source material is not cited here or, as a rule, in the notes to the various chapters. But of special importance for the first century of the crusades is the *Historia* of Archbishop William of Tyre (d. 29 September 1186), ed. *RHC Hoc.* 1 with the important autobiographical chapter XIX, 12 ed. **R. B. C. Huygens,** in *Latomus,* 21 (1962), 811ff. A new edition by Huygens *Guillaume de Tyr, Chronique,* 2 vols. (*Corpus Christianorum. Continuatio mediaevalis,* 63, 63A) (1986). There are excellent introductions to the Arab chronicles in **C. Cahen,** *La Syrie du Nord à l'époque des croisades* (1940), 33–93, and for the thirteenth century in **H. L. Gottschalk,** *Al-Malik al-Kāmil von Egypten und seine Zeit* (1958), 6–19. Cf. also *Historians of the Middle East,* ed. **B. Lewis** and **P. M. Holt** (1962) and **J. Sauvaget,** *Introduction à l'Histoire de l'Orient musulman: élements de bibliographie,* 2nd edn., ed. **C. Cahen** (1961). On all points of detail see **C. Brockelmann,** *Geschichte der arabischen Literatur,* 2nd edn., 2 vols. (1943–9); Supplement: 3 vols. (1937–42). **G. Graf,** *Geschichte der christlichen arabischen Literatur,* 5 vols. (1944–53). On the Syriac and Armenian chronicles cf. also **A. Lüders,** *Die Kreuzzüge im Urteil syrischer und armenischer Quellen* (1964).

CHARTERS: Most important are the papal charters, listed together with a summary of their contents in Ph. Jaffé, *Regesta pontificum Romanorum* (as far as 1198), 2nd edn., 2 vols. (1885–8); A. Potthast, *Regesta pontificum Romanorum* (1198–1304), 2 vols. (1874–5), as well as the registers of the thirteenth-century papal chancery edited by the Ecole française de Rome and supplemented by P. Pressutti, *Regesta Honorii papae III*, 2 vols. (1888–95). Register of Innocent III: Migne, *Patrologia Latina*, vols. 214–7. R. Hiestand, *Vorarbeiten zum Oriens pontificius*, 3 vols. (1972–85). vols. 1 and 2 contain the unedited papal charters for the Templars and Hospitallers, vol. 3 those for the secular and monastic churches in the Holy Land. Byzantium : *Regesten der Kaiserurkunden des Oströmischen Reiches*, ed. F. Dölger, in 5 parts covering 565–1453 (1924–65). In contrast the charters of the Western emperors and kings are of little value. Important Italian collections are: G. L. F. Tafel and G. M. Thomas, *Urkunden zur älteren Handels- und Staatsgeschichte der Republik Venedig mit besonderer Berücksichtigung auf Byzanz und die Levante*, 3 vols. (1856–7). C. Imperiale di Sant'Angelo, *Codice diplomatico della repubblica di Genova*, 3 vols. (1936–42). G. Müller, *Documenti sulle relazioni delle città toscane coll' Oriente cristiano* (1879). The charters of the Holy Land itself are listed in R. Röhricht, *Regesta regni Hierosolymitani* (1893), together with the *Additamentum* (1904). An important new publication is *Le cartulaire du chapitre du Saint-Sépulcre de Jérusalem*, ed. G. Bresc-Bautier (1984).

MODERN WORKS: H. E. Mayer, 'Aspekte der Kreuzzugsforschung', *Geschichte und Gegenwart. Festschrift Karl Erdmann* (1980), 75ff. Mayer, 'America and the Crusades', *Proceedings of the American Philosophical Society*, 125 (1981), 38ff. (both on the development of crusading research). Mayer, *Bibliographie zur Geschichte der Kreuzzüge* (1960; 2nd, unaltered edn. 1965), supplemented by H. E. Mayer, 'Literaturbericht über die Geschichte der Kreuzzüge' (1958–67), *Historische Zeitschrift*, Sonderheft, 3 (1969), 642ff. In vol. VI of Setton, *A History of the Crusades* (see below) a selective bibliography of the subject compiled by Mayer will be published which will aim at a full listing of all works published after 1967. New literature on the subject is generally briefly reviewed by Mayer in *Deutsches Archiv*. Less easily accessible for the general public, but more comprehensive are the annual bibliographies in the *Bulletin of the Society for the Study of the Crusades and the Latin East*, 1ff. (1981ff.). P. Alphandéry, *La Chrétienté et l'idée de Croisade*, ed. A. Dupront, 2 vols. (1954–9). J. A. Brundage, *Medieval Canon Law and the Crusader* (1969). M. Villey, *La Croisade. Essai sur la formation d'une théorie juridique* (1942). *A History of the Crusades*, ed. K. M. Setton, 5 vols. so far (1955–85), sixth and last volume in the press. K. M. Setton, *The Papacy and the Levant (1204–1571)*, 4 vols. (1976–84). S. Runciman, *A History of the Crusades*, 3 vols. (1951–4). R. Grousset, *Histoire des Croisades*, 3 vols. (1934–6). P. Rousset, *Histoire des Croisades* (1957). M. Zaborov, *Krestonoscy na vostoke* (The Crusaders in the East) (1980). L. Bréhier, *L'Église et les Croisades* (5th edn. 1928). B. Kugler, *Geschichte der Kreuzzüge* (2nd edn. 1891; an excellent account despite both its age and the emotional style in which it is written). B. Z. Kedar, *Crusade and Mission. European Approaches toward the Muslims* (1984). C. Cahen, *Turcobyzantina et Oriens christianus* (1974). J. Richard, *Orient et Occident au moyen âge: contacts et relations (XIIe–XVe siècle)* (1976). Richard, *Les relations entre l'Occident et l'Orient au moyen âge* (1977).

Richard, *Croisés, missionnaires et voyageurs* (1983). **H. E. Mayer,** *Kreuzzüge und lateinischer Osten* (1983). The last five titles were published in the Variorum Collected Studies Series and are listed here because their topics cover so wide a range as to make it impossible to list them in the notes to individual chapters. Of great general interest for the subject is *Crusade and Settlement. Papers read at the First Conference of the Society for the Study of the Crusades and the Latin East and presented to R. C. Smail,* ed. **P. W. Edbury** (1985). **F. W. Wentzlaff-Eggebert,** *Kreuzzugsdichtung des Mittelalters* (1960). **G. Spreckelmeyer,** *Das Kreuzzugslied des lateinischen Mittelalters* (1974). For a Marxist point of view see **W. Spiewok,** 'Die Bedeutung des Kreuzzugerlebnisses für die Entwicklung der feudalhöfischen Ideologie und die Ausformung der mittelalterlichen deutschen Literatur', *Weimarer Beiträge* 9/10 (1963/4), 669ff. Cf. also the important works cited in note 75, especially **J. Prawer.** *Histoire du royaume latin de Jerusalem,* vols. 1 & 2 (1969–70). *The Cambridge Medieval History,* vol. 4: *The Byzantine Empire,* Parts I and II (1966–7). **G. Ostrogorsky,** *History of the Byzantine State* (2nd edn. 1968). **A. A. Vasiliev,** *History of the Byzantine Empire,* 2nd edn., 2 vols. (reprinted 1961). **R. J. Lilie,** *Byzanz und die Kreuzfahrerstaaten (1096–1204)* (1981). **H. G. Beck,** *Kirche und theologische Literatur im Byzantinischen Reich* (1959). **W. Norden,** *Das Papsttum und Byzanz* (1903). **C. Brockelmann,** *History of the Islamic Peoples* (1949). **B. Spuler,** *Geschichte der islamischen Länder,* 2 vols (Handbuch der Orientalistik, 6, 1952–3). *The Encyclopedia of Islam,* 4 vols. and supplement (1908–38). A new edition of this is being published. **R. Roolvink** and others, *Historical Atlas of the Muslim People* (1957). **E. De Zambaur,** *Manuel de généalogie et de chronologie pour l'histoire de l'Islam* (1927). **S. Lane Poole,** *The Mohammadan Dynasties* (2nd edn. 1925). **N. Daniel,** *Islam and the West. The Making of an Image* (1960). **R. W. Southern,** *Western Views of Islam in the Middle Ages* (1962). **E. Sivan,** *L'Islam et la croisade. Idéologie et propagande dans les réactions musulmanes aux croisades* (1968). Forthcoming is **M. Köhler,** *Allianzen und Verträge zwischen Kreuzfahrern und islamischen Herrschern vom ersten Kreuzzug bis zum Fall Akkons 1291.*

NOTES

1. S. Runciman, *The Eastern Schism* (1955).
2. B. Lewis, 'The Ismā'īlites and the Assassins', in *A History of the Crusades*, ed. K. M. Setton, 1 (1955), 99ff.; M. G. Hodgson, *The Order of the Assassins* (1955).
3. C. Cahen, *Pre-Ottoman Turkey. A General Survey of the Material and Spiritual Culture ca. 1071–1330* (1968); Cahen, 'La première pénétration turque en Asie Mineure', *Byzantion*, 18 (1946–8), 5ff.; Cahen, 'En quoi la conquête turque appellait-elle la croisade?', *Bulletin de la Faculté des Lettres de Strasbourg*, 29 (1950), 118ff. There is an expanded English version of this article: Cahen, 'An Introduction to the First Crusade', *Past and Present*, 6 (1954), 6ff.
4. W. Holtzmann, 'Studien zur Orientpolitik des Reformpapsttums und zur Entstehung des ersten Kreuzzuges', *Historische Vierteljahresschrift*, 22 (1924–5), 167ff.; Holtzmann, 'Die Unionsverhandlungen zwischen Kaiser Alexios I. und Papst Urban II. im Jahre 1089', *Byzantinische Zeitschrift*, 28 (1928), 38ff.; F. L. Ganshof, 'Robert le Frison et Alexis Comnène', *Byzantion*, 31 (1961), 57ff. The letter by Emperor Alexios to Robert I of Flanders has been much discussed. It was dated by Ganshof to 1089–90, but Erdmann (below, n. 5), 365f., and Joranson (*American Historical Review*, 55, 1950, 811ff.) wrote it off as a forgery intended to propagate the crusade of Bohemund I of Antioch against Byzantium, and dated it to 1105. However C. Cahen, 'La politique orientale des comtes de Flandre et la lettre d'Alexis Comnène', *Mélanges d'Islamologie* (Memorial volume A. Abel, 1974), 84ff., raises such fundamental objections to 1105 that this date can no longer be upheld. This does not mean that one should agree with M. de Waha, 'La lettre d'Alexis Comnène à Robert Ier le Frison', *Byzantion*, 47 (1977), 113ff., who argues, against the evidence of the sources, that the letter is basically authentic but was addressed to Count Robert II of Flanders while he was on the First Crusade; D. C. Munro, 'Did the Emperor Alexios I ask for Aid at the Council of Piacenza 1095?', *American Historical Review*, 27 (1922), 731ff.; P. Charanis, 'Byzantium, the West and the Origin of the First Crusade', *Byzantion*, 19 (1949), 17ff.
5. General bibliography for chapter two: C. Erdmann, *Die Entstehung des Kreuzzugsgedankens* (1935); English translation, *The Origin of the Idea of the Crusade* (1977), especially for the Holy War. Contrary points of view in J. Gilchrist, 'The Erdmann Thesis and the Canon Law, 1083–1141', *Crusade and Settlement* (above, p. 293), 37ff. I have not yet seen J. Riley-Smith, *The First Crusade and the Idea of Crusading* (1986); Alphandéry (above, p. 292), vol. 1; P. Rousset, *Les origines et les caractères de la première croisade* (1945); Rousset, *Histoire d'une idéologie. La croisade* (1983); J. Riley-Smith, *Crusades* (below, n. 108). E. O. Blake, 'The Formation of the Crusade Idea', *Journal of Ecclesiastical History*, 21 (1970), 11ff.; B. Lacroix. 'Deus le volt! La théologie d'un cri', *Etudes de civilisation médiévale* (Festschrift E. R. Labande) (1974), 461ff.; E. Delaruelle, 'L'idée de croisade dans la littérature clunisienne du XIe siècle et l'abbaye de Moissac', *Annales du Midi*, 75 (1963), 419ff and H. E. J. Cowdrey, 'Cluny and the First Crusade', *Revue bénédictine*, 83 (1973), 285ff. have persuasively argued that the role Cluny played in the origins of the crusades, should not be overemphasized, particularly in respect of the holy war in Spain. After the Council of Clermont, of course, Cluny did support the crusade proclaimed by Urban II, himself a Cluniac. Cowdrey accepts that Cluny's contribution to the Peace of God movement and to the definition of a knightly ethos helped to prepare the ground for the crusades, but naturally insists that this was not Cluny's intention.

6. For the debate between Cowdrey and myself (above, p. 10): H. E. J. Cowdrey, 'Pope Urban II's Preaching of the First Crusade', *History*, 55 (1970), 177ff. H. E. Mayer, *The Crusades* (1972), 290, n. 6. The implications of Cowdrey's work reach far beyond the problems of the crusade, and, if he is right, then very considerable revisions might have to be made to the current interpretations of the papacy's eastern policy in the eleventh century.

7. S. Mähl, 'Jerusalem in mittelalterlicher Sicht', *Die Welt als Geschichte*, 22 (1962), 11ff.; R. Konrad, 'Das himmlische und das irdische Jerusalem im mittelalterlichen Denken', *Speculum historiale* (Festschrift J. Spörl) (1965), 523 ff. Among the Muslims the idea of the holiness of Jerusalem, propagated by the mystics, did not become important until after the conquest of Edessa by Zengi in 1144. From then on the reconquest of Jerusalem was high on the political agenda. Cf. E. Sivan, 'Le caractère sacré de Jérusalem dans l'Islam au XIIe–XIIIe siècles', *Studia Islamica*, 27 (1967), 149ff.

8. Some of Alphandéry's views have already been modified or denied by his editor A. Dupront, 'La spiritualité des croisés et des pèlerins d'après les sources de la première croisade', *Pellegrinaggi e culto dei santi in Europa fino alla Ia crociata* (1963), 456ff. and, more energetically, by Blake'(above, n. 5), 14.

9. B. Kötting, *Peregrinatio religiosa. Die Wallfahrten der Antike und das Pilgerwesen der alten Kirche* (1950); E. D. Hunt, *Holy Land Pilgrimage in the Later Roman Empire, A.D. 312–460* (1982); P. Maraval, *Lieux saints et pèlerinages d'Orient. Histoire et géographie des origines à la conquête arabe* (1985); H. Leclercq, 'Pèlerinages aux Lieux saints', *Dictionnaire d'archéologie chrétienne et de liturgie*, 14 (1939), 65ff.; C. Vogel, 'Le pèlerinage pénitentiel', *Pellegrinaggi e culto dei santi in Europa fino alla Ia crociata* (1963), 37ff.

10. R. H. W. Regout, *La doctrine de la guerre juste de St. Augustine à nos jours* (1934). Erdmann (above, n. 5); F. H. Russell, *The Just War in the Middle Ages* (1975); E. D. Hehl, *Kirche und Krieg im 12. Jahrhundert. Studien zu kanonischem Recht und politischer Wirklichkeit* (1980).

11. C. Erdmann, 'Die Aufrufe Gerberts und Sergius IV. für das Hl. Land', *Quellen und Forschungen aus italienischen Archiven und Bibliotheken*, 23 (1931–2), 1ff.; A. Gieysztor, 'The Genesis of the Crusades. The Encyclica of Sergius IV', *Medievalia et Humanistica*, 5 (1948), 3ff.; 6 (1950), 3ff.

12. M. Defourneaux, *Les Français en Espagne aux XIe et XIIe siècles* (1949); H. E. J. Cowdrey, 'The Mahdia Campaign of 1087', *English Historical Review*, 92 (1977), 1ff.

13. H. E. J. Cowdrey, 'Pope Gregory VII's Crusading Plans of 1074', *Outremer* (below, n. 75), 27ff.; I. S. Robinson, 'Gregory VII and the Soldiers of Christ', *History*, 58 (1973), 169ff.; J. Riley-Smith, 'The First Crusade and St. Peter', *Outremer* (below, n. 75), 41ff.

14. G. Duby, *La Société aux XIe et XIIe siècles dans la région mâconnaise* (1953); Duby, 'Au XIIe siècle: les "Jeunes" dans la société aristocratique', *Annales. Économies, Sociétés, Civilisations*, 19 (1964) 835ff., trans. C. Postan, in Duby, *The Chivalrous Society* (1977), 112ff.; cf. also R. Fossier in *Comptes rendus des séances de l'Académie des Inscriptions et Belles-Lettres* for 1971, p. 261; G. Duby, *The Knight, the Lady and the Priest* (1983). Differing viewpoint in J. Riley-Smith, 'Earliest crusaders' (below, n. 32), 721ff.; D. Herlihy, 'The Agrarian Revolution in Southern France and Italy', *Speculum*, 33 (1958), 23ff.

15. A. Gottlob, *Kreuzablass und Almosenablass* (1906); N. Paulus, *Geschichte des Ablasses im Mittelalter*, 3 vols. (1922–3; very apologetic); B. Poschmann, *Der Ablass im Lichte der Bussgeschichte* (1948). My thesis that originally crusading indulgences were proclaimed without an adequate basis in the decree of the Council of Clermont and that it was only much later that theological and canonistic doctrine provided support for the practice, had briefly been touched upon by Vogel (above, n. 9), 85f. in 1963. This was unknown to me when I published the German original of this book in 1965. When it came to my knowledge, it was a welcome confirmation of my thesis from a great expert in canon

law—and this despite the fact that Vogel, in the final analysis, came to the same conclusion as that reached by Brundage, *Medieval Canon Law* (below, n. 17), 145–8, namely that true plenary indulgences were not granted by the Church before the crusading decree of the Fourth Lateran Council in 1215. From my point of view what matters in Vogel's paper is his conviction that canon 2 of Clermont released the faithful only from all penance, and from nothing else. He accepts, moreover, that as well as the pronouncements which, he argues, repeat the equation: crusade = equivalent of all penance, there were other texts (after Clermont but before Lateran IV) stating the equation: crusade = indulgence. To that extent Vogel, although he saw clearly that the Clermont decree and many of the non-canonist texts from after the council were irreconcilable, was still the prisoner of Poschmann's view that at this date *remissio peccatorum* still meant nothing more than release from penance. But in this case the crusade would hardly have been called a *novae poenitentiae via* (Ekkehard of Aura, *Hierosolymita*, 304) because it would have imposed on the sinner a burden in most cases harder than the penance that had been or would have been levied on him, without assuring him of his release from purgatory. Moreover, when Orderic Vitalis, *Historia ecclesiastica*, ed. M. Chibnall, 5, 16–18, wrote that Urban II absolved the crusaders from all their sins and released them from all penance, it is hard to see why Orderic mentioned them separately (and put the emphasis on the remission of sins), if, as argued by Riley-Smith, 'Death on the First Crusade', *The End of Strife*, ed. D. Loades (1984), 17, public opinion clearly understood that the first meant only the second. In fact there is more support for Vogel's and Riley-Smith's arguments in the Chronicle of Montecassino, MGH, SS 34, 475: *ultramarinum iter ad sepulcrum Domini a Saracenis eripiendum in penitentiam et remissionem peccatorum suorum illis iniunctum fide promptissima se arripere spoponderunt certi et indubii redditi, quod, quicquid aversi ... illis contingeret, loco penitentiae a Domino recipiendum, ut tamen se a preteritis nequitiis continerent.* Here we have both terms and then only one equation: crusade = penance. Yet here too there is a sense of novelty, for otherwise there would have been no need to stress that the crusaders went off confident of the promised reward, surely unnecessary if all that had been offered was something entirely within the tradition of centuries. Moreover, the phrase *a Domino recipiendum* suggests that the promise had a transcendental aspect, essential for the remission of sins, but not essential and not found, certainly not in canon 2 of Clermont, in the traditional penitential system. When the chronicler spoke first of penance and remission of sins and then, later in the same sentence, only of penance, he may have had in mind the distinction which William of Tyre, a trained canon lawyer, put into Urban's mouth at Clermont: *Nos autem ... fidelibus Christianis, qui contra eos arma susceperint et onus sibi huius peregrinationis assumpserint, iniunctas sibi pro suis delictis poenitentias relaxamus. Qui autem ibi in vera poenitentia decesserint, et peccatorum indulgentiam et fructum aeternae mercedis se non dubitent habituros.* It looks as though William was well aware not only of what had been promised at Clermont but also of the theological impasse created by the premature grants of plenary indulgences to all crusaders. Although it flatly contradicted what pope Eugenius III had stated in *Quantum praedecessores*, referring expressly to rules established by Urban II, William tried to find an escape route of his own, arguing that release from penance had been promised to those participants who survived, and an indulgence in the full sense to those who died on crusade. Theologically this would have been much less objectionable, and indeed Riley-Smith (as above), 19ff., has shown that from 1098 on, in the crusading armies as well as in the writings of later chroniclers, there was a massive rise in the belief that those who died on crusade were martyrs, even though the Church never canonized a man just for that. But the promise of a martyr's crown was surely insufficient to raise armies as big as those of the First Crusade if only because the vast majority of people presumably wanted to return alive. On the other hand, if William's distinction was in the reward as originally promised, then it would be easy to see how all the crusaders might misunderstand it and eagerly look forward to the maximum reward even if they did not die. Although Riley-Smith, 17, disagrees with my interpretation of the indulgence and its preaching, he also concludes that the crusaders expected a full release from temporal punishment for past sins, obviously something considerably more than just a release from penance and more too than had been promised at Clermont.

16. General bibliography for chapter three: F. Chalandon, *Histoire de la première croisade* (1925); H. von Sybel, *Geschichte des ersten Kreuzzuges* (2nd edn. 1881, important on account of a critical evaluation of the sources which long remained authoritative). R. Röhricht, *Geschichte des ersten Kreuzzuges* (1901). Riley-Smith, *First Crusade* (above, n. 5); Rousset, *Origines* (above, n. 5); J. Prawer, 'The Jerusalem the Crusaders Captured: a Contribution to the Medieval Topography of the City', *Crusade and Settlement* (above, p. 293), 1ff; G. Constable, 'The Financing of the Crusades in the Twelfth Century', *Outremer* (below, n. 75), 64ff. (also for later crusades); H. E. J. Cowdrey, 'Martyrdom and the First Crusade', *Crusade and Settlement* (above, p. 293), 46ff.; H. E. Mayer, 'Zur Beurteilung Adhémars von Le Puy', *Deutsches Archiv*, 16 (1960), 547ff., and including a summary of the debate between Hill and Brundage. Mayer's last paragraph needs revising in the light of Guibert of Nogent, *Gesta Dei per Francos*, RHC Hoc. 4, 121, 140, 148. See also J. Richard, *Journal des Savants* (1960), 49ff.; J. C. Andressohn, *The Ancestry and Life of Godfrey of Bouillon* (1947); G. H. Hagspiel, *Die Führerpersönlichkeit im Kreuzzug* (1963) needs to be used with caution; cf. *Deutsches Archiv*, 20, 261f. By contrast G. Waeger, *Gottfried von Bouillon in der Historiographie* (1969), is an excellent study. H. E. Mayer, *Mélanges sur l'histoire du royaume latin de Jérusalem* (Part I: *Études sur l'histoire de Baudouin Ier roi de Jérusalem*) (*Mémoires de l'Académie des Inscriptions et Belles-Lettres*, N.S., 5, 1984), 10ff. on Baldwin I and Godfrey before the crusade. P. Gindler, *Graf Balduin I. von Edessa* (1901); R. B. Yewdale, *Bohemund I Prince of Antioch* (1924); see also the fine article by Girgensohn, 'Boemondo I', *Dizionario biografico degli Italiani*, 11 (1969), 117ff.; R. L. Nicholson, *Tancred. A Study of His Career and Work* (1940). C. W. David, *Robert Curthose Duke of Normandy* (1920). J. H. and L. L. Hill, *Raymond IV Count of Toulouse* (1962); J. A. Brundage, 'An Errant Crusader: Stephen of Blois', *Traditio*, 16 (1960), 380ff.; P. Rousset, 'Étienne de Blois, croisé fuyard et martyr', *Genava*, N.S., 11 (1963), 183 ff.; Lilie, *Kreuzfahrerstaaten* (above, p. 293). F. Chalandon, *Les Comnène. Études sur l'Empire byzantin au XIe et XIIe siècle* I: *Essai sur le règne d'Alexis Ier Comnène* (1900); L. Dasberg, *Untersuchungen über die Entwertung des Judenstatus im 11. Jahrhundert* (1965). Better is H. Liebeschütz, 'The Crusading Movement in its Bearing on the Christian Attitude towards Jewry', *Journal of Jewish Studies*, 10 (1959), 97ff.

17. The privileges are clearly summarized in the canons of the Lateran Council of 1123 where they are all attributed to Urban; cf. Mansi, *Sacrorum Conciliorum nova et amplissima collectio*, 21, 284.There is a more elaborate summary in *Quantum praedecessores*, the bull for the second crusade (see above, p. 94). On the canonistic doctrine at the end of the twelfth century see J. A. Brundage, 'The Crusade of Richard I. Two Canonical Quaestiones', *Speculum*, 38 (1983), 443ff. The leading expert on the Council of Clermont believes, as do most historians, that some of the organizational framework for the crusade was set up at Clermont itself: R. Somerville, 'The Council of Clermont and the First Crusade', *Studia Gratiana*, 12 (1976), 323ff. On the crusader's vow see A. Noth, *Heiliger Krieg und Heiliger Kampf in Islam und Christentum* (1966), 120ff. Objections by J. A. Brundage, 'The Army of the First Crusade and the Crusade Vow', *Medieval Studies*, 33 (1971), 334ff. See also Brundage, *Medieval Canon Law and the Crusader* (1969), *passim*, on the crusader's position in canon law, but especially pp. 30–114 on the vow, expanding on his studies in *Traditio*, 24 (1968), 77ff.; *Catholic Historical Review*, 52 (1966), 234ff.; *Traditio* 22 (1966), 289ff. See also *Deutsches Archiv*, 22, 673 and *Historische Zeitschrift*, Sonderheft, 3, 678f.

18. H. Hagenmeyer, *Le vrai et le faux sur Pierre l'Hermite* (1883); E. O. Blake and C. Morris, 'A Hermit Goes to War: Peter and the Origins of the First Crusade', *Studies in Church History*, 22 (1985), 79ff., make a very cautious but interesting attempt to rehabilitate the older theory that it was Peter, returning from Jerusalem, who inaugurated the First Crusade, preaching it even before Clermont. The authors succeed in showing that there was a tradition to this effect in Flanders, along the Lower Rhine and in north-west Germany. They argue that the failure of Peter's premature popular crusade led, later on, to this tradition being obscured by the French emphasis on Urban II and the council of Clermont. This may be true but this alone does not make the north-west German tradition any more credible than the French one. The authors also cast doubts on the roles of Robert d'Arbrissel and the abbot of St.-Bénigne. But while it is true that there is no direct evidence that either of them preached the crusade, the fact remains that the former undoubtedly received a papal preaching commission (in February 1096) and the latter, as a prelude to the crusade and at the pope's request, brought about peace between the king of England and the duke of Normandy by the summer of 1096 and then accompanied the Norman crusaders as far as Pontarlier. It is therefore difficult to escape the conclusion generally drawn from these facts and it is, at least, arguable that preaching the crusade was part of their activities. F. Duncalf, 'The Peasants Crusade', *American Historical Review*, 26 (1920–1), 440ff. On preaching the crusade in general see C. Morris, 'Propaganda for War: the Dissemination of the Crusading Ideal in the Twelfth Century', *Studies in Church History*, 20 (1983), 79ff.

19. J. Riley-Smith, 'The First Crusade and the Persecution of the Jews', *Persecution and Toleration* (Studies in Church History, 21, 1984), 51ff. believes that the crowds of the Peasants' Crusade were, in fact, well disciplined troops under experienced captains. At least so far as the army of Peter the Hermit is concerned, St. Bernard in his widely circulated letter no. 363 (below, p. 96, copy addressed to Speyer) thought otherwise, firmly attributing this group's failure to premature departure and a lack of experienced leadership. Riley-Smith also believes that contemporaries were honestly convinced that the Jews deserved to be punished as enemies of Christ and that this was not merely a façade to conceal less worthy motives.

20. It is possible that Raymond believed there were threats to the hereditary rights of his descendants in Provence and Toulouse, but on this point further research is needed. Raymond's exceptional position among the leaders of the First Crusade has recently been disputed by J. Richard, 'Les Saint-Gilles et le comté de Tripoli', *Islam et chrétiens du Midi* (1984), 65ff.

21. J. Richard, 'Quelques textes sur les premiers temps de l'église latine de Jérusalem', *Recueil Clovis Brunel*, 2 (1955), 421. Mayer, 'Adhémar' (above, n. 16); R. Hiestand, *Legaten* (below, n. 90), has raised convincing objections.

22. The discussion between Lilie, *Kreuzfahrerstaaten* (above, p. 293), 10–20, and H. Möhring, *Historische Zeitschrift*, 234 (1984), 603 (Lilie's rejoinder to this part of this otherwise rather careless review in R. J. Lilie and P. Speck, *Varia I*, Poikila Byzantina, 4, 1984, 125, n. 11) on the reputed vassalitic status of the leaders of the crusade *vis-à-vis* the emperor in Constantinople (and, consequently, on a possible feudal tenure, by the crusaders, of the former parts of the Byzantine Empire extending east and south of Antioch as far as Jerusalem) has been rendered obsolete by J. H. Pryor, 'The Oath of the Leaders of the First Crusade to Emperor Alexius I Comnenus', *Parergon*, N.S., 2 (1984), 111ff. He shows that the crusaders swore oaths of fealty but did not pay homage, thus did not become Alexius's vassals. L. Buisson, *Erobererrecht, Vasallität und byzantinisches Staatsrecht auf dem ersten Kreuzzug* (Berichte aus den Sitzungen der Joachim-Jungius-Gesellschaft der Wissenschaften Hamburg 2,7 for 1984, published 1985), was written before the author could have known Pryor's work, but is still useful for drawing the reader's attention to applications of the Norman law of conquest during the First Crusade.

23. According to Anna Comnena the fight took place on Maundy Thursday but on this point modern Byzantinists accept the date given by Albert of Aix; cf. Dölger, *Regesten der Kaiserurkunden des Oströmischen Reiches*, no. 1196. Following the Byzantine custom Alexius adopted several of the leaders of the crusade in order to demonstrate their dependent position; cf. F. L. Ganshof, 'Recherche sur le lien juridique qui unissait les chefs de la première croisade à l'Empereur byzantin', *Mélanges P. E. Martin* (1961), 49ff.

24. Bohemund's 'house chronicle', the *Gesta Francorum*, tells of a secret arrangement whereby Bohemund was to receive Antioch but this is a later interpolation (inserted *c*. 1105 or even after 1108) designed to give support to Bohemund's claim to Antioch. Cf. A. C. Krey, 'A Neglected Passage in the Gesta', *The Crusades and other Historical Essays Presented to D. C. Munro* (1928), 57ff., recently questioned by R. Hill, *Anonymi Gesta Francorum et aliorum Hierosolimitanorum* (1962), 12f., n. 2 and by H. Oehler, 'Studien zu den Gesta Francorum', *Mittellateinisches Jahrbuch*, 6 (1970), 74ff.

25. Cf. L. A. M. Sumberg, 'The "Tafurs" and the First Crusade', *Medieval Studies*, 21 (1959), 224ff; M. Rouche, 'Cannibalisme sacré chez les croisés populaires', *La religion populaire*, ed. Y. M. Hilaire (1981), 29ff. offers the absurd view that cannibalism was one of the reasons for the success of the crusade.

26. S. Runciman, 'The Holy Lance found at Antioch', *Analecta Bollandiana*, 68 (1950), 197ff.

27. J. France, 'The Crisis of the First Crusade from the Defeat of Kerbogha to the Departure from Arqa', *Byzantion*, 40 (1970), 276ff., believes that originally Raymond was not serious about marching from Maarat an-Numan to Jerusalem.

28. H. E. Mayer, 'The Beginnings of the Lordships of Ramla and Lydda in the Latin Kingdom of Jerusalem', *Speculum*, 60 (1985) 537ff.

29. This has often been seen as a clerical attempt to establish a kind of theocracy in the Crusader States; cf. J. Hansen, *Das Problem eines Kirchenstaates in Jerusalem* (1928). Emphatically, and rightly, critical of this view is J. G. Rowe, 'Paschal II and the Latin Orient', *Speculum*, 32 (1957), 471ff. On Arnulf of Rohes cf. R. Foreville, 'Un chef de la première croisade: Arnoul Malecouronne', *Bulletin philol. et hist. du Comité des travaux hist. et scientif.* 1953-4 (1955), 377ff.

30. On Godfrey's title in the East, formerly believed to be *advocatus sancti Sepulchri*, i.e. Defender of the Holy Sepulchre, see now J. Riley-Smith, 'The Title of Godfrey of Bouillon', *Bulletin of the Institute of Historical Research*, 52 (1979), 83 ff. He builds up an impressive case, arguing that Godfrey only styled himself Duke of Lower Lorraine. As we have no charters issued by Godfrey in the East, the question cannot be answered with absolute certainty—a pity since the answer would provide important insights into Godfrey's relations with the Church. To Riley-Smith's list of references for an advocacy at the Holy Sepulchre should be added William of Tyre, *Historia*, XX, 22, ed. Huygens 942, who calls King Amalric of Jerusalem the *defensor et advocatus* of the holy places of the Passion and Resurrection.

31. R. Blanchard, *Asie occidentale* (Géographie universelle, 1929); R. Thoumin, *Géographie humaine de la Syrie centrale* (1936); F. Dussaud, *Topographie historique de la Syrie antique et médiévale* (1927); F. M. Abel, *Géographie de la Palestine*, 2 vols. (2nd edn. 1933-8); G. Dalman, *Arbeit und Sitte in Palästina*, 7 vols. (1928-39). Meteorological measurements for 1928-33 are given in the *Zeitschrift des Deutschen Palästina-Vereins*, 52-5 (1929-32) and 57 (1934); M. Alex, *Klimadaten ausgewählter Stationen des Vorderen Orients* (Beihefte zum Tübinger Atlas des Vorderen Orients, A 14, 1985).

32. General bibliography for chapter four: A. Wollf, *König Balduin I. von Jerusalem* (1884); R. L. Nicholson, *Joscelyn I Prince of Edessa* (1954); A. Herzog, *Die Frau auf den Fürstenthronen der Kreuzfahrerstaaten* (1919); B. Hamilton, 'Women in the Crusader States: the Queens of Jerusalem (1100-1190)', *Medieval Women* (Festschrift R. Hill), ed. D. Baker (1978), 143ff. Cf. also the biographies listed above, n. 16. J. Riley-Smith, 'The motives of the earliest crusaders and the settlement of Latin Palestine 1095-1100',

English Historical Review, 98 (1983), 721ff.; Mayer, 'Pontifikale von Tyrus' (below, n. 90); B. Hamilton, 'Ralph of Domfront, Patriarch of Antioch (1135–40)', *Nottingham Medieval Studies*, 28 (1984), 1ff.; R. Hiestand, 'Ein unbekannter Bericht über das Konzil von Antiochia 1140', *Annuarium historiae conciliorum* 1988 (forthcoming; see the text in Hiestand, *Vorarbeiten*, above, p. 292, 3, 160, no. 46). F. Chalandon, *Les Comnène* II: *Jean II Comnène et Manuel Ier Comnène* (1912); E. Sivan, 'La genèse de la contre-croisade: un traité damasquin du début du XIIe siècle', *Journal asiatique*, 254 (1966, published 1967), 197ff. On the Frankish–Muslim *condominia* see in general below, n. 145. On the early ones see Röhricht, *Geschichte* (below, n. 75), 84; Grousset, *Croisades* (above, p. 292), 1, 249, 679; Richard, *'Comté de Tripoli'* (below, n. 75), 18, 25; Runciman, *Crusades* (above, p. 292), 2, 96; Prawer, *Histoire* (below, n. 75), 1, 274f.; C. Cahen, 'Compléments aux Historiens des Croisades: extraits d'Ibn abî Tayyi', *Studi in onore di Francesco Gabrieli* (1984), 143f.

33. It is generally accepted that the text of the letter in William of Tyre X, 4 is not genuine. Nevertheless it is hardly possible to deny the existence of a letter with contents very similar to this.

34. S. Runciman, 'The Crusades of 1101', *Jahrbuch der österreichisch-byzantinischen Gesellschaft*, 1 (1951), 3ff.

35. On this war see J. G. Rowe, 'Paschal II., Bohemund of Antioch and the Byzantine Empire', *Bulletin of the John Rylands Library*, 49 (1966), 165ff.; Kindliman (below, n. 51), 119ff.; Lilie, *Kreuzfahrerstaaten* (above, p. 293), 65 ff., and the helpful study by G. Rösch, 'Der "Kreuzzug" Bohemunds gegen Dyrrhachion 1107–1108 in der lateinischen Tradition des 12. Jahrhunderts', *Römische Historische Mitteilungen*, 26 (1984), 181ff., who demonstrates Bohemund's pseudo-success. Buisson (above, n. 22), 72, 77f., has recently advanced the interesting and not implausible hypothesis that in the treaty of Devol Bohemund did not receive Antioch as a fief but as a grant for life under the Byzantine institution of *pronoia*. Pending discussion of this suggestion by Byzantinists the older theory has been retained here.

36. In truth the constitutional position was even more complicated than this; see J. Richard, *Comté de Tripoli* (1945), 26–43.

37. H. E. Mayer and M. L. Favreau, 'Das Diplom Balduins I. für Genua und Genuas Goldene Inschrift in der Grabeskirche', *Quellen und Forschungen aus italienischen Archiven und Bibliotheken*, 55–6 (1976), 22ff.

38. Lilie, *Kreuzfahrerstaaten* (above, p. 293), 82 (cf. his modifications in Lilie, *Handel und Politik zwischen dem byzantinischen Reich und den italienischen Kommunen*, 1984, p. 72ff.) interprets this incorrectly as an offensive alliance. The treaty, however, only stipulated Pisan neutrality.

39. H. E. Mayer, *Mélanges* (above, n. 16), 49ff., also on the accession of Baldwin II.

40. G. Bautier, 'L'envoi de la relique de la Vraie Croix à Notre-Dame de Paris en 1120', *Bibliothèque de l'École des Chartes*, 129 (1971), 387ff.; H. E. Mayer, 'The Concordate of Nablus', *Journal of Ecclesiastical History*, 33 (1982), 531ff.; Mayer, 'Jérusalem et Antioche au temps de Baudouin II', *Comptes rendus des séances de l'Académie des Inscriptions et Belles-Lettres* (1980), p. 717ff.

41. J. G. Rowe, 'The Papacy and the Ecclesiastical Province of Tyre', *Bulletin of the John Rylands Library*, 43 (1960), 160ff.

42. *Die geistlichen Ritterorden Europas*, ed. J. Fleckenstein and M. Hellmann (1980) contains the especially important study by R. Hiestand, 'Die Anfänge der Johanniter', p. 31ff. There is no good modern history of the Templars. Closest to it is the series of biographies of the Masters of the Templars by M. L. Bulst-Thiele, *Sacrae domus militiae Templi Hierosolymitani magistri* (1974); M. Melville, *La vie des Templiers* (2nd edn. 1974); M. Barber, 'The Origins of the Order of the Temple', *Studia monastica*, 12 (1970), 219ff., argues for 1129 rather than 1128 as the year of the foundation of the Templars. Some strange older theories that the institution of Military Orders was

influenced by Islamic models have been satisfactorily refuted by A. J. Forey, 'The Emergence of the Military Order in the Twelfth Century', *Journal of Ecclesiastical History*, 36 (1985), 175ff.; J. Riley-Smith, *The Knights of St. John in Jerusalem and Cyprus ca. 1050–1310* (1967); J. Delaville Le Roulx, *Les Hospitaliers en Terre Sainte et à Chypre* (1904); A. Luttrell, *The Hospitallers in Cyprus, Rhodes, Greece and the West 1291–1440* (1978); P. Bertrand de la Grassière, *L'ordre militaire et hospitalier de St.-Lazare de Jérusalem* (1960); Sh. Shahar, 'Des lepreux pas comme les autres', *Revue historique*, 267 (1982), 19ff. (the last two titles need to be used with caution); A. J. Forey, 'The Order of Mountjoy', *Speculum*, 46 (1971), 250ff.

43. On the succession of Baldwin II: R. Hiestand, 'Zwei unbekannte Diplome der lateinischen Könige von Jerusalem aus Lucca', *Quellen und Forschungen aus italienischen Archiven und Bibliotheken*, 50 (1970), 25ff.; Hiestand, 'Chronologisches zur Geschichte des Königreichs Jerusalem um 1130', *Deutsches Archiv*, 26 (1970), 220 ff. H. E. Mayer, 'Studies in the History of Queen Melisende of Jerusalem', *Dumbarton Oaks Papers*, 26 (1972), 98ff., also on the revolt of Hugh of Jaffa. But I would no longer maintain that the designation of 1131 changed the marriage contract of 1129. Rather it confirmed the contract (Hiestand and Hamilton, *Women*, above, n. 32, 149f.). On the problem of the *haeres regni* see H. E. Mayer, 'The Succession of Baldwin II of Jerusalem. English Impact on the East', *Dumbarton Oaks Papers*, 39 (1985). Attention should be drawn especially to the fact that R. C. Smail presented, in an as yet unpublished lecture in Jerusalem, a different interpretation of the problem of joint rule. He believes that Melisende's constitutional position after 1143 was already unclear to contemporaries. This should be borne in mind above, pp. 91 and 108.

44. H. E. Mayer, 'The Origins of the County of Jaffa', *Israel Exploration Journal*, 35 (1985); William of Tyre reports only one revolt of Roman, i.e. the one together with Hugh of Jaffa. J. Richard, *The Latin Kingdom of Jerusalem* (1979), 95 thinks there were two distinct revolts at different times. Mayer, 'Queen Melisende' (above, n. 43) also has two revolts but at different dates, while J. Prawer, *Histoire de Jérusalem* (below, n. 75) 1, 318, n. 8 and *Crusader Institutions*, 27, n. 3 and 438, thinks in terms of two separate but simultaneous revolts of Roman and Hugh. On Hugh's revolt Mayer, 'Queen Melisende', 102ff. But I do not now believe that Hugh revolted in favour of the designation of 1131 and against the marriage contract of 1129 since I no longer see the two as being contradictory.

45. P. Deschamps, *Les châteaux des croisés en Terre Sainte*, 3 vols. of text and 3 vols. of plates (1934–73); M. L. Favreau-Lilie, 'Landesausbau und Burg während der Kreuzfahrerzeit. Safad in Obergalilaea', *Zeitschrift des Deutschen Palästina-Vereins*, 96 (1980), 67ff.; Huygens (below, n. 76); G. Saadé, 'Histoire du Château de Saladin', *Studi medievali*, 3rd series, 9 (1968), 980ff.; A. Grabois, 'La cité de Baniyas et le château de Subeibeh pendant les croisades', *Cahiers de civilisation médiévale*, 13 (1970), 43ff.; J. Riley-Smith, 'The Templars and the Castle of Tortosa in Syria: An Unknown Document Concerning the Acquisition of the Fortress', *English Historical Review*, 84 (1969), 278ff. (most interesting); M. Braune, 'Die mittelalterlichen Befestigungen der Stadt Tortosa-Tartus. Vorbericht der Untersuchungen 1981–1982', *Damaszener Mitteilungen*, 2 (1985), 45ff.

46. W. H. Rüdt de Collenberg, 'Les premiers Ibelins', *Moyen Age*, 71 (1965), 433 ff., refuted by H. E. Mayer, 'Carving up Crusaders: The Early Ibelins and Ramlas', *Outremer* (below, n. 75), 101ff.; Mayer, 'Ramla and Lydda' (above, n. 28).

47. H. E. Mayer, 'Kaiserrecht und Heiliges Land', *Aus Reichsgeschichte und Nordischer Geschichte* (Festschrift Karl Jordan, 1972), 193ff.; R. C. Smail, 'The International Status of the Latin Kingdom of Jerusalem, 1150–1192', *The Eastern Mediterranean Lands in the Period of the Crusades*, ed. P. M. Holt (1977), 23ff.; Hiestand (below, n. 48), 119.

48. General bibliography for chapter five: B. Kugler, *Studien zur Geschichte des zweiten Kreuzzuges* (1866); G. Constable, 'The Second Crusade as Seen by Contemporaries', *Traditio*, 9 (1953), 213ff.; H. Gleber, *Papst Eugen III.* (1936); J. Leclercq, 'L'encyclique de St.-Bernard en faveur de la croisade', *Revue bénédictine*, 81 (1971), 282ff.; Leclercq, *Études de civilisation médiévale* (Festschrift R. Labande, 1974), 479ff.; E. Delaruelle, 'L'idée de croisade chez St.-Bernard', *Mélanges de St.-Bernard* (1953), 53ff.; E. Willems, 'Citeaux et la seconde croisade', *Revue d'histoire ecclésiastique*, 49 (1954), 116ff.; L. Schmugge, 'Zisterzienser, Kreuzzug und Heidenkrieg', *Die Zisterzienser* (1980), 57ff.; H. Tüchle, 'Ein Hildegard- und ein Bernhardbrief aus der ehemaligen Ochsenhausener Klosterbibliothek', *Studien und Mitteilungen zur Geschichte des Benediktiner-Ordens*, 79 (1968), 17ff.; G. Constable, 'A Report of a Lost Sermon by St. Bernard on the Failure of the Second Crusade', *Studies in Medieval Cistercian History Presented to Jeremiah O'Sullivan* (1971), 49ff.; E. Vacandard, *Vie de St.-Bernard*, vol. 2 (4th edn. 1910); P. Rassow, 'Die Kanzlei St. Bernhards von Clairvaux', *Studien und Mitteilungen zur Geschichte des Benediktiner-Ordens*, 34 (1913), 243ff.; W. v. Bernhardi, *Konrad III.* (1883); P. Lamma, *Comneni e Staufer*, 2 vols. (1955–7); R. Hiestand, '"Kaiser" Konrad III., der zweite Kreuzzug und ein verlorenes Diplom für den Berg Thabor', *Deutsches Archiv*, 35 (1979), 82 ff.; A. J. Forey, 'The Failure of the Siege of Damascus in 1148', *Journal of Medieval History*, 10 (1984), 13ff., explains the failure purely in military terms and rejects all theories of sabotage. On the motives of Louis VII of France at the Bourges assembly see the noteworthy remarks by A. Grabois, 'The Crusade of King Louis VII: a Reconsideration', *Crusade and Settlement* (above, p. 293), 94ff.; F. Chalandon, *Comnène*, vol. 2 (above, n. 32); Chalandon, *Histoire de la domination normande en Italie et en Sicile*, vol. 2 (1907).

49. The best survey of the polemical literature is contained in E. Caspar, 'Die Kreuzzugsbullen Eugens III', *Neues Archiv*, 45 (1924), 285ff., together with a text of the March bull.

50. But L. Grill, 'Die Kreuzzugsepistel St. Bernhards *Ad peregrinantes Jerusalem*', *Studien und Mitteilungen zur Geschichte des Benediktiner-Ordens*, 67 (1956), 237ff. was wrong to believe that Bernard also wrote to Spain. The existence of such a letter had frequently been assumed but the version found by Grill in a manuscript from Ripoll is merely an unaddressed late copy of the encyclical no. 363 on the Jerusalem crusade. P. Knoch, 'Kreuzzug und Siedlung. Studien zum Aufruf der Magdeburger Kirche von 1108', *Jahrbuch für die Geschichte Mittel- und Ostdeutschlands*, 23 (1974), 1ff. On the Wendish Crusade: M. Bünding, *Das Imperium Christianum und die deutschen Ostkriege* (1940), 35ff., reprinted in *Heidenmission und Kreuzzugsgedanke im der deutschen Ostpolitik des Mittelalters*, ed. H. Beumann (1963) which deals with subsequent developments in this area. H. D. Kahl's study in this volume, 'Zum Ergebnis des Wendenkreuzzuges von 1147', p. 275ff., adopts a much more positive view than most other historians; F. Lotter, *Die Konzeption des Wendenkreuzzugs* (1977). That some of the Saxon bishops should intentionally have sabotaged the crusade, is a totally unproved speculation by H. D. Kahl, *Slawen und Deutsche in der brandenburgischen Geschichte des 12. Jahrhunderts*, vol. 1 (1964), 186–235, especially p. 225. On the discussion of Bernard's notorious alternative see B. Z. Kedar's summing-up, *Crusade and Mission* (above, p. 292), 70f.

51. W. M. Daly, 'Christian Fraternity, the Crusaders and the Security of Constantinople', *Medieval Studies*, 22 (1960), 59ff.; S. Kindlimann, *Die Eroberung Konstantinopels als politische Forderung des Westens im Hochmittelalter* (1969).

52. On the following see Lamma (above, n. 48); P. Rassow, *Honor imperii. Die neue Politik Friedrich Barbarossas* (1940); K. Heilig, 'Ostrom und das deutsche Reich um die Mitte des 12. Jahrhunderts', *Kaisertum und Herzogsgewalt im Zeitalter Friedrichs I.* (1944), 159ff.; H. Vollrath, 'Konrad III. und Byzanz', *Archiv für Kulturgeschichte*, 59 (1977), 321ff.

53. F. Kurth, 'Der Anteil niederdeutscher Kreuzfahrer an den Kämpfen der Portugiesen gegen die Mauren', *Mitteilungen des Instituts für österreichische Geschichtsforschung, Ergänzungsband*, 8 (1911), 133ff.; R. Hiestand, 'Reconquista, Kreuzzug und heiliges Grab. Die Eroberung von Tortosa 1148 im Lichte eines neuen Zeugnisses', *Gesammelte Aufsätze sur Kulturgeschichte Spaniens*, 31 (1984), 136ff.

54. Gerhoh of Reichersberg, *De Investigatione Antichristi*, MGH, Libelli de lite, 3, 374ff., 380ff.; *Annales Herbipolenses*, MGH, Scriptores, 16, 3; Bernard of Clairvaux, *De Consideratione II*, 1, in Migne, *Patrologia Latina* 182, 741.

55. General bibliography for chapter six: Histories of the crusades above p. 293; crusader states below, n. 75; Saladin below, n. 60; collapse of the kingdom of Jerusalem below, n. 66; Chalandon (above, n. 32); Lilie, *Kreuzfahrerstaaten* (above, p. 293); N. Elisséeff, *Nūr ad-Dīn*, 3 vols. (1967); Sivan, *Islam et la croisade* (above, p. 293). On the civil war of 1152 Mayer, 'Queen Melisende' (above, n. 43). R. C. Smail, 'Latin Syria and the West 1149–1187', *Transactions of the Royal Historical Society*, 5th series, 19 (1969), 1ff.

56. Having on one occasion dated the Tripoli assembly to the summer of 1150 and, on another, to the summer of 1152 (Mayer, 'Queen Melisende' above, n. 43, 158ff., Mayer, 'Mélanges', below, n. 59, 138f.), I am now inclined, on the basis of a renewed examination of the text of William of Tyre XVII, 18–19, to believe that there must in fact have been two assemblies at Tripoli, one in 1150 before Melisende's fall from power, dealing with the Antioch marriage problem, and a second one after her fall, dealing with a marital crisis in the ruling family of Tripoli (see above, p. 112). After reporting the first matter William expressly says that everybody returned home. Since he then goes on to report the second, this implies that there must also have been a second assembly.

57. On the status of the double county of Jaffa-Ascalon dealt with above, p. 112, see H. E. Mayer, 'The Double County of Jaffa and Ascalon: One Fief or Two?', *Crusade and Settlement* (above, p. 293), p. 181ff., to be supplemented by *Livre de Jean d'Ibelin* c. 177, *RHC Lois* i, 279f., expounding his theory that the 'quatre baronnies' (see above, p. 159), of which Jaffa-Ascalon was one, were indivisible. On the dealings of Hugh II of Jaffa with regard to Ascalon see Mayer, *Bistümer* (below, n. 90), 137–56. On Reynald of Châtillon see G. Schlumberger, *Renaud de Châtillon* (2nd edn. 1923); B. Hamilton, 'The Elephant of Christ: Reynald of Châtillon', *Studies in Church History*, 15 (1978), 97ff., puts his career after his return from captivity in a more favourable light (see above, p. 115). In view of Reynald's open defiance of the crown (see above, p. 134) it is not easy to share this opinion.

58. The 18th of February, was, it is true, the feast of Bishop Simeon of Jerusalem, a local saint, but none of the sources mentions this. Indeed the Old French translator of William of Tyre doing his best to associate the coronation with a festival of the Church says that it took place a few days before the feast of the *cathedra Petri* (22 February).

59. H. E. Mayer, 'Ein Deperditum König Balduins III. von Jerusalem als Zeugnis seiner Pläne zur Eroberung Ägyptens', *Deutsches Archiv*, 36 (1980), 549ff.; G. Schlumberger, *Campagnes du roi Amaury de Jérusalem en Égypte* (1906); G. Wiet, *L'Égypte arabe de la conquête arabe à la conquête ottomane* (Paris, no date); H. E. Mayer, 'Mélanges sur l'histoire du royaume latin de Jérusalem' (Part II: 'Le service militaire des vassaux à l'étranger et le financement des campagnes en Syrie du Nord et en Égype au XIIe siècle'), *Mémoires de l'Académie des Inscriptions et Belles-Lettres*, N.S., 5 (1984), 139ff.

60. 'Saladin', *Enzyklopädie des Islam;* 'Ayyubids', *Encyclopedia of Islam*, new edn.; S. Lane-Poole, *Saladin and the Fall of the Kingdom of Jerusalem* (1898); H. A. R. Gibb, 'The Achievement of Saladin', *Bulletin of the John Rylands Library*, 35 (1952), 44ff.; A. S. Ehrenkreutz, *Saladin* (1972; a demythologization which needs to be used with caution; cf. *Speculum*, 49, 1974, 72ff.). Against Gibb's image of Saladin see P. M. Holt, 'Saladin and His Admirers: A Biographical Reassessment', *Bulletin of the School of Oriental and African Studies*, 46 (1983), 235ff. On Saladin in the western sources see J. Hartmann, *Die Persönlichkeit des Sultans Saladin im Urteil der abendländischen Quellen*

(1933). On the cult of Saladin in modern Islam, in particular as a consequence of a Damascus dinner speech by the German emperor William II in 1898, see W. van Kampen, *Studien zur deutschen Türkeipolitik in der Zeit Wilhelms II.* (1968; text of the speech p. 408) and, in more detail, W. Ende, 'Wer ist ein Glaubensheld, wer ist ein Ketzer?' (part II: 'Die Saladins-Legende der Gegenwart'), *Die Welt des Islams*, N.S., 23–4 (1984), 79ff.; H. Möhring, *Saladin und der Dritte Kreuzzug* (1980); R. B. C. Huygens, 'La campagne de Saladin en Syrie du Nord (1188)', *Colloque d'Apamée de Syrie. Bilan de recherches archéologiques* (1972), 273ff. On Saladin's army see D. Ayalon, 'Aspects of the Mamluk Phenomenon', *Der Islam*, 53 (1976), 196ff.; 54 (1977), 1ff., and Ayalon, 'Mamlukyyat', *Jerusalem Studies in Arabic and Islam*, 2 (1980), 321 ff.; M. C. Lyons and D. E. P. Jackson, *Saladin. The Politics of the Holy War* (1982); A. Hartmann, *an-Nāṣir li Dīn Allāh (1180–1225). Politik, Religion, Kultur in der späten ʿAbbāsidenzeit* (1975); E. Sivan, 'Saladin et le Calife al-Nāsir', *Scripta Hierosolymitana*, 23 (1972), 126ff.; A. Helbig, *al-Qāḍī al-Fāḍil* (1908).

61. Lilie's theory (*Kreuzfahrerstaaten*, above, p. 293, 317ff.) presupposes both that Amalric purposely betrayed Byzantium more than once, i.e. in 1168 as well as 1169, and that Byzantium failed to notice. If Amalric really had set out prematurely in 1168 only in order to be able to conquer Egypt without Byzantine help, it is hard to see why the Byzantines should once again lay out enormous sums of money for the conquest of Egypt the following year, and even give their commander written instructions to do nothing without Amalric's approval. Lilie's thesis (p. 323) is mainly based on his view that Amalric, on the evidence of his charter for Pisa of 17 September 1169, did not want a Byzantine fleet at all, but instead wished to conquer Egypt with Pisan aid. But M. L. Favreau-Lilie's forthcoming book on the Italians in the crusader states (below, n. 96) will show that in 1169 Amalric still wanted to abide by the terms of the 1168 treaty with Byzantium. In a startling interpretation of the charter for Pisa and combining this with the evidence of Amalric's 1169 charter for the Hospitallers—which I had previously misunderstood—Favreau-Lilie is able to demonstrate how Egypt was to be partitioned in 1168 and 1169: Jerusalem was to get the interior together with Cairo and Bilbais and Rosetta as its only port, while all the rest was to go to Byzantium. That Amalric issued his charter for Pisa of 1169 in order to create, as I believe, a counterweight to Byzantium, is denied by both Lilie and Favreau-Lilie on the grounds that there is no direct evidence for Pisan participation in the campaign.

62. J. L. La Monte, 'To What Extent was the Byzantine Empire the Suzerain of the Latin Crusading States?', *Byzantion*, 7 (1932), 253ff.; S. Runciman, 'The Visit of King Amalric I to Constantinople in 1171', *Outremer* (below, n. 75), 153ff.

63. M. G. S. Hodgson, *The Order of the Assassins* (1955); B. Lewis, *The Assassins. A Radical Sect in Islam* (1968); C. E. Nowell, 'The Old Man of the Mountain', *Speculum*, 22 (1947), 497ff; F. M. Chambers, 'The Troubadours and the Assassins', *Modern Language Notes*, 64 (1949), 245ff.; J. Hauzinsky, *Muzułmanska sekta asasynów w europejskim pismiennictwie wieków srednich* (The Islamic Sect of the Assassins in European Medieval Literature, 1978).

64. H. Möhring, 'Heiliger Krieg und politische Pragmatik: Salahadinus Tyrannus', *Deutsches Archiv*, 39 (1983), 417ff., argues unconvincingly on the basis of an alleged letter of condolence from Saladin to King Baldwin IV, known only in a 15th-c. Arabic chancery manual, that towards the end of Amalric's rule he was in formal alliance with Saladin. But, other inconsistencies apart, Möhring's theory obliges him to postulate an 1174 treaty violation by Amalric because he maintains that in that year Amalric was involved in a pro-Fatimid plot against Saladin, once again planning the conquest of Egypt, this time in alliance with the Normans.

65. C. Brand, 'The Byzantines and Saladin, 1185–1192: Opponents of the Third Crusade', *Speculum*, 37 (1962), 167ff., interpreting the alliance as the corner-stone of Byzantine foreign policies 1185–92, certainly overstates his case; see e.g. *Deutsches Archiv*, 18, 601f.

But to deny that the alliance ever existed (H. Möhring, 'Byzanz zwischen Sarazenen und Kreuzfahrern', *Das Heilige Land im Mittelalter*, ed. W. Fischer and J. Schneider, 1982, 64ff.) goes too far. The letter written by the *qadi* al-Fadil to Saladin in the summer of 1189 merely asserts that the alliance with Byzantium was (now) valueless. The most thoughtful discussion of this problem is to be found in Lilie, *Kreuzfahrerstaaten* (above, p. 293), 218ff. and in Lilie and Speck, *Varia I* (above, n. 22), 151ff.

66. On the following cf. M. W. Baldwin, *Raymond III of Tripolis and the Fall of Jerusalem* (1936); H. van Werveke, 'Filips van de Elzas en Willem van Tyrus', *Mededelingen van de koninkl. Vlaamse Academie voor Wetenschappen, Letteren en Schone Kunsten van Belgie*, Kl. der letteren, 33 (1971), 3ff. (an apologia on Philip's behalf); A. C. Krey, 'William of Tyre', *Speculum*, 16 (1936), 149ff.; R. Hiestand, 'Zum Leben und zur Laufbahn Wilhelms von Tyrus', *Deutsches Archiv*, 34 (1978), 345ff.; P. W. Edbury and J. G. Rowe, 'William of Tyre and the Patriarchal Election of 1180', *English Historical Review*, 93 (1978), 1ff. Literature on Reynald of Châtillon above, n. 57. H. E. Mayer, 'Die Herrschaftsbildung in Hebron', *Zeitschrift des Deutschen Palästina-Vereins*, 101 (1985). On Agnes of Courtenay see Hamilton, 'Queens of Jerusalem' (above, n. 32), and Hamilton, 'The Titular Nobility of the Latin East: The case of Agnes of Courtenay', *Crusade and Settlement* (above, p. 293), 197ff. (both very good); R. L. Nicholson, *Joscelyn III and the Fall of the Crusader States* (1973) needs to be used with extreme caution; cf. *Deutsches Archiv*, 30, 596; B. Z. Kedar, 'The Patriarch Eraclius', *Outremer* (below, n. 75), 177ff.; Kedar, 'The General Tax of 1183 in the Crusading Kingdom of Jerusalem: Innovation or Adaptation?', *English Historical Review*, 89 (1974), 339ff.; H. E. Mayer, 'Latins, Muslims, and Greeks in the Latin Kingdom of Jerusalem', *History*, 63 (1978), 175ff.; R. Hiestand, 'Chronologisches zur Geschichte des Königreichs Jerusalem im 12. Jh.', *Deutsches Archiv*, 35 (1979), 542ff. Literature on Saladin above, n. 60. F. Groh, *Der Zusammenbruch des Reiches Jerusalem* (1909); L. Usseglio, *I marchesi di Monferrato in Italia ed in Oriente durante i secoli XII e XIII*, 2 vols. (1926); J. Riley-Smith, 'Corrado marchese di Monferato', *Dizionario biografico degli Italiani*, 29 (1983), 381ff. (an excellent article). On the battle of Hattin see R. C. Smail, 'The Predicaments of Guy of Lusignan, 1183–1187', *Outremer* (below, n. 75), 159ff.; H. E. Mayer, 'Henry II of England and the Holy Land', *English Historical Review*, 97 (1982), 721ff.; J. Prawer, 'La bataille de Hattin', *Israel Exploration Quarterly*, 14 (1964), 160ff., and P. Herde, 'Die Kämpfe bei den Hörnern von Hittin und der Untergang des Kreuzritterheeres', *Römische Quartalschrift für christl. Altertumskunde u. Kirchengeschichte*, 61 (1966), 1ff. with conflicting views on the course of the battle; B. Z. Kedar, 'Ein Hilferuf aus Jerusalem vom September 1187', *Deutsches Archiv*, 38 (1982), 112f.

67. Ehrenkreutz, *Saladin* (above, n. 60), 204ff., mistakenly believes that there was only one siege of Tyre and criticizes Saladin on the grounds that it came too late. In fact Tyre was besieged for the first time in August 1187. The attempt by Möhring, *Saladin* (above, n. 60), 36ff., to bring this siege forward to July has been disproved by Lilie, *Varia I* (above, n. 22), 163ff., especially 164, n. 80.

68. General bibliography for chapter seven: H. E. Mayer, 'Die Stiftung Herzog Heinrichs des Löwen für das Hl. Grab', in *Heinrich der Löwe*, ed. W. D. Mohrmann (1980), 307ff.; Mayer, Henry II (above, n. 66). On the crusading taxes see Kedar, 'General Tax' (above, n. 66) and below, n.69; P. Zerbi, *Papato, impero e 'respublica christiana' dal 1187 al 1198* (2nd edn., 1980); Lamma (above, n. 48); R. Chazan, 'Emperor Frederick I, the Third Crusade and the Jews', *Viator*, 8 (1977), 83ff.; G. Kleemann, *Papst Gregor VIII.* (1912); Y. Congar, 'Henry de Marcy, abbé de Clairvaux, cardinal-évêque d'Albano et légat pontifical', *Studia Anselmiana*, 43 (1958), 1ff.; A. Cartellieri, *Philipp II. August, König von Frankreich*, vols. 1 and 2 (1900–6); J. Richard, 'Philippe Auguste, la Croisade et le royaume', *La France de Philippe Auguste*, ed. R. H. Bautier (1982), 411ff.; H. van Werweke, 'La contribution de la Flandre et du Hainaut à la troisième croisade', *Moyen*

Age, 78 (1972), 55ff.; J. Gillingham, *Richard the Lionheart* (1978); K. Norgate, *Richard the Lion Heart* (1924). J. O. Prestwich, 'Richard Coeur de Lion: *rex bellicosus*', in *Riccardo Cuor di Leone nella storia e nella leggenda* (Accademia Nazionale dei Lincei. Problemi attuali di scienze e di cultura 253, 1981) 3ff. J. Gillingham, 'Richard I and the Science of War in the Middle Ages', *War and Government in the Middle Ages* (Festschrift J. O. Prestwich, 1984), 78ff.; H. E. Mayer, 'Die Kanzlei Richards I. von England auf dem Dritten Kreuzzug', *Mitteilungen des österreichischen Instituts für Geschichtsforschung*, 85 (1977), 22ff.; J. Gillingham, 'Roger of Howden on Crusade', in *Medieval Historical Writing in the Christian and Islamic Worlds*, ed. D. O. Morgan (1982), 60ff.; H. Fichtenau, 'Akkon, Zypern und das Lösegeld für Richard Löwenherz', *Archiv für österreichische Geschichte*, 125 (1966), 11ff. On the rebuilding of Ascalon see Pringle, 'Walls of Ascalon' (below, n. 100). A. J. Forey, 'The Military Order of St. Thomas of Acre', *English Historical Review*, 92 (1977), 481ff. On Saladin see above, n. 60; on Conrad of Montferrat above, n. 66; on Henry of Champagne below, n. 126.

69. F. A. Cazel, 'The Tax of 1185 in Aid of the Holy Land', *Speculum*, 30 (1955), 385ff.

70. E. Eickhoff, *Friedrich Barbarossa im Orient. Kreuzzug und Tod Friedrichs I.* (1977); S. O. Riezler, 'Der Kreuzzug Kaiser Friedrichs I.', *Forschungen zur deutschen Geschichte*, 10 (1870), 1ff.; K. Fischer, *Geschichte des Kreuzzuges Kaiser Friedrichs I.* (1870). On the German–Byzantine conflict 1189–90, see K. Zimmert, *Byzantinische Zeitschrift*, 12 (1903), 42ff.; 11 (1902), 303ff.; C. Cahen, 'Selǧukides, Turcomans et Allemands au temps de la troisième croisade', *Wiener Zeitschrift für die Kunde des Morgenlandes*, 56 (1960), 21ff.; P. Scheffer-Boichorst, 'Das Grab Barbarossas', *Gesammelte Schriften*, 2 (1905), 154ff.

71. M. Tumler, *Der Deutsche Orden im Werden, Wachsen und Wirken bis 1400* (1955); W. Hubatsch, 'Montfort und die Bildung des Deutschordensstaates im Heiligen Lande', *Nachrichten der Akademie der Wissenschaften in Göttingen*, phil.-hist. Klasse 1966, 161ff.; M. L. Favreau, *Studien zur Frühgeschichte des Deutschen Ordens* (no date [1974]); U. Arnold, 'Entstehung und Frühzeit des Deutschen Ordens', *Die geistlichen Ritterorden Europas*, ed. J. Fleckenstein and M. Hellmann (1980), 81ff.; Arnold, 'Jerusalem und Akkon. Zur Frage von Kontinuität oder Neugründung des Deutschen Ordens 1190', *Mitteilungen des Instituts für österreichische Geschichtsforschung*, 86 (1978), 416ff. It is true that Arnold upholds the case for continuity only by splitting Henry, head of the community at Acre, in two, in order to be able to place between these two halves a Master Ulrich who Favreau regards as the head of the German hospital in Jerusalem. Arnold also demands proof that the Jerusalem hospital held land in Germany. Although such proof does not exist, it is unthinkable that, for example, Conrad III in 1125 and 1148 or Frederick Barbarossa in 1148, should not have made donations to the German hospital in Jerusalem. Even Arnold admits, however, that the old arguments in favour of the theory of continuity will no longer do.

72. Peter of Blois, *De Hierosolymitana peregrinatione acceleranda*, in Migne, *Patrologia Latina*, 207, 1057ff.; *Passio Reginaldi*, ibid. 957ff.; Radulf Niger, *De re militari et triplici via peregrinationis Ierosolimitane*, ed. L. Schmugge (1977).

73. The attempt by P. E. Williams, 'The Assassination of Conrad of Montferrat: Another Suspect?', *Traditio*, 26 (1970), 381ff., to lay the crime at the door of Henry of Champagne, merely because, as Conrad's successor, he profited from it, is not helpful. It was by no means certain that he would be the next husband of Conrad's widow, and it was on this that the succession depended.

74. H. Toeche, *Kaiser Heinrich VI.* (1876); E. Traub, *Der Kreuzzugsplan Kaiser Heinrichs VI.* (1910); W. Leonhardt, *Der Kreuzzugsplan Kaiser Heinrichs VI.* (1913); but cf. Dölger, *Kaiserregesten*, no. 1619. On Lesser Armenia see *The Cilician Kingdom of Armenia*, ed. T. S. R. Boase (1978).

75. Particularly important for the kingdom of Jerusalem in general are: J. Prawer, *Histoire du royaume latin de Jérusalem*, 2 vols. (1969–70); J. Richard, *Le royaume latin de Jérusalem*

(1953; English translation as: *The Latin Kingdom of Jerusalem*, 2 vols., 1979); R. Röhricht, *Geschichte des Königreichs Jerusalem* (1898, still of fundamental importance); J. Prawer, *Crusader Institutions* (1980); *Outremer—Studies in the History of the Crusading Kingdom of Jerusalem Presented to Joshua Prawer*, ed. B. Z. Kedar *et al.* (1982). Setton, *Crusades* (above, p. 292), vol. 5: *The Impact of the Crusades on the Near East* with important chapters by J. Prawer and J. Richard, reached me only in January 1986 and thus too late for me to take account of their findings. J. L. La Monte, *Feudal Monarchy in the Latin Kingdom of Jerusalem* (1932); J. Riley-Smith, *The Feudal Nobility and the Kingdom of Jerusalem* (1973); H. E. Mayer, *Probleme des lateinischen Königreichs Jerusalem* (1983); M. Benvenisti, *The Crusaders in the Holy Land* (1970); *Crusade and Settlement* (above, p. 293), part II, *passim;* A. Ben-Ami, *Social Change in a Hostile Environment. The Crusaders' Kingdom of Jerusalem* (1969) is unhelpful. J. Prawer and M. Benvenisti, *Atlas of Israel* IX/10 (1970) contains an index of place names; C. Du Cange, *Les familles d'Outremer*, ed. E. G. Rey (1869) is the basic work on genealogy; S. De Sandoli, *Corpus inscriptionum crucesignatorum Terrae Sanctae* (1974). For reasons of space this chapter concentrates on the kingdom of Jerusalem. On the other crusader states see: C. Cahen, *La Syrie du Nord à l'époque des croisades et la principauté franque d'Antioche* (1940); J. Richard, *Le comté de Tripoli sous la dynastie toulousaine* (1945); Richard, 'Le comté de Tripoli dans les chartes du Fonds de Porcellet', *Bibliothèque de l'École des Chartes*, 130 (1972), 339ff. On Cyprus see below, n. 123.

76. On the history of the settlement see J. Riley-Smith, 'Earliest crusaders' (above, n. 32); J. Prawer, 'The Assise de Teneure and the Assise de Vente. A Study of the Landed Property in the Latin Kingdom', *Economic History Review*, 2nd series, 4 (1951), 77ff.; Prawer, 'The Settlement of the Latins in Jerusalem', *Speculum*, 27 (1952), 490ff.; Prawer, 'Colonization Activities in the Latin Kingdom of Jerusalem', *Revue belge de philologie et d'histoire*, 29 (1951), 1063ff.; R. B. C. Huygens, *De constructione castri Saphet. Construction et fonctions d'un château fort franc en Terre Sainte* (1981). For differing views see D. Pringle, 'Reconstructing the Castle of Safad', *Palestine Exploration Quarterly*, 117 (1985); J. Prawer, 'Jewish Resettlement in Crusader Jerusalem', *Ariel. A Review of Arts and Sciences in Israel*, no. 19 (1967), 60ff.

77. Prawer, *Crusader Institutions* (above, n. 75), 11f., 351f. Richard, *Documents chypriotes* (below, n. 123), 67; Richard, 'Fonds de Porcellet' (above, n. 75), 361ff.; Favreau-Lilie, 'Landesausbau' (above, n. 45), 79, n. 63; Mayer, *Bistümer* (below, n. 90), 77, 176. For a different interpretation Riley-Smith, *Feudal Nobility* (above, n. 75), 7 and Riley-Smith, 'Earliest crusaders' (above, n. 32), 734f.

78. *Tenure en bourgeoisie*, also known as *héritage*, was the principal legal institution under which free, non-noble Franks held property predominantly consisting of real estate within or near towns or Frankish settlements. The nobility also held genuine *héritages* but they often tried to represent feudal holdings as *héritages* because they were very much simpler to alienate than fiefs.

79. The number of inhabitants in medieval Acre is disputed, and will remain so until the military establishment allows archaeologists to determine the course of the Eastern wall of the city. Prawer, *Crusader Institutions* (above, n. 75), 182, 380f. gives an estimate of 40,000 Latins (i.e. not counting members of other creeds), whereas D. Jacoby, 'Crusader Acre' (below, n. 96), 41, without making an estimate of population, calculated that the town covered an area of 33 hectares. Inevitably this would necessitate a drastic downward revision of Prawer's population estimate, because the density of even a population of 10,000 would be 30,000 per square kilometre (for comparison: the density in New York is 9,500 per square kilometre on average, but 25,000 in Manhattan). Yet a figure as low as 10,000 may be too little since even at a relatively early date the population seems to have spread beyond the city walls. By 1120 there is charter evidence for a suburb (*suburbium*) of Acre and this cannot be explained away simply by assuming that the suburb consisted only of a few houses at a crossroads (so D. Jacoby, 'Suburb of Acre',

Outremer, above, n. 75, 206f.). The reader cannot be warned strongly enough against the hollow demographic speculations advanced by J. C. Russell, 'The Population of the Crusader States', in Setton, *Crusades* (above, p. 292), 5, 295ff., a chapter in which 'perhaps' and 'probably' are, perhaps, the most frequently used words. We are told that Syria (are we to include Palestine in this or not?) included 110,000 square kilometres of inhabited area settled by 2.3 million villagers (not counting townspeople) in 11,000 villages! (But we have only *c.* 900 identified place names for the whole of Crusader Palestine). One also finds such gems as a statement that the fortress of Krak des Chevaliers in North Syria (above, p. 88) covered 35 hectares (p. 306)—though this makes the castle as big as his estimate for the whole of Beirut on the following page. The reference is in reality to Kerak in Jordan and indicates the area of the whole town, the fortress of which is much smaller (*c.* 220 × 100 metres).

80. A. D. Von den Brincken, *Die "Nationes Christianorum Orientalium" im Verständnis der lateinischen Historiographie von der Mitte des 12. Jh. bis in die zweite Hälfte des 14. Jh.* (1973); M. R. Morgan, 'The Meaning of Old French Polain, Latin Pullanus', *Medium Aevum*, 48 (1979), 40ff.

81. On the king and nobility see J. Prawer, 'Les premiers temps de la féodalité dans le royaume de Jérusalem', *Tijdschrift voor rechtsgeschiedenis*, 22 (1954), 401ff.; Prawer, 'La noblesse et le régime féodale du royaume latin de Jérusalem', *Le Moyen Age*, 65 (1959), 41ff.; Prawer, 'Étude sur le droit des Assises de Jérusalem: droit de confiscation et d'exhérédation', *Revue historique de droit français et étranger*, 4th series, 39 (1961), 520ff.; 4th series, 40 (1962), 29ff. All of these studies are now available in English in Prawer, *Crusader Institutions* (above, n. 75); J. Riley-Smith, 'Further Thoughts on Baldwin II's établissement on the Confiscation of Fiefs', *Crusade and Settlement* (above, p. 293), 176ff. On the feudal geography see R. Röhricht, 'Studien zur mittelalterlichen Geographie und Topographie Syriens', *Zeitschrift des Deutschen Palästina-Vereins*, 10 (1887), 195ff. and the much more penetrating articles by G. Beyer in the same journal (Mayer, *Bibliographie* above, p. 292, nos. 3012, 3019, 3028, 3057, 3062, 4402).

82. Edbury and Rowe, 'William of Tyre' (above, n. 66), 11f. deny that this was the standard procedure. Hiestand, 'Wilhelm von Tyrus' (above, n. 66), 350f., has, however, argued convincingly against these doubts; cf. also Kedar, 'Eraclius' (above, n. 66), 188.

83. On crusader sealing practice in general H. E. Mayer, *Das Siegelwesen in den Kreuzfahrerstaaten* (Abhandlungen der Bayerischen Akademie der Wissenschaften, phil.-hist. Klasse, N.F. 18, 1978), especially 59ff. On the baronial coinage see D. M. Metcalf, *Coinage* (below, n. 100), 24ff. and P. W. Edbury, in *Coinage in the Latin East*, ed. Metcalf and Edbury (1980), 50ff. (well worth reading).

84. M. Greilsammer, 'Structure and Aims of the Livre au Roi', *Outremer* (above, n. 75), 218ff.

85. The Assises of the Haute Cour: *RHC Lois* 1; M. Grandclaude, *Étude critique sur les livres des Assises de Jérusalem* (1923).

86. J. Richard, 'Les statu de femme dans l'Orient latin', *Recueils de la Société Jean Bodin*, 12 (1962), 377ff.

87. Riley-Smith, *Feudal Nobility* (above, n. 75), 40–98; Riley-Smith, 'Some Lesser Officials in Latin Syria', *English Historical Review*, 87 (1972), 1ff.; Riley-Smith, 'The survival in Latin Palestine of Muslim administration', *The Eastern Mediterranean Lands in the Period of the Crusades*, ed. P. M. Holt (1977), 9ff.

88. Metcalf, *Coinage* (below, n. 100), 9ff.; A. A. Gordus and D. M. Metcalf, 'Neutron activation analysis of the gold coinage of the Crusader states', *Metallurgy in Numismatics*, 1 (1980), 119ff.; P. Balog and J. Yvon, 'Monnaies à légendes arabes de l'Orient latin', *Revue numismatique*, 6th series, 1 (1958), 133ff. The theory of A. S. Ehrenkreutz, 'Arabic Dinars Struck by the Crusaders', *Journal of Economic and Social History of the Orient*, 7 (1964), 167ff., that with their poor imitations the crusaders intended to undermine the Fatimid currency, is now generally rejected.

89. R. C. Smail, *Crusading Warfare* (1956). See also the works cited above, n. 45. P. W. Edbury, 'Feudal Obligations in the Latin East', *Byzantion*, 47 (1977), 328ff.; Mayer, 'Mélanges' (above, n. 59), 93ff.; Gillingham, 'Science of War' (above, n. 68).

90. W. Hotzelt, *Kirchengeschichte Palästinas im Zeitalter der Kreuzzüge* (1940); G. Fedalto, *La Chiesa latina in Oriente*, 3 vols. (1977–8); B. Hamilton, *The Latin Church in the Crusader States. The Secular Church* (1980); R. Hiestand, *Vorarbeiten zum Oriens pontificius*, 3 vols. (1972–85); Hiestand, *Die päpstlichen Legaten auf den Kreuzzügen und in den Kreuzfahrerstaaten vom Konzil von Clermont bis zum vierten Kreuzzug (Habilitationsschrift* Kiel 1972, typescript; forthcoming); H. E. Mayer, *Bistümer, Klöster und Stifte im Königreich Jerusalem* (1977); Ch. Coüasnon, *The Church of the Holy Sepulchre* (1974); V. C. Corbo, *Il Santo Sepolcro di Gerusalemme*, 3 vols. (1981); B. Z. Kedar, 'Palmarée, abbaye clunisienne du XIIe siècle en Galilée', *Revue bénédictine*, 93 (1983), 260ff.; H. E. Mayer, 'Sankt Samuel auf dem Freudenberge und sein Besitz', *Quellen und Forschungen aus italienischen Archiven und Bibliotheken*, 44 (1964), 35ff.; B. Hamilton, 'The Cistercians in the Crusader States', in Hamilton, *Monastic Reform, Catharism and the Crusades* (1979), no. X; B. Z. Kedar, 'Gerard of Nazareth, a Neglected Twelfth-Century Writer in the Latin East', *Dumbarton Oaks Papers*, 37 (1983), 55f.; E. Friedman, *The Latin Hermits of Mount Carmel* (1979); H. E. Mayer, 'Das Pontifikale von Tyrus und die Krönung der lateinischen Könige von Jerusalem', *Dumbarton Oaks Papers*, 21 (1967), 141ff.; Runciman (above, n. 1). Von den Brincken (above, n. 80); P. Kawerau, *Die jakobitische Kirche im Zeitalter der syrischen Renaissance*, 2nd edn. (1960); R. W. Crawford, 'William of Tyre and the Maronites', *Speculum*, 30 (1955), 222ff.; K. S. Salibi, 'The Maronite Church in the Middle Ages and its Union with Rome', *Oriens christianus*, 42 (1958), 92ff.; Salibi, 'The Maronites of Lebanon under Frankish and Mameluk Rule', *Arabica*, 4 (1957), 288ff. On the 'Easter Fire miracle' see A. S. Tritton, 'The Easter Fire of Jerusalem', *Journal of the Royal Asiatic Society* (1963), 249ff.; S. Schein (below, n. 138).

91. R. B. C. Huygens, 'Guillaume de Tyr étudiant. Un chapitre (XIX, 12) de son "Histoire" retrouvé', *Latomus*, 21 (1962), 811ff. On the statutes of Odo de Châteauroux see B. Z. Kedar, 'Ecclesiastical Legislation in the Kingdom of Jerusalem: the Statutes of Jaffa (1253) and Acre (1254)', *Crusade and Settlement* (above, p. 293), 230, n. 19, and Hill, *Cyprus* (below, n. 123), 3, 1067f.

92. R. Hiestand, 'Legat, Kaiser und Basileus', *Aus Reichsgeschichte und Nordischer Geschichte* (1972), 141ff.

93. J. Prawer, 'Étude préliminaire sur les sources et la composition du "Livre des Assises" des Bourgeois', *Revue historique de droit français et étranger*, 4th series, 32 (1954), 198ff., 358ff.; Prawer, *Crusader Institutions* (above, n. 75), 263ff.

94. R. B. Patterson, 'The Early Existence of the funda and catena in the Twelfth Century', *Speculum*, 39 (1964), 474ff., argued, but on insufficient grounds (cf. H. E. Mayer, *Historische Zeitschrift*, Sonderheft 3, 1969, 715) for an earlier origin of these courts. What must have existed at this earlier stage were the fiscal offices known as *funda* and *catena* but hardly the courts which developed out of them.

95. J. L. La Monte, 'The Communal Movement in Syria in the Thirteenth Century', *Haskins Anniversary Essays* (1929), 117ff.; J. Prawer, *Crusader Institutions* (above, n. 75), 46ff. J. Riley-Smith, 'The Assise sur la ligece and the Commune of Acre', *Traditio*, 27 (1971), 179ff.; H. E. Mayer, 'On the Beginnings of the Communal Movement in the Holy Land: the Commune of Tyre', *Traditio*, 24 (1968), 443ff.; Mayer, 'Zwei Kommunen in Akkon?', *Deutsches Archiv*, 26 (1979), 434ff.; J. Richard, 'La féodalité de l'Orient latin et le mouvement communal: un état des questions', *Structures féodales et féodalisme dans l'Occident méditerranéen (Xe–XIIIe siècles)* (1980), 660ff.; J. Riley-Smith, 'A Note on Confraternities in the Latin Kingdom of Jerusalem', *Bulletin of the Institute of Historical Research*, 44 (1971), 301ff.; cf. Mayer, *Deutsches Archiv*, 27, 615f.; J. Richard, 'La confrérie des Mosserins d'Acre et les marchands de

Mossoul au XIIIe siècle', *L'Orient syrien*, 11 (1966), 451ff.; Richard, 'La confrérie de la croisade: à propos d'un épisode de la première croisade', *Études de civilisation médiévale* (Mélanges E. R. Labande, 1974), 617ff.

96. M. L. Favreau-Lilie, *Die Italiener im Hl. Land vom Ersten Kreuzzug bis zum Tode Heinrichs von Champagne* (forthcoming 1988) will be fundamental. In addition H. E. Mayer, *Marseilles Levantehandel und ein akkonensisches Fälscheratelier des 13. Jh.* (1972); Favreau, 'Heinrich von Champagne' (below, n. 126). Favreau, 'Italienische Levante-Piraterie' (below, n. 126); J. Riley-Smith, 'Government in Latin Syria and the Commercial Privileges of Foreign Merchants', in D. Baker, *Relations between East and West in the Middle Ages* (1973), 109ff.; J. Prawer, 'I Veneziani e le colonie veneziane nel regno latino di Gerusalemme', *Venezia e il Levante fino al sec. XV*, 1 (1973), 625ff.; Mayer and Favreau (above, n. 37). D. Jacoby, 'L'expansion occidentale dans le Levant: les Vénitiéns à Acré dans la seconde moitié du treizième siècle', *Journal of Medieval History*, 3 (1977), 225ff.; Jacoby, 'Crusader Acre in the Thirteenth Century: Urban Layout and Topography', *Studi Medievali*, 3rd series, 20 (1979), 1ff.; D. Jacoby, 'Venetian Anchors for Crusader Acre', *The Mariner's Mirror*, 71 (1985), 5ff.; D. Abulafia, 'Crocuses and Crusaders: San Gimignano, Pisa and the Kingdom of Jerusalem', *Outremer* (above, n. 75), 227ff. M. L. Favreau, 'Zur Pilgerfahrt des Grafen Rudolf von Pfullendorf. Ein unbeachteter Originalbrief aus dem Jahre 1180', *Zeitschrift für die Geschichte des Oberrheins*, 123 (1975), 31ff. (on money deposits in Venice); R. H. Bautier, 'La collection de chartes de croisade dite "Collection Courtois"', *Comptes-rendus des séances de l'Académie des Inscriptions et Belles-Lettres* (1956), 382ff.; D. Abulafia, 'Invented Italians in the Courtois Charters', *Crusade and Settlement* (above, p. 293), 135ff.

97. W. Heyd, *Histoire du commerce du Levant au moyen âge*, 2 vols. (1885–6); A. Schaube, *Handelsgeschichte der romanischen Völker des Mittelmeergebiets bis zum Ende der Kreuzzüge* (1906); C. Cahen, 'Un texte peu connu relatif au commerce oriental d'Amalfi au Xe siècle', *Archivio storico per le provinze Napoletane*, 34 (1953–4), 3ff.; Cahen, 'Le commerce d'Amalfi dans le Proche-Orient musulman avant et après la croisade', *Comptes-rendus des séances de l'Académie des Inscriptions et Belles-Lettres* (1977), 291ff.; A. O. Citarella, 'Patterns in Medieval Trade: The Commerce of Amalfi Before the Crusades', *Journal of Economic History*, 28 (1968), 531ff.; B. Z. Kedar, 'Mercanti genovesi in Alessandria d'Egitto negli anni sessanta del secolo XI', *Miscellanea di studi storici*, 2 (1983), 21ff.; E. Bach, *La cité de Gênes au XIIe siècle* (1955); D. Abulafia, 'Marseilles, Acre and the Mediterranean, 1200–1291', *Coinage in the Latin East*, ed. P. W. Edbury and D. M. Metcalf (1980), 19ff.; J. H. Pryor, 'Commenda: the Operation of the Contract in Long-Distance Commerce at Marseilles during the 13th Century', *Journal of European Economic History*, 13 (1984), 397ff.; C. Cahen, 'L'alun avant Phocée', *Revue d'histoire économique et sociale*, 41 (1963), 433ff.; G. Wiet, 'Les marchands d'épices sous les sultans mamlouks', *Cahiers d'histoire égyptienne*, 7 (1955), 81ff.

98. J. Prawer, *Crusader Institutions* (above, n. 75), 201ff.; E. Sivan, 'Réfugiés syro-palestiniens au temps des croisades', *Revue des études islamiques*, 1967 (1968), 135ff.

99. J. Prawer, 'Études de quelques problèmes agraires et sociaux d'une seigneurie croisée au XIIIe siècle', *Byzantion*, 22 (1953), 5ff.; 23 (1953), 143ff.; C. Cahen, 'Le régime rural syrien au temps de la domination franque', *Bulletin de la Faculté des Lettres de Strasbourg*, 29 (1950–1), 286ff.; J. Richard, 'Le casal de Psimolofo et la vie rurale en Chypre au XIVe siècle', *Mélanges d'archéologie et d'histoire*, 59 (1947), 121ff.; J. Riley-Smith, 'Some Lesser Officials in Latin Syria', *English Historical Review*, 87 (1972), 1ff. (an excellent study).

100. M. de Vogüé, *Les églises de Terre Sainte* (1860); C. Enlart, *Les monuments des croisés dans le royaume de Jérusalem*, 2 vols., 2 albums (1925–8). In the future D. Pringle, *Church Buildings of the Crusader Kingdom of Jerusalem: a Corpus* (planned for 1987; in the meantime cf. Pringle, *Revue biblique*, 89, 1982, 92ff.); M. Pillet, 'Notre-Dame de

Tortose', *Syria*, 10 (1929), 40ff. On the main gate of Jerusalem (today called the Damascus Gate) in the crusader period see J. B. Hennessy, 'Preliminary Report on Excavations at the Damascus Gate, Jerusalem, 1964–6', *Levant*, 2 (1970), 22ff.; Deschamps, *Châteaux* (above, n. 45); Z. Goldmann, 'The Hospice of the Knights of St. John in Akko', *Archaeology*, 19, no. 3 (1966), 182ff.; D. Pringle, 'King Richard I and the Walls of Ascalon', *Palestine Exploration Quarterly*, 116 (1984), 133ff.; on earlier building phases at Ascalon see B. Z. Kedar and W. G. Mook, *Israel Exploration Journal*, 28 (1978), 173ff.; D. Pringle, 'Some Approaches to the Study of Crusader Masonry Marks in Palestine', *Levant*, 13 (1981), 173ff.; M. Barash, *Crusader Figural Sculpture in the Holy Land* (1971); *Crusader Art in the Twelfth Century*, ed. J. Folda (1982); H. Buschhausen, *Die süditalienische Bauplastik im Königreich Jerusalem von König Wilhelm II. bis Kaiser Friedrich II.* (1978); cf. on this work the unanimous objections by Folda and Burgoyne, *Art Bulletin*, 63 (1981), 321ff., by Z. Jacoby, *Zeitschrift für Kunstgeschichte*, 47 (1984), 400ff., as well as by Pace (see below); Z. Jacoby, 'Le portail de l'église de l'Annonciation de Nazareth au XIIe siècle', *Monuments et Mémoires de la Fondation E. Piot*, 64 (1981), 141ff.; Z. Jacoby, 'The Tomb of Baldwin V, King of Jerusalem, and the Workshop of the Temple Area', *Gesta*, 18 (1979), 3ff.; Z. Jacoby, 'The Workshop of the Temple Area in Jerusalem in the Twelfth Century: its Origin, Evolution and Impact', *Zeitschrift für Kunstgeschichte*, 45 (1982), 325ff.; V. Pace, 'Sculpture italienne en Terre Sainte ou sculpture des croisés en Italie? A propos d'un livre récent', *Cahiers de civilisation médiévale*, 27 (1984), 251ff., has reservations about the Temple Area Workshop and cautions that monumental sculpture in Apulia needs to be more thoroughly investigated before far-reaching conclusions one way or the other can be drawn. B. Kühnel, 'Steinmetzen aus Fontevrault in Jerusalem', *Wiener Jahrbuch für Kunstgeschichte*, 33 (1980), 83ff. A considerable discussion has developed on the two lintels on the Southern façade of the Church of the Holy Sepulchre: A. Borg, 'Observations on the Historiated Lintel of the Holy Sepulchre, Jerusalem' *Journal of the Warburg and Courtauld Institutes*, 32 (1969), 25ff.; Borg, 'The Holy Sepulchre Lintel', ibid., 35 (1972), 389ff.; N. Kenaan, 'Local Christian Art in Twelfth-Century Jerusalem', *Israel Exploration Journal*, 23 (1973), 167ff., 221ff. Objections by L. Y. Rahmani, 'The Eastern Lintel of the Holy Sepulchre', ibid., 26 (1976), 120ff.; W. Fleischhauer, 'Das romanische Kreuzreliquiar von Denkendorf', *Festschrift Georg Scheja* (1975), 64ff.; H. Meurer, 'Kreuzreliquiare aus Jerusalem', *Jahrbuch der Staatlichen Kunstsammlungen in Baden-Württemberg*, 13 (1976), 7ff.; Meurer, 'Zu den Staurotheken der Kreuzfahrer', *Zeitschrift für Kunstgeschichte*, 48 (1985), 65ff. On Godefroid of Huy see P. C. Claussen, 'Goldschmiede des Mittelalters', *Zeitschrift des Deutschen Vereins für Kunstwissenschaft*, 32 (1978), 49 and 83; D. M. Metcalf, *Coinage of the Crusades and the Latin East in the Ashmolean Museum Oxford* (1983); G. Schlumberger, *Sigillographie de l'Orient latin* (1943); R. B. C. Huygens, *Latijn in Outremer. Een blik op de Latijnse letterkunde der kruisvarderstaten in het Nabije Oosten* (1964); B. Z. Kedar, 'Gerard of Nazareth, a Neglected Twelfth-Century Writer in the Latin East', *Dumbarton Oaks Papers*, 37 (1983), 55ff.; Huygens, 'Guillaume de Tyr étudiant' (above, n. 91); cf. also Huygens, *Studi medievali*, 3rd series, 5 (1964), 1ff., and *Latomus*, 25 (1966), 139ff., as well as *Sacris Erudiri*, 27 (1984), 461ff.; Hiestand, 'Wilhelm von Tyrus' (above, n. 66). The attempt by R. C. Schwinges, *Kreuzzugsideologie und Toleranz. Studien zu Wilhelm von Tyrus* (1977), to turn William into an early champion of tolerance is fundamentally wide of the mark; cf. Mayer, *Deutsches Archiv*, 34, 255ff., and H. Möhring, ibid., 39, 439ff.; D. Jacoby, 'La littérature française dans les états latins de la Mediterranée orientale à l'époque des croisades: diffusion et création', *Essor et fortune de la Chanson de Geste dans l'Europe et l'Orient latin. Actes du IXe Congrès international de la Société Rencesvals pour l'étude des Epopées Romanes* (1984), 617ff.; C. Cahen, 'Le premier cycle de la croisade (Antioche-Jérusalem-Chétifs)', *Le Moyen Age*, 63 (1957), 311ff.; U. T. Holmes and W. M. McLeod, 'Source Problems of the "Chétifs", a Crusade Chanson de Geste', *Romanic Review*, 28 (1937), 99ff.; M. Bertram, 'Johannes von Ancona: ein Jurist des 13. Jh. in den Kreuzfahrerstaaten', *Bulletin of Medieval Canon Law*, N.S., 7 (1977), 49ff.; K. Weitzmann, *Studies in the Arts at Sinai* (1982); Weitzmann, 'Crusader Icons and maniera greca', *Byzanz und der Westen. Studien zur Kunst des europäischen Mittelalters*, ed. I. Hutter (Sitzungsberichte der österreichischen Akademie der Wissenschaften, philos.-hist. Klasse 432, 1984), 143ff.; O. Demus, 'Zum Werk eines venezianischen Malers auf dem Sinai', ibid., 131ff., has advanced the theory that those icons which Weitzmann tentatively ascribed to a Venetian atelier in Acre were the work of the painter of two portraits of saints preserved in the Museo Civico Correr in Venice. Must we, by the way, totally exclude twelfth-century Jerusalem as a place where icons in the *maniera greca* could have been painted? According to the legend about the picture of the Virgin at Sardenai near Damascus which can be traced to the late twelfth century, the icon had been purchased in Jerusalem in the year 1′370 of the era of Alexandria, i.e. AD 1059 (*Magistri Thietmari peregrinatio*, ed. J. C. M. Laurent, *Medii aevi peregrinatores IV*, 2nd edn. 1873, 14: *interrogavit, ubi venundarentur ycone;* cf. Matthew Paris, *Chronica maiora*, 2, 485. On the date 1059 see P. Devos, 'Les premières versions occidentales de la légende de Saidnaia', *Analecta Bollandiana* 65, 1947, 271); J. Folda *et al.*, 'Crusader Frescoes at Crac des Chevaliers and Marqab Castle', *Dumbarton Oaks Papers*, 36 (1982), 177ff. (with fine descriptions but very speculative historical conclusions; cf. Mayer, *Deutsches Archiv*, 40, 370); H. Buchthal, *Miniature Paintings in the Latin Kingdom of Jerusalem* (1957); J. Folda, *Crusader Manuscript Illumination at Saint-Jean d'Acre, 1275–1291* (1976); the attempt to turn Acre into a cultural centre is not convincing. Concerning those manuscripts said to have been illuminated at Acre in the purest Parisian style by a 'Hospitaller Master' who allegedly first illuminated a manuscript of Ste.-Geneviève in Paris but then emigrated to Acre because after the death of St. Louis in 1270 the Paris market is supposed to have collapsed (as if the king were the only patron of the arts in Paris), before finally returning to Europe, see the objections by H. Stahl, *Zeitschrift für Kunstgeschichte*, 43 (1980), 416ff.; R. H. Hoppin, 'The Cypriot–French Repertory of the Manuscript Torino, Biblioteca Nazionale, J.II.9', *Musica Disciplina*, 9 (1957), 79ff. (Edition by the same scholar in 4 vols. under the same title Corpus mensurabilis musicae 21, 1–4, 1960–3); J. Richard, 'La Fauconnerie de Jean de Francières et ses sources', *Le Moyen Age*, 67 (1983), 893ff.

101. J. S. Beddie, 'Books in the East during the Crusades', *Speculum*, 8 (1933), 240ff. The legacy of books by the dean of Chartres in *Gallia christiana*, new edn. 8, col. 1200; A. Maier, 'Die Handschriften der "Ecclesia Sidonensis"', *Manuscripta*, 11 (1967), 39ff; Kedar, 'Gerard of Nazareth' (above, n. 100). On the Castilian Bible see *La Fazienda de Ultramar*, ed. M. Lazar (1965). On the commentary by St. Chrysostom see Hiestand, *Vorarbeiten* (above, p. 292), 3, 201, no. 67. On Aimery and Hugh Etherianus see Migne, *Patrologia Latina* 202, 230f.

102. General bibliography for the Fourth Crusade: Among the monographs the only useful one is D. E. Queller, *The Fourth Crusade. The Conquest of Constantinople 1201–1204* (1978); J. Longnon, *Les compagnons de Villehardouin. Recherches sur les croisés de la quatrième croisade* (1978); D. E. Queller, *Medieval Diplomacy and the Fourth Crusade* (1980); A. Luchaire, *Innocent III. La question d'Orient* (1907); H. Roscher, *Papst Innocenz III. und die Kreuzzüge* (1968; very good). I have not yet seen Ch. M. Brand, 'The Fourth Crusade: Some Recent Interpretations', *Mediaevalia et Humanistica*, 12 (1984), 33ff., although it is said to have appeared. E. Winkelmann, *König Philipp von Schwaben* (1873). On Boniface of Montferrat see Usseglio (above, n. 66); E. H. McNeal, 'Fulk of Neuilly and the Tournament of Ecry', *Speculum*, 28 (1953), 371ff; E. E. Kittel, 'Was Thibaut of Champagne the Leader of the Fourth Crusade?', *Byzantion*, 51 (1981), 557ff; Ch. M. Brand, 'A Byzantine Plan for the Fourth Crusade', *Speculum*, 43 (1968), 462ff; P. Schreiner, 'Genua, Byzanz und der 4. Kreuzzug. Ein

neues Dokument im Staatsarchiv Genua', *Quellen und Forschungen aus italienischen Archiven und Bibliotheken*, 63 (1983), 292ff.; Ch. G. Ferrard, 'The Amount of Constantinopolitan Booty in 1204', *Studi Veneziani*, 13 (1971), 95ff.

103. The best summary of the nineteenth-century debate is E. Gerland, 'Der vierte Kreuzzug und seine Probleme', *Neue Jahrbücher für das klassische Altertum*, 13 (1904), 505ff., now supplemented by D. E. Queller and S. J. Stratton, 'A Century of Controversy on the Fourth Crusade', *Studies in Medieval and Renaissance History*, 6 (1969), 233ff. Also fundamental is W. Norden, *Der vierte Kreuzzug im Rahmen der Beziehungen des Abendlandes zu Byzanz* (1898). Since Gerland wrote the most important contributions have been: E. Faral, 'Geoffrey de Villehardouin: la question de sa sincérité', *Revue historique*, 177 (1936), 537ff.; H. Grégoire, 'The Question of the Diversion of the Fourth Crusade. An Old Controversy solved by a Latin Adverb', *Byzantion*, 15 (1940–41), 158ff.; A. Frolow, *Recherches sur la déviation de la IVe croisade vers Constantinople* (1955); J. Folda, 'The Fourth Crusade, 1201–1203. Some Reconsiderations', *Byzantinoslavica*, 26 (1965), 277ff. (very important). The pope is blamed for the deviation by M. A. Zaborov, *Vizantiiskii vremennik*, N.S., 5 (1952), 152ff., and by S. de Mundo Lo, *Cruzadas en Bizancio. La cuarta cruzada a la luz de la fuentes latinas y orientales* (1957; a Buenos Aires dissertation not often found in European libraries). Innocent III found a tireless and forceful defender in J. Gill, 'Franks, Venetians and Pope Innocent III 1201–1203', *Studi Veneziani*, 12 (1970), 85ff. (see also below, n. 105). Most recent studies on the Venetian share in what happened are: R. Cessi, 'Venezia e la quarta crociata', *Archivio veneto*, 81 (1951), 1ff. and D. E. Queller and G. W. Day, 'Some Arguments in the Defense of the Venetians on the Fourth Crusade', *American Historical Review*, 81 (1976), 717ff.

104. J. Ebersolt, *Orient et Occident*, 2nd edn. (1954), 82ff. If a list of the relics given to the abbey of Corbie in Picardy by the chronicler Robert de Clari were authentic, he would have stolen nearly the whole relic collection of the chapel of the Bucoleon palace in Constantinople.

105. Latin Empire, Venetian, and Genoese possessions: J. Longnon, *L'Empire latin de Constantinople et la principauté de Morée* (1949); E. Gerland, *Geschichte des lateinischen Kaiserreichs von Konstantinopel*, 1 (1905); K. Hopf, *Geschichte Griechenlands vom Beginn des Mittelalters bis auf die neuere Zeit*, 2 vols. (1867–8); R. L. Wolff, *Studies in the Latin Empire of Constantinople* (1976); P. E. Schramm (and R. Elze), *Herrschaftszeichen und Staatssymbolik*, 3 (1956), 837ff.; J. Déer, *Byzantinische Zeitschrift*, 54 (1961), 306ff., places more emphasis on the Byzantine influence on the coronation of the Latin emperors. W. Norden (above p. 293); J. Gill, *Byzantium and the Papacy 1198–1400* (1979; to be used with great caution); N. Oikonomidès, 'La décomposition de l'Empire byzantine à la veille de 1204 et les origines de l'Empire de Nicée: à propos de la "Partitio Romaniae"', *XVe Congrès international d'études byzantines* (1976); R. Pokorny, 'Zwei unedierte Briefe aus der Frühzeit des lateinischen Kaiserreichs von Konstantinopel', *Byzantion*, 55 (1985), 180ff.; R. Spence, 'Gregory IX's Attempted Expeditions to the Latin Empire of Constantinople: the Crusade for the Union of the Latin and Greek Churches', *Journal of Medieval History*, 5 (1979), 163ff.; B. Hendrickx, 'Les institutions de l'Empire latin de Constantinople (1204–1261): La cour et les dignitaires', *Byzantina*, 9 (1977), 187ff.; Hendrickx, 'Les institutions de l'Empire latin de Constantinople (1204–1261): La chancellerie', *Acta classica. Proceedings of the Classical Association of South Africa*, 19 (1976), 123ff.; L. Santifaller, *Beiträge zur Geschichte des Lateinischen Patriarchats von Konstantinopel und der venezianischen Urkunde* (1938); E. A. R. Brown, 'The Cistercians in the Latin Empire of Constantinople and Greece', *Traditio*, 14 (1958), 63ff.; R. Clair, 'Les filles d'Hautecombe dans l'Empire latin de Constantinople', *Analecta sacri ordinis Cisterciensis*, 17 (1961), 261ff.; F. Thiriet, *La Romanie vénitienne au moyen âge* (1959); Thiriet, *Études sur la Romanie gréco-vénitienne (Xe–XVe siècles)* (1977); R. J. Loenertz,

Byzantina et Franco-Graeca, 2 vols., ed. P. Schreiner (1970–8); Loenertz, *Les Ghisi.*
Dynastes vénitiens dans l'Archipel 1207–1390 (1975); M. Balard, *La Romanie génoise*
(XIIe-début du XVe siècle), 2 vols. (1978).

106. Ch. Perrat and J. Longnon, *Actes relatifs à la principauté de Morée 1289–1300* (1967);
J. Longnon and P. Topping, *Documents sur le régime des terres dans la principauté de*
Morée au XIVe siècle (1969); D. Jacoby, *La féodalité en Grèce médiévale. Les Assises de*
Romanie. Sources, application et diffusion (1971); A. Bon, *La Morée franque. Recherches*
historiques, topographiques et archeologiques sur la principauté d'Achaie (1205–1430), 2
vols. (1969); Longnon (above, n. 105). Longnon, 'Le prince de Morée chansonnier',
Romania, 65 (1939), 95ff.; R. J. Loenertz, 'Aux origines du despotat de l'Épire et de la
principauté d'Achaie', *Byzantion*, 43 (1973), 360ff.; P. Topping, *Studies on Latin Greece*
(1977); D. Jacoby, 'The Encounter of Two Societies: Western Conquerors and
Byzantines in the Peloponnesus after the Fourth Crusade', *American Historical Review*,
78 (1973), 873ff.; Jacoby, 'Les états latins en Romanie: phénomènes sociaux et
économiques (1204–1350 environ)', in D. Jacoby, *Recherches sur la Méditerranée*
orientale du XIIe au XVe siècle (1979), no. 1; Jacoby, 'Les archontes grecs et la féodalité
en Morée franque', *Travaux et mémoires*, 2 (1967), 421ff.; G. G. Litavrin, 'Le problème
de la symbiose dans les États latins formés sur le territoire de Byzance (faits sociaux et
économiques 1204–1261)', *XVe Congrès international d'études byzantines* (1976);
E. Dade, *Versuche zur Wiedererrichtung der lateinischen Herrschaft in Konstantinopel*
1261–1310 (1937); D. J. Geanakoplos, *Emperor Michael Palaeologus and the West*
(1959).

107. R. I. Burns, 'The Catalan Company and the European Powers 1305–1311', *Speculum*,
29 (1954), 751ff.; K. M. Setton, *Catalan Domination of Athens*, 2nd edn. (1975); Setton,
Athens in the Middle Ages (1975); D. Jacoby, 'La compagnie catalane et l'État catalane
de Gréce. Quelques aspects de leur histoire', *Journal des Savants* (1966), 78ff.; K. M.
Setton, *Europe and the Levant in the Middle Ages and the Renaissance* (1974); A. E.
Laiou, *Constantinople and the Latins: The Foreign Policy of Andronicus II, 1282–1328*
(1972); Ph. P. Argenti, *The Occupation of Chios by the Genoese and their Administration*
of the Island 1346–1566, 3 vols. (1958); Argenti, 'The Mahona of the Giustiniani.
Genoese Colonialism and the Genoese Relationship with Chios', *Byzantinische*
Forschungen, 6 (1979), 1ff.

108. H. Pissard, *La guerre sainte en pays chrétien* (1912); P. Belperron, *La croisade contre les*
Albigeois et l'union de Languedoc à la France (1942); *Paix de Dieu et guerre sainte en*
Languedoc (1969); N. Housley, *The Italian Crusades. The Papal–Angevin Alliance and*
the Crusades against Christian Lay Powers, 1254–1343 (1982; cf. *Journal of Ecclesiastical*
History, 34, 283f.) is an excellent book, although I am not convinced by that part of it
which attempts to prove that all these 'political' crusades (on this term see now
E. Kennan, 'Innocent III, Gregory IX and Political Crusades: a Study in the
Disintegration of Papal Power', in: *Reform and Authority in the Medieval and*
Reformation Church, 1981, 15ff.) were authentic crusades. In the debate initiated in my
Geschichte der Kreuzzüge (1965), 261ff., and in *The Crusades* (1972), 281ff., between
those, like myself, who advocate a narrow definition of 'crusade' (only to Jerusalem) and
those, like J. Riley-Smith, *What Were the Crusades?* (1977), 11ff. (cf. on this Mayer,
Speculum, 53, 1978, 841ff.), who advocate a wider one (against all enemies of the
Church), Housley comes down squarely on the side of the wider definition. I shall not
carry on this debate in this book except in this note, partly for lack of space, partly
because it would seem to me that the fronts have become hardened on both sides.
Housley (p. 3) dismisses as a 'prejudice' the opinion that these wars disguised as
crusades represented an abuse on the part of the Church. In 'Crusades against
Christians: their Origins and Early Developments, *c.* 1100–1216', *Crusade and*
Settlement (above, p. 293), 17ff., Housley has recently, and with great erudition,
investigated the theoretical and practical approaches towards warfare against heretics

and other non-pagan enemies of the Church as early as the 11th c. But this is to do what Erdmann, *Entstehung* (above, n. 5), 246f. did before him, namely, to put holy war and crusade into the same category. The ecclesiastical abuse lay, it seems to me, not in the fact that Christians were being fought, for one cannot apply to the 13th c. the standards of the Enlightenment, but in the fact that the institution of the crusade was used to finance and conduct such wars. Moreover, in spite of his efforts, Housley is unable to show a plenary indulgence for surviving participants of such wars (as opposed to those killed in them, which was not a novelty) before Innocent III, and it was the plenary indulgence for survivors which was characteristic of the Holy Land crusades. Housley's (p. 23) *pièce de résistance*, Pope Innocent II's promise of reward 'as at the Council of Clermont' made in 1135 for all soldiers participating in a war against Roger II of Sicily, was not a crusading indulgence since all that was remitted at Clermont was penance (above, p. 30), and even Housley admits, though on the grounds of the absence of any evidence for taking the cross and the vow, that there may not have been a crusade in 1135. Many contemporaries believed that the extension of the crusading idea was a scandal—though for an attempt to deny this see Siberry (below, n. 143)—and Housley (p. 24), correctly realizing the danger this presents for his theory, argues that the criticism was in no way representative of public opinion, but merely reflects the attitude of isolated and prejudiced individuals. The discussion during the crusading conference at Cardiff in 1983 showed both that the wide definition of the crusades attracts little support outside England (though see now M. Markowski, 'Crucesignatus: its origins and early usage', *Journal of Medieval History*, 10, 1984, 157ff., who also disregards public opinion and fails to see that what is at issue is not Church doctrine but the extent to which society found that doctrine acceptable) and that in England too there are critical voices, e.g. C. J. Tyerman, 'The Holy Land and the Crusades in the Thirteenth and Fourteenth Centuries', *Crusade and Settlement* (above, p. 293), 105ff.—E. Christiansen, *The Northern Crusade. The Baltic and the Catholic Frontier, 1100–1525* (1980; cf. *English Historical Review*, 97, 122f.).

109. Even more than Miccoli (see below), P. Raedts, 'The Children's Crusade of 1212', *Journal of Medieval History*, 3 (1977), 279ff., denies that the participants were children; he believes that they were lower class adults. Some may have been, but not necessarily either the majority of them or their leaders. It is in the logic of Raedt's argument that he also denies that the idea of innocent children as the 'chosen ones' could have been a formative factor but there are so many contemporary parallels that the contribution of these images to the unfortunate undertaking can hardly be disputed. G. Miccoli, 'La crociata dei fanciulli del 1212', *Studi medievali*, 3rd series, 2 (1961), 407ff.; U. Gäbler, 'Der "Kinderkreuzzug" vom Jahre 1212', *Schweizerische Zeitschrift für Geschichte*, 28 (1978), 1ff., is an iconoclastic study which argues that no crusade was intended, only a pilgrimage to Jerusalem. But this is not what the sources say.

110. General bibliography for the Damietta crusade: H. L. Gottschalk, *al-Kāmil* (above, p. 291); R. Röhricht, *Studien zur Geschichte des fünften Kreuzzuges* (1891); H. Hoogeweg, 'Der Kreuzzug von Damiette', *Mitteilungen des Instituts für österreichische Geschichtsforschung*, 8 (1887), 188ff.; 9 (1888), 249ff.; J. Clausen, *Papst Honorius III.* (1895); J. P. Donovan, *Pelagius and the Fifth Crusade* (1950). On John of Brienne see below, n. 126; P. B. Pixton, 'Die Anwerbung des Heeres Christi: Prediger des Fünften Kreuzzuges in Deutschland', *Deutsches Archiv*, 34 (1978), 166ff.; J. A. Brundage, 'The Crusader's Wife: A Canonistic Quandary', *Studia Gratiana*, 12 (1967), 425ff.; Brundage, 'The Crusaders Wife Revisited', ibid. 14 (1967), 241ff.

111. Kedar, *Crusade and Mission* (above, p. 292), 213, n. 56 pointed out that as early as 1909 P. Alphandéry showed this to be no more than an isolated rhetorical flourish. But in fact Alphandéry later changed his mind and I am here adopting the position he took in his *La chrétienté et la croisade* (above, p. 292), 2, 150.

314   Notes

112. F. Kempf, 'Das Rommersdorfer Briefbuch des 13. Jh.', *Mitteilungen des österreichischen Instituts für Geschichtsforschung*, Ergänzungsband, 12 (1933), 502ff.

113. The decree is printed in Mansi, *Sacrorum conciliorum nova et amplissima collectio*, 22, 1058ff. On the crusading taxes see A. Gottlob, *Die päpstlichen Kreuzzugssteuern des 13. Jahrhunderts* (1892).

114. M. Roncaglia, 'San Francesco d'Assisi in Oriente', *Studi Francescani*, 50 (1953), 97ff.; Roncaglia, *St. Francis of Assisi and the Middle East*, 3rd edn. (1957); G. Basetti-Sani, *Mohammed et St.-François* (1959). L. Lemmens, *Die Franziskaner auf dem Sion (1336–1551)*, 2nd edn. (1925); O. van der Vat, *Die Anfänge der Franziskanermissionen und ihre Weiterentwicklung im Nahen Orient und in den mohammedanischen Ländern während des 13. Jh.* (1934). Instructive on the 14th and 15th centuries is S. Schein, 'La Custodia Terrae Sanctae franciscaine et les Juifs de Jérusalem à la fin du moyen âge', *Revue des études juives*, 141 (1982), 369ff.; E. R. Daniel, *The Franciscan Concept of Mission in the High Middle Ages* (1975); Kedar, *Crusade and Mission* (above, p. 292), 120ff.; J. Richard, *La papauté et les missions d'Orient au moyen âge (XIIIe–XVe siècles)* (1977), as well as Richard's collected studies and other works quoted in n. 136; B. Altaner, *Die Dominikanermissionen des 13. Jh.* (1924).

115. Metcalf, *Coinage* (above, n. 100), 22f., argues that this is numismatic as well as constitutional nonsense. But to attribute these coins to a mint in Acre when the word *Damiata* appears in the legend, is difficult, and John had, after all, been promised in 1218 that he would be the ruler of all lands conquered in Egypt (*Estoire de Eracles, RHC Hoc. 2*, 329).

116. Fundamental is J. Richard, 'L'Extrême-Orient légendaire au moyen âge. Roi David et Prêtre Jean', *Annales d'Éthiopie*, 2 (1957), 225ff. (also in Richard, *Orient et Occident au moyen âge*, 1976, no. XXVI); P. Pelliot, 'Mélanges sur l'époque des croisades', *Mémoires de l'Académie des Inscriptions et Belles-Lettres*, 44 (1951), 73ff.

117. From this point on the—in any event somewhat dubious—numbering of the crusades lacks all consistency. Many scholars do not count the Damietta crusade at all and, for them, Frederick II's crusade of 1228–9 is the fifth and Saint Louis's first crusade (1248–50) the sixth. Others count the Damietta crusade, but not Frederick II's. Still others count the Damietta crusade as the fifth, Frederick II's as the sixth, and Saint Louis's as the seventh.

118. On the *passagium* Alphandéry (above, p. 292) 2, 131ff.; Schaube (above, n. 97), 195ff., 201ff.; A. M. Chazaud, 'Inventaire et comptes de la succession d'Eudes, comte de Nevers', *Mémoires de la Société des Antiquaires de France*, 32 (1871), 169ff.

119. For the Christian picture of the heathen: Wentzlaff-Eggebert (above, p. 293), 247ff. For knowledge of Islam: Southern and Daniel (above, p. 293), especially Daniel, 309ff. (on the question of idolatry). U. Monneret de Villard, *Lo studio dell'Islam in Europa nel XIIe nel XIII secolo* (1944). On the translations of the Koran: M. Th. d'Alverny, 'Deux traditions latines du Coran au moyen âge', *Archives d'histoire doctrinale et littéraire du moyen âge*, 16 (1947–8), 69ff.; J. Kritzeck, *Peter the Venerable and Islam* (1964); F. A. Rouleau, 'The Yangchow Latin Tombstone as a Landmark of Medieval Christianity in China', *Harvard Journal of Asiatic Studies*, 17 (1954), 345ff.

120. On the crusade of Frederick II: H. M. Schaller, *Kaiser Friedrich II., Verwandler der Welt* (1964); E. Kantorowicz, *Kaiser Friedrich II.*, 2 vols. (1927–31); R. Röhricht, 'Die Kreuzfahrt Kaiser Friedrichs II.', in Röhricht, *Beiträge zur Geschichte der Kreuzzüge*, 1 (1874), 1ff.; E. Kestner, *Der Kreuzzug Kaiser Friedrichs II.* (1873). On the coronation of 1229 in Jerusalem see Mayer, 'Pontifikale' (above, n. 90), 200ff.; Gottschalk, *al-Kāmil* (above, p. 291); H. Heimpel, 'Hermann von Salza', in Heimpel, *Der Mensch in seiner Gegenwart* (1954), 87ff.; W. Jacobs, *Patriarch Gerold von Jerusalem* (1905).

121. The apparently peculiar lengths of the time arranged for truces are the result of the difference between the Christian and Muslim year.

122. F. Kampers, *Die deutsche Kaiseridee in Prophetie und Sage* (1896), 73ff.; H. M. Schaller, 'Das Relief an der Kanzel von Bitonto: ein Denkmal der Kaiseridee Friedrichs II.', *Archiv für Kulturgeschichte,* 45 (1963), 295ff. Different views have been expressed by R. Neu-Kock, 'Das Kanzelrelief in der Kathedrale von Bitonto', ibid., 60 (1978), 253ff. This study does not, however, force us to abandon Schaller's interpretation. The controversy over Frederick's II 'self-coronation' between A. Brackmann and E. Kantorowicz (*Historische Zeitschrift,* 140, 1929, 534ff.; 141, 1930, 457ff.) was not very fruitful.

123. General bibliography for Cyprus: J. Richard, *Documents chypriotes des Archives du Vatican* (1962); Richard, *Le Livre des Remembrances de la Secrète du Royaume de Chypre (1468–1469)* (1983); G. Hill, *A History of Cyprus,* vols. 2 and 3 (1948); L. de Mas Latrie, *Histoire de l'île de Chypre sous le règne des princes de la maison de Lusignan,* 3 vols. (4 vols. in the reprint because additional papers by Mas Latrie have been added) (1970, repr.); J. Richard, 'Le peuplement latin et syrien en Chypre au XIIIe siècle', *Byzantinische Forschungen,* 7 (1979), 157ff. On the conflict of 1271 over military service see Mayer, 'Mélanges' (above, n. 59), 106ff.; D. Jacoby, 'The Rise of a New Emporium in the Eastern Mediterranean: Famagusta in the Late Thirteenth Century', *Meletai kai Hypomnemata* (the periodical of the Foundation Archbishop Makarios III at Nicosia), 1 (1984), 145ff.; J. Richard, 'La situation juridique de Famagouste dans le royaume des Lusignans', in Richard, *Orient et Occident au moyen âge* (1976), no. XVII; Richard, 'Une économie coloniale? Chypre et ses ressources agricoles au moyen âge', *Byzantinische Forschungen,* 5 (1977), 331ff.; M. L. von Wartburg, 'The Medieval Cane Sugar Industry in Cyprus: Results of Recent Excavation', *The Antiquaries Journal,* 63 (1983), 298ff. During the excavations at Palaeopaphos a most interesting medieval two-phase mill for the grinding and pressing of sugar cane as well as an installation for cleaning the vessels used in the crystallizing procedure were unearthed. The boiling tract and the crystallizing compartments themselves have not yet been found. D. Jacoby, 'Citoyens, sujéts et protégés de Venise et de Gênes en Chypre du XIIIe au XVe siècle', *Byzantinische Forschungen,* 5 (1977), 159ff.; J. Richard, 'Une famille de Vénitiens blancs dans le royaume de Chypre au milieu du XVe siècle', *Rivista di studi bizantini e slavi* (Festschrift A. Pertusi), 1 (1981), 89ff.; L. de Mas Latrie, 'Histoire des archevêques latins de l'île de Chypre', *Archives de l'Orient latin,* 2ª (1884), 207ff.; J. Richard, 'Le royaume de Chypre et le Grand Schisme', *Comptes-rendus des séances de l'Académie des Inscriptions et Belles-Lettres* 1965 (1966), 498ff.; W. H. Rudt de Collenberg, 'État et origine du haut clergé de Chypre avant le Grand Schisme d'après les registres des papes du XIIIe et du XIVe siècle', *Mélanges de l'École française de Rome, moyen âge–temps modernes,* 91 (1979), 197ff.; J. Gill, 'The Tribulations of the Greek Church in Cyprus 1196–ca. 1280', *Byzantinische Forschungen,* 5 (1977), 73ff.; J. Richard, 'Chypre du protectorat à la domination vénitienne', *Venezia e il Levante fino al secolo XV,* ed. A. Pertusi, I, 2 (1973), 657ff.; W. H. Rudt de Collenberg, 'Le royaume et l'église de Chypre face au Grand Schisme (1378–1417), *Mélanges de l'École française de Rome, moyen âge–temps modernes,* 94 (1982), 621ff.; P. W. Edbury, 'The Crusading Policy of King Peter I of Cyprus, 1359–1369', *The Eastern Mediterranean Lands in the Period of the Crusades,* ed. P. M. Holt (1977), 90ff., suggests that the crusade of Peter I was chiefly intended to promote the position of Famagusta in Mediterranean trade. Edbury, 'The Murder of King Peter I of Cyprus (1359–1369)', *Journal of Medieval History,* 6 (1980), 219ff.; J. Richard, 'La révolution de 1369 dans le royaume de Chypre', *Bibliothèque de l'École des Chartes,* 110 (1952), 108ff.; C. Enlart, *L'art gothique et de la Renaissance en Chypre,* 2 vols. (1899).

124. Until recently many historians—unfortunately including myself—assumed that Amalric (or Amaury) and Aimery were one and the same name. Therefore two kings of Jerusalem have often been referred to as Amalric I and Amalric II. Here, following the

316 *Notes*

terms they themselves employed on their seals, they are referred to as Amalric and Aimery.

125. W. Hubatsch, 'Der Deutsche Orden und die Reichslehnschaft über Cypern', *Nachrichten der Akademie der Wissenschaften in Göttingen* (1955), 245ff.; Hubatsch, 'Montfort' (above, n. 71); H. E. Mayer, 'Die Seigneurie de Joscelin und der Deutsche Orden', *Die geistlichen Ritterorden Europas*, ed. J. Fleckenstein and M. Hellmann (1980), 171ff.

126. Crusader states 1192–1244: P. Richter, 'Beiträge zur Historiographie in den Kreuzfahrerstaaten', *Mitteilungen des Instituts für österreichische Geschichtsforschung*, 13 (1892), 255ff.; 15 (1894), 561ff.; M. R. Morgan, *The Chronicle of Ernoul and the Continuations of William of Tyre* (1973). See also the literature quoted above, n. 75; Herzog (above, n. 32); H. Bettin, *Heinrich II. von Champagne, seine Kreuzfahrt und Wirksamkeit im Hl. Lande* (1910). M. L. Favreau, 'Graf Heinrich von Champagne und die Pisaner im Königreich Jerusalem', *Bollettino storico Pisano*, 47 (1978), 97ff.; Favreau, 'Die italienische Levante-Piraterie und die Sicherheit der Seewege nach Syrien im 12. und 13. Jahrhundert', *Vierteljahrschrift für Sozial- und Wirtschaftsgeschichte*, 65 (1978), 461ff.; M. L. Favreau-Lilie, 'La cacciata dei Pisani dal regno di Gerusalemme sotto la reggenza di Enrico conte di Champagne e un diploma di Boemondo conte di Tripoli per il commune di Pisa', *Bollettino storico Pisano*, 54 (1985), 107ff. (mostly on Tripoli, but also on the king's conflict with Ralph of Tiberias); G. A. Loud, 'The Assise sur la ligece and Ralph of Tiberias', *Crusade and Settlement* (above, p. 293), 204ff. (unconvincing); L. Böhm, *Johann von Brienne, König von Jerusalem, Kaiser von Konstantinopel* (1938); J. M. Buckley, 'The Problematical Octogenarianism of John of Brienne', *Speculum*, 32 (1957), 315ff.; J. L. La Monte, 'John d'Ibelin, the Old Lord of Beirut', *Byzantion*, 12 (1937), 417ff.; H. Müller, *Der Longobardenkrieg auf Zypern* (1890); G. N. Bromiley, 'Philipp of Novara's Account of the War between Frederick II of Hohenstaufen and the Ibelins', *Journal of Medieval History*, 3 (1977), 325ff., expresses doubts concerning the objectivity of Philip who has, however, always been considered a partisan of the Ibelins; his memoirs remain indispensable as a source. M. L. Bulst-Thiele, 'Zur Geschichte der Ritterorden und des Königreichs Jerusalem im 13. Jh. bis zur Schlacht bei La Forbie am 17. Oktober 1244', *Deutsches Archiv*, 22 (1966), 197ff.; R. Röhricht, 'Acte de soumission des barons du royaume de Jérusalem à Frédérick II', *Archives de l'Orient latin*, 1 (1881), 402f. On the vexing problem of the date of the appointment of Alice of Cyprus as regent of Jerusalem (above, p. 258): P. Jackson, 'The End of Hohenstaufen Rule in Syria', *Bulletin of the Institute of Historical Research*, 59 (1986), 20ff., and D. Jacoby, 'The Kingdom of Jerusalem and the Collapse of Hohenstaufen Power in the Levant', *Dumbarton Oaks Papers*, 40 (1986), 83ff. Both scholars opt firmly for 1242 and do so on the basis of impressive new evidence. But the evidence for 1242 is not sufficient to dismiss the legal argument of the anti-imperialists (John of Jaffa, Philip of Novara) that Alice's appointment as regent took place *after* Conrad had come of age (15th year completed in Jerusalem and Germany = 25 April 1243) as a simple 'red herring' (Jackson, 36). If it were, then it would be hard to see why the anti-imperialists fabricated the story in the first place and why they succeeded in deceiving everyone. We know for a fact that the matter of Conrad's age played a role in the debate even before the appointment of Alice as regent. The barons, in 1241, petitioned the emperor to remove Filangieri and, in return, offered to restore Hohenstaufen rule in the whole country under Simon de Montfort until Conrad came of age and arrived in person in the East. In 1242, if this date be accepted, the emperor granted their request and recalled Filangieri. He also tried to secure the appointment of a new lieutenant, in all probability Thomas of Acerra. That he proposed to have him appointed in Conrad's name rather than in his own, may have been intended as a further conciliatory gesture. It was he after all, not Conrad, who had been at war with them. Conrad could not formally make such an appointment until he came of age, and

in 1242 this was still a year away. Yet although the offer of 1241 had not also included the explicit promise to accept a lieutenant appointed by Conrad (Jackson's interpretation, 29, to the contrary is not borne out by the text of the source), precisely because he was still a minor, it had none the less been so submissive that the emperor was bound to assume that any such proposal, intended as a conciliatory gesture, would be accepted as such, provided that the legal requirement had been met, i.e. that Conrad really had come of age. After King Henry (VII) of Germany had been deposed in 1235 there remained only one legitimate heir to the empire and all of Frederick's kingdoms: Conrad IV. In his will of 1250 (MGH Constitutiones, 2, 385) Frederick left the empire and 'especially Sicily' to Conrad who was already king-elect of Germany and heir of Jerusalem. Frederick did this although by that time he had another legitimate son, Henry-Carlotto, born in 1238 from his marriage to the English Isabella. It may very well be that he planned this concentration of power in Conrad's hands as early as the deposition of Henry (VII) but refrained from making it public because the union of Sicily and the empire was unacceptable to the papacy. Under Sicilian (though not under German) law, however, Conrad came of age when he completed his fourteenth year on 25 April 1242. The *Constitutiones regni Siciliae*, 3, 30 provided that the guardianship for minor fiefholders lapsed when the heir reached his *pubertas* which in Roman law was defined as commencing *post quartum decimum annum completum* (Justinian, *Institutiones*, I, 22), even though the same Constitutions 2, 42 fixed the majority of commoners at eighteen (Huillard-Bréholles, *Historia diplomatica Friderici II*, 4, 139, 113). Frederick himself had attained his majority in Sicily after having completed his fourteenth year (Böhmer-Ficker, *Regesta imperii*, 5,1, no. 598a). It is a priori difficult to see what Sicilian majority might have to do with the Hohenstaufen position in the East, although Frederick had based himself on German law when claiming the revenues of Cyprus in 1228 (*Gestes des Chiprois*, §127) and had, with the same lack of legality and by appointing Filangieri legate not of the emperor but of the empire in Syria, effectively claimed that the kingdom of Jerusalem formed part of the empire, an action against which the pope protested ineffectually as early as 1231 (Böhmer-Ficker, *Regesta imperii*, 5, 3 no. 6865). Could it, perhaps, be that Frederick was looking for any kind of legal excuse to have Conrad's majority announced in order to be able to make a conciliatory move towards the Palestinian barons? This theory, speculative though it may be, would at least for the first time resolve the contradiction between the chronicles placing the events firmly in 1241 and Conrad's coming of age in Jerusalem in 1243.

127. While the Ibelins themselves seem to have claimed descent from the counts of Chartres, which is certainly wrong, J. Richard argued in the *Bulletin de correspondance hellénique*, 74 (1950), 99, n. 3, for Pisan origins.

128. Lesser Armenia: Article on Armīnya, *Encyclopedia of Islam*, new edition; *The Cilician Kingdom of Armenia*, ed. T. S. R. Boase (1978); L. M. Alishan, *Léon le Magnifique* (1888); Alishan, *Sissouan ou l'Arméno-Cilicie* (1899); W. H. Rüdt-Collenberg, *The Rupenides, Hethumides and Lusignans. The Structure of the Armeno-Cilician Dynasties* (1963); H. Hellenkemper, *Burgen der Kreuzritterzeit in der Grafschaft Edessa und im Königreich Kleinarmenien* (1976).

129. P. Jackson, 'The Crusades of 1239–1241 and their Aftermath', *Bulletin of the School of Oriental and African Studies*, 50 (1987), 32ff. (fundamental). On the rebuilding of Ascalon see Pringle, 'Walls of Ascalon' (above, n. 100).

130. E. R. Daniel, 'Apocalyptic Conversion: The Joachite Alternative to the Crusade', *Traditio*, 25 (1969), 127ff., corrected by Kedar, *Mission* (above, p. 292), 114.

131. J. Richard, *Saint Louis, roi d'une France féodale, soutien de la Terre Sainte* (1983; a *tour de force* of historical biography); W. C. Jordan, *Louis IX and the Challenge of the Crusade* (1979); as an example of how not to write history: V. Rittner, *Kulturkontakte und soziales Lernen im Mittelalter* (1973; cf. H. E. Mayer, *Historische Zeitschrift*, 219, 1974,

392ff.); E. Delaruelle, 'L'idée de croisade chez St. Louis', *Bulletin de littérature ecclésiastique*, 61 (1960), 241ff.; cf. J. Richard, 'St. Louis dans l'histoire des croisades', *Bulletin de la Société d'émulation du Bourbonnais*, 55 (1970), 229ff.; Richard, 'La politique orientale de St. Louis. La croisade de 1248', *Septième centenaire de la mort de St. Louis. Actes des colloques de Royaumont et de Paris* (1976), 197ff.; A. Schaube, 'Die Wechselbriefe König Ludwigs des Hl.', *Jahrbücher für Nationalökonomie und Statistik*, 70 (1898), 603ff., 730ff.; Cahen, *Journal Asiatique*, 1970, 8ff., has convincingly argued that Frederick did not betray Louis's crusading plans to Egypt; L. J. Friedman, *Text and Iconography for Joinville's Credo* (1958).

132. B. Z. Kedar, 'The Passenger List of a Crusader Ship, 1250', *Studi medievali*, 3rd series, 13 (1972), 267ff., disagrees on the grounds that on this ship most of the passengers were non-nobles travelling separately, surprisingly enough 9 per cent of them women. But one such list is insufficient evidence on which to base so considerable a revision of our picture of the social composition of crusading armies. Moreover, as Kedar pointed out, the ship was at Messina on 30 July 1250. This means that the passengers knew of the 1249 conquest of Damietta before they put to sea. The intended settlement of Egypt called mainly for non-nobles. For the crusade itself there were other priorities.

133. J. Richard, 'La fondation d'une église latine en Orient: Damiette', *Bibliothèque de l'École des Chartes*, 120 (1962), 39ff.

134. G. Schregle, *Die Sultanin von Ägypten* (1961); H. L. Gottschalk, 'Die ägyptische Sultanin Šağarrat ad-Durr in Geschichte und Dichtung', *Wiener Zeitschrift für die Kunde des Morgenlandes*, 61 (1967), 41ff.; article on Bahriyyah, *Encyclopedia of Islam*, new edition. Fundamental are the papers by D. Ayalon, *Studies on the Mamluks of Egypt (1250–1517)* (1977), and also Ayalon's studies above, n. 60; P. M. Holt, 'The Position and Power of the Mamluk Sultan', *Bulletin of the School of Oriental and African Studies*, 38 (1975), 237ff. R. Irwin, *The Middle East in the Middle Ages: The Early Mamluk Sultanate 1250–1382* (1986) was published too late for me to use.

135. On King Henry of Cyprus as regent see H. E. Mayer, 'Die Kreuzfahrerherrschaft 'Arrābe', *Zeitschrift des Deutschen Palästina-Vereins*, 93 (1977), 198ff. On the administrative reform of 1251 see Mayer, *Proceedings of the American Philosophical Society* (below, n. 138) and Prawer, *Crusader Institutions*, (above, n. 75), 290ff.

136. J. Richard, *La papauté* (above, n. 114) and, continuing his research, the many studies in the three volumes of his collected papers, *Orient et Occident au moyen âge: contacts et relations* (1976); *Les relations entre l'Orient et l'Occident au moyen âge* (1977); *Croisés, missionnaires et voyageurs* (1983); P. Pelliot, 'Les Mongols et la papauté', *Revue de l'Orient chrétien*, 23 (1922–3), 3ff.; 24 (1924), 225ff.; 28 (1931–2), 3ff.; G. Soranzo, *Il papato, l'Europa cristiana e i Tartari* (1930); I. de Rachewiltz, *Papal Envoys to the Great Khans* (1971); Altaner (above, n. 114); G. G. Guzman, 'Simon of St. Quentin and the Dominican Mission of the Mongol Baiju. A Reappraisal', *Speculum*, 46 (1971), 232ff. (other studies by Guzman on Simon of St. Quentin have become obsolete because of J. Richard's fine edition of the report, 1965); P. Pelliot, *Recherches sur les chrétiens d'Asie centrale et d'Extrême-Orient* (1973, published posthumously); Rouleau (above, n. 119); C. W. Troll, 'Die Chinamission im Mittelalter', *Franziskanische Studien*, 48 (1966), 109ff.; 49 (1967), 22ff. On the Nestorians: E. Tisserant, 'Nestorienne (Église)', *Dictionnaire de théologie catholique;* F. Nau, 'L'expansion nestorienne en Asie', *Annales du Musée Guimet*, 40 (1913), 193ff.; H. Cordier, 'Le christianisme en Chine et en Asie centrale sous les Mongols', *T'oung pao*, 18 (1917), 49ff.; J. Dauvillier, *Histoire et institutions des Églises orientales au moyen âge* (1983); J. M. Fiey, 'Les pèlerinages des Nestoriens et Jacobites à Jérusalem', *Cahiers de civilisation médiévale*, 12 (1969), 113ff.

137. Articles on Čingiz-Khan and Čingizids, *Encyclopedia of Islam*, new edition. Pelliot and Richard (above, n. 136) and the volumes of Richard's collected studies (above, n. 136), especially 'The Mongols and the Franks', *Journal of Asian History*, 3 (1969), 45ff.;

G. A. Bezzola, *Die Mongolen in abendländischer Sicht 1220–1270* (1974); J. J. Saunders, *The History of the Mongol Conquests* (1971); J. A. Boyle, *The Mongol World Empire 1206–1370* (1977); W. Barthold, *Zwölf Vorlesungen über die Geschichte der Türken Mittelasiens* (reprint, 1962); B. Spuler, *Geschichte der islamischen Länder. Die Mongolenzeit* (1953); Spuler, *Die Mongolen in Iran. Politik, Verwaltung und Kultur der Ilchanzeit 1220–1350*, 2nd edn. (1965); *The Cambridge History of Iran*, V: *The Saljuk and Mongol Periods* (1968). Especially important is the chapter by I. P. Petruschevsky on the agricultural, social, and economic developments, all the more so since Petruschevsky's fundamental work in Russian on Iranian agriculture in the 14th and 15th centuries (1960) has still not yet been translated into any language except Persian. This chapter seems to highlight the unfortunate consequences of the Mongol invasion for the old urban civilization of Central Asia. However, B. Lewis, 'The Mongols, the Turks and the Muslim Polity', *Transactions of the Royal Historical Society*, 5th series, 18 (1968), 49ff., cautions against overestimating the extent of Mongol destruction; L. Olschki, *Guillaume Boucher, a French Artist at the Court of the Khans* (1946).

138. For background secondary works for this chapter see the general histories of the kingdom of Jerusalem (above, no. 75) and Prawer (above, n. 95). In addition R. Röhricht, 'Études sur les derniers temps du royaume de Jérusalem', *Archives de l'Orient latin*, 1 (1881), 617ff.; 2a (1884), 365ff.; Röhricht, 'Der Untergang des Königreiches Jerusalem', *Mitteilungen des Instituts für österreichische Geschichtsforschung*, 15 (1894), 1ff.; E. Stickel, *Der Fall von Akkon* (1975; open to considerable criticism in the topographical details). On the *bailliage* see Riley-Smith (above, n. 75), also H. E. Mayer, 'Ibelin versus Ibelin: The Struggle for the Regency of Jerusalem 1253–1258', *Proceedings of the American Philosophical Society*, 122 (1978), 25ff. (also on the affair between John of Jaffa and Plaisance of Cyprus), partly disputed by P. W. Edbury, 'John of Jaffa's title to the county of Jaffa and Askalon', *English Historical Review*, 98 (1983), 115ff.; rejoinder by Mayer, 'John of Jaffa, His Opponents and His Fiefs', *Proceedings of the American Philosophical Society*, 128 (1984), 134ff.; P. W. Edbury, 'The Disputed Regency of the Kingdom of Jerusalem 1264–6 and 1268', *Camden Miscellany*, 27 (1979), 1ff., with important revisions. On the new sealing formula: Mayer, *Siegelwesen* (above, n. 83), 59ff. On the role of the Military Orders: J. Prawer, 'Military Orders and Crusader Politics in the Second Half of the XIIIth Century', in *Die geistlichen Ritterorden Europas*, ed. J. Fleckenstein and M. Hellmann (1980), 217ff.; S. Schein, 'The Patriarchs of Jerusalem in the Late Thirteenth Century: seigneurs espiritueles et temporeles?', in *Outremer* (above, n. 75), 279ff. On Geoffrey of Sergines see the fine biographical sketch by J. Riley-Smith, *What Were the Crusades?* (1977), 65ff.; P. Jackson, 'The Crisis in the Holy Land in 1260', *English Historical Review*, 95 (1980), 481ff.; J. Richard, 'Les comtes de Tripoli et leurs vassaux sous la dynastie antiochienne', in *Crusade and Settlement* (above, p. 293), 213ff.; J. Riley-Smith, 'The Templars and Teutonic Knights in Cilician Armenia', in *Cilician Kingdom* (above, n. 128) 92ff.; N. Housley, 'Charles II of Naples and the Kingdom of Jerusalem', *Byzantion*, 54 (1984), 527ff.

139. G. Caro, *Genua und die Mächte am Mittelmeer*, 2 vols. (1895–9); Mayer, 'Ibelin' (above, n. 138), 51ff. On the Tripolitan revolt of 1258 see Richard, 'Porcellet' (above, n. 75), 353ff. and Richard, 'Comtes de Tripoli' (above, n. 138).

140. P. Hilsch, 'Der Deutsche Ritterorden im südlichen Libanon', *Zeitschrift des Deutschen Palästina-Vereins*, 96 (1980), 174ff.; M. L. Favreau, 'Die Kreuzfahrerherrschaft Scandalion (Iskanderūne)', ibid., 93 (1977), 12ff.; M. L. Favreau-Lilie, 'The Teutonic Knights in Acre after the Fall of Montfort (1271)', in *Outremer* (above, n. 75), 272ff. On Casel Imbert see Mayer, *Siegelwesen* (above, n. 83), 66ff., 90ff.

141. On Baibars see P. Thorau, *Sultan Baibars I. Ein Beitrag zur Geschichte des Vorderen Orients* (forthcoming 1987), the most detailed biography; A. A. Khowaiter, *Baibars the*

First: *His Endeavours and Achievements* (1978); *Encyclopedia of Islam*, new edition, article of Baybars I.

142. R. Sternfeld, *Ludwigs d. Hl. Kreuzzug nach Tunis und die Politik Karls I. von Sizilien* (1896); R. Lefèvre, *La crociata di Tunisi del 1270 nei documenti del distrutto archivio angionio di Napoli* (1977); Y. Dossat, '*Alfonse de Poitiers et la préparation financière de la croisade de Tunis: les ventes de forêts (1268–1270)*; in *Septième centenaire de la mort de St.-Louis. Actes des colloques de Royaumont et de Paris* (1976), 121ff. On the crusade of Prince Edward, B. Beebe, 'The English Baronage and the Crusade of 1270', *Bulletin of the Institute of Historical Research*, 48 (1975), 127ff.; but see S. Lloyd, 'The Lord Edward's Crusade, 1270–1272: Its setting and significance', in *War and Government* (above, n. 68), 120ff., who shows against Beebe that the recruiting of the English crusaders was by and large restricted to the households of Edward himself and of the king. The best description of the crusade still in Röhricht, 'Études' (part I) (above, n. 138). Cf. also on English crusading affairs A. J. Forey, 'The Crusading Vows of the English King Henry III', *Durham University Journal*, 65 (1973), 229ff.

143. L. Gatto, *Il pontificato di Gregorio X* (1959); V. Laurent, 'La croisade et la question d'Orient sous le pontificat de Grégoire X', *Revue historique du Sud-Est européen*, 22 (1945), 105ff.; B. Roberg, *Die Union zwischen der griechischen und der lateinischen Kirche auf dem II. Konzil von Lyon* (1964); cf. also Roberg in *Annuarium historiae conciliorum*, 5 (1973), 241ff.; 15 (1983), 96ff., and S. Schein, *The West and the Crusade* (forthcoming); P. A. Throop, *Criticism of the Crusade. A Study of Public Opinion and Crusade Propaganda* (1940); E. Siberry, *Criticism of Crusading 1095–1274* (1985), mainly directed against Throop, is useful as a rich collection of material and for its study of twelfth-century crusading criticism, but it is a curiously one-sided piece of work. While the defenders of the papacy with regard to the crusades against heretics and the Hohenstaufen are taken at face value, the critics are throughout dismissed as a small circle of determined enemies of the papacy (3), as influenced by personal interests or coloured by prejudice (181), as men without an audience. Even contemporary statements such as 'as *everyone* says in truth' are dismissed as representing only the views of a small literary circle. In the case of Guillem Figueira, the author of a virulent attack on papal policy, his work is twice labelled a 'savage denunciation' (9, 167) while of Gormanda of Montpellier we hear only that she 'challenged' Guillem's views (167) (no mention of the fact that she was just as savage.) We are told that there is 'no evidence that he represented a large body of opinion' (174), although in 1274 the inquisition received information leading to a rather different conclusion: the suspect stated that he had often heard Guillem's poem sung and had frequently recited it himself in public (9). The quantitative problem, the fact that there is much more evidence for criticism than for support of crusades not directed to the Holy Land, is all too easily shrugged off; the critics were simply 'more vociferous' than the supporters (187, 219), as if the Roman popes had not themselves been the most vociferous of all. The opponents, troubadours, *trouvères, Minnesänger*, we are told, had their attitude shaped by 'location and circumstances' and 'we have no real means of assessing their effect upon public opinion' (11), even though we know that many of them were wandering minstrels whose very way of life consisted of travelling from castle to castle to sing their songs and spread their ideas. More than anyone else Hostiensis developed the canonistic doctrine that crusades against all enemies of the Church were of equal value, yet even he had to admit that there was a great deal of opposition in Germany to the crusade against the Hohenstaufen. Hostiensis has been adduced in evidence more than once (*Speculum*, 53, 842; *English Historical Review*, 99, 863)—but apparently to no effect. Both Housley, *Italian Crusades* (above, n. 108, 37) and Siberry (182) show an astonishing reticence when it comes to Hostiensis and mention his report in the briefest fashion only, giving no space to the arguments of the critics. They objected *maxime quia non invenitur in iure*

expressum argumentum. Put on the spot, Hostiensis—though quick enough to plug the gap when back at his desk—had been able to come up with nothing better than: *Plura sunt negotia quam vocabula*—a very poor rejoinder. Moreover it is hard to deny that enthusiasm for all forms of crusading, even crusades to the Holy Land, was waning in the second half of the thirteenth century. By stopping in 1274, Siberry avoids having to deal, e.g. with the revealing refusal of France and the Military Orders to support Gregory X in his scheme for a new Holy Land crusade (above, p. 282), discussed at great length by Throop. And she ignores altogether a telling indication that enthusiasm was waning, the fact that the indulgences granted simply for listening to a crusading sermon, first instituted by Innocent III in 1213, tended to grow longer and longer as the century wore on and people became less interested in hearing them. The literature on the subject (Paulus, Throop, Purcell) suggests the following development: Honorius III 10–20 days, Gregory IX 10–40 days, Innocent IV up to 60 days, Urban IV 40–100 days, Clement IV and Gregory X 100–405 days! M. Purcell, *Papal Crusading Policy, 1244–1291* (1975), to be used with great caution; cf. H. E. Mayer in *Zeitschrift für Kirchengeschichte*, 88, 336ff.

144. In theory the degree of relationship to Conradin should have decided who has to be regent. In 1264 it had been different because then the issue was the appointment of a deputy for a regent who was a minor. Thus at that time it had been correct to take the degree of relationship to the regent.

145. J. Richard, 'Un partage de seigneurie entre Francs et Mamelouks: Les "Casaux de Sur"', *Syria* 30 (1953), 72ff.; P. M. Holt, 'The Treaties of the Early Mamluk Sultans with the Frankish States', *Bulletin of the School of Oriental and African Studies*, 43 (1980), 67ff.; Holt, 'Qalāwūn's Treaty with Acre in 1283', *English Historical Review*, 91 (1976), 802ff.; Holt, 'Qalāwūn's Treaty with Genoa in 1290', *Der Islam*, 57 (1980), 101ff.; Michael Köhler, 'Munāsafāt: Gebietsteilungen zwischen Kreuzfahrern und islamischen Herrschern im 12. und 13. Jahrhundert', *Zeitschrift der deutschen morgenländischen Gesellschaft*, supplement 6 (1985), 155ff., has grave deficiencies; cf. H. E. Mayer in *Deutsches Archiv*, 41 (1985), 697. A wider treatment of this problem by Köhler is planned (above, p. 293).

146. Secondary literature see above, nn. 114, 136, and 137. Also D. Sinor, 'Les relations entre les Mongols et l'Europe jusqu'à la mort d'Arghoun et de Bela IV', *Cahiers d'histoire mondiale*, 3 (1956), 39ff.; J. M. Fiey, *Chrétiens syriaques sous les Mongols* (1975); J. A. Boyle, 'The Il-Khans of Persia and the Princes of Europe', *Central Asiatic Journal*, 20 (1976), 25ff. On an offer of alliance made by Hulagu as early as 1262 see P. Meyvaert, 'An Unknown Letter of Hulagu, Il-Khan of Persia, to King Louis IX of France', *Viator*, 11 (1980), 245ff.; with proper chronology by J. Richard, 'Une ambassade mongole à Paris en 1262', *Journal des Savants* (1979), 295ff.

147. On the later crusades see now the standard work by Setton, *Papacy* (above, p. 29f.); Schein (above, n. 143) and Housley, *Italian Crusades* (above, n. 108); L. Thier, *Kreuzzugsbemühungen unter Papst Clemens V.* (1973); A. Luttrell, 'The Crusade in the Fourteenth Century', in *Europe in the Late Middle Ages*, ed. J. R. Hale and others (1965), 122ff.; J. Delaville Le Roulx, *La France en Orient au XIVe siècle*, 2 vols. (1886); S. Schein, The future regnum Hierusalem. A Chapter in Medieval State Planning', *Journal of Medieval History*, 10 (1984), 95ff.; Schein, 'Gesta Dei per Mongolos 1300. The Genesis of a Non-Event', *English Historical Review*, 94 (1979), 805ff.; C. J. Tyerman, 'Marino Sanudo Torsello and the Lost Cause: Lobbying in the Fourteenth Century', *Transactions of the Royal Historical Society*, 5th series, 32 (1982), 57ff.; A. J. Forey, 'The Military Orders in the Crusading Proposals of the Late 13th and 14th Centuries', *Traditio*, 36 (1980), 317ff.; B. Z. Kedar and S. Schein, 'Un projet de passage particulier proposé par l'Ordre de l'Hôpital 1306–1307', *Bibliothèque de l'École des Chartes*, 137 (1979), 211ff.; J. Delaville Le Roulx, *Les Hospitaliers à Rhodes*

(1310–1421) (1913); A. Luttrell, *Hospitallers in Cyprus, Rhodes, Greece and the West (1291–1440)* (1978); Luttrell, *Latin Greece, the Hospitallers and the Crusades* (1982); J. Goñi Gaztambide, *Historia de la bula de la cruzada en España* (1958); article on Croisade (bulle de la) in *Dictionnaire de Droit canonique*, 4 (1949), 780ff.

MAP 1   Central and East Asia

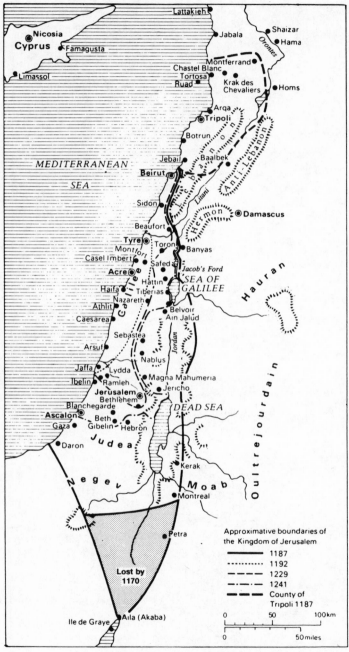

Lattakieh
Nicosia
Cyprus
Famagusta
Jabala
Shaizar
Hama
Limassol
Montferrand
Chastel Blanc
Tortosa
Ruad
Krak des Chevaliers
Homs
Arqa
Tripoli
MEDITERRANEAN
Botrun
Jebail
Baalbek
Beirut
SEA
Litani
Sidon
Hermon
Damascus
Beaufort
Tyre
Toron
Banyas
Montfort
Casel Imbert
Safed
Jacob's Ford
Acre
SEA OF GALILEE
Hattin
Hauran
Haifa
Tiberias
Nazareth
Athlit
Belvoir
Caesarea
Ain Jalud
Sebastea
Jordan
Arsuf
Nablus
Jaffa
Lydda
Magna Mahumeria
Ibelin
Ramleh
Jericho
Jerusalem
Bethlehem
Blanchegarde
DEAD SEA
Ascalon
Beth
Gaza
Gibelin
Hebron
Daron
Judea
Oultrejourdain
Kerak
Negev
Moab
Montreal

Approximative boundaries of
the Kingdom of Jerusalem
———— 1187
·········· 1192
– – – – 1229
–·–·– 1241
– – – County of
Tripoli 1187
0   50   100 km
0   50 miles

Lost by 1170

Petra

Ile de Graye
Aila (Akaba)

MAP 2   Southern Syria and Palestine

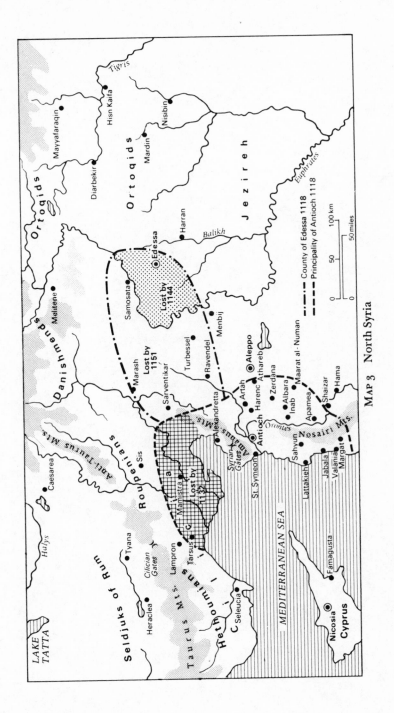

MAP 3   North Syria

LAKE
TATTA

Tigris

Mayyafaraqin

Hisn Kaifa

Nisibin

Mardin

Diarbekir

O r t o q i d s

J e z i r e h

Euphrates

Harran

Balikh

Edessa

Samosata

Lost by
1144

Menbij

Ravendel

Turbessel

Marash
Lost by
1151

Sarventikar

Aleppo

Artah
Harenc Athareb

Zerdana

Albara
Inab

Maarat al-Numan

Shaizar

Hama

Apamea

Sahyun

Nosairi Mts.

Antioch

Oronies

Alexandretta

Amanus Mts.

Syrian
Gates

St. Symeon

Lattakieh

Jabala

Valania

Margat

MEDITERRANEAN SEA

Famagusta

Nicosia

Cyprus

C. Seleucia

Tarsus

Lampron

Cilician
Gates

Heraclea

Tyana

Sis

Caesarea

Halys

Seljuks of Rum

Anti-Taurus Mts.

Danishmends

Melitene

R o u p e n i a n s

C i l i c i a

Mamistra

Lost by
1132

Taurus Mts.

Hethoumians

Danishmends

Ortoqids

Ortoqids

········ County of Edessa 1118
— — — Principality of Antioch 1118

0   50   100 km
0   50 miles

INDEX

This index comprises personal and place names as well as selected subjects. In the alphabetical listing the Arabic article *al* has not been taken into account. For a plurality of persons bearing the same name the listings are in hierarchical order, the clergy taking precedence over the laity.

Baldwin II, Latin Emperor of
Constantinople 205, 207–8, 266
Baldwin I (Baldwin of Boulogne), count of
Edessa, king of Jerusalem 42, 44,
48–50, 60, 62–3, 65–6, 68–70, 72, 75,
88, 92, 152, 154, 175, 187
Baldwin II (Baldwin of Bourcq), count of
Edessa, king of Jerusalem 42, 48,
59, 63, 65–8, 70, 72–7, 80–4, 91,
108–9, 154, 158, 168
Baldwin III, king of Jerusalem 82, 91,
102–3, 108–18, 126, 153, 158, 161,
163
Baldwin IV, king of Jerusalem 116,
127–8, 130–3, 163–4, 247, 302
Baldwin V, king of Jerusalem 128,
130–3, 163–4, 190, 250
Baldwin of Boulogne *see* Baldwin I, king
of Jerusalem
Baldwin of Bourcq *see* Baldwin II, king of
Jerusalem
Baldwin of Flanders *see* Baldwin I, Latin
Emperor of Constantinople
Baldwin, lord of Ramleh 88, 130
Balian *see* Barisan
Balikh River 66
Balkans 20, 44, 64, 98, 140, 214, 269
banking 79, 185, 264, 266, 277–9
Banu as-Sufi, Damascene family 108
Banyas, Palestinian bishopric and
town 87, 103, 113, 119, 123, 129,
171
al-Bara, Syrian bishopric 53
Barbastro (Spain) 26
Barcelona 29, 212
Bar Hebraeus, Syriac writer 270
Bari (Italy) 3, 20
Barin *see* Montferrand
Barisan the Old, constable of Jaffa,
castellan and lord of Ibelin 88, 110,
112
Barisan II of Ibelin, lord of Ramla 128,
135
Barisan III of Ibelin, lord of Beirut 256
Barsauma, Jacobite monastery 175
Bartolomeo Embriaco, mayor of
Tripoli 285
Basle, German bishopric and town 34,
140
Baudri of Dol, chronicler 12
Bavaria 64–5, 137
Bavarians 64, 98
Beaufort, Palestinian castle 88, 136, 247,
259, 278, 281

Beaulieu, French abbey 13
Beauvais, French bishopric 148
Bedouins 71, 88, 157, 168
beguines 172
Beirut, Lebanese bishopric, lordship,
town 54, 68–9, 76, 103, 109, 115,
120, 126, 132–3, 150, 161, 163, 171,
179, 189, 247–8, 254, 278, 284–5, 306
Beisan, Palestinian castle and
lordship 59, 172
Belgrade 42
Bellapais, Cypriot abbey 241
Belvoir, Palestinian castle 88, 136, 163
Benedict of Alignan, bishop of
Marseilles 193
Benedictines 172
Benevento, battle of 211
Beqaa, Lebanese plain 60, 90
Berkyaruk, Seldjuk sultan 50
Bernard of Valence, patriarch of
Antioch 61, 75
Bernard, abbot of Clairvaux 34–5, 77–8,
82, 93–9, 104–5, 140, 155, 230, 234,
296
Bernard of Blois, hermit 73
Bernardus (Teutonicus), Venetian
financier 141
Bernold of Constance, chronicler 7
Berry, French region 39, 190
bers (= barons) *de terre* 210
Bertha of Sulzbach (Irene), Byzantine
Empress 98, 115
Bertrand of Saint-Gilles, count of
Toulouse and Tripoli 43, 68, 70
Bertrand of Gibelet, Tripolitan
baron 274
Bertrand Mazoir, Antiochene baron
163
Besançon (Burgundy) 64
Bethany, Palestinian double
monastery 91, 111, 172
Beth Gibelin (Bait Gibrin), Palestinian
fortress and settlement 79, 88, 155
Bethlehem, bishopric, town 12–13, 55,
59, 63, 74, 82, 103, 112–13, 123, 163,
172, 191, 215, 236
Bethlehem-Ascalon, double
bishopric 113
Bethphage, locality on the Mount of
Olives 194
Bible translation 192
bigamy 71, 74–5, 144
Bilbeis (Egypt) 118, 120, 302
bisancii saracenati 168

Melfi (Italy) 17–18
constitutions of 238
Melisende, queen of Jerusalem 82, 84–5,
91–2, 102–3, 108, 110–12, 116, 175
Melisende of Lusignan, princess of
Antioch 250–1, 283
Melisende, countess of Tripoli 115
Melisende Psalter 116
Melitene (Anatolia) 46
menagerie 167
Mendicant Orders 172, 231, 241; see also
Dominicans, Franciscans
mercenaries 7, 40–1, 79, 135, 161, 165,
169, 179, 212, 245, 254
Mergecolon, Palestinian lordship 247
Mersivan (Anatolia) 64
Mesopotamia 5, 51, 59, 122, 143, 185,
221, 226, 259, 263, 265, 269–70
Messina (Italy) 145–6, 150, 219
metal work 191
mète du sel 169
Metz, German bishopric 100, 103
Michael VIII Palaeologus, Byzantine
Emperor 208, 211
Michael II, despot of Epirus 211
Miles of Plancy, seneschal of Jerusalem
127
Military Orders 77–80, 89, 117, 129,
136, 149, 160, 169–70, 173–4, 185,
188, 223, 228–9, 242, 244, 277–9,
282, 284–7; see also Hospitallers,
Templars, Teutonic Knights
exemption of from tithes 78, 173, 188
Masters of the 103, 132, 220, 224, 273
sale of fiefs to 163, 278–9, 284
military service 119, 157, 169–70, 174,
205, 210, 243
outside the kingdom 170, 243
refusal of 159–60; see also *Assise sur la
ligece*
militia Christi 19–20
militia sancti Petri 19–20
mills 154–5, 182
Milly (family) 109
Minnesänger 320
minting see coinage
Mirabel, Palestinian castle and
lordship 110–11, 186
mission, Christian 224, 231, 269, 281;
see also conversion
Mistra, Peloponnesian fortress 209, 211
Moab (Jordan) 58, 88, 136
Mohammad ibn Malik-Shah, Seldjuk
sultan 70

Monembasia (Greece) 211
money fief *see* fief
Mongka Khan, Great Khan of the
Mongols 269–70, 275
Mongols 212, 226, 230, 256–7, 259,
265–9, 271, 275–8, 280–1, 284
Monophysites 49, 156
Monotheletes 157
Montferrand (Barin), Syrian castle 86
Montferrat, Piemontese family 103, 247,
249; see also Boniface of Montferrat,
Conrad of Montferrat
Montfort, Palestinian castle 234, 282
Montgisard, battle of 131
Montjoie:
hill in Acre 273
hill near Jerusalem 55, 80, 172
Montmusard, suburb of Acre 149
Montpellier (France) 182
Montreal (Shobak), Transjordanian
castle 71, 136
Moors 287
Morea (= Peloponnese) 204–6, 209–12
Morphia, countess of Edessa, queen of
Jerusalem 73
mosaics 123
Mosserins 180, 185
Mosul 49, 54, 66–7, 69–71, 73, 80–1, 86,
92, 107, 122, 124–5, 147, 180, 225
Mount Carmel 172, 221
Mount Hermon 58
Mount of Olives (Jerusalem) 55, 172
house of canons on 172
Mount Pilgrim (Tripoli) 65, 68
Mount Sinai 136, 175, 194
Mount Sion 169, 172
Mount Tabor 172, 217
Mousay (France) 42
al-Mu'azzam, ruler of Syria and
Palestine 221–3, 225, 235–6
music in crusader states 195
al-Mustali, Fatimid caliph 4
al-Mustasim, Abbasid caliph 270
Myriocephalum, battle of 124

Nablus, Palestinian crown demesne and
town 75–6, 111, 119, 129–32, 158,
171; see also concordate (council) of
Nablus
Nachmanides, Spanish rabbi 157
Namur 98
Naples (Italy) 211–12, 233, 283
an-Nasir, Ayubid ruler of Aleppo 265
an-Nasir, Ayubid ruler of Damascus 236

Thessalonica, Greek town and Latin
kingdom 44, 104, 126, 199, 204,
206–7, 209
Thessaly 204, 212
Thiemo, archbishop of Salzburg 64–5
Thierry, count of Flanders 114
Thietmar, German pilgrim 136
Thomas of Capua, cardinal 232
Thomas Becket, archbishop of
Canterbury 135
Military Order of Saint Thomas of
Canterbury 149
Thomas of Acerra, lieutenant of
Jerusalem 316
Thoros, prince of Edessa 48–9
Thoros II, prince of Lesser Armenia 114
Thrace (Greece) 44, 204, 207–8, 212
Thuringia 142
Tiberias, Palestinian bishopric, lordship,
town 59, 63, 65, 69–70, 103, 127,
133–5, 171–2, 257; see also Galilee,
principality of
timber 117, 183, 185
tithes, ecclesiastical 74–5, 157, 173, 175,
188, 206
exemption from 78, 157, 173, 188
royal tithe on Cyprus 246
Saladin tithe 139–40
Toghtekin, ruler of Damascus 69–71, 73,
81, 123
Toledo (Spain) 192
Tolomeo of Lucca, writer 243
Tonkin (Asia) 269
tooling of ashlar masonry 190
Toron, Palestinian lordship and
castle 88, 103, 109, 131, 134, 236,
281
Toron Aghmid, locality near Beirut 278
Tortosa (Spain) 105
Tortosa, Tripolitanian bishopric, castle
and town 54, 65, 68, 76, 89, 123,
136, 163, 189, 273, 286–8
Toul, German bishopric 103, 140
Toulouse, French county 68, 218, 261
Tournai (Flanders) 55
Tours (France) 39
Tower of David (Jerusalem) 56–7, 61,
111, 256
trade 117, 122, 126, 168–9, 177, 183–5,
219, 244, 275
contracts 183–4
goods exported and imported 185
interplay with politics 183

privileges see commercial privileges
Transjordan see Oultrejourdain
Transoxania, region north-east of Oxus
River 256, 268–9
Trapani (Italy) 282
transport of crusaders 145, 199, 229; see
also pilgrims
treason 84, 159
treasurer in Achaia 210
Treasury of Merits 24, 26, 32–3
Trebizond, Empire of 206
tributes 119, 150, 168
Trier (Germany) 39–40, 98
Tripoli, Lebanese bishopric, commune,
county, town 54, 65, 67–8, 73–4,
76, 79–80, 83, 86, 88–9, 109–10, 112,
115, 118, 123, 130–1, 134, 136, 139,
142, 149–50, 152, 156, 163–4, 172,
177, 245, 247–8, 252–3, 274, 276–7,
282, 285, 301
troubadours 227, 320
trovères 320
Troyes (France) 103, 247
council of 77
truces 114, 125, 131, 134, 139, 149, 223,
227, 233, 247, 249, 257, 273, 282,
284–5
True Cross 57, 74–5, 135, 146, 191, 203,
224
Tunis 282
Turanshah, Ayubid sultan of Egypt 263,
265, 280
Turbessel, Edessenian fortress and
lordship 49, 53, 65, 70, 92
Turcomans 49, 141
turcopoles 79, 154, 169, 240
turcopoliers 167, 169
Turin, peace of 209
Turkestan 256
Turks 5, 10, 41, 47–8, 51–3, 101, 105,
108, 125, 157, 212–13, 246, 256,
264–5, 267–8, 287
Tuscany 185
Tutush, Seldjuk ruler in Syria
49–50
Tyana, Anatolian town 47–8
Tyre, Palestinian archbishopric,
commune, crown demesne, lordship,
town 54, 68–9, 75–7, 81, 88, 109,
111, 120, 131, 136, 139, 141–2, 144,
148–9, 156, 158, 161, 168, 171, 177,
181–2, 185, 188, 192–3, 225, 234,
247, 255–6, 258, 272, 275, 284–6

Ukraine 269
Ulrich, bishop of Passau 64
union:
of Armenian church with Rome 151,
253
of Greek Orthodox church with
Rome 2–3, 6–7, 20, 200, 206,
208, 217
of the Maronites with Rome 175–6
Unur, ruler of Damascus 108
Urban II, pope 5–10, 14, 18–21, 23,
27–30, 33, 36, 38–40, 44–5, 53, 61,
76, 94–5, 216, 294, 296
Urban III, pope 138–39
Urban IV, pope 272, 275, 321

Valania (Buluniyas), Syrian bishopric and
town 67, 163, 173
Vallombrosa, Italian monastery 9–10, 33
Varangian Guard 7, 203
vegetables 154
Vendômois 216
Venice 75, 86, 181–2, 185, 198–201,
205–6, 208–9, 212, 217, 229, 273
Venetians 3, 62, 76, 100, 168, 181–2,
185, 188–9, 199–206, 208, 244,
246, 269, 273–5, 285
white Venetians 245
Venetian quarter in Acre 181
Verdun, Lorraine bishopric, county 42
Verona (Italy) 103, 138
Veronese 205
Vézelay (France) 95, 145
Via Egnatia 43–4
vice-chancellor of Jerusalem 166
Victor III, pope 6
Vienna 149
Vikings 1, 15–16
vilains 186, 189, 211, 246
Villehardouin, dynasty in Achaia 206
vineyards 188
Visconti, Genoese family 184
viscounts:
baronial 112, 166, 177
as presidents of *cour des bourgeois* 177,
182
Italian 182
royal 158, 166, 188
royal of Nicosia 167
Viterbo (Italy) 93
treaty of V. 211
Volga River 269
Volkmar, German crusader 40

vow, crusading 38–9, 208, 219

Walter of Brienne, count of Lecce, duke
of Athens 212
Walter, lord of Caesarea 83
Walter the German, lord of
Mergecolon 247
Walter Sans-Avoir, knight 40
Walther von der Vogelweide, German
poet 220
war:
abroad 119, 170
chest 51
church teaching on 14–20
Holy 3, 12, 14, 16–20, 28, 313; *see
also jihad*
strategy 91, 169–70
tactics 147, 170
War of the Lombards 242, 254, 258, 277
War of St. Sabas 181, 273, 275, 278, 281
Welf, family 104, 137, 217
Welf IV, duke of Bavaria 64
Welf VI, duke of Spoleto 98, 103
Welsh 89
Wends 99–100
Wendish crusade 99–100, 215, 230
William I, archbishop of Tyre 77
William II, archbishop of Tyre 77, 116,
120, 127, 129–30, 133, 156, 166,
173–5, 192, 194
chronicle of William of Tyre 116
William of Chartres, chaplain of Saint
Louis 264
William of Malmesbury, chronicler 43
William of Newburgh, chronicler 137
William of Rubroek, Franciscan 193,
269–70
William of Tripoli, Dominican 193
William I the Conqueror, king of
England 2, 44
William II Rufus, king of England 2, 44
William II, king of Sicily 138–9, 149
William I de Champlitte, prince of
Achaia 206
William II Villehardouin, prince of
Achaia 209, 211–12
William IX, duke of Aquitaine 64, 85
William II, count of Nevers and
Auxerre 64
William Longsword, marquis of
Montferrat 130, 164
William Cassinese, Genoese notary 184
William of Queivillers, pilgrim 228–9